THE IRRESISTIBLE URGE TO PREACH

*A Collection of
African American "Call" Stories*

William H. Myers

WIPF & STOCK · Eugene, Oregon

Wipf and Stock Publishers
199 W 8th Ave, Suite 3
Eugene, OR 97401

The Irresistible Urge to Preach
A Collection of African American "Call" Stories
By Myers, William H.
Copyright©1991 by Myers, William H.
ISBN 13: 978-1-4982-7835-5
Publication date 12/9/2015
Previously published by Eerdmans, 1991

The McCreary Center for African American Religious Studies Vol. 1

The Irresistible Urge to Preach   by William H. Myers

Editor: **William H. Myers**
Ashland Theological Seminary, Ashland, OH

Associate Editors:
Kelley Brown
Howard University Divinity School, Washington, DC

Cheryl Gilkes
Colby College, Waterville, ME

Clarice Martin
Princeton Theological Seminary, Princeton, NJ

James Earl Massey
Anderson University School of Theology, Anderson, IN

Ella P. Mitchell
Interdenominational Theological Center, Atlanta, GA

Henry H. Mitchell, III
Interdenominational Theological Center, Atlanta, GA

Renita Weems
Vanderbilt University Divinity School, Nashville, TN

Gayraud S. Wilmore
Interdenominational Theological Center, Atlanta, GA

    The purpose of this series is to encourage relevant works for the Black church by helping to underwrite the financial burden of publication. By making an avenue possible that takes seriously the importance of scholarship in this manner, it is hoped that even more fruitful studies will emerge. The primary goal of this series will be to focus on works that are written for the wider audience of the Black church, not the academy. Those writing for the academy have numerous outlets; this is not the case for those who wish to write for the wider audience in the Black church.

    The McCreary Center for African American Religious Studies is a community-based theological center located in the Hough area of Cleveland, Ohio. It began in 1984. The Black Church Studies Program at Ashland Theological Seminary, Ashland, Ohio, takes place in this inner-city center to truly contextualize Black students' ministerial preparation. The Center's primary objective is to expose the Black seminary student to the best African American religious scholars in America, while at the same time giving support to these scholars in their research and teaching.

"When you're born, preaching is in you. And when the time comes it stirs, God stirs it up... at night I'd go home to bed. I'd go to sleep, I'd go to preaching. I'd wake up in the morning, I'd be tired. Preaching all night.... So that's the way it is, and I've been knowing it from a boy. And I used to play, me and my sister and other kids would play church, and I'd always be the preacher. And I'd get in the wagon, they'd have boxes and things all around on the ground, and I'd get in the wagon and preach.... So a preacher is a preacher, just like I was born Black."

Bishop Elmer E. Cleveland, Ephesians Church of God in Christ, Berkeley. Quoted in Gereald L. Davis, *I Got the Word in Me and I can Sing It, You Know* (Philadelphia: University of Pennsylvania Press, 1985): ix.

Dedication

To

The Reverend Carey McCreary, D. D.

Founder and Pastor of the New Mount Zion Baptist Church
in Cleveland, Ohio, for thirty-three years

My Father in the faith, surrogate father in life, friend, and uncle

My dearly beloved pastor for thirty years

One who exemplifies every day what it means to be called by God

"*If* I proclaim the gospel, this gives me no ground for boasting, for an obligation is laid on me, and woe to me if I do not proclaim the gospel! For if I do this of my own will, I have a reward; but if not of my own will, I am entrusted with a commission. What then is my reward? Just this: that in my proclamation I may make the gospel free of charge, so as not to make full use of my rights in the gospel. For though I am free with respect to all, I have made myself a slave to all, so that I might win more of them."

(I Corinthians 9: 16 -19, NRSV)

Contents

Acknowledgments		xii
Preface		xiii
"The Irresistible Urge to Preach"		xxii
1.	"We Would Rather Have an Unqualified Man Than a Qualified Woman"	2
2.	Starting a Church in the Garage at Age Eight	11
3.	The Law Student Who Became Bishop	16
4.	The Bishop Who Swore Never to Be a Preacher	18
5.	The Woman No One Would Allow in Seminary	20
6.	The Lutheran Who Became a Baptist	25
7.	Cracked in God's University of Hard Knocks	34
8.	"Confess the Call or Die"	38
9.	Preaching at Camp at Age Fifteen	42
10.	The Mississippi Preacher Who Founded a Convention	44
11.	Damascus Road in an Emergency Room	49
12.	When God Appeared as a Light	54
13.	"Choose Me and Live, or Take Your Chances with Satan"	58
14.	When God Called at 3:45 Every Morning	60
15.	Acceptance of the Call at a Funeral	64

Contents

16. "Now That Your Grandmother Is Gone, You Must Move Up" — 71

17. Movies and Dancing or Preaching: Which Will It Be? — 74

18. Young Preacher Influences Future Baptist Congress President — 76

19. Boy Preachers Yes, Girl Preachers No — 78

20. From a Seventh Grader to the Leading Revivalist — 81

21. A Divine Seizure — 84

22. "God's Yes Was Louder Than My No" — 88

23. A Scary Question at Ordination — 95

24. "Fear Not, I Have Chosen You . . ." — 99

25. The Troubler of Biblical Waters — 104

26. When God Spoke through Tchaikovsky's Symphony #4 in F Minor — 111

27. The Preacher Who Is Also Mayor — 114

28. God Called through a Little Boy without Shoes — 116

29. "I Think I'm Going Crazy" — 124

30. "You Are No Longer to Work with the Dead, but with the Living Dead" — 137

31. When Her Father Said, "I Won't Support You if You Go to Seminary" — 143

32. From a Physical Education or Music Major to District Superintendent — 147

Contents

33. "Are You Ready to Preach?" — 151
34. "Nobody with Your Color Eyes Can Be a Preacher" — 157
35. "The Calling Came as a Fact That I Was Raised by God" — 169
36. "Who in the World Would Marry a Woman Preacher?" — 172
37. Considered Most Likely to Be Bishop in High School — 179
38. Influenced by an Old Testament Professor — 183
39. The Most Dominant President of a Baptist Convention — 186
40. When God Spoke in a New York Traffic Jam — 188
41. "It Was like My Body Was on Fire" — 195
42. Two Similar Accidents – Is God Speaking to Me? — 197
43. "I Would Not Be a Boy Preacher" — 199
44. "I Was Down in the Motor Pool Preaching to Trucks" — 201
45. Rebellious Soldier in Two Armies: Man's and God's — 204
46. "God, If You Want Me to Preach, Wake Me Up at 3:00 or 4:00 o'Clock in the Morning" — 211
47. One Regret: Daddy King Wasn't There — 213
48. "I Don't Come from a Lineage of Preachers" — 216
49. "I Never Wanted to Be a Preacher" — 220
50. From a Broadcasting Career to Preaching — 226
51. Called While Reading a Score of Chopin — 230

Contents

52.	Betwixt and Between: Blinded at High Noon	233
53.	The Presence of God in the Wind	242
54.	"I Didn't Call You to Be Your Father's Clone"	245
55.	When a White Candle Turned Red	254
56.	"In the Same Year That Mama Died, I Also Saw the Lord"	259
57.	Has Anyone Written More on Black Preaching?	264
58.	"I Made a Bargain with God"	270
59.	The Urge to Preach	275
60.	The Influence of Being a Preacher's Kid	277
61.	"I Had No Choice"	280
62.	Awakened by the Hand of God	283
63.	An Overwhelming Burden	286
64.	Isolation, Separation, and Confrontation with the Brutality of Fraternities	289
65.	"Called from My Mother's Womb"	300
66.	Called in the Midst of a Medical Mishap	304
67.	Rebellion of an AME Preacher's Kid	307
68.	Under a Magnolia Tree Looking Up, When God Spoke	311
69.	An Irresistible Compulsion	320
70.	"A Constant Inclination toward Ministry"	322
71.	"I Was Anti-religious and Anti-God"	324

Contents

72. The Saxophone Player Who Heard the Call of God — 326

73. The Dean of Black Preachers: — 328
    He Didn't Want to Be a Preacher

74. "I Tried to Avoid it; I'm Going to Die" — 331

75. "No, No, No, Young Man. Not Money; Service, Service" — 334

76. When the Preacher Came, Everything Seemed Better — 337

77. "...All Right God, I Tell You What, — 338
    I'm Gonna Fleece You"

78. No Girl Friends If You Are a Teenage Preacher — 346

79. Confirmation of a Woman Preacher by Women Preachers — 350

80. "The Next Time You Hear That Voice, — 360
    Answer Yes, Lord"

81. Unnatural Light in a Dark Room — 362

82. Awakened at Four o'Clock; "I Had Been Preaching" — 372

83. Lost on the Pacific When God Spoke — 378

84. "The Lord Is Calling...You Can't Ignore That" — 384

85. "You Know What I Want You to Do" — 388

86. From Marginal Roman Catholic to — 392
    Muslim to CME Preacher

Appendix A: Selected Data — 397

Appendix B: Index of Call Stories by Author — 404

Acknowledgments

Gratitude goes to a host of people: All of the individuals included in the study for giving of their time; to Jeremiah Wright, Jr., for going out of his way to introduce me to many of the women included in this volume; to Henry H. Mitchell III and Ella Mitchell for doing the same with both men and women; to Fred Cleveland of Aaron Press for his devotion to the publication of the entire corpus, without which a very large part of it would undoubtedly never have seen the light of day. I am also grateful to my copy editor, Stephen A. Jones, whose excellent editorial suggestions saved me untold errors.

I am especially grateful to the following people who believed in me enough to support my work financially, without hesitation: Arthur Kemp, Berthella Brooks, James and Callie Melton, Pamela Canzater, William and Vivian Bryant, Hardin Martin Sr., Gerry McClamy, Carrie Hinton, Patricia Smothers, Willie and Idelle Cook, David and Mary Ann Turner, Lillie Gilchrist, Walter Chavers, Joe Funchess, Thomas Ragland, C. Jay Matthews I, Ethel Pye, Henry Fagin, Barbara Lee, Barbara Waller and Eric Walker.

Special thanks goes to my family for the untold time and funds that they were denied as this project went forth by one "called" to complete it, no matter what the costs.

Preface

I have spent my entire life in the nurturing embrace of the "Black Church." From my earliest recollections, which begin at age five, I was a participant in the African Methodist Episcopal (AME) Church. I participated in the Sunday school and worship experience at St. James AME on Davis street in Meridian, Mississippi. I don't remember much about my religious experience during those years; perhaps it is because they were very difficult years of growing up without any knowledge of a mother or father. I have no memory of the faces or names of any Sunday school teachers, preachers, elders or deacons. I recall no sermons, only two songs and a few lines from prayers.

However, two thoughts have lingered with me throughout the years about that community. One is that the community instilled in me the value of religious education in such a way that, between the ages of five and eleven, I tried to learn everything I could about the Bible. I don't even remember the process that brought this about; I assume it was Sunday school. It became so much a part of me that I initiated correspondence with the American Bible Society in New York to learn more, even at this early age. The second is that the community was given strongly to prophesying about which children in the community were going to "grow up to be somebody." Often, while on my way to school, I would pass the older prophetesses of the community who would sit on their porches and prophesy about children as they passed by. "There goes Big Bubba," one would say, "he's going to be a preacher." Others in the community agreed that I was going to be somebody, but they held out for a doctor or a teacher. Though obviously not as vivid as some of the stories in this collection, this was my first introduction to the notion of a call to preach, though I did not think of it in such terms at the time. Twenty years later when I returned for the first time to that community, one of the older prophetess's first question addressed to me as I entered her house was, "So, which one are you?" She wanted to know whether I was a doctor, teacher or preacher. She had not forgotten.

After I moved to Cleveland, Ohio, where I joined the New Mount Zion Baptist Church and became a part of the Baptist community of faith, I was introduced to the riveting testimonials, conversion stories and call stories that have become so much a part of my religious pilgrimage. I remain a member of that community which has nurtured me in my Christian faith to this hour. During all of these years I have listened to countless call stories in sermons, casual conversations and testimonies from Baptists as well as from those in other parts of the Black church. No call story was more enchanting than that told by my own pastor, the Rev. Cary McCreary, numerous times over the years. In addition, I have participated in at least twelve councils brought together to license or ordain candidates for the ministry. There, oral articulation of the call is a requirement.

For the last nine years I have taught at a seminary that has over fifty different denominations represented in its student body. I have listened to many stories from students who were wrestling with their call to preach, and I attempted to give them some direction, particularly African American students.

Some people are enthralled by novels, plays, or movies. Some of these things hold my interest for a while as well. However, I admit to being captivated by oral call stories for as long as I can remember. My fascination and interest in this phenomenon that attempts to articulate the mystery of a divine-human encounter in oral communication has not diminished over the years. As I began work on the analysis of call narratives some years ago, biblical and extra-biblical, it was as if I had been born to do it; that is, I felt called to research the call to preach. (Some of my dearest, most revered friends have suggested that this is nothing more than my attempt to resist my own call to preach. I plead no contest.) As an active participant in the Black church, I intuitively knew a number of things about call stories, but I had never seriously raised academic questions about them in any systematic way or brought any methodological tools to bear on them, especially their relationship to biblical call narratives.

Discussion of call, whether public or private, is not a new phenomenon in the Black church. People are very familiar with the concept and process of the call to preach and stories about it. Like conversion stories and testimonials they are heard in part

Preface

in sermons, testimonials, and rituals leading to ordination. This oral phenomenon has a long history, as works quoted throughout this work will attest. *God Struck Me Dead,* a collection of nineteenth century conversion narratives, contains stories that describe, at least in part, calls to preach that occurred along with conversion to the Christian faith.

The collection in this work is an attempt to give call narratives the recognition that they are due in the religious experience of African Americans in the Black church. These eighty-six stories were collected in tape-recorded interviews over a six year period from 1985 to 1991. The corpus represents at least eight different denominations, it is one-fourth female, it covers every geographical area in this country and it spans three different generations. Some of the people interviewed are recognized nationally and internationally; others are recognized nationally, regionally or locally. This kind of mixture adds to the scholarly significance of the study by including people with a diversity in background, recognition and theological tendencies.

Scholars as diverse as literary critics, narrative theorists, folklorists, anthropologists and biblical experts—to name a few—have highlighted the importance of stories. Storytelling brings together a story, a storyteller and a hearer/reader. Recently, in the last decade or so, scholars in biblical and theological disciplines have begun to accentuate the importance of story. They are finally catching up with literary critics on the importance of the reader. Of even greater significance, for me, is that much of recent scholarship is rejecting the bias toward the content of language as the center of understanding and hermeneutical inquiry to the exclusion of the effect of form and structure on the hearer/reader.

The bias toward content over form, especially as it relates to stories, is a modern development. Such was not the case with the ancients. And it is certainly not true of the African or African American experience. Storytellers in the African American religious experience have always been concerned with the experience they could evoke from the hearer by the way they shaped the story. The artistic form of the African American performed sermon is an example. The cultural phenomenon of sermonizing in many African American contexts is designed to have an emotive impact on the hearer. The frequency of the refrain "tell the story," heard from the lips of the hearers in an African

American preaching experience, is sufficient evidence of the storyteller's craft. In other words, the hearer (reader) and the hearing (reading) experience is paramount.

Other examples of this phenomenon in the African American religious experience are testimonials, especially conversion stories, and call stories. More than anything else, the storytellers want to persuade; they want their hearers to believe their story. Content is important in this regard, but the contours of the story, how it is told, may be even more important. Storytellers in African American churches know this, and it is evident in the shape their stories take.

However, it should not be inferred that this phenomenon is so "folksy" that content is abandoned strictly for the sake of form. Certainly one could find extreme examples of this in the African American context as in any other, but it is not the norm. Without culturally relevant content, the eloquent artistry of the storyteller will ultimately be called into question by the hearers —if not the present hearers, then surely a new generation of hearers. Various types of "telling" and re-telling live on in African American churches, even today. The point is simply this: storytelling in the African American religious experience elevates the importance of story form, as well as the experience of the hearer of the story, in ways not taken seriously heretofore.

Scholars who have taken seriously the equal importance of *how* stories are told with *what* is told use a variety of technical terms to make this distinction. "Story" refers to the content: what is told. "Narrative" refers to the discourse: how it is told. "Story" is the storyteller's attempt to reconstruct the chronological account of what happened. "Narrative" is the oral or written words that the hearer or reader experiences as articulated by the storyteller.

The significance of these distinctions for African American call stories will be made more evident in the companion volume to follow. For now, my task in this book is to tell these gripping stories as I heard them. Indeed, they are stories meant to persuade. Therefore, my role in this book is like that of John the Baptist: I must decrease so that the storytellers and their stories might increase. I must fade into the background as an unobtrusive researcher so that the reader/hearer might meet the storyteller in the story at the intersection of the telling experience and the reading/hearing experience. I will rise again in the second book, which calls for the researcher to be much more intrusive.

Three important points need to be made: (1) Theological or ideological persuasion was not a criterion for selection of these stories. A good demographic mixture was the most important factor. Many in this collection do not agree ideologically or theologically on a host of issues, but each has a call story worth considering. (2) The biographical data are information received at the time of the interview. Generally, it was not possible to keep up with changes that occurred in eighty-six people's lives over six years, but a few alterations were made when information was readily available. (3) The oral form of these stories is as important as the content. Although there has been slight editing to make the corpus more readable, retention of the spoken voice is given priority throughout this work. Hence the speakers syntax has been retained at crucial places because it will prove significant in the scholarly analysis in the second volume.

Indeed, more should be said about this last point. As an African American religious studies scholar I live in two worlds — the academic community and the African American religious community. I know many of the people in this study well, and I respect all of them. I am very familiar with call stories. I approach them with great reverence. In addition, however, I am a scholar who uses critical tools of analysis to further the broader community's understanding of certain phenomena.

Although the detailed critical analysis of this body of material will occur primarily in the second volume, I had to make some decisions in this volume. I wanted to present the storyteller's story, not my story, but I also had to insure that the reader would understand what I heard the storyteller say. This dual objective necessitated some difficult choices. Every attempt was made to be consistent throughout the document.

All of those interviewed, except two or three, told their stories orally without the requirement that they be able to alter the written version before it was published. Many of them are excellent writers, and if given the opportunity to edit their stories they would have changed many literary and stylistic idiosyncrasies. However, one of the objectives of the study was to capture these idiosyncrasies so that they could be analyzed as well. Moreover, I did not want the editorial process to be so intrusive that what started out as oral African American stories turned out to be non-African American when published.

Some editorial decisions reflected in this document are as follows:
1. Brackets were used sparingly.
2. Confusing statements were eliminated if they didn't effect the flow of the story. Sometimes a word or two needed to be added (in square brackets). The latter is an infrequent occurrence.
3. What I recognized as common African American speech patterns (what linguists call BEV, Black English vernacular), such as beginning a sentence with "so" or "and," or using "there" for "then," were allowed to remain in the stories. If they were too repetitious, some were eliminated but others retained so that the pattern could be recognized for analytical purposes later.
4. The most difficult decision was what should be done with obvious grammatical errors. This was made even more difficult by some patterns that are very important to narrative analysis, even when they appear to be grammatically incorrect. For example, an incorrect use of a present tense verb when a sentence calls for a past tense may be an example of a storyteller retrospectively re-living part of an experience at that very moment. That difference alone may not be sufficient to prove it is such an example, but in conjunction with other narrative analysis it could prove decisive. Therefore, to change the verb because it is not grammatically correct would be uncritical and premature at this stage.

When the context suggested that it might be important for critical analysis, the interviewee's form of the verb was retained in every instance, even if there was doubt. When there was clearly a pattern throughout the story that this was the storyteller's preferred grammatical usage, it was retained; if overly repetitious so that clarity was effected, some instances were reduced. When it was an obvious error that the storyteller would change if given the opportunity, it was changed.

The size of this collection and the significance of the study made a two-volume work necessary. Most publishers wanted me to choose between the publication of all the stories or publication of all the detailed analysis of the stories. I held out for both. A thorough scholarly analysis of the stories was as important to me as making the stories available in published form. Moreover, publication of all eighty-six stories rather than a limited selection that another editor would determine was paramount to me. Only Aaron Press offered me the option to publish all of these stories and in one volume. Therefore, this

Preface

volume is primarily devoted to making the stories available in print and saying something about the whole collection only in a very brief and general way. The companion volume (forthcoming), will contain a detailed analysis of these stories as a corpus, as well as a critical analysis of the call to ministry from an African American perspective.

Three people included in this volume have died since their stories were collected: J.H. Jackson (Baptist), T.Oscar Chappelle (Baptist), and Eugene Morgan (AME Zion). May they live on through their stories captured in this volume.

There are many other people whom I wish I had included in this collection. It was not because of a lack of effort. After years of attempts to get interviews with some people, time and money proved to be the final decision-maker, and the work had to be closed. There are African Americans in other denominations–Episcopalians, Presbyterians, Penecostals and others—that I did not even have time to pursue. In addition, my initial goal was to insure that the study would be at least one-third female. This proved to be the most difficult task of all, and the ratio slipped to one-fourth.

This study was not a funded research project. This situation limited to a large degree how much I could do and, to some extent, how it could be done. Hopefully, my research will encourage future studies in this area that will receive funding. Such a development will unshackle the researcher from the limitations faced here.

William H. Myers
Ashland Theological Seminary
Ashland, Ohio
November, 1991

"*I was in the field ploughing, a sunshiny morning; there came a west wind as a fire and lifted me up, and showed me a ladder from the northwest, that passed right along by me, about two miles from me; the voice told me to go to it and be baptized. I saw the church, and in it twelve people, and in the pulpit a colored man preaching. I could see half his body; the twelve people were in front of him, and I saw myself sitting behind him in the pulpit, and by that spirit and that sign I was showed I was called to preach.*"

Roland Steiner,"*Sol Lockheart's Call.*"
Journal of American Folk-Lore
13 (March, 1900): 67-70.

"*I* would often talk about my call to the ministry in the sense of an urging, not even an urgency. I think that came later for me, but urgings and tuggings at heartstrings in mind and soul came first."

Sharon Austin, Assistant Pastor,
Ebenezer Baptist Church,
Atlanta, Georgia

"*T*he urge to preach became overwhelmimg. I found myself preaching for the five miles I had to walk to my job. All while I was working I was preaching."

Joseph Blake, Pastor,
Sacred Trinity Baptist Church,
Cleveland, Ohio

"*I*t has never been my desire to do anything else but preach. I mostly articulate it with words of a divine call motivated by an inward urge to preach the gospel. And I could say a ton of more words, but I don't think it will come any more crystal clear than a divine urge to preach the gospel."

E. Theophilus Caviness, Pastor,
Greater Abyssinia Baptist Church,
Cleveland, Ohio

"*I* cannot remember when I did not carry in the inner core of my being the urge to preach. I can recall vividly a dream concerning the ministry at the age of four or five. It has been a consciousness, an inner consciousness throughout my life. However, I did not always acknowledge that. This inner awareness, urge, grew stronger as the years passed. And its acknowledgment was not made public until I reached the age of seventeen."

Otis Moss, Jr., Pastor,
Olivet Institutional Baptist Church,
Cleveland, Ohio

"The Irresistible Urge to Preach"

"*I had the urge, that desire to preach when I was some eight or nine years old. It is an urge; it's an inner urge that one has that is only satisfied when you yield to it.... Dr.E. L. Harris used to tell us that if a man can keep from preaching he ought not to preach, because if he can keep from preaching that is a sign that he hadn't been called to preach. You don't preach because you want to; you preach because you can't help yourself. Have you read of Jeremiah's frustration? He felt that God had let him down; he felt like he had gone out on a limb. He said, 'I guess I'm through with it.' But then when you hear from him again he's on his mission and he said the reason is that, 'although I intended to go no further the word was like fire.' So you have that inner urge, it haunts you, and you only have a sense—a feeling—of satisfaction when you yield to it. The reason I wanted to do it was what had been laid on my own heart. It is not something I wanted to do because I had seen somebody else do it, but necessity, as the apostle Paul said, was laid on me.*"

Ceasar A. W. Clark, Pastor
Good Street Baptist Church, Dallas, Texas.

An important theme common to this collection of stories whether stated explicitly or implicitly, is the belief that the call to preach is an urge that one cannot, without great price, resist. Many in this study would argue that it cannot be resisted, period. Ultimately, God will have the final say.

This theme is captured explicitly in the call story and life of the Reverend Dr. Caesar Clark. Certain aspects of his preaching career allow us to see this clearly. For example, he has been responding to this urge for more than six decades. He is arguably, one of the leading African American revivalists in America. That he preaches thirty-five revivals a year, two of which are ten days each and the remaining five days each, may clinch the argument.

Moreover, when we consider how long he has been preaching, his uncanny mastery and utilization of a familiar African American sermonic art form consistently for six decades, then the theme of this book is illustrated vividly. Observe how the urge in Clark's story is connected to a number of other important issues. It is divinely given in such a way that it cannot be successfully resisted. Complete satisfaction, peace, and fulfillment in life are not possible until one yields. Biblical rhetoric, especially other biblical call narratives that support this theme are utilized. Ultimately, the inability to resist the urge is a kind of litmus test for a divine call. Resistance may continue for weeks for some, but years for others.

That a divine call is described as an internal urge, in the stories presented in this collection as well as in some biblical call narratives, highlights the subjective self-understanding of the call. To say that they are subjective is not a negative assertion. The same is true of every biblical call narrative. To speak of these narratives as subjective self-understandings is to emphasize both the importance and complexity of these retrospective accounts. For too long the experiential encounter with the divine has been looked upon with a jaundiced eye, simply because we can never know everything about that intensely personal moment. Yet there is much that we can learn, because the mystery of the experience is not only concealed but revealed in the retrospective story. Again, this is also true of biblical call narratives.

We learn that many interpret their experiences as evolving, while others see theirs as sudden. In some instances the experiences are cataclysmic, peculiar, mysterious, inexplicable. Those whose experiences were spectacular often refer to having visions or dreams, hearing voices or seeing images and a host of other unusual phenomena. Others relate phenomena, though not as mysterious, that are just as providentially intriguing in terms of timing, lack of options, and other types of confirming events. For some the call was expected; for others it was not.

Responses to the experiences are as varied as the experiences themselves. Some were reluctant and defiant, while others responded immediately. Resistance and reluctance to accepting the call have many motivations: ambiguity, economics, other career preferences, poor image of the profession, treatment of those in the profession, gender pressures (on women), inappropriate or inadequate models—to name several.

A number of positive and negative factors influenced those interviewed in this collection. The leading positive influence was a Christian environment in early childhood; this was primarily the home and church. In the absence of religious parents, other religious family members such as grandparents, aunts and uncles were influential. Although the church was key even when there was a religious home, it was even more the case when there was no such home. The value of the church as an influencing factor in the lives of these individuals is beyond measure. In a number of cases we observe the interesting effect that "playing church" had on some during childhood.

Another important positive influence was religious individuals. The key person in the church was the pastor, though there are many cases where other religious people were influential as well. In some instances people in the larger church were named as influential figures, e.g., Sam Proctor, Gardner Taylor, James Earl Massey, Henry Mitchell and Agnes Alston. It is evident in these stories that these people would not have known how much of an influence they were at the time.

The negative factors that proved to be obstacles were numerous: the low economic standards of those in the ministry; the negative dynamics of being a "PK"(preacher's kid); expectations about lack of freedom for those entering the professional ministry; the lack of adequate and varied images of those in the ministry; resistance to women because of gender; and early childhood predictions are a few.

In this volume, the actual stories are given primary consideration. It is the voice of the callee that is to be heard and appreciated. Analytical observations have been brief and general. In the companion volume, examination of these stories proceeds from three different angles:content, structure and hermeneutics.

In that volume, the examination of the content of the stories reveals that the call to preach can be understood as a process, a "rite of passage." Six stages of call are identified: early religious exposure, experience, struggle, search, sanction and surrender. This is not to suggest that every call includes all stages but that types of call stories can be usefully defined and described in such a way.

This analysis of the structure of the material demonstrates that it consists of "story" and "narrative." There is a difference between the "experiental moment" and talking about it one hour, one year or ten years later. From this analysis it is demonstrated that three different types of calls to preach can be identified.

In view of the fact that callees are telling a story, often many years removed from the actual event, we should expect that retrospective interpretation is a significant part of the narratives. Hence, analysis of these stories helps to uncover some of the explicit and implicit hermeneutics (interpretation) resident in them. This analysis allows us to wrestle with some important contemporary hermeneutical issues for the Black church, especially women in the preaching ministry, and criteria for validation of a call to the preaching ministry.

The stories that follow represent a phenomenon that is primarily oral. Their importance can be observed in the fact that, though oral, they have not ceased to exist in the life of the Black church; they are indicative of a longstanding tradition; moreover, their present significance can be observed in rituals carried out in a very large part of the Black church.

Up to now, such stories have not been treated with the attention they are due in view of their place in the life of the Black church. Sermons and conversion stories, which fall into the same category of oral phenomena have, however, received extensive treatment in recent times. Although a call story, or part of one, may appear here and there as part of a larger life history, e.g., in a biography, no one has examined call stories as a genre, stories that can stand alone. This present volume seeks to focus much-needed attention on these stories.

"God started on me when I was a little boy. I used to grieve a lot over my mother. She had been sold away from me and taken a long way off. One evening I was going through the woods to get the cows. I was thinking about Mama and crying. Then a voice spoke to me and said, 'Blessed art thou. An obedient child shall live out the fullness of his days.' I got scared because I did not know who it was that spoke nor what he meant....

After this, one day, I was putting a top on our little log house that I was building. It was broad open day, and I was as wide awake as ever I was in this world. I had just got in position to fit on the first rafters when a voice called my name three distinct times. It called, 'Oh, William! Oh, William! Oh, William! I hollered and answered, 'Hey!' But nobody answered. I looked around and began to wonder about the voice. It sounded so strange. It seemed to come from afar off, and still it seemed to be right at me. I never have been able to find out what it meant.

When God called me I had applied in hell, but my name wasn't on the roll.... As I went along, a voice called out, "Oh, William! Oh, William! Oh, William!' When he said that he turned me around out of the big road into a little path, my face being toward the east. He spoke again and said, 'Go preach my gospel to every creature and fear not, for I am with you, an everlasting prop."

Hooked in the heart, in Clifton H. Johnson, ed., *God Struck Me Dead: Religious Conversion Experiences and Autobiographies of Ex-slaves* (Philadelphia: Pilgrim Press, 1969): 19-21.

"*Yer see I am a preacher. De Lord call me once when I was workin'.* . . . *He call me and told me, in imagination, you know, that he wanted me to preach. I told him I didn't know enough—that I was ig'nant, and the folks would laugh at me. But he drew me on and I prayed. I prayed out in the woods, and every time I tried to get up from my knees He would draw me down again. An' at last a great light came down sudden to me, a light as big as the moon, an' struck me hard on the head and on each shoulder and on the bress, here and here and here.* . . *And den same time warm was in around my heart, and I felt that the Book was there. An' my tongue was untied, and I preach ever since and is not afraid. I can't read de Book, but I has it here, I has de text, and de meanin', and I speaks as well as I can, and de congregation takes what the Lord gives me.*"

American Missionary 13 (February 1869): 28.
Quoted in Albert J. Raboteau
*Slave Religion: The "Invisible Institution in the Antebellum South,*8787
(Oxford: Oxford University Press, 1978): 237

Lucille Abernathy
Cleveland, Ohio

The Reverend Lucille Abernathy was born in Hattisburg, Mississippi, on March 8, 1944, called to preach in 1978, and ordained an American Baptist minister in 1985. She is the niece of one of the leaders of the Civil Rights movement, the Reverend Ralph David Abernathy of Atlanta, Georgia. Presently, she is pastor of the Hough Avenue United Church of Christ in Cleveland, Ohio. She has a BA from Bishop College, Dallas, Texas and an MDiv from Princeton Theological Seminary. Interview recorded June 13, 1990.

1

"We Would Rather Have an Unqualified Man Than a Qualified Woman"

If you are in communication with God, there is a voice within you that you hear. The only thing I can equate it with is where in the Scriptures it says, *"My sheep will know my voice."* When God speaks to you, you are in conversation with God. I used to be in conversation with God all the time when getting direction for my life and what I was doing. As a young person, I remember at 16 to 17, I was a Cub Scout leader. I was a den mother at this age because none of the mothers would take the troop. So I became a den mother with the kids, and secretary of the Sunday School. I was always doing something in the church. I've always done that as long as I can remember.

It was around age thirty-four when I started to deal with this thing about a call to the ordained ministry. It was a thing where I heard the voice. A voice spoke to me as I was leaving prayer meeting. I remember that we had noonday prayer service. I had taken my lunch break to come to noonday prayer service, and I was teaching school down on 30th Street. I was getting ready to rush back to school for my afternoon class and the voice said, "You can't do what I want you to do and keep teaching school." I didn't understand it. But it came back again. And it was as if going back to school was robbing me from doing whatever God wanted me to do.

So after that I can't tell you exactly how the call came, but it was to the ordained ministry. It was like, "You are to go into the ordained ministry." I didn't know what ordination meant. I kept seeking after people to tell me what it meant to be ordained. They would want to know why, and I kept saying, "Because I feel like God is saying I'm to be ordained." But they would not tell me. The way I finally found out about ordination was through the Executive Minister of the Cleveland Baptist Association (CBA). Our church was dually aligned with the National Baptist and American Baptist. I don't even remember how that took place.

I remember my pastor saying, "Well, you had better be quiet about this, because you don't know what you are talking about and you can't tell anybody." I was trying to be obedient because I respect pastors, and our pastor was our friend and everything.

So, every time I would go to prayer meeting I felt like I needed to tell people, especially at the testimony period. I could never do it because the pastor would say, "No, don't do it." And finally, one day: It was like it was burning; it was driving me crazy. Inside me was like this overwhelming thing to just tell them. It was like, if you tell them you will have peace inside. So, finally I just told them. Everybody got real quiet, and nobody said anything. I remember talking to the pastor again and him saying, "Well, you can be a teacher or a counselor, but God didn't call you to preach." I said, "I never said God called me to preach." That was my whole thing throughout the process. God never called me to preach. He didn't. He said, "Ordained ministry," and I said, "Whatever that means, that's what I have to do."

So when I went down to CBA, I asked, "What does it mean to be ordained. What do you have to do, and what do you do after you get ordained?" Then they told me about school. Then I went through the whole struggle that if I have to go back to school, where do I go to school? My daughter said, "You know where you have to go."

So I went to Bishop College. When we were at the National Baptist Congress my pastor took me to Bishop, and I met the dean of the religion department. It was like, "Oh God, I know I have to be here." I had never been to Texas before in my life, but knew when I was there that this was where I had to be. I was so ill at ease that I left before the Congress was over. That night, at 2:00 o'clock in the morning, I called the airport to see when was the first flight back to Cleveland, because I did not want to be in Texas. I cried all the way to the airport, because I knew I was gonna have to be there. Yet, I thought that by leaving I wouldn't have to be there.

That was in August. I had written a letter and received a letter in response, a very supportive letter. It was the first supportive letter I had ever gotten from a man that said, "There are a lot of men that say, 'dah dah dah dah'." I still have that letter, because that was my first written validation that God really does call women.

Now, what I went through trying to validate it was part of what I had said earlier about this guy from Denver coming to our church that summer. Everything fell into place. That summer a minister from Denver came to do a revival at our church. I ended up at an after-revival reception with him, and the conversation for some strange reason in this group of ministers turned to women in ministry. This pastor from Denver said, "Well, I used to be like you all, but God convicted me and converted me that he does call women." He said, "Right now I have two or three women on my staff, and they take part in the service." I was sitting there and my mouth dropped open, because this is what I asked God for. I said, "God, show me another Black Baptist woman in ministry, and then I won't question you anymore." Prior to that the people at CBA had invited me to go to a girl's ordination at First Baptist, but it was a White girl. You know in the Black church we don't always validate what people do in the White church. "They'll do anything," as some people say. So, I can't use that as validation, because I'm in a Black church. I needed to see a Black woman.

Well, this man went on talking about these women in the ministry, and I was just thanking the Lord. Well, something strange happened. My pastor was invited to go there [Denver] to do something, and the church was invited to go. So, the Lord said, "You have to go." And I'm saying, "I have to go to Denver?"

"We Would Rather Have an Unqualified Man Than a Qualified Woman"

Now, we're going to Denver, right. Seems like everything fell in place for me to go. I got a ticket cheap enough to go. I think the occasion was his brother's ordination, I think it was. Anyway, so I went to Denver and saw these women in the pulpit being a part of the service and everything. I talked to my pastor's brother. They were very open, their father is a pastor. Both of them are pastors. But they are totally different as far as what they think theologically. The brother was all for women in ministry, but my pastor was definitely, "God doesn't call women."

After this experience in Denver, and I call it "My Mountaintop Experience," because Denver was so high, I came home and said, "Okay God, you called, I'm doing whatever you say, you showed me what I needed to know." I no longer felt that I had to argue with people or convince people that God had called me. Prior to that, people would want to tell you why you weren't called rather than validate what God was doing. I just came home with the conviction that God had called me, and I believe that where God leads, he will provide.

From then on, it was just a process of "What do you want me to do?" My whole process of school fell in place. School was a trying situation. Because, again, you are confronted with all these men who don't believe God calls women. Here I am in a Black Baptist school, in a religion department with all Black Baptist men. Some men who were sponsors or supporters of the school resented the fact that I was a woman in a male-dominated position. It was strange, but I went with a peace. I didn't have to validate it for anybody anymore. I just had to do whatever God called me to do, which was to train and to learn.

During my second year, a strange thing happened. The Lord spoke to me. We had a minister's alliance which included all of the ministers on campus. It was like a fraternity or whatever. The first year I visited, but I didn't get involved, because women weren't welcomed, to put it nicely. Basically, I was the only woman in most of my classes, because all I took was religion. I already had all the other courses. So, it was time for the second year. The Lord just put on my heart that I was supposed to run for office. I said to the Lord, "I don't even go; they don't want me in there. Why should I run for office?" President was what it was. The Lord said to me, "You're going to run." "No, Lord," I said, but finally, of course, being obedient I gave in. Being obedient, I won. Strange things happened. Even to the point that some of the ministers threatened to stop supporting the school, because they allowed this woman to be president of this group. They had the guys fearful at one point that they would never preach in their churches, because they let a woman do this. It was tremendous in that it was a continuation of validation by God in what he had called me to do. Some of the people were even bold enough to say, "We would rather have an unqualified man than a qualified woman, because women aren't supposed to lead the men."

But God validated it in such a way that that year we were one of the most powerful organizations that there had been. We accomplished a lot of things that year. We preached in different churches. We had one minister call the group on the carpet, a minister out of Houston, when we went to Houston. He said, "I'm going to be different than the rest of you, because I have heard about the way you all have treated this woman. Unless you start accepting women and everything else you are not going to preach in my church." He turned the tables on them. I saw that as God's continuing validation of what he had called me to be. Because everybody, including the adult males, as well as the campus people, had said, "God didn't call this woman and this is gonna go down the tubes." What God showed us was that through the process of whatever we did, it did prosper. To me that was part of the validation.

Going back to deal with the call itself, I guess the hardest part is being alone in it—being alone in it and not having anybody else around you to say, "Yeah, this is wonderful, celebrate it." Everybody in my church, where I had been all my life (and this was always strange to me, because I had been in that church since I was three years old), was turned-off by my announcement. I had worked in every department of the church, done everything that you do, but they were so programmed to believe that God did not call women, that they could not accept the fact that he called me.

When I came home from seminary, there was a little lady, she was very elderly, and had been my teacher when I was three years old. She had been in this church all her life. She said to me, "When you went away to school, I thought that was the worst thing you could have ever done, but now I see what God has done." So, it took all those years, but it was another confirmation that God does call women and that women could finally recognize and appreciate it.

One of my prayers, because of my own struggle, was that

"We Would Rather Have an Unqualified Man Than a Qualified Woman"

"God always uses me to help validate somebody else's call, and maybe that's why I know about you." That was my prayer, after I became comfortable with the idea that I was called. I wanted to be able to be there for somebody else, because I didn't have anybody.

Even in my family, my in-laws more than my family, it was awful, because they don't believe that God calls women. My mother-in-law went through this thing that my husband was awful, because he was going to let me go to school and do all this other stuff. It was terrible, but the blessing was in my immediate family, meaning my husband and children. I had always raised my children to know that God was first in my life, that they were a gift to me from God and that they did not come before God. They knew that from day one, from the time they could understand anything I taught them: that God would always be first and they would always be second. So that when it came time for me to deal with my call, there was my support.

Even when I went away to school, my kids stayed at home with my husband. That was another whole big incident related to my call, because these same church people who teach you and tell you that you are supposed to follow Christ were the first ones to say, "No, God didn't call you to leave your children. God made you a mother and a wife first." Church people, including in-laws, were saying, "Your children are going to be juvenile delinquents, your daughters are going to be pregnant, your husband is going to leave you and have some other women." All these things were comments that church people planted as advice to me. I would tell people, "If my husband leaves me, then God didn't want me to have him," and I honestly believed that. I said, "I could stay home and my husband could leave me." I said, "Look at all the people around you who are divorced and whose husbands are running around. Staying there doesn't keep him there." And, I said, "As for my children, I believe that if God called me, God's going to take care of my children." They didn't get pregnant, they are not juvenile delinquents, and they love God.

When I left to go to school, my husband, who did not even go to church at that time, started going to church every Sunday, taking his kids to Sunday School. We never used to talk about the Bible. When I would call home, my husband would start saying, "You know what happened in Sunday School today?" And we would start carrying on conversations about God and the Bible. This man was not that kind of person before I went to school.

I always say that a lot of things that are associated with my call I would have missed the enjoyment of, if I had neglected my call. I would have robbed myself and my family of a whole different kind of relationship with God. Consequently, when I was in school and I wanted to quit, my daughter would say, "Mother, you know you can't quit, God's going to do such and such." There were never any real problems. Their father was there, which gave them another whole dimension of family life. When I was there, he really didn't care for them in the same way that I did. He didn't know what size shoes they wore, what size dress or pants. But because I went away, he had to learn that stuff. He had to care in a different kind of way. Before it was "He's daddy and he's there" but then it became "Daddy takes us here and daddy does that." It just added to our relationship. Everything that happened because of my call has been positive. The negatives were the struggle of accepting it, and knowing that that's what God was saying when everybody around you was saying, "God doesn't say that." And it's all the people that you respect and love. These people were people that I had known all of my life who were saying, "God doesn't do that." And I was saying, "Well, if he doesn't do it, then why am I getting this, why am I hearing this?"

I finally had to "one-on-one" say, "Lord, what are you saying? If you show me, I'll do it." He showed me, and I couldn't help but do it. It hasn't been real easy. But now it's a whole lot better than it was, because that was ten years ago. Eleven years ago, it was totally different. Since that time, and I can honestly say, because of that time, there have been other women who have come forth and said, "I was dealing with my call, and I waited to see what was happening to you." I thank God that I really answered it. I even thank him for the struggle now that I'm out of that aspect of it. The greatest part of it was not having that human validation, but that became the greatest asset too; because then you know it's just you and God. And you know for sure, no man called you.

You get into situations like when I first came here to my present church and said, "God, are you sure you called me?" "Are you sure you want me to be here? Are you sure I didn't hear you wrong?" I don't think that's any different for any man that goes through it. That is, in the fact that there are points of uncertainty once you find yourself in situations. I don't think that you are so uncertain, rather it's that you just don't want to

"We Would Rather Have an Unqualified Man Than a Qualified Woman"

be in that situation, and, you are looking for a way out. But all of the positive things from it I wouldn't trade them, even to the degree that when I was in school, part of my call was to remain Baptist, and I couldn't understand that. I said, "Lord, why do I have to be Baptist when the Baptists won't accept me?" When I was in seminary, people would say to me, "Well, who do you think is going to ordain you?" First, it started at Bishop. I actually ended up being licensed in Texas, which I didn't think would happen there, because it's a male chauvinist preacher area. But this Black American Baptist minister near the college, Mt. Tabor—he died since—he licensed me. He said, "Whenever you are ready to do your trial sermon, just let me know, we'll do it. I'm American Baptist, it'll be valid." I prayed about it, because I don't rush into anything. I wanted to be sure that it's where God wants it to happen. So, I was licensed Baptist.

In seminary, people kept saying, "You're not going to be ordained. Who's going to ordain you? You are going to have to start your own church." You know people will always tell you what's going to happen to you. I said, "Well, I have to go with whatever the Lord is saying." It kept impacting on me, "You gotta remain Baptist." People actually came to me and offered to pay tuition and everything else. I got invited to be United Methodist, A.M.E. and Presbyterian; I worked in the Presbyterian church and they wanted to ordain me Presbyterian. I said, "I'm sorry, I can't." I really didn't have all the money for school, and they were going to pay full-tuition and everything, plus the United Methodists will promise you a position when you graduate if you are United Methodist. So you don't even have to worry about placement.

I couldn't do it, mainly because part of my call was to remain Baptist. I did not understand it, but I did trust God. When I came home and went back to my church where I grew up, I knew that I would never be ordained there and I couldn't continue being there, because I was making them terribly uncomfortable. It was like an all-out attack to make me leave.

Finally, it got to the point where I said, "Lord, I can't go there anymore, I have to resign." It hurt me to my heart, because I loved my church. I loved my church and the people in it. I wrote a letter of resignation asking for a letter to transfer. They refused to give me a letter until I found a church. I didn't have any place I wanted to go. I said, "Lord, I can't go anywhere until you send me."

Somebody from CBA knew what I was going through. This white guy called me up and said, "We can ordain you, and you can be part of our church, but its not the Black church." I said, "Well, I don't think that is where God is leading. I don't think it's ordination as much as it is that I needed a place where I can do ministry where God wants me to be. Then finally they told me to go visit this church on Lee Road, Lee Road Baptist. I went and really didn't like it and really wasn't quite ready to join a church; but I went because they had asked me to go visit. The next Sunday, the Lord led me to go back, but I said, "I don't want to go, Lord." I went, and I think about the second or third time I went, they opened the doors of the church. I was going up there and I didn't know why.

The minister said, "I take by your coming forward, you've come to join this church." I was speechless. I never answered him. I was just standing there. It was like the Spirit moved me there. I guess I joined the church there, and it was one of the best things that could have ever happened to me.

I was there a little less than a year before they voted to ordain me. They were the most wonderful people and accepted all of my gifts. I taught Bible class for adults. They just went all out and did for me what I would have expected my home church to do. But it was like God kept giving me that scripture, "*A prophet is without honor in his own country,*" to let me know that I was not to be at my home church, I was to be right where he had placed me. Since then he's done nothing but bless me.

It was kind of strange, because there were a few people in my home church that came forward and said different things; they may have come to the ordination or the installation here. But the most difficult part was letting go of people and things you held dear. It was just letting you and God be, and just letting everybody else go by the wayside. Because when you love and respect people they can have too much of an influence on you the wrong way.

That's what God did for me. He moved the people. At first it was real strange. It's always real lonely, always really lonely. But then God will do something to make you satisfied.

Charles G. Adams
Detroit, Michigan

The Reverend Charles Gilchrist Adams was born in Detroit, Michigan, on December 13, 1936, called to preach before he was born and ordained a Baptist minister in 1961. He has a BA from the University of Michigan and an MDiv from Harvard Divinity School. He serves as the President of the Progressive National Baptist Convention, Inc. Considered by many to be one of the best pulpiteers of our day, he is sought after constantly as a revivalist throughout the country and preacher throughout the world. Reverend Adams pastors the Hartfield Memorial Baptist Church of Detroit, Michigan. Interview recorded October 24, 1991.

2

Starting a Church in the Garage at Age Eight

There has never been a moment in my consciousness of being alive and being a person that I have not understood myself as having been called and commissioned to preach. I deeply and sincerely believe that my call to preach came before my birth. My only Biblical reference to that possibility is the call of Jeremiah as he acknowledged that he was called before he was born. Jeremiah 1:4-5 says, *Then the word of the Lord came unto me saying, Before I formed thee in the belly, I knew thee; and before thou camest forth out of the womb I sanctified thee, and I ordained thee a prophet unto the nations.* I think that is what happened to me.

There was no preacher in my household for me to identify with. My parents were very devout Christian people, and my father's father was a pastor in South Carolina, but I never saw him until I was about twelve or thirteen years old, and I had confessed the call to preach long before then. My grandmother's father, my great-grandfather on my mother's side, was a preacher;

but he died in 1903. He died at forty-one, after preaching a sermon in South Carolina. His son, my grandfather's brother, was Dr. Gordon B. Hancock, pastor of Moore Street Missionary Baptist Church in Richmond, Virginia, and professor of sociology and economics at Virginia Union University. I had seen him very rarely and infrequently, because he lived all the way in Richmond and travelled in the forties mostly by train. So, we didn't get together very often. I could not really identify with him as a significant person in my life at the time that I acknowledged the call to preach. Neither can I pinpoint any day or hour, because as I said before, it has always been a part of my consciousness that I was to preach the gospel. I knew that I was born to do it, and that a compulsion was upon me, is upon me and will be upon me to preach the gospel, and to be a prophet; that is, to speak for God. I think a prophet is not just one who gives prognostications and predictions, but one who represents the presence and activity of God in politics, economics, foreign policy, domestic policy, in issues of social change. I think a prophet has to address those issues, and I feel compelled to do so.

I can remember that as a very young child I knew that I was to be a preacher, but I also wanted the distinction and the comfort that would go along with being a doctor. So, I had in my heart and in my mind a desire to be both a physician and a pastor. But my mother, who was a very intelligent woman, and obviously did not know about the career of Albert Schweitzer, told me when I was about seven or eight years old that I could not be a doctor and a preacher, and I would have to choose between them. Secretly, I'm sure that she harbored in her heart the desire that I would be a doctor, that I would choose that. I wanted to please her, so when she told me that I could not be both, I said, "Well, if you name it, I will be it." With great love, with love that permits and encourages the freedom of the beloved, she told me, "No, that's for you to choose, not for me. I can't make that choice for you." Then instinctively, without hesitation and with no doubt in my mind I said, "Well, I've got to preach," and she said, "Well, be the best one you can be." That was when I was seven or eight years old.

As I went through grammar school, I began to organize the church for children in the backyard and the garage. We didn't have an automobile, so the garage was empty, and I made it into the church. I would have the children in the neighborhood gather into the garage. I would teach them the Sunday school lesson, I would preach the sermon; and I would also receive an offering, I'm sorry to say. This went on until I made it into a formal Bible school. During the summer months we would have Bible school. Those who were advanced students would have classes for those who were under them in age and in grade, and I was the sort of principal and architect of the whole thing for children who were both older and younger than myself. I had gotten the model from a Lutheran storefront mission that was located in our neighborhood. A white Lutheran pastor would have a Bible school, and it was so rare and ingenious that his little storefront could not hold the people who wanted to attend. So there was a market for it, and I exploited that market by organizing my own little Bible school in the backyard and garage of our humble dwelling.

When I got to junior high I received my first invitation (I was thirteen) to preach in a real church. It was the junior church of a Christian Methodist Church in the neighborhood. In those days they called it the Colored Methodist Church. They had a junior church, and they invited this little Baptist boy who had acknowledged the call to preach, who had organized a Bible school in his backyard and garage, and who had preached to the children in the neighborhood. They said, "You come and preach in a real church." On the fourth Sunday in November 1950, I preached, at the age of thirteen, my first sermon. It came from the book of Romans: *The wages of sin is death, but the gift of God is eternal life through our Lord Jesus Christ.* I don't know what I said. I think I talked about what happened in the preceding chapters of Romans and how it led up to that particular statement which was very vivid and very cutting. I knew then that by taking the high road that meant that I could be led to life and lead others to life, and by taking the low road I would be driven to death and would mislead others to destruction. I tried to preach that as best as I could at age thirteen.

Shortly after that, I had to make a decision about what high school I would attend and what would be my area of concentration. I decided to go to Cass Technical High School in Detroit and concentrate in chemistry and biology, which was the pre-medical curriculum. I had given up being a doctor; but I wanted a mind that was sharp and clear, a mind that had been challenged by the rigor and the exactitude of the sciences. I wanted to go into preparation with a disciplined mind, so I took that curriculum and graduated. Then, I went to Fisk University for two years and transferred to the University of Michigan, where I majored in the history of the ancient near east so that I would have a good background for the study of the Bible. From there, I went to Harvard Divinity School, where I concentrated more in Old Testament history and theology than any other single discipline.

I took a pastorate in Boston, the first pastorate that I had. Concord Baptist Church was the largest Black Baptist Church in New England. I served them for almost seven years before being called to my present pastorate, which is my home-based church where I met the Lord and where I also first met a prophetic ministry. My predecessor, Charles Andrew Hill, was not only an excellent spiritual leader, a very upright man, a family man, a very intelligent man, college-trained, seminary-trained. He was also an activist—a fighter for racial justice, economic justice, social justice, community development, and people empowerment. He was very much interested in Black people being organized in Detroit and voting intelligently and being active in public life. He was connected with the left-wing movement of the Democratic party, the Henry Wallace people, which pulled out in the forties and became the Progressive party. He would tell them, "Don't vote Democratic, don't vote Republican, vote Progressive." He helped to organize the labor movement right in the sanctuary, in the late thirties, when it was considered subversive and un-American to do this. He was fighting for the rights of workers. He fought for the right of Black teachers to be hired by the Detroit Board of Education and to receive equal pay. When they were first hired, they got a salary that was not equal to the salary that was being paid to whites. He fought for them to get equal pay for equal work.

On the one hand I had the spiritual focus, while on the other hand I also had the political focus. It was the spiritual that drove me into political interest and concern, but I have never sought political office. It wasn't politics that drove me into the church to use it as a political stomping horse. Therefore, I think that we are free of a criticism that is often levelled by persons who want to discredit the Black church. They say that it is purely a social organization or a political battering-ram, but that it is not really a spiritual and theological community. Well, I beg to differ. I think that it is the spiritual and the theological that drives us into the social, political, economic, and academic realities, demands and challenges.

I was also influenced by my grandfather's pastor. My grandfather came out of the country, but the country never came out of my grandfather. He didn't want to join a church where the minister was real sophisticated and at times was unemotional. He wanted to be in a church where you could count on a visitation by the Holy Ghost every time you went in there. He was a deacon in a less sophisticated church, and his pastor was a Mississippian who was unlettered, but one of the most brilliant men that I have ever met, Rev. A. M. Martin. He was a very, very studious man, but highly spiritual in morals and stature. He would preach with his whole little body. He was pliant and very demonstrative in his preaching. He would leap on the table and across the pews. He was very pliant and dramatic. It was under him that my spiritual depths were plumbed and shaken.

My ministry has three foci. It has the spiritual focus, the intellectual focus—which I saw in this unlettered man as well as my pastor, Rev. Charles A. Hill—and then it has the political and social focus, which I saw in Hill and eventually in my uncle who was pastor and professor of sociology and economics at Virginia Union University. So I have tried in my ministry to be all three: spiritual, first and foremost and throughout; secondly, academically and intellectually informed and honest; and thirdly, politically relevant and courageous. So that's the call.

John Hurst Adams
Atlanta, Georgia

Bishop John Hurst Adams was born in Columbia, South Carolina, on November 27, 1929, called to preach in 1946, and ordained an Elder in the African Methodist Episcopal Church in 1952. He received a BA from Johnson C. Smith University, and an STB and STM from Boston University. He is the Bishop of the sixth Episcopal District of the AME Church, headquartered in Atlanta, Georgia. Interview recorded June 23, 1989.

3

The Law Student Who Became Bishop

I guess the best way to start this story is to tell you that I grew up in a very religious home. My father was an AME minister before me. My mother was a very, very avid and devout Christian woman. The combination of those two parental influences was always there. This was always very, very important; and I assume in many respects that the nurturing which they gave me as a child, groomed me to be called to preach.

I remember as a junior high and senior high school fellow, my particular, most joyous play, was playing church — being the preacher and trying to preach to my friends, many of whom were also from religious homes. Along with my sister, we used to play church; and I think I was just acting out what I felt and wanted, though at the time we were just playing. Conversely, I was resisting making that a life commitment, which I eventually had to do. It would be junior high, very early junior, when I think — as I look back on it, that it was clear to me where I was headed — where I thought I did not want to go.

The truth of the matter is that I ran from this during my college days, because I think the imperative, the call to preach, the imperative to be a minister and serve black folks through the black church was there. But I fought it, ran from it, evaded it. When I finished college, continuing this evasion and resistance to the call to preach, I decided to go to law school.

I left college, at Johnson C. Smith, and went to Cleveland, to go to Western Reserve University Law School. I guess it's now Case Western, after the merger. And it was there, in Cleveland, that I joined St. John AME Church as a watch-care member. At that time the Reverend Charles S. Spivey, Sr. was the pastor of St. John. This intense struggle in my life between the call to preach and my decision to go to law school became more than I could handle. So, I started talking to him about it, and he helped me considerably to clarify my call.

Then, I finally went through a long series of discussions with my own father, after some discussions with Dr. Spivey. It became clear that this call was for real, that I would fight it and resist it and disobey it at my own peril, and that I would be displeased with myself the rest of my life if I didn't go on and do what the Lord wanted me to do: that was preach, pastor and work through the instrument of the black church to do what I could to liberate and elevate black folks. That's not a very dramatic story. I wasn't struck by lightning, and didn't fall off no mountain top. I think I was groomed and nurtured, and I was converted. The call was there, and I just tried to walk away from it as much as I could, but I couldn't. So, I finally did give in. I've been very pleased with that decision ever since. It's a simple, easy story.

I tried to go other routes, and the Lord interfered, circumstances interfered, and my own happiness interfered. People who knew and loved me interfered. Everything just kept pushing me where I was supposed to be. When that was done, that confusion, that discontent with my own life was over. I just got on, enjoyed the struggle of being, trying to be a good Christian since then: And that's exactly what I mean, enjoy the struggle, trying to be a good preacher.

Herman L. Anderson, Sr.
Charlotte, North Carolina

Bishop Herman L. Anderson, Sr., was born in Wilmington, North Carolina, on February 23, 1923, called to preach in 1956, and ordained an elder in the African Methodist Episcopal Zion Church in 1958. He has a BS from Tuskegee Institute and a BD from Hood Seminary. Interview recorded July 17, 1989.

4

The Bishop Who Swore Never to Be a Preacher

My story would begin, I suppose, with the background of my parentage and the experiences I had prior to coming to the ministry. I grew up in a parsonage where, as a young fellow, I resented the manner in which the members of churches treated my father, the pastor, and expected the children to be paragons of virtue. At that time, I decided that the last thing in the world I would be was that I would be a preacher. So, when I came of age and went to school, instead of going to our school where we used it to develop ministers, I went far away from home.

I went to Tuskegee, Alabama, to attend Tuskegee Institute to earn a degree in commercial industries, which included trade and business administration. Upon leaving there, I practiced that trade, went into the service—into the Navy—and returned to Mobile, Alabama, where my father was pastoring at that time at an AME Zion church. There, I met my wife. We married and moved back to my hometown, which was Wilmington, North Carolina, where I went into business and finally ended up teaching at the high school there.

During those days, I felt a restlessness that would not go away, along with an emptiness or lack of purpose. There was an absence of purpose to my life. I was not a regular churchgoer. After my father came to preach at that church, I became active in that local church as a steward, a member of the trustee board, a board composed of young—as they would say, "young Turks" who felt that the pastor wasn't doing a good job (he could have done a better job) in handling the finances of the church. We suggested some possible scenarios, and each time we would suggest something, he would let us know that he was the pastor and we were going to do it his way. Each time I would go away thinking that there must be a better way, there has got to be a better way.

With those thoughts on my mind, one night I found myself on my knees saying to the Lord, "I'll go if you want me to go." At that time I told my wife, and we sold the house. I took my children up to Salisbury, North Carolina, to Hood Seminary and returned to school to attend the seminary there. From there on, I've been giving him my all. I've been a full-time pastor. Since I've been in the ministry, I have pastored four churches before being elected as General Secretary of our church, and four years later as Bishop of the church.

Agnes Alston
Baltimore, Maryland

The Reverend Agnes Alston was born in Norfolk, Virginia, on August 31, 1921, called to preach in 1938, and ordained by the Christian Community Church in 1952. She received a BA from Queens College, New York, and a BTh degree from Payne Theological Seminary. She serves as associate minister at Gillis Memorial Community Church in Baltimore, Maryland. Interview recorded June 15, 1989.

5
The Woman No One Would Allow in Seminary

I was fifteen years old when I received the call to the ministry, at which time I was a member of a Baptist church here in Baltimore. Prior to that, I had been what they considered an unusual child, very spiritual with a great determination to become an adult Christian in that particular church. But when I said to the pastor and the officers of that church that the Lord had called me to the ministry, and that I was going to prepare myself to become a minister, it was then that they felt that I was no longer that peculiar child or that spirit-filled child, but that I was a confused child. I remained in that church about six months, and at the end of six months I attended the Gillis Memorial Christian Community Church. At that time it was CME and I talked with the pastor, Reverend Theodore C. Jackson, Sr., who gave me the kind of spiritual nourishment and advice that was needed, and gave me the opportunity to begin my ministry in Gillis Memorial Methodist Church.

When I was thirteen and fourteen years old, churches

The Woman No One Would Allow in Seminary

were inviting me to speak to small youth groups, to talk to the children who were part of the conventions. Of course, it gave me an opportunity to go to the convention. I think all of that was leading up to my ministry. I felt encouraged to do this. I was still in school, still in high school. I knew the Lord was using me for this, I really did. The churches in this city, I imagine, they felt the same thing, because they were constantly inviting me to come and talk to youth groups.

I want to give you a personal experience that I had. I was on an errand for Mrs. Pauline Wells-Lewis, who sits up in that front office now. I was singing and praying as I was walking up the street when I crossed Winchester and Cary Street—just like we're sitting here talking now. (And I know that God speaks to us through his word, but I was not as much in the word of the God as I later grew into it.) As I walked along the street—I had been very apprehensive about getting up before people, really coming out with the word of God, that type of thing—and just as clear as we're sitting here now, I heard, "Use what you have," because I had been very apprehensive about it. It was as though he was really speaking to my mind, telling me to "use what you have." I was a child and I was very afraid to really go into the preaching ministry, and this is what I wanted to know. So, I knew I wanted to be a preacher at fifteen. I knew this, but I was still very apprehensive about it; and I was constantly singing and praying and asking the Lord to lead me. That was my first experience of really hearing or feeling that the Lord was speaking directly to my soul, to me. I came back, and I shared it with the members of our church and shared it with Mrs. Lewis who sits up in the office. And they all said to me, "Well, you have to obey what the Lord says. But, you know, you're still a child and you're out here playing with all the other kids, you're going places with other kids and you're wondering how they're going to receive you." But I kept praying, I continued to pray.

I was taught to pray by my grandmother; I prayed about everything. I prayed about going to school, I prayed about my class work, I prayed about just whatever happened to me daily. I was constantly praying about it. And so I went to the Lord with my ministry, and I asked him if he really wanted me to be that kind of preacher, then he would have to show me. I was available to him, and he would have to lead me, and he did just that.

I remained at Gillis and remained Methodist, until 1947. But during that time, Reverend Jackson and that very small congregation decided that I was not only to prepare myself spiritually, but educationally, to become the greatest minister that I could be. So they sent me from Baltimore to Queens College in Flushing, New York; and after two years there, they sent me on to Wilberforce University and Payne Theological Seminary. My ministry at that time had begun to grow, not only preaching, but ministering to people, talking to young people, talking to older people, trying to win souls for Christ, trying to strengthen those who believed that they were Christians, and trying to encourage other people to get closer to the Lord. And the Lord began to bless my ministry.

When I went to Queens College in New York—and at that time you know what it was like all those years—there were only six black students. When I graduated, there was three of us left. And it was rough, a very rough experience, but like I said, I prayed about everything. Things got real bad for me there, and everybody was really kind of prejudiced. I thought that prejudice was only here in Baltimore and in the South, but they were very prejudiced there. But the Lord brought me through, the same when I went to Wilberforce. These were sanctions to me, because when I stepped on the Wilberforce campus, Dean Spivey said to me that he thought I should be over on the college side and not seminary because there were no women at the seminary.

See, I tried every seminary, that's another reason I know that God called me to the ministry. I tried every seminary that somebody would tell me about. At Gammon, they had no place for women to live. I tried Allen, they had no accommodations for women in the seminary. So I finally ended up in all of the southern schools, the Black schools. The only place that would accept me was Wilberforce; but I had to live on the college side, in the dormitory with the girls; because there were no women over in the seminary. Again, that was a sanction to me. I was told when I arrived there that I would never finish. The Lord blessed me and I knew that he was sanctioning my ministry, because I finished. In fact, in everything that I have done, I have received a sanction from the Lord.

I came back to Baltimore (my grandmother passed, and I needed to be working rather than traveling), and I asked the Lord to really lead me the way that I was supposed to go. I wanted to have Sundays free. I wanted to be free to do evangelistic work during the summer. You know which way he led me? Into education. I went back to Northern State University to get a degree, so that I could get into the public school system. Then I prayed again and asked God how he could use me there in the public school system. So, for the first five years, he used me in a classroom situation, and he really, really used me. I know he used me, because there was a class in that school when I went there that nobody had been able to control for two years. They had eight teachers in two years in that class. I went in that class, and I stayed for five years in that particular school. I followed that class for three years because they were seventh graders. That's why I know the Lord uses my ministry, and not so much in the pulpit. You see, I'm a preacher, it's true; but I have more than a pulpit ministry. I took my ministry to the school with me so that I could touch the lives of those children there, not necessarily spiritually, but touch their lives so that morally they would be different people. And I kept praying and asking God, "Where are you going to take me from here?" and "How can I ever get to the place that I can really minister the way you want me to minister, even in the Baltimore city school system?"

I went on to study at John Hopkins University. At the time, Hopkins was not really particularly interested in accepting black women; they had a few black men, but I went anyway. When I finished—in psychology and guidance—I became a principal in the Baltimore city school system, and the Lord used my ministry in ministering to mothers and fathers and healing wounded people. For thirty-one years, you know, he just used me at that particular place in his ministry. When I retired I came here, and I have had a full-time ministry in this church (Gillis Memorial Community Church) with my pastor, and I really have enjoyed it. The only thing I can tell you is that I know that God placed his sanction upon the ministry that he called me to and the way that he has used me throughout these fifty, almost fifty-one years now.

My ministry in Baltimore has grown. The Lord blessed me in 1979 to organize the Interdenominational Women Ministerial Alliance in Baltimore City, Maryland and Washington, DC. That organization has begun to grow. The purpose of the organization was to encourage women ministers to prepare themselves to be the kind of ministers that they really believed in their heart that God had chosen them to be, educationally, spiritually—not necessarily just hanging around the pulpit, but getting out in the community and serving people throughout our city. The organization has grown, and these women have not only grown spiritually but educationally. We have seven of them who have now received their masters from Howard University. Some are now at St. Mary's Seminary. The Lord has just really blessed them—blessing not only my ministry, but blessing the ministry of women in Baltimore City.

Sharon Austin
Atlanta, Georgia

The Reverend Sharon Austin was born in Jamaica, New York, on May 7, 1955, called to preach in 1975, and ordained a Baptist minister in 1981. She has a BS from Barry College and an MDiv from Emory University's Chanler School of Religion. She is the associate pastor of Ebenezer Baptist Church in Atlanta, Georgia. Interview recorded June 23, 1989.

6

The Lutheran Who Became a Baptist

I think I would like to start with the time that I met with pastor Joseph Roberts just prior to my licensing and the time of meeting with the deacon board before the preaching of my trial sermon.

One significant incident in my growing process in ministry was a conversation that I had with pastor Roberts. Just prior to the meeting with the deacon board for the official blessing and permission of sorts to go on to the trial sermon stage, I can remember wondering how I could approach my concern with him, how to even go about phrasing the question. In essence the question was, "How can I authentically articulate to them, honestly and with intregrity intact, my experience of being called to ministry?" From my limited exposure and the basis on which I made these judgments, it seems to fall so far outside of the realm of that which I had experienced others articulate, particularly in the Baptist church. I could clearly see, whenever I would rethink and recall my call in light of what I heard others share based on their own experiences, that mine just didn't seem to hook up.

I am a former Lutheran, a former northern New Yorker,

a suburban Lutheran. Nothing is probably farther from that than to be in the south and to be Baptist and to hear the call story shared by many of my male colleagues in ministry. That I have been called, I have no doubts; that it is authentic, I have no doubt. I really didn't, but in my youth and in my immaturity, I found myself floundering just a little bit. I say that, and stress "floundering," because I am, for the most part, a confident person. I always have been. I can be confident and wrong, but I am confident. So, this whole experience was new to me; because probably for the first time in my life, I found myself saying, "Now wait a minute, what is this? Can we figure this out and find a resolution with empirical data and all of that? When we add this up, two plus two we want to get four every time." In this whole call to ministry, things were just like a very new experience.

I think I had the advantage of having a father who is in ministry, but who was called to ministry at maybe a third stage in life — if you want to look at ministry as profession, career or direction. So, I was well aware of the point at which my father entered ministry, when I was a teenager. I was old enough to remember and had the opportunity to see firsthand the transitions that one goes through and, sort of, how that happens in the context of a close-knit family situation. So, I guess if I took heart in anything prior to asking pastor Roberts, it was my father's experience. But then I was so refreshed, so relieved to hear pastor Roberts, whose thoughts were in essence, "Be yourself." It is all right to be yourself. Don't try to make anything up. Don't try to phrase it or to say it in a way which you think will make it authentic to others. Talk about it, share out of your own experience, the ways in which God has moved and touched you in your own life. I think that particular word to me was important, not only for the purposes of articulating the call and working with that deacon board with the trial sermon, but for integrity and honesty in ministry and in life. I think that is why it stands out; and that is the reason why I would want to begin there.

I would often talk about my call to the ministry in the sense of an urging, not even an urgency. I think that came later for me, but urgings and tuggings at heartstrings, in mind and soul came first. I came to Georgia to attend undergraduate school at Berry College in Rome, Georgia. Rome is a medium-sized southern town, at least it was in the early '70s. Berry College is a small, predominantly-white, religiously-oriented, but nondenominational liberal arts college. It had, maybe in a little more sophisticated way, all of the vestiges of small southern towns. You know the racial implications and all of that. I mean, there were maybe sixty black students, and this includes those from the Caribbean and from countries in Africa as well as African-American students, out of a total population of 1,600 students. So we were a very distinct minority.

Yet I have to admit and continue to be grateful for the fact that it was the faculty and the religion and philosophy departments of that college that—I won't say authenticated the call, because that doesn't come from people—did encourage me to pursue in academic and formal ways that which I had begun to express to them. I kept thinking that, yes, God is calling me. I went on and finally claimed that, somewhere around the end of my junior year. I felt that I was called to ministry but continued to limit myself by the role models that I did not see, namely women in parishes, especially in the Baptist tradition, the Black Baptist tradition in particular.

And so I kept saying, I must be called to a lay ministry, such as serving as a missionary. I just used that as an example, and serving as a missionary is the thing that keeps coming back to me as I recall those years. My professors, two of whom were Caucasians, one of whom was Hispanic—in fact Jorge Gonzalez, and his brother Husto Gonzalez, who was a professor of mine at Berry, said, "First of all, you do not have to limit yourself in ministry. You can wait for the revelation and the unfolding of God's will for your life. And second, you do not have to allow this period of uncertainty to be one in which you cannot still incorporate some structure and some learning, and in that context, do some growing." So, it was my college professors who encouraged me to pursue seminary education.

Several years after I had been in Atlanta and, I guess, even after seminary here, people asked me why I didn't attend Interdenominational Theological Center And I have had very few people who actually believed that I didn't know about Interdenominational Theological Center. My professors, out of the three, two had direct contact with Emory and with Candler School of Theology. One, in particular, went through Candler; the other had done a graduate program in philosophy at Emory. So they were actually encouraging me out of their own experience and their own personal knowledge that this was one school they could recommend to a student of theirs without reservation. I really didn't know there was an ITC until I came to Atlanta and actually had enrolled and begun my studies at Candler School of Theology.

My call process and experience, as I remember it, was a time of questioning everything from my sanity to my faith in some ways. Growing up in the Lutheran Church in New York gave me a very strong foundation and appreciation for teaching and for Christian education. The preaching was important to proclaim the word on Sunday morning, but it was not quite as paramount as it sometimes appears to be in the Black church. I did at least have an appreciation for the various expressions and areas of ministry that did not have to be limited to or always focused upon preaching. That appeared to be a safeguard for me; I was saying, "Now, Lord, I know you are not calling me to be a preacher per se, you are still calling me to do ministry, and that can take a number of forms, such as missionary work or teaching." So, I think I used my former experience as a way of saying "You are not quite crazy, because there are some more acceptable forms of ministry that you can pursue, particularly as a woman."

The call and the comfort of visualizing myself as minister in a number of areas, especially when I thought about parish ministry and the preaching piece, actually came much later. I never thought I would be in ministry. I did not make that conscious decision early on. There are persons that I speak to who say, "I always knew I was always going to be a preacher." I was called at a very early age and sort of grew up with the assumption that, really, ministry was not my case. I had gone from the artist, to the pre-med, and the point of being called to ministry really focused on a career as a clinical psychologist. I was not a religion major in undergraduate school. I was a psychology major, planning, as I said, to move on through psychology and obtain a graduate degree. But something in my head would not let the religion studies go. It was more than just a compatible discipline with psychology. I have always seen myself as a person with a deeply rooted spirituality and a deep and abiding and tenacious faith. When I began to feel and to believe that God did not want me to just let it remain there, but wanted to me to incorporate that in a very integral sense of my life, then it began to make some sense.

To this day, one of the areas in which I have been told that I am most effective is the area of counseling in the ministry. One of my real loves in ministry is counseling; and so, I guess, have been blessed to have a way in which my chosen love is still incorporated and very compatible with God's will and calling in my life. That is a blessing, because I have sometimes heard people talk about the call to ministry as though it was sort of antithetical with everything else that they were about and ever hoped to do. They talk about the call as though they feel they have to do it and have to hear God's call. God makes a way and he makes certain that you sort of stay on that path, because that is God's chosen path for you. To some there is a certain resentment to that.

I don't have a resentment about ministry at all. It is such a part of my life and my personality. As I think of who I am, sometimes I have a difficult time even conceiving of [ministry] as a profession or career, paid employment. I have said to people on a number of occasions that ministry is the one area of my life that I really wish I did not have to be compensated for. I mean, I feel that strongly about it, but the realities are that if I am going to do this full time, I have to at least get a love offering every now and then.

Another part of that call process in those early years which sticks in my mind was a conversation I had with my parents. It really was, I guess, something of a situation of having to build confidence. How do you call your parents 600 miles away and tell them that you believe that God is calling you to ministry? This has no precedent. This isn't connected with anything that you discussed with them prior to your undergraduate career or any of the applications that you plan to send to graduate school. This just seems to have been laid upon you. How do you tell them and still come across sounding like a person who is lucid and sane and hasn't taken total leave of her senses?

I got two very different responses from my parents, both of which were supportive. My dad did not have a problem believing [in my call], because he had already gone through his own sort of miraculous call experience as a middle-aged man. He had already dealt with the nay-sayers and those who sort of wondered if Austin finally had lost it. And so, I received his support as one who was himself less than a decade in the ministry. My mother approached it, I think, in the true sense of what we have to come to know and to call and to consider as mothering and nurturing, as that sort of concern for the well-being of the child. She said, "Oh, Sharon, you know, I don't know now. Do you think you're really ready?" She was just really concerned as to how I would be seen.

I had always been a bright child intellectually. My parents were called by teachers early on, not because I was a behavior problem, but [to discuss] "What are your dreams or plans for this child, because we see something in her." So my mother was just concerned that folks might see me as sort of off the top, and I must admit that I feel that the role models and the images to which she had been exposed—I don't want to be too detailed and graphic at this point, because there are folks who may fit this visual image who are just on target—she just had seen some women who professed to be in ministry in various stages or areas, who did seem a bit fanatical and a little off track. I'll just say it that way. So, I think, she wondered if I had come into contact or been exposed to something in college, you know, that was a passing sort of phase; if I was going to drop out of school and pick up my Bible, you know, and stand on the street corner.

I don't know what she was thinking, but she was very concerned for me. She saw that at that point, maybe it was sort of being outside of the realm of the Sharon that she had known for twenty, twenty-one years. But it has been wonderful to see the grace of God and the unfolding of all of this. In more recent years, my mother has gone back even before the experiences that she shared with me regarding teachers in elementary school, and said she can remember lying in the hospital bed in labor with me and looking at a clock as the hours went by and thinking and feeling even then that there was something special about this child. (I was the first one so she didn't have a basis for comparison. I've had three, and I think they are all special. But I don't know that she has had that experience—not that she didn't think that all of her children were special; but they could have been special in another sense).

So, it has been wonderful. I don't want to say that everyone has jumped on the bandwagon because this has turned out fairly well. But now folks are saying bits and pieces along the line, you know, the Lord had a hand in this early on. I mean, in a way that I can see. He's just been wonderful. A great person, a great influence in my life. Besides my parents in this whole call process is my grandmother, my mother's mother, who is still living and an active churchwoman. She knows more about the rules, regulations, policy in Baptist churches than most preachers that I know, because she made that a study. She had a little bit of a struggle, I think, early on; because my grandmother knows the Bible— and can quote it, you know, chapters—and sort of wondered, "Well, now see how this fits in with the overall structure and the placement of men and women in the general order of things, if you will."

But God has been good and allowed me to see my grandmother supportive. She was never against me, in all fairness. It wasn't so much that, but it was just outside of the realm of her experience. I sort of figured if my grandmother, soon to be an octogenarian, can make that transition and lift her granddaughter in the circle of her rich tradition as a Baptist of some seventy years, or however long she had been in the Baptist church, that there's hope for the rest of the world.

So, when I hear people say, "You know, I've got a problem with women in ministry and I am struggling with this, and I don't quite see it," and so forth, I think of my grandmother. And I think, here is a woman who for me embodies the church and really knows the substance and the essence of the church, as well as the traditions and the practices under which we sort of govern ourselves or allow ourselves to be governed — and she has come to an acceptance of this.

After hearing me preach for the first time—in fact, my parents and my grandmother heard me for the first time in person on the same day in my dad's church last fall—my grandmother came up afterward and, in her own sort of quietly cerebral way, took pride in the fact that while preaching, I didn't stumble and I didn't falter; I just went on and got it out. That meant a lot to her. I was confident in what I was saying. That's priceless. I will never forget that.

I guess what I am saying in my story is really not that long nor is it elaborate, but I have had my calling authenticated, not only by God in the sense that you think of the spirit of God and this awareness into which we grow as we come to know God's will for our lives, but in the part which we will play in the whole scheme of things. And God has seen to it that my call has been authenticated over and over, and over and over, and over again, because this is the kind of lifestyle that will leave one questioning and constantly struggling with doubt on every hand. Every time I think, "What if there really is a possibility that this wasn't for me, and maybe I got this thing confused?," you know, the Lord steps in with two or three experiences, sort of lifting me on every side. It often seems to come from the most unexpected places. It is not from those who are sort of young and like-minded, formally trained, exposed to the world, well-traveled and well-read. It is from the grandmothers who say, "Baby, you sure, sure showed your shape this morning." Then it's eigth grade; can't read but you know the word of the Lord and they see you as representing that in a meaningful and significant way, and the focus just comes out. "I've never met your father. I want to shake your hand. I've got to hug you." Tears and all of that. To see folks lifted and to have them share that with me is an authentication of the call for me.

I just firmly believe that the Lord has seen to it that [this authentication] has been done for, you know, this last decade and that I've just come to expect it. I don't look for it, but I know that God sees to it that it is done over and over and over again. That's been a source of confidence. That's been my strength, even though I still question myself sometimes—you know, "Where shall I go from here?" Ebenezer is not a final resting place, I don't believe. I feel the Lord, even now, tugging and causing me to look in some new directions. I don't have to worry about the outcome. I don't know what's going to happen, but I know that the outcome will be right. In that sense, it will be good, even though it may be hard or not quite what I had in mind, because I didn't have any of this in mind. And it has not come out too badly. So I'll let the Lord be in charge of it. He really has not done badly.

"*Between* four and five years after my sanctification, on a certain time, an impressive silence fell upon me, and I stood as if some one was about to speak to me, yet I had no such thought in my heart. But to my utter surprise there seemed to sound a voice which I thought I distinctly heard, and most certainly understood, which said to me, 'Go preach the Gospel!' I immediately replied aloud, 'No one will believe.' Again I listened, and again the same voice seemed to say, 'Preach the Gospel; I will put words in your mouth, and will turn your enemies to become your friends.'

At first I supposed that Satan had spoken to me, for I had read that he could transform himself into an angel of light, for the purpose of deception. Immediately I went into a secret place, and called upon the Lord to know if he had called me to preach, and whether I was deceived or not; when there appeared to my view the form and figure of a pulpit, with a Bible lying thereon, the back of which was presented to me as plainly as if it had been a literal fact.

In consequence of this, my mind became so exercised that during the night following, I took a text, and preached in my sleep. I thought there stood before me a great multitude, while I expounded to them the things of religion. So violent were my exertions, and so loud were my exclamations, that I awoke from the sound of my own voice, which also awoke the family of the house where I resided. Two days after, I went to see the preacher in charge of the African Society, who was the Rev. Richard Allen... to tell him that I felt it my duty to preach the gospel.... But as to women preaching, he said that our Discipline knew nothing at all about it—that it did not call for women preachers....

O how careful ought we to be, lest through our by-laws of church government and discipline, we bring into disrepute even the word of life. For unseemly as it may appear now-a-days for a woman to preach, it should be remembered that nothing is impossible with God."

Jarena Lee, AME preacher, from the 1836 edition of
The Life and Religious Experience of Jarena Lee in *Sisters of the Spirit: Three Black Women's Autobiographies of the Nineteenth Century* (Bloomington: Indiana University Press, 1986): 35-36.

E. K. Bailey
Dallas, Texas

The Reverend Dr. Ervin Kinsley Bailey was born in Marshall, Texas, on December 19, 1945, called to preach in 1964, and ordained a Baptist minister in 1969. He received a BA from Bishop College, an MDiv from Southwestern Baptist Seminary and a DMin from United Theological Seminary. He pastors the Concord Missionary Baptist Church in Dallas, Texas. Interview recorded August 14, 1989.

7

Cracked in God's University of Hard Knocks

Well, like so many other children of ministers, I'm a "PK" (preacher's kid), and when I first became aware of my existence on the planet Earth, I was in San Antonio, Texas, having been born in Marshall, Texas, about 150 miles southeast of Dallas. My dad moved when I was two years old to San Antonio, where we stayed ten years. It was there that I became aware of myself and my family.

It was also there that I can recall mimicking and marking the preacher. Some things I'm not all that proud of now, but they happened. Like when we used to take out our BB guns and go out and shoot, what we called then, chi-chi birds, sparrows; the main purpose was so I could preach their funerals. We would go out behind the garage, I'd bury them, and, oh, we'd have a funeral. We'd have church. I can remember that. That should have taken place, I guess, somewhere around seven, eight years old. My older brother had a little BB gun, and we'd take that gun and do that. I can remember these scenes with my sister, sitting them down and preaching to them. So even at that very early age, I was not so much aware of a call, but aware that there was something in me, prodding me to mimic my father. I didn't really know all the ramifications of it at that time, but it was something that fulfilled me.

At the age of nine I remember telling my dad (we were still in San Antonio) that I knew that I would eventually be a preacher, but I wasn't ready yet. He asked me, "How long have you thought about this?" I said, "Well, a couple years." He asked me, "Why are you telling me now?" I said, "Because we had a nine-year-old preacher come to our church, and I was nine; so I identified with him." That was the first public airing or articulating the feelings that were churning underneath my skin.

After that I put the call on the back burner. It was there, but dormant. All through high school I was aware of the presence of an invisible power moving, urging me toward the pulpit. But I thought I had better things to do. Plus I had seen, like so many other preacher's kids, my dad go through so much, so many problems with churches, court battles, physical battles, and I didn't want that. Going through high school, I did well in football and wrestling, got scholarships in those areas.... What I thought I was going to pursue [was] an acting career; but God had different plans for me.

My best friend in high school, Bernard Henderson, used to tell me the reason I was so bad and was the leader of a gang was that I felt like I had to do all of that to suppress the call to preach. When he mentioned it, we'd have a fist fight, because I told him I wasn't going to preach. He could see that all of this rebellion and antagonism in me was a cover-up for something much deeper, but I never told him, never admitted it during those high school years.

Between my high school year and my college year, my daddy was tragically killed. We had since moved to California. That put my education on hold for a year. Instead of going to Arizona State to play football, I stayed at home. That was, perhaps, the most pivotal year in the whole of my life. Even to this point, because it was during that year—piggybacking on the tragedy, the death of my dad—that God got my undivided attention. Two months after my dad died, my stepmother, who had been with me since I was six years old (or I had been with her), asked me out of the house. We never had a very good relationship; we tolerated each other because dad was the hub of the family, kept all the various spokes in line and in place. But with that centerpiece gone, we were to have nothing in common; so two months after his death, she asked me out and I got out. I was seventeen at the time.

I went over to my brother's house, and it was a situation there where nobody in his family liked any part of my family but him. My dad had fired my brother's wife's mother—if you can follow the intricacy of all of that—as a musician. So I woke up that first night that I stayed with them, at about four o'clock (my brother worked at the post office, and he was preparing to leave). And I heard all this arguing going on. I heard my brother say, "Well, if he has to go, I'm going, too." That's my brother. So he walked out. About 7:30, his wife being a school teacher, she left. At about nine o'clock I left, and I never went back.

From that point, for the next nine months I lived in the street. I slept in parked cars, slept in parks, slept in basements of empty houses, slept on the sidewalk, slept in yards, under trees for all those nine months. I remember how painful that was, especially seeing how I came from a middle-class family. Now being totally outdoors, I didn't know where I was going to eat or sleep. The clothes I had were those on my back. It was a blow for my ego, but it was very real to me, a very real experience.

The reason why I shared all that is because it was the "university of hard knocks" that God used to cause me to submit to the call. Because I was a hard nut to crack. I was going to preach, and I'd been knowing it since a child. So, I remember one night, having walked all night long from Berkeley to Oakland, I sat down on the corner of Lakeshore and Mandana on a bus stop bench. (I go by there periodically and just thank the Lord; it's a shrine in my pilgrimage.) I remember tears coming down my face. It was cold that time of morning, the wind whipping through the tattered clothes I had on. It's difficult to go that far back . . . I've told this story many-a-day, and I ain't never had this kind of effect. And I said, "Lord, you've been the God of my father, and I've been knowing through a secondhand experience, his experience. If you are willing, I need you to do something about this situation. And if preaching is what I have to do, I'll do it."

It was that night, I don't remember the date. It must have been sometime in the latter part of July, first part of August, because I also said, "If I'm going to preach, I need to go to school." I had been a fair to poor student most of my academic pilgrimage, but my dad—although he didn't spend a lot of time with me personally—was kind of like an eggheaded genius, brilliant mind, studied all the time. So my example for preaching was that of studying. I tacked on to my surrender, "If you gonna call me to preach, I gotta go to school." I had been turned down academically at a couple of schools, because in high school I didn't major in studies, I majored in doing other things. But my dad had made a lot of friends across the years. He'd been president of the Texas State [Baptist] Convention, president of the California State Baptist Convention. So one of the parishioners, a layman, a Mr. Goady, called Dr. T. M. Chambers, Sr. He was in Los Angeles, and I asked him to call President Curry, president of Bishop College. Well, first of all he asked me, "What are you going to do about your life?" I said, "I don't know." He said, "What are you going to do about school?" I said, "I don't know." "Wouldn't you like to go?" I said, "It doesn't make any difference to me." He said, "Why don't you go to school where your dad went?" I said, "I'm not going to Marshall." Bishop had been in Marshall. He said, "I think I heard that Bishop moved to Dallas." I said, "Well, if it's in Dallas, I'll go."

So, Tim Chambers made the call, and President Curry, who knew my dad, told him, "Send him on." So, Mr. Goady bought me a bus ticket, bought me two pairs of pants, two coats, a couple shirts. I packed up my daddy's suitcase, got on the Trailways, and went to Texas. I arrived there on the ninth of September 1964, and for the first time I saw, literally, about 100 preachers my age. I had seen several young preachers in California (we moved to California), but to see so many young fellows my age also gave me kind of, like, a support system to make my calling public.

So, after arriving on the ninth of September, on October 11, 1964, I went to church with some friends to Hamilton Park First Baptist in Dallas, where Reverend Jesse Lee Foster was preaching that morning. He was talking about you can't stay on both sides of the fence, love one and hate the other. When he opened the doors, I hit the floor, and walked down the aisle. Even then, it was still tough for me to admit that I had been called, but I acknowledged I wanted to join the church. He looked at me and said, "Is there anything else?" I said, "Yeah, man, I've been called to preach." He said, "I could see something else was in you." So, the very next Sunday night, I was up preaching about Moses on my first sermon, and that was twenty-five-years ago.

Joseph L. Blake, Jr.
Cleveland, Ohio

The Reverand Joseph L. Blake, Jr., was born in Bamford, Alabama on August 14, 1927, called in 1932, and ordained a Baptist minister in 1962. He received a BTh degree from American Baptist Theological Seminary. He pastors the Sacred Trinity Baptist Church in Cleveland, Ohio. Interview recorded November 17, 1988.

8

"Confess the Call or Die"

The call to the ministry is quite a lengthly process. The first knowledge that I had was when I was a boy in a country town called Bamford, Alabama. My father was a Baptist minister, and every Sunday when we come from church, I would get in the wagon and have the other children to sit down. I would verbally do my father's whole sermon. Many Sunday evenings, my father, mother and grandmother would sit on the front porch, and they would just observe how closely I had listened.

After we moved from Bamford, at the age of six I stopped preaching. My father told a lady, "I noticed since we moved to Leeds, my boy has stopped preaching." And this lady started calling me the "down-home preacher." After I was ten years of age, I thought singing was the thing for me to do in the church. We had a family aggregation, and everywhere we would go the people would say, "You gonna be a preacher."

After getting all wrapped up in singing and loving to sing under the direction of my sister, I just became overwhelmed with doing whatever I could on God's program. At the age of twelve, the Fall term of the country school began, and this particular morning I was noticing my mother trying to cook, and my sister was donning her clothing. My brother had a butcher knife cutting some cardboard to put in the bottom of his shoes. Being one of a poor family, I said to my mother, "I'm not going to school anymore." Mama said, "Why?". I said, "I'm gonna find a job, because you all need too much for me to not try to help." My mother thought for a moment, and she said, "Boy, you going to school." I said, "Naw, mama, I'm not going to school." My grandmama spoke up and said, "Well, Bee, don't you think his reasoning ought to be understood?" Mama said, "Well, son, if this is the way you feel toward your family, go ahead."

So I got a job at a sawmill as a water boy, and when I was paid, I gave the money to my mother. I worked there until I was sixteen. The joy of my life was to see the expression on mama's face. How religious I was toward helping the family. I refused even a penny of that money, but if mama thought I needed a pair of socks, she would buy it. I was very faithful in the church and I just loved to be around older men. The Spirit of the Lord was just continously dwelling on preaching.

Now, the preaching aspect I believe is one of the dynamics of a Holy God being poured upon an unholy man. His understandings of God come according to his ability to understand. The urge to preach became overwhelmimg. I found myself preaching for the five miles I had to walk to my job. All the while I was working, I was preaching.

When I was sixteen years of age, I moved to Cleveland upon the encouragement of my aunt, who felt that I could get a better job and make more money. My mother said to me, as I was going to the train station, "Son, don't forget the Lord; join the church and be faithful, and the Lord is going to bless you." I joined the Corinthian Baptist Church and I was very faithful, singing in the choir, working on the trustee board.

The urge to preach overwhelmed me again, but I just determined in my heart that I was not going to preach. After I was eighteen years of age, I began to slacken my activities in the church, because I got tired of hearing an inward voice saying, "Preach."

I took up gambling. Never could drink alcohol, but I became very successful in gambling. In 1949 I was gambling at this particular place. I had gambled from Friday night to Sunday evening about dusk dark. And a voice spoke to me and said, "Get up from the table." I collected my money and got up and went into the living room of this house, and just sat down in a dark room. I wasn't there more than five minutes when the door came down. The police raided the place. They shined a flashlight in my face and ordered me out of the house. As soon as I got out of that house, I began to tremble and the Lord spoke to me again, "This is my protection."

As I went home, I was useless, because I was always afraid of a jail record. I said then, "Lord, forgive me." And I reactivated myself into the church. In 1950 I became restless. I couldn't sleep, and I could work all day; all night long I would just roll and tumble. The Lord said, "You're not going to rest until you acknowledge the call." I went to church and prayer meeting, but the devil kept insisting that you can preach without open confession. When I would leave the church, whether Sunday night or Sunday morning, I was still restless.

On the first Sunday in August 1950, the Lord said, "You confess or you die." After communion that Sunday night, the pastor had given the benediction, and I went back and I talked to him. "Pastor Cole," I told him, "I can't hold out any longer, the Spirit of the Lord has been on me a long time to preach." The church lit up just like a building when the lights are out. Everybody in that congregation began to cry and shout. The pastor said, "I knew it from the day you came here."

I preached my trial sermon about a month later. One of the associate ministers and his wife, who was quite studious, said to me, "You won't make a preacher, you are illiterate, your diction is terrible, your English is terrible and your knowledge of the Bible is terrible." He even objected that the pastor gave me a license.

I left that church after my trial sermon more disturbed, but those words are still alive in me today. I determined as a result of what this minister and his wife said to me that I was going to do a good job. I went home and prayed, and I just told the Lord that I was poor and nobody in my family had enough money to loan me five dollars, but I needed an education. I needed to finish high school and I needed a knowledge of the Bible. I asked God to open a way.

I had been classified 4-F by the Selective Service in 1945. That Monday, the day after I preached my trial sermon, I received a letter from the Selective Service saying that I had been reclassified from 4-F to 1-C. A week from that Monday, I received another letter saying that I had been reclassified from 1-C to 1-A. And a week from that Monday, I received another letter saying that "Your friends and neighbors have chosen you to represent your country in the United States Armed Services."

It was later that I learned that that was the answer to the prayer, because I was able to join the army and put my mother and ten sisters and brothers on an allotment. After I came to Cleveland, my oldest sister's husband walked off and left her; and I was supporting my sister and three children. I was able to take one-half of the seventy-eight dollars a month I was making and give it to my sister. After going into the army, I was able to wash and iron, because mama taught me to make old-fashioned starch. I washed and ironed; and the twenty weeks that we were in special training, I made more than $12,000 washing and ironing. For two and one-half years I didn't spend one penny of my income. I didn't take a furlough. I was able to go on weekend passes, and the Lord opened a door for me to get a free flight from the Army camp to Alabama and see my parents at least once a month. While I was in the army, I finished my high school. I learned to be a typist, I learned to be a projectionist, and I got credit for one year of studies from the University of New York.

When I received my discharge, the late Rev. O. M. Hoover encouraged me to go to the American Baptist Theological Seminary. I was able to go, still support my family and begin some direct ministerial and theological training. I feel very strongly that God's call carries dynamics according to one's ability to understand these processes.

One interesting note about an episode between my first sermon and the Sunday night after Thanksgiving when I returned from the army [regarding] the minister that said I would not make a preacher: I brought the Sunday morning message. The Lord moved on their hearts (that minister and his wife) and caused both of them to be spellbound to the extent that, after the benediction, they couldn't even move from their seats. And almost spontaneously they screamed and said, "I was wrong." God can do anything but fail. It has been that experience that has made me more determined to preach the gospel of Jesus Christ. Because, whatever your needs, God has a way to supply them.

Charles Booth
Columbus, Ohio

The Reverend Dr. Charles Booth was born in Baltimore, Maryland, on February 4, 1947, called to preach in 1961, and ordained a Baptist minister in 1970. He has a BA degree from Howard University, an MDiv from Eastern Baptist Seminary and a DMin from United Theological Seminary. He pastors the Mt. Olive Baptist Church in Columbus, Ohio. Interview recorded July 7, 1989.

9

Preaching at Camp at Age Fifteen

From my earliest recollection, I have always wanted to preach, and I've always been enamored with the church experience, the worship experience, and with the preacher. I can remember as a child always being eager to get to church on Sunday morning, primarily to see my pastor and to hear what he had to say.

I recall at the age of fourteen announcing to my mother that I knew that I was to preach, at which point she quickly halted me. She came out of Tidewater, Virginia, out of a place called Glouchester County. It was the kind of environment that said you did not play with God, you did not play with the Bible, you did not play with the church. She felt that I was a bit young to be talking about preaching and the call to preach. She said, "If it's of God and for real, you'll come to a point and place where you will not be able to contain yourself. At that point, I think we should move ahead with some kind of public acknowledgment."

It was not until three years later, when I was seventeen years old and a senior in high school in Baltimore, Maryland, that I reached that point. She instructed me to go and talk with my pastor, Dr. A. J. Payne of a local Baptist Church in Baltimore. He scheduled me to preach my initial or trial sermon on the sixteenth of October, 1964.

An interesting thing occurred before that. When I was approximately fifteen years old, I went to a Methodist youth camp. Even though born and raised in the Baptist tradition, my closest friends were United Methodist, so I belonged not only to the Baptist Youth Fellowship with my own church in Baltimore, but to the Methodist Youth Fellowship of Metropolitan United Methodist Church there in Baltimore. I served as the chaplain of the group. I remember at about fifteen we went on a weekend camp experience in Maryland, and I'll never forget it. I was in charge of the worship experience on that Sunday morning, and as the chaplain of the group, I was to preach or to bring the message. So, actually, my first sermon was preached when I was about fifteen years old to a group of young people in a Methodist camp situation, even though the formal announcement of my call to the ministry did not occur until two years later in October of 1964. So, that is my call as I know it and as I have related it across these years.

L. Venchael Booth
Columbus, Ohio

The Reverend L. Venchael Booth was born in Covington County, Mississippi, on January 7, 1919, called to preach in 1936 and ordained a Baptist minister in 1941. He received an AB from Alcorn A & M College, a BD from Howard University School of Religion, and an MA from the University of Chicago. He is considered to be the founder of the present-day Progressive National Baptist Convention, Inc. and served as its President from 1971 to 1974. He pastors the Olivet Baptist Church in Cincinnati, Ohio. Interview recorded July 6, 1989.

10

The Mississippi Preacher Who Founded a Convention

I was born in Covington County, Mississippi. Our nearest town was eight miles away; I was born and reared in a Christian home on the farm. The farm experience lends itself to growing thoughts about God, because on the farm you are part of growth—animals, plant life, as well as other members of your family. You watch them grow. You see animals being born. You adopt pets of your own. In the process, as you go to church and Sunday School and are taught by leaders and teachers, you begin to form your ideas about God. So God became a reality to me at a very early age—because it was a part of my family upbringing.

My great-grandfather was a philosopher and a teacher of a sort. He might have been a preacher. My grandfather was a preacher, and I was old enough at the time that my father started preaching to understand what he was doing and to remember the year in which he started. It was 1928. I was born in 1919, so I was not even a teenager.

My religious experience with a desire to be a minister started before I was formally converted or gave a formal expression of my conversion, which was at the age of thirteen. In those days we had revival periods. I was impressed with the evangelists who came to conduct the revivals. I was also impressed with my own minister, who was a very fine and progressive man, I thought, the Reverend Dr. R. G. Gray from Mississippi.

In those early experiences I felt converted and called, but I knew that I was in a family in which you, first of all, had to offer some proof of your conversion and be certain of your call to the ministry. So I confessed Christ and was baptized at the age of thirteen and then I progressively moved toward the ministry as I moved through high school. I decided upon finishing high school that I could afford to take the risk of announcing my call to ministry. Back in those days you, had to announce your call to the ministry formally to a church group or at a church meeting, and the church would grant your hearing to examine your call. So at seventeen, I wrote a letter to my parents informing them of my call to the ministry and expressing the hope that they would permit me to go into the ministry.

The letter was not answered, but I did hear them discussing it one night as I laid in bed. My father said, "Well, if he's called to the ministry, Fido has been called." That was our little dog. Well, I knew then that he was not convinced, but I also knew that I would be leaving home and going to college very shortly thereafter. It was the year 1936. I had finished high school and was going to college.

I announced my call to the ministry, and the church gave me a hearing. When they heard me, there was considerable weeping and emotion on the part of some who had watched me grow up. I preached on "Trust in the Lord and do good" from Psalm 37: 3. That text became my guide post as I went out into life, because the text reads, *Trust in the Lord and do good; so shalt thou dwell in the land, and verily thou shalt be fed.*

I went away to college with the intention to work my way through school, and was fortunate to get matriculated the very first year. There was a janitor there. His name was Reverend Lowells. I adopted him as a friend, and he adopted me. He would take me out into the community preaching. This was Alcorn A & M College in Mississippi, which is now Alcorn State University. I recall very, very vividly, going to nearby churches in the community, and Reverend Lowells would ask people to let me preach. He said, "This boy's a preacher. He's a good preacher." So I went to Rodney several times to preach. Rodney was on the edge of Mississippi and Louisiana, and the floods would come very ferociously through Rodney. The water would get up so high, and you could see the water lines on the old buildings. I'd like to go back there now and see how the place is. Anyway, I would preach in Rodney and nearby places where they would listen to me. So, this janitor kept on talking to the chaplain at the college at that time. The chaplain was Mrs. Lucretia. It seemed right at that time. He kept asking the chaplain to let this boy preach in chapel. "This young man is a preacher, let him preach," he said.

One evening she decided that she didn't want to speak herself, so she had me preach. I spoke to the student body and they were so impressed that they literally picked me up and carried me back to the dormitory, hoisted high. From then on my wings were spread. I always felt that the minister or the young preacher could always conduct himself as a preacher in spite of the fact that he was just a student in school. So, I would work with the YMCA and with the superintendent of Sunday school and would encourage other young people to go to the Sunday school on Sunday mornings. I would even wake some of them up in the dormitory where I lived.

My call to the ministry was almost a thing of birth. I never had any other view or any other position or desire. So, I went through college with that desire, and when I finished, the president said that I had been a very exemplary student. He said, "I'm going to do something that I've never let anybody else do. I am going to let you read the scripture at the baccalaureate service." So, I read the scripture for the baccalaureate service, and Bishop A. P. Shaw of the Methodist church delivered the sermon. There was a recognition on my part that I should magnify the call by training.

Despite the fact that I was offered a position as a dean of a small Baptist college in Mississippi, upon finishing college I refused to accept it. I matriculated at Gammon Theological Seminary in Atlanta, Georgia, where I spent one year. After spending a year there, a very fine Methodist theological seminary, I decided that I wanted to go on to Howard, where I had been invited in the first place by Dr. Benjamin Mays who was then dean of the school of religion. But while I was at Gammon, he came to Morehouse as President of Morehouse College.

I went over to Morehouse to talk with President Mays. I met him one morning on his way to his office. I said, "Dr. Mays,

I want to talk with you, but I know you're much too busy to talk with me." He said, "Well, if you have to talk with me, I'll take the time to talk with you." So I talked with him. When I told him I didn't want to stay at Gammon any longer, because when I went into the History class, they were always talking about the Methodist Church, and so forth and so on—that was my little story. "Now wait a minute, history is just history. It is not Baptist history or Methodist history, it's just history," he said. "But why didn't you come to Howard when I invited you?" I told him that I just didn't see my way clear. I didn't even have train fare. So he said to me, "May I help you in any way to go to Howard then?" I said, "No, thank you, I think I can make it." He said, "Well, I will write Mrs. Pollard, who was my secretary, and tell her to help you get straightened out and get a job and so forth. I can do that." I went on to Howard and finished.

I toyed with the idea of going to Harvard. Dr. Mordecai W. Johnson was president of Howard at that time, and he suggested I might go to Harvard. But I discovered that I had to have a reading knowledge of German. I couldn't get that down my throat and in my head, so I decided I couldn't go to Harvard.

I went to the University of Chicago, where I only had to have a reading knowledge of French. I went first to the Chicago Theological Seminary. I did almost a year there, but I didn't stay with it and didn't like it. I kept going back home. Then I matriculated at Divinity School and enrolled in church history. I finished with a master's in church history. That has very little to do with the call, but I think it says something about the determination of the call. Because I have always felt like, and I feel this even today when I am coming to the close of my ministry, that I am still not worthy of the call.

I have still not fulfilled the call as I should have liked to have done. But I am still working at it. So my ministry has been a very interesting one. I've pastored in Virginia, First Baptist Church for a couple of years, then a few months in Lacon, Illinois, at a small church that was hardly preached in for a number of years. I cleaned it up and preached there for a while. Then I got the call to First Baptist Church in Gary, Indiana in 1944. I stayed there from '44 to '52. I accepted the call to Cincinnati to Zion Baptist Church, where Dr. Wheeler is now. I stayed there thirty-one years, built the church there, paid for it and so on. Then left there in 1984 and came here.

In 1961, of course, I issued the call for the convening of

a meeting of a group that eventually became the Progressive National Baptist Convention. We started out with some other name at the time. Now, after thirty years, I'm still contending for the integrity of that body. We do have a serious question there, but I think it can be resolved. It involves the general secretary, because there seems to be some conflict or confusion about the powers of the president and the general secretary. So, that is my little story in a very roundabout way, but the call has been with me so early that I cannot really determine when it was, but I certainly discovered it by the time I was thirteen. I actually entered the ministry at seventeen. I am now seventy, so you know how long that's been.

Julia Brogdon
Cleveland, Ohio

The Reverend Dr. Julia Brogdon was born in Warren, Ohio, on September 27, 1938, called in 1935, and ordained by the Disciples of Christ (Christian Church) in 1979. She has a BA from Wilberforce, an MRE from Garrett Theological Seminary and a DMin from Chicago Theological Seminary. She pastors the Freedom Christian Church in East Cleveland, Ohio. Interview recorded March 8, 1990.

11

Damascus Road in an Emergency Room

I think that part of me has always known that I had a calling without really being able to clarify that. I've always felt that God had something that I was to do that was special for me. I labored under the understanding, however, when I was in early elementary school, that I was going to be a nurse, primarily because so many people in my family were already heavily invested in that particular area in the South and North. I felt for me, personally, I wanted to be involved with really helping people, because I did a great deal of volunteer work in the hospitals. I used to hang around on a lot of the weekends and had instructed even the nurses that if there were terminally-ill persons who had no one visiting them, that I would be willing to do that, and I did for a great length of time.

I've been involved in the church all of my life. I remember, in Sunday school, from when I was nine years old, my teacher was chairman of the deacon's board, deacon Leslie. For twenty some years. I used to raise so many questions with him that he decided that he would make me his assistant teacher. So, I began at, nine years old, teaching every other Sunday. Of course, that ended a lot of my questions, because once I started, I stopped raising all these questions. But the beautiful thing about him was that he was very mild-mannered and very heavily committed and vested in the word. He never stopped to correct me or to chastise me. What he consistently did with me instead was to pull me aside and just continually feed me Scripture. That, I really enjoyed with him. I had a great deal of respect for him. At that time I did not see myself teaching. I got involved in it simply because of respect for him and thought, perhaps, that teaching was just something that he wanted me to do. I didn't see myself in that area.

But I can recall going across the bridge, the First Street Bridge, in elementary school one day, and all of a sudden, just seemingly out of nowhere, I began to sense the presence of God. I began to feel with my spirit. I know now that there were questions being raised with me in regards to my future. I didn't know at that time how to reply to the questions that were being raised within me, but I knew that it meant, again for me, that God had special work for me to do. I found, however, that I would be able to wait until I became a nurse and did some other things; and then I could get involved, perhaps, and see what that calling looked like.

There was a lady in our church, Reverend Anna Lee Caldwell, that used to shout; there was heavy shouting in our church. There was something about the way she shouted that always disturbed me. When she shouted, she would cry, "Holy." Her husband and everyone would go after her, and I used to say to my mother, "That lady shouted again." My mother would ask me, "What is it about her?" I said, "I don't know, Mama, but every time she shouts and cries 'holy,' it disturbs me in ways that no one else did." For some reason, I kept watching her. I remember that she was licensed and ordained when I was growing up there at Second. The pastor that did this felt that she was called.

At that particular time, I didn't realize that there was a problem with women being called into the ministry. Because, once again, my church was large, liberal and all of these other things. So I saw all this happening. She was placed on the pulpit and served there for seven years in a row. She was called Reverend. She was an active part of what was happening and heavily invested in the congregation. There were no problems that I knew of with her being there. Later on, I discovered when this pastor resigned (the one who had baptized me), that our association had made a decision (after a lady was ordained in Youngstown, Ohio, by Reverend Lonnie Simon) that any church condoning, sympathizing, or going along with women ministers would have to withdraw from the association. I think that was the time that I began to realize that Second was not a typical church. There were many things that we were doing that were not reflective of what the larger bodies were doing. I think that was a very hurried experience, because I saw her being taken down. I saw her sitting in the audience, and for a few years I saw her sit there very wounded and very troubled. The people had a great deal of ambivalence relative to how they should be with her, because they loved her. They had accepted her as a minister, but in our congregation the way that the pastor saw a person determined the response of the congregation. So they were very torn between their loyalty to the pastor and their loyalty and involvement to one who had grown up in our midst. I kept feeling the pull of all that as a youngster. I did not understand it personally, but I could feel the pain of the congregation, as well as her.

I was baptized when I was nine years old. My mother thought that I needed to wait. My dad didn't go to church. I waited as long as I thought I could, and then I made the decision that I wasn't going to wait any longer. I went up to join the church that morning, and one of the Sunday school teachers felt that I was too young to join church, and deacon Leslie, who was chairman of the board, stood up and told them to leave me alone and that I was ready. I was prepared. I did know what I was doing. Once again he came to my rescue and I was told later by some other persons (the deacon, one of the ladies that sat at the pool), that when I came up out of the pool that they could see in the spirit, like a dove that was around me. They said they knew then that God had special work for me to do.

My great-grandmother said to me, a few years later, that she sent for me when she heard that a number of people wanted to know what was going on with me, because the Lord was really dealing heavily with me. My great-grandmother sent for me. She lived to be over a hundred and ten. She said to me, "You have to understand, child, that man did not call you, so man will never know what to do with you. God called you, and God will always know what to do with you. So, you go back, and you go ahead and play; but never forget what I've told you." Ma Abbey was sort of the matriarch of our family. When she sent for you, you had to go immediately. If you didn't, she would come after you. She was never able to read or write. She would not talk really about it; she talked about being a slave. She would not talk about coming from Africa. Both of her brothers, twin brothers, lived to be over a hundred. She had never been sick a day in her life. She had all her own teeth and a head full of white hair. She wore high-heeled shoes, and everything had to be matching-mink stoles and all of this. She used to say to me that she had to be together.

She said that she had really, in a sense, felt responsible for my calling. She said she had prayed that God would put a minister in our family before she died and that God had promised her he would. She said she thought that it would be one of the men. But when I was born with gray hair, she knew that was a sign to her that I was going to be different. My mother said that the startling thing to her was that I had these tight eyes and gray hair. Everyone tells me that's all they can remember about me as a babe. My great grandmother knew that, sooner or later, I would have to come to her and she would have to tell me that I was the result of her prayers. Even though on my father's side there are twenty-six ministers, she said to me, "It's not because of them that you were called. It is because of me, because I have an understanding with God." She also told us that her understanding with God meant that she wasn't going to die until she got ready. Okay, we soon learned that she seemed to have an understanding with God, because she lived to be way over a hundred and ten. She made a decision that she was ready to go home to be with the rest of her children. Within that week, she was gone. So it appeared that she did have an understanding with God.

She called me her praying child. She said I was also marked by prayer; that my grandmother, who was one of her daughters, was a tremendous prayer woman; that my mother prayed a lot; and she said, I too, was marked by prayer. So, she would send for me at various intervals and just share with me a part of the story. She would make me count up her grandchildren, her great-grandchildren, and just share her wisdom with me and always have that time to spend with me. I guess I appreciate it now more than I did even then. But I felt real drawn to her. There were things that she shared with me that she didn't share with others. She would ask me how I felt about being called by the Lord. That was something that at that time I really could not explain to her. I just knew down in my spirit that God wanted me to do something special. What that would be, I would have to wait and see.

When I was sixteen years old, I was going to a dance near Youngstown. Coming back from this dance in Youngstown, we were driving alone. I remember just a car light coming at us; I guess I was knocked unconscious immediately. I'm told that our car looked like you picked up a biscuit and smashed it, because the people thought that everyone in our car was dead. We were hit by two cars from the side and the back. Some of our friends that had gone to that dance that night had gone to the morgues in the area looking for our bodies. They thought we were dead. We ended up at St. Elizabeth Hospital, there in Youngstown. It was there in that hospital in Youngstown when they rolled me into the emergency room—I had a gash in my head where they gave me seven stitches and cervical spine injuries, no feeling in my feet—while I was lying there to be stitched up, that I heard a voice, wherein the Lord said to me, asked me—like a Damascus Road experience—the Lord said, "You know that you have work to do for me." I said, lying there with the doctor stitching me up, "I'll go." Just those two words, "I'll go," It was in saying "I'll go" as I laid there, that there was a tremendous peace that came over me; and I knew that no one heard it but me. But that has followed me. When they wheeled me out of there in a wheelchair, we learned that the driver of the car was dead. Of the other car, the other person died a few days later. I had a great deal of time in going back home and reflecting on that experience.

I have never been able to get around that experience, because the Lord settled for me in that emergency room as he reminded me that I already knew that I had work to do for him. So my commitment was—and I got these words from deacon McLaughlin—"I'll go," and that has been my song, since a teenager, relative to my call. If the Lord wants somebody, who am I to say?

Cecelia Williams Bryant
Baltimore, Maryland

Reverend Cecelia Williams Bryant was born in Yonkers, New York, on October 31, 1946, called in 1955 and ordained an African Methodist Episcopal elder in 1982. She received a BA and MA from Boston University and an MA from Howard University. She founded a church on the Ivory Coast in West Africa and has recently returned to the United States with her husband, Bishop John Bryant. Interview recorded June 15, 1989.

12

When God Appeared as a Light

My first experience with God was when I was nine. We lived in the projects in Yonkers, New York. At that time—right outside the kitchen, we had the linen shelf—the Holy Spirit came to me and told me, "When you become a lady, you are going to go to Africa and be a missionary." I told my mother about it, and it was a major experience in my life. I know it was toward the Christmas season. There were ten of us, and we would identify for our parents three things that we wanted for Christmas. Then they would try to get one of them, because there were so many of us. My mother, subsequent to that announcement, asked me what I wanted for Christmas. I told her I wanted a Bible, and she said, "What else?" I said, "No, that's all I want." She waited a while and came back and told me, "Well, you know, get your list together, daddy will be home."

My father was a cook on the Silvermeter Railroad, which meant he was home every third day. I told my mother I wanted a Bible. So, when my father came in, obviously she had discussed it with him, and he said, "Well, you know Geraldine (she was my best friend downstairs) says she wants a Chatty Cathy." That was big then—the doll that talked. And I told him I didn't want a Chatty Cathy, I wanted a Bible, and that was all I wanted. So they got me a Bible for Christmas. That was the first significant experience with God in my conscious mind.

When I was about thirteen—again it was during the Christmas holidays—there was a little girl that lived downstairs from us. It was very late; the stores were open late. I was taking her to the store to pick up some milk or something. When we got to the top of the steps on the outside of the projects, a light came out of the sky and shone down on us. I told her to wait a minute, don't move. She said, "What is it?" I said, "It's God." And as I said, "It's God," the light left. What is significant is five years ago I spoke in New Jersey at a women's conference, and that same little girl, now a grown woman, came up to me and said, "Cecelia, I never forgot about the light that came when I was a little girl when you were taking me to the store and you told me it was God." It was my second main experience with the supernatural.

I had a number of supernatural experiences in childhood. My mother heard me once trying to negotiate with God in my prayers. My father, who was in the second World War, became ill and was hospitalized. I was trying to make an agreement with God that if he would heal my father, then I promised I would always be good, and do things for God. So I was praying, and my mother was sitting on the bed. She was saying, "You can't negotiate with God. Your father's health is a decision that obviously God has made." It seemed perfectly reasonable to me that that was a good exchange. Since God was God, God could heal my father. In order to facilitate that, I would do things to help God out with this big world that we have.

Subsequent to that, there were a number of experiences. But to get to the actual call to preach, again, it was around Christmas time, and John [Bryant] was pastoring at Bethel Church in Baltimore. He stood up and preached "Life from a Broken Lamb," which is the sermon he was preaching when the Holy Spirit came to me and said, "Preach." I just froze. Three times during the sermon, the Holy Spirit came to me and said, "Preach." The next thing I knew, I was standing in front of the church; John was opening the door to the church and I was standing there. Obviously, I was already a member and I said the Lord had called me to preach. He announced it to the congregation. When he announced it, I left. I went straight out the door and went home. As soon as I got back into the parsonage, I collapsed in the chair that was by the door. The Lord gave me a ministry of encouragement and said, "It will make you an even better wife and mother." It was as though the Lord had grabbed hold of all my anxieties around saying yes to this call. When the Holy Spirit gave me that ministry of encouragement, I felt at peace about the calling.

Since then, the Lord has been operating in the way that God operates, and has had me to preach the power of God to heal to and use me in many instances to pray for people and they were blessed with healings. The irony is that when we came back from Africa, John and I went to see my father, who was still in the hospital from when I was thirteen. Within a split second of seeing each other I was about to be upset, but then the Lord gave me the spirit of grace. That's kind of my call story and encounters with God.

"I then began to question the reality of my call to the ministry; and endeavored to bring it to the test by laying my heart before the Lord, and solemnly praying to the God of my salvation, that if it were His will for me to go out to preach the gospel, He would give me a token thereof by opening my way before me at the end of three months; and, if otherwise, that He would remove from my mind the weighty impression, which clogged me with care, kept me as a prisoner on parole, and blighted every other prospect in life. I accordingly waited very quietly until the time was nearly expired, watching carefully the signs of the time: but all was still dark; and not only so, I was also attacked with a severe fit of sickness and rendered unable to attend to my school. I then concluded that I had been mistaken, and endeavoured to attribute my past impressions to the zeal of imagination; for I thought, if it had really been the design of God to send me forth to preach the gospel, He would have disposed my affairs so as to open my way, and suitably replenish my purse for the journey; but instead of this being the case, my situation became more and more irksome, and hemmed in with difficulties... and in prayer I said to my heavenly master, in reference to my mnistry, 'Now I know that I am mistaken; and I am not going out at all.'

I had no sooner uttered these words, than a dreadful and chilling gloom instantaneously fluttered over, and covered my mind; the Spirit of the Lord fled out of my sight, and left me in total darkness... The members of the class inquired why I did not preach to people? 'You see,' said they, 'how the people flock to hear you, and yet you do not preach to them.' This went like a dagger to my heart; for it was evident to all that I had displeased my God... I then laid my case before some of the church; but none of them could administer any comfort to me. I also consulted some of the Society of Friends, but they could give me no instructions, because my business was not with mortal man, but with the living God.

Zilpha Elaw, Methodist Episcopal preacher,
from the 1846 edition of her *Memoirs* in
*Sisters of the Spirit: Three Black Women's
Autobiographies of the Nineteenth Century*
(Bloomington: Indiana University Press, 1986): 86-87.

John Bryant
Baltimore, Maryland

Bishop John Bryant was born in Baltimore, Maryland, on June 8, 1943, called in 1953 and ordained an African Methodist Episcopal elder in 1966. He has a BA from Morgan University, an MTh from Boston University and a DMin from Colgate Rochester Seminary. He serves as Bishop of the fourteenth Episcopal District. Interview recorded June 15, 1989.

13

"Choose Me and Live, or Take Your Chances with Satan"

I could say that my first recollection is made up of my desire to be a preacher. I've wanted to be a preacher all my life. My father's a preacher and that had a lot to do with it. I, however, establish 1953 as the time of my call. I was ten years old, and I dreamed that Satan was after me and was out to kill me. I was being chased by him, and he was out to kill me. And Jesus stepped between us and said to me in the dream, "Choose me and live, or take your chances with him." I responded in the dream, "I choose you, I have always wanted to." When I woke up, I was very much aware of the dream. It's funny, I am a person who doesn't remember. At that point in my life, I didn't remember dreams. And the only two dreams I remembered until I was about thirty-something was that one, and [the one where] I dreamed that I was at my brother's funeral. When I woke up, at that time, I was brought into consciousness by my mother, who told me my brother had just died. It was unusual for me to remember the dream, because I had always said I don't dream because I never remembered. That was my first dream that I remembered and that's what it was.

Choose Me and Live, or Take Your Chances with Satan

Now of course I was ten years of age, so I would say as a person I was a very normal, typical kid. If anything, I was considered more, as my mother would like to say, mischievous. So, the older I got, I kept wondering, Could this be true, for a couple of reasons. One is that people never affirmed it in me because of my behavior. I stayed in trouble in school and then I was very poor in academics. In the church, being a minister's son, I never displayed any leadership, so I did not display any of the gifts that I thought were typical for a preacher. Then it came to me in my late teens, because my father said I couldn't preach until I graduated from high school. It came to me that preachers were poor and also, in that day and time, people didn't affirm preachers. In other words, when I was with my friends and adults would say, "What do you want to be?" [I would say,] "I want to be a lawyer." "What do you want to be?" "I want to be a doctor." "What do you want to be?" "I want to be a preacher." "Oh, what do you want to do that for?" So, it wasn't an affirmation like it is now for the ministry.

And then feeling as I did at that time, that I did not have the gifts, that my behavior wasn't what it ought [to be], and I had given my parents trouble. I had a conversation [with my father] when I was nearing close to the time. I kept holding onto it, though, because I was very well aware that I felt God had called me. I just couldn't put my life in sync with that call. I said to my father at the time, "You know, I'm supposed to get ready to preach now but you know what my life has been, the trouble I have given y'all. I just can't understand how God can use me." He said, "Well, I know what you mean, but I can tell you this: that if God called you, he will prepare you. The life you now live will not be the life you will live. The key is for you to be certain that God called you."

So I received the date for my trial sermon. In my church it's called a trial sermon. For my friends, it was a joke; they couldn't believe it. The girl I was going with said she knew better than anyone else I'd never be a preacher. I just couldn't fathom it until I was preaching. It wasn't that great, but it was clear; it became crystal clear that this is where I belong and that this was God's intention for my life. I was eighteen at that time—that's close to thirty years ago—and it was clear.

Vivian C. Bryant
Southfield, Michigan

The Reverend Vivian C. Bryant was born in Detroit, Michigan, on June 25, 1938, called in 1984 and ordained an African Methodist Episcopal elder in 1991. She received a BA from Michigan State University, an MA from Wayne State University and an MA and MDiv from Ashland Theological Seminary. Interview recorded May 28, 1989.

14

When God Called at 3:45 Every Morning

Actually, the Lord called me into the ministry approximately three years before I accepted the call. There were many reasons why I didn't accept it initially. First of all, I'm a woman, and I've been brought up in a Baptist church; and in the Baptist church there were no women ministers. I had never heard a woman preach. I had been told by men all of my life that women did not do that—preach, so that was one reason why I didn't accept the calling. Another reason I didn't accept the calling was that I was, at that time, in my late forties, and I thought, you know, that was absolutely too old for anybody to venture into any new beginnings. So that was my second reason. The third reason for my reluctance was the unknown. I didn't know what it involved. I didn't know what it entailed. I didn't really know what it meant. Therefore, I was reluctant for those three reasons.

Every morning at 3:45, I was awakened. I could not go back to sleep. It was an idea that just kept coming in my mind that I was supposed to preach. I could see myself in a pulpit.

I wasn't asleep, I was awake, but I could see myself in a pulpit. I could see myself preaching, I could hear myself preaching. That was every morning at 3:45. Normally I get up at 5:30, and I was awakened at 3:45, so it was very clear to me that I was being called into the ministry. But, as I said, for the three reasons that I mentioned, I didn't accept it. I didn't want that. It was an awesome responsibility as I thought about it, to do that, and I didn't want that. So I tried to ignore it. And every morning at 3:45, I was wide awake. I could never go back to sleep. I would leave my bedroom and go into the family room and just sit there. I just couldn't believe it. I would talk to the Lord and tell him why he couldn't call me; you know, I didn't understand why he would call me. I would tell him I was a woman; I kept telling him that. That was the first thing I would say all the time, "Lord, don't you know I'm a woman?" And then I would tell him that I was too old and that I definitely did not want to go back to school; that's not what I had in mind to do. And then I would ask him questions like, "Why would you call me?" It was almost a confrontation with him, a verbal confrontation. I would just say, you know, "This is not what I want to do. I'm going to retire in the next few years, and when I retire, preaching's not on my agenda." I would talk to him like that.

You know, one time I remember, before I accepted, I asked him, "Why would you call me? I'm a woman. Why would you call me to the ministry?" And an answer came to me so plain that, I mean, I just had to drop down to the floor and I started crying. Because the answer that came to me, Dr. Myers, was, "I've called so many men and they're not doing what I want them to do." Now, that was the thing that made me really realize that I had something to do. And I thought about it, because my husband and I married when my daughter was nine years old. And see, I was in the Baptist church. My father had been superintendent of the Sunday school for forty-four years, and all I knew was the Baptist church. Then I married my husband, who was an African Methodist Episcopal person. I never heard of that in my life. I had never been in an AME church in my life. But, you see, the Lord was putting me in place so that I could answer the call, and that's what made it very clear to me, because I had never thought of leaving the Baptist church. I knew that I was very, very strong in my belief. My father's being superintendent of Sunday school contributed to that. I had been in church all of my life. I joined the church when I was eight years old, and I remember that very day. So I was very strong in the Lord and I was very strong in my religion. My husband was not. He was a babe in Christ, as it were.

I volunteered to go over to this AME church that I had never heard of before. But it was the Lord who was moving me into place. So I thought about that too. Then, as I said, in the morning he would wake me up, the Holy Spirit would wake me up and just talk to me about this and give me this idea about preaching. But I consider that a whisper.

Then he began to really shout at me. I mean, I would drive along and I would hear a sermon on the radio and the sermon would be "Come before Winter," this kind of thing, and it would hit me. At that time, I did not know that you could not enter the ministry in the AME church after the age of fifty. And when I accepted, I was forty-nine and a half. See, that was the screaming on his part. I mean, I would hear songs, and people would confirm it. I was the women's day speaker at Dr. Evans' church. He brought me into his study and he said, "Sister Bryant, here are some books that you should look at. I believe the Lord has called you." And this was a Baptist minister. People would come up to me and ask me, "Why aren't you accepting your calling?" and "Don't you know you're called?" Everywhere I would go, I would hear this; and it was on the upswing, because I would begin to speak almost every month someplace. I mean, they called me out in Los Angeles; I spoke out there and I would come back. Then one of my friends sent me a tape from a Baptist institute in the Ministerial Alliance in Los Angeles; E. V. Hill made a comment about women preachers, and it was very negative. When I heard that, I began to cry, because it grieved my spirit that here was a man who was called, who would not understand that the Lord could call anyone he wanted to call. And I thought, "Why would I take this so personally?" There I was, crying over a tape I'm listening to.

At that time I said, "I'm going to accept this thing; because I have to get some sleep. But first I'm going to talk to my daughter and my husband, and see what they say about it. If they say no, then that's going to do it. Or, if they say yes, then I'll speak to my pastor." I spoke to my daughter and my husband, and my daughter's words were, "What took you so long?" My husband's response was, "I've known you were called all along. You're very different." And, I mean, there was no negative word from them at all. It was as if the Lord had prepared them for my final acceptance, even though I hadn't accepted at that point.

I made an appointment with my pastor and I went to talk to him. In the meantime, I had prepared three pages of why the Lord should not call me into the ministry, and I had these three pages written out. I am a woman, you know, and it took me three pages to say all those things. I had it in my hand, so if my minister said, "No," I would say, "You see, I knew it." And I went in there with these three pages, and my pastor said to me, "I have been looking at you for years, because I knew you were called. If anyone I've ever met was called, I knew the Lord had called you." And he said, "I was just waiting." And the thing about it is this man had had a heart attack and bypass, and he wanted to move onto something else. He was waiting for me to come into the fold before he left the church to go to another. I mean, he was just waiting for me. And, so, he said, "What is that you have in your hand?" I had these three things and I told him. He said, "Don't you know the Lord knows all those things?" (He was a very wise, wise man.) And I didn't. On my way out, I started singing "Have Thine Own Way, Lord." From that night, up until last night, I have slept all night, each night. And that's it.

Delores Carpenter
Washington, D. C.

Dr. Delores Carpenter was born in Towson, Maryland, on July 26, 1944, called in 1960, and ordained [by the] Free Will Baptists in 1962. She has a BA from Morgan State University, an MDiv from Howard University School of Divinity, an MA from Washington University (St. Louis) and an EdD from Rutgers University. She is a professor on the Howard University Divinity School's faculty and senior pastor of the Michigan Park Christian Church in Washington, D C. Interview recorded June 16, 1989.

15

Acceptance of the Call at a Funeral

It seems like I always knew God and was very interested in God and the things of God. As soon as I learned to read, I was reading religious material, even before I went to school. My grandmother was a semi-invalid, so she had religious people in the home all the time. As a young girl I would be around, and I would do things for her. She had lost one leg and she became fairly immobile. I was the oldest grandchild, and I would be called upon to do this or that for her. So I was always by her side up until I was nine years old. My mother was working and I was at home.

I will say this, however, to go back even further. My mother had been in a Pentecostal church when she carried me. And I think I realize something now about this whole issue of why I finally found a church that had a rhythm to the gospel—a beat—and why I felt very much at home with that. It's something that I discovered recently. My mother had been involved in a Pentecostal church while she was carrying me. She was a member of Perkins Square Baptist Church in Baltimore and at the same time a member of Mt. Calvary Holy Church's junior church. She had been going to church, therefore, before I was born. I was hearing this gospel music, shouting, praising God, the holy dance, and all of this. When I was young, the first time I saw my mother do the holy dance it frightened me. It made a kind of compatibility for that kind of thing that I didn't understand. But some people would say to you, "Well, I don't do anything." They would think this was some kind of pretense or exaggeration, or excessive emotionalism. I would say that it was nurture, and nurture starts in the womb. And, so, even before being born I went to church a lot.

My mother moved with my grandmother. I'm not sure about all of the details of this, because it was a semi-rural family from Sparks, Maryland, which is above Towson, Maryland, where people had been slaves. My great-great-grandmother was a slave. I knew her until I was eight years old. She stayed on the farm. So we went back and forth between these communities. People kind of migrated from Sparks to Towson to Baltimore. So my mother's family had lived in all three of these places.

When I was born we went back to Towson, and I spent a lot of time with my grandmother. She was a woman who prayed a lot. Her mother and father were members of the Church of God in Christ. So, as I mentioned at Hampton [Hampton University Ministers' Conference, June 5-9, 1989], during those first nine years of my life, I saw my grandmother writing religious tracts, and I helped her look up the correct spelling. She only had a third grade education. I saw the deacons from the Missionary Baptist Church bringing her communion. I saw the pastor-preachers coming in and plugging in their outlets for the microphones for the street meetings. There was a bar across the street from my grandmother's house that they targeted. It was a real tiny community out there. She got a tent for the preachers. The Jehovah's Witnesses would come in, and we would sit around and study.

My mother gave me a golden book of Bible stories. This is going to be very important to this story. I guess if I can remember reading "See Spot run, see Dick, see Jane," I was also learning to read this book of Bible stories. And I would tell all the other children. My grandmother said I preached my first sermon when I was five years old. I've seen my children do this — it's just a natural thing. I saw my daughter Susan (she was six when we moved here) go to the typewriter and type out an order of service, preach the sermon and read a children's story called

"Woofey and the Prodigal Son," which is a very popular children's story. So I've seen it replicated in my own daughter. I would apparently memorize these stories out of this book of beautiful pictures, mainly Old Testament stories about Moses, David and Samson. Then I would have all the children sit down, and I would tell them these stories.

Well, this would turn out to be very important to my call— playing church. It was just something we did. We imitated people in church and we took different roles, my cousins and I. We had quite an extended family that was very close-knit. One of my aunts had seven children and an uncle had fourteen children. But I was the oldest grandchild and I was precocious and smart, because I had to do grocery shopping when I was eight, I had to go to the bank, and I had to go pay the rent. Since my grandmother couldn't get out and my mother was working, I learned to do a lot of things at a very young age. I had a lot of responsibility. So that led to, I guess, a certain amount of assertiveness. I was a kind of little leader of a band of relatives and friends. I didn't just do this with religious things, but everything.

When I was nine, my mother moved to the city. We moved out of my grandmother's house, and she got a place of her own that she was very proud of. My cousins were already relocated in the city and we started going to Sunday school. I went with my cousins. It was down the street from a Free Will Baptist Church, and we had moved two or three times and finally we moved right across the street from this Free Will Baptist Church. It was relatively small with about a hundred people, and it was in that church that I heard that good singing, the rhythms again. And I had not really been in a church where people would clap their hands and sing like that. This was a Kinston, North Carolina transplant. The pastor and his family and most of the members of that church in Baltimore were from Kinston, I was very excited about what I saw there. I fell in love with the church. I was there every time the doors opened. The minister used to have quizzes for young people. He would question us in the bulletin, and whoever gave the best answer would get a prize. But he stopped doing it, because I would win every time. So I just started working in that church.

One day I was at home (I was almost thirteen) and my cousins were with me, and we were playing church. We had learned these new songs. We were singing the song, "He's

Acceptance of the Call at a Funeral

Calling Me." This was something we sang at church. We were in the junior choir. When you became a teenager you moved up to the number two choir. So, by this time, at thirteen I was eligible for the number two choir and my cousins were in the junior choir. But we knew this song, and we liked it a lot. *He's calling me, he's calling me, every day of my life I can hear Jesus calling me.* We were clapping our hands, and all of a sudden, I couldn't stop clapping my hands. I began to feel that I was moving to a different level of consciousness. I was aware of where I was and what we were doing, but I was also aware of something pulling me to go inside, like an inscape. And so, even after they stopped singing, I kept clapping. I closed my eyes. It just seemed like the instinctive thing to do. As I closed my eyes I saw this field. It was a big huge field, the grass was kind of tall, and I started walking. And my dilemma was, Was I going back to the reality of where my cousins were, or was I going to walk on across the field? So I decided that I'm gonna go for it, I'm going on across the field. And so, I did. I actually never remembered seeing myself walking, because I kind of went out of it. It was a sense of the unconscious, because I have no memory of what happened to me after that.

When I did become conscious again, I was lying on the bed kicking my feet and laughing, just laughing and laughing and laughing. When I finished, I wanted to go tell my mother what had happened to me. She was ironing, and when I went to tell her what had happened to me, I couldn't speak English. I opened my mouth to say to her whatever it was—you know, "Gee, Mom, guess what happened to me?" And it came out different, just gibberish. I got so frustrated that I stopped trying. My mother was very helpful to me. She understood. I didn't. She understood. She understood all the time.

Of course, I had to discover it and unload all of this, and it was going to take years to do that. Actually, it was going to take me three years to preach my first sermon. But when I was thirteen, that's the incident that got all of it started. That raised the question for me. And so my search started for the meaning for these various things. They described how I had moved all around in the room. This was one of the most joyful feelings that I had ever had in my life. It was a very, very high feeling, a very happy feeling. So we would sing that song. Of course, everytime I would hear it in church I couldn't help but be reminded of this experience and wonder what did it mean.

So I got very, very "religious" at this point, and I would pray a lot and read the Scripture a lot. I knew it was something significant but I didn't know what. I said, "Well, maybe it means God is calling me," because I had heard people talking about being called to the ministry. I had heard people talk about that. I would pray about it, and in my heart I felt that's what it was, that God was calling me to dedicate my life to him. My first line of thought was that I was going to be like my grandmother, who had gifts of healing and prophecy. See, I had read all about the spiritual gifts in the Bible and all that. I studied all these types of things. And I was very impressed with that—you know, Jesus healing and helping people, my grandmother praying for people and all that.

But as time went on (this is where it breaks down in my memory), I can't remember how it got translated actually into being called to preach. I finally knew that I was going to be a minister, but I still didn't know about preaching. But once, I remember praying to God and saying, "I want the gifts of healing and prophecy. I give you my life, I want the gifts of healing and prophecy." There was no audible voice but something inside said to me, "I want you to preach, and all these gifts will be added to you." And there was a time when that actually came to me as an inspiration, but I don't know all the sequence or steps that led up to me understanding that.

Now, the first person that I told this to was a woman in our church. And she told me that it was the devil, because God did not call women to preach. I was fourteen then, and I cannot tell you the devastation I felt. I was plunged into a very, very deep depression. My grades dropped in school. I would go to church because I couldn't stay away. I would cry and cry and cry. But I guess people around me knew I was struggling. The minister in the church knew, and as I related in my sermon in Hampton, so did the minister's daughter, who was the assistant pastor. I really admired her a lot. She was a very grand lady. And I was inspired by her faith journey and story of her struggle with leukemia. She took a very special interest in me. So, through it all I was still active in the church. I did a lot of things: teaching vacation church school, doing young people's Christian league and doing mid-week services at this time. The congregation saw that I had a great knowledge of the Bible. This was the thing that was the authority in the church. So, at a very young age I had quite a lot of leadership going on in that congregation.

Acceptance of the Call at a Funeral

It was Reverend Sister Johnson who would ask me those probing questions, "Do you have anything you want to tell me?" And I'd say, "No." I didn't even want to think it really. I went downtown one day, and I ran into her—the woman that I loved and had spent so much time with and had questioned about God and especially about the Holy Spirit, because she was the one person in the church who was always talking about the Holy Spirit. That was going to be a big key in understanding what had happened to me. And so she would say, "You just shouldn't do this and do that." I'd say, "Why can't you dance and why can't you do this and this?" She would say, "Well, when you get the Holy Spirit, you'll understand these things." I didn't really know what she was talking about, "Get the Holy Spirit." But I knew that there was something that she knew about God, that there was something in what she was saying to me that was the key to my own relationship with God, and that I was going to dedicate myself to God.

I had seen her in the hospital, and the last time I saw her, she said, "Delores, why don't you do what God wants you to do?" I went home and I got sick. I went and got in the bed. It was at her funeral, that instead of the prepared statement, I announced that God had called me to preach. I announced that I was going to do what God had called me to do. It was as though a mantle had been laid down, the one that she had, and I picked it up.

Now, the pastor of the church had been very worried about me, because he could see that I was really struggling. I was one of those people in the church that if anybody preached I'd get happy. There was one preacher, who would say, "Oh, Sis Causion, I love to come here. I always know one person who's gonna get happy whenever I preach." I'd go up for prayer on a few occasions, and I'd fall out in the Spirit. And I remember one woman said, "You kept us here all night long, but you don't look any different to me." So everybody kind of knew that I was struggling. It was so bad that my mother was so concerned. My grades were dropping in school and so was my general mood.

My mother sought some help by talking to the pastor of the church. So, I looked up one Sunday, and my whole extended family was there. This was very unusual. The pastor preached a special sermon trying to reach me. Now, later I found out he knew that I was being called to the ministry. So, when I told him that I had this great thing to tell him, after I had struggled and finally I was ready he looked up and said to me, "I know." That blew my mind. Apparently many people felt I was going to do something, but they didn't know what. It was very wonderful to have that burden lifted from me and to just strike out.

Not long after that we set the trial sermon date, and I preached my trial sermon in February, 1960. But, the pastor had a stroke suddenly and died. I remember the pulpit was draped in black and people asked me, "Are you going to cancel your trial sermon?" I said, "No, we're going to go ahead with it." I preached three nights in a row. I preached in my church; I preached in my mother's church; I preached in the church where I was a member of the Tuesday night youth church. (I belonged to St. Paul, but I'd go to Tuesday night church in this other church.) So, I started out with three trial sermons. It was just one thing after another. That's how all of this got started. That's pretty much the story of the call.

Mack King Carter
Fort Lauderdale, Florida

The Reverend Dr. Mack King Carter was born in Ocala, Florida, on February 4, 1947, called in 1956 and ordained a Baptist minister in 1966. He received a BA from the University of Florida, and an MDiv and DMin from Southern Baptist Seminary (Louisville). He pastors the Mt. Olive Baptist Church in Fort Lauderdale. Interview recorded March 14, 1990.

16

"Now That Your Grandmother Is Gone, You Must Move Up"

My calling into the gospel ministry, though I would have to clarify it and articulate it much better later on, was not anything that was overwhelmingly dramatic. I grew up in a Christian home. I learned at my grandmother's knees the practicalities of theology out of an agrarian background—I learned the practicalities of theology from my grandmother, who was a second or third grade scholar. I learned the rudiments of Christianity or the rudiments of Christ from my grandmother and my mother and my father. So, I had the benefits of a Christian home.

I knew from the year 1953, when I made a commitment (though as a child I made a commitment) to Jesus Christ. I could not articulate all of the theologies and the psychology of making a commitment to Christ, but I was certain in 1953 that the Lord had laid his hands upon me, and in a very real sense. I became a deacon of the church at the age of ten years. The first great event was when I committed my life to Christ in 1953 at the age of six. The next great event in my life, as I evolved into the call, was in 1957 when I, at the age of ten years, was placed on the deacon board in my church, which is the New Bedford Baptist Church in Ocala, Florida.

The next great event in the evolvement towards my call was in 1960 with the passing of my grandmother when I was thirteen years of age. This was a very traumatic experience for me, because to me part of my being had been severed from me. I never will forget as I was walking to school after the Christmas holidays in 1961. As we went into a new year (my grandmother passed December 19, 1960), I never will forget as I was walking down Maple Street in Ocala, Florida on my way to school — I was attending elementary school then — just as I crossed the railroad that separated Maple Street from Beech Street, I had a revelatory experience. A voice spoke within me and said, "Now that your grandmother is gone, you must move up now. You must get eager in your commitment, you must get eager in the faith." The voice that spoke within me was not saying that you must take her place. God does not require us to take another's place, but to fill our own space. As I was walking to school, that was an overwhelming experience in January 1961. Almost from that point, my life changed.

Then finally in 1966, while I was attending college at Florida Memorial College in St. Augustine, Florida, I had gone to church down at the Shiloh Baptist Church in St. Augustine, pastored by the Reverend J. D. Wright. He preached a sermon that Sunday about Jacob wrestling with the angels. As he preached that Sunday, he talked about the struggle that the angel had with Jacob and the constant struggle that we have in making decisions. And as I was walking back to the campus from the Shiloh Baptist Church, there was an overwhelming sense of oughtness, to quote Immanuel Kant. There was an overwhelming sense of oughtness which said, beyond a shadow of doubt, "Now is the time." It was at that time that I made my personal commitment to the gospel ministry.

However, as the years have passed on, I have learned and as I have pursued the New Testament in a far deeper sense, I articulate my calling in a little different fashion since that particular event. First of all, I think the whole issue of the call has been misunderstood not only by Blacks, but it's been misunderstood by White people also. In a broad sense, in the New

Testament there is no such thing as "the call to preach" as we have articulated. Everybody is called to preach in a New Testament sense, and the call to preach is inseparable and cannot be extricated from the call to salvation. When I'm called to salvation, I'm also called to preach in the sense of spreading the word. What we have confused with a call to preach is the cultural phenomenon of sermonizing. Sermonizing is not Biblical, sermonizing is cultural. And in this sense there is a paralysis in our pew, because they come to watch us do what we call preaching. In fact, it is not necessarily New Testament preaching (it can be), but it is sermonizing.

Therefore, usually we would say that in my case, prior to really coming to grips with this, I was saved in 1953 and I was called to preach in 1966. I personally articulate it in this fashion now. I was saved in 1953 and I was called to preach in the New Testament sense in 1953; but I received a special anointing in 1966 to be a pastor-teacher, upon which I later would go on and receive training for the gift that God had given me in this particular area.

So, I guess you could say my calling was just God preparing—or it would be just like my mother would make me, as a baby, some pants that would fit a person who was nineteen years of age; and I just simply grew religiously and spiritually to the point until when I reached that particular position. Then God said, "It's time to step into these trousers that were already made for you nineteen years ago," because I was nineteen years of age when I was anointed to be a pastor-teacher.

E. Theophilus Caviness
Cleveland, Ohio

The Reverend E. Theophilus Caviness was born in Marshall, Texas, on May 23, 1928, called in 1945 and ordained a Baptist minister in 1945. He has a BA from Bishop College and a BD from Eden Theological Seminary. He pastors the Greater Abyssinia Baptist Church. Interview recorded June 4, 1990.

17

Movies and Dancing or Preaching: Which Will It Be?

Basically, I think this matter of ministry was a divine kind of impulse, motive and motivation since the earliest part of my life. That is, whenever I came to that point of understanding, it has always been my basic feel and motive that I was designed and called to preach. It was a verbal kind of calling as much as it was an innate, inward, constraining, compelling kind of motivation. It was something that was almost innate and inculcated within my bones that I was destined, pushed, constrained, and motivated to preach. And that's always been the motivating factor. I guess at six years of age I was already doing these kinds of things: watching preachers, listening to preachers, being inspired by preachers, watching their mannerisms and everything. It has never been my desire to do anything else but preach. I mostly articulate it with words of a divine call motivated by an inward urge to preach the gospel. And I could say a ton more words, but I don't think it will come any more crystal clear than a divine urge to preach the gospel, a divine call to be an ambassador and emissary and person for dispensing the Bible truth. And that has always been a part of me and seemingly my destiny to do that, and I have never deviated from it.

I guess being born in a religious setting, and being an ardent participant in Black church activities, and brought up in that confine probably gave me the framework for preaching. But this actually was almost a Jeremiah-kind of impelling that the Lord wants you. "You are designed, I created you for this and you must do it." It's a divine must. You've got to do it. You've got no choice but to do it. And it was that Bible teaching and the kind of things that was indelibly impacted upon my mind and heart: that Jesus Christ died that your sins might be forgiven. Forgiving is forgiveness, and calls for some action on your part to pass the word along to others who might not be of such divine blessing.

I had been pushed in this direction from six on up. But I acknowledged it at seventeen, because I had some other little things that I had to work out. Things that were delineated in terms of the world more then than now. Back there, you didn't go to movies on Sundays, you didn't dance, dancing was considered a sin. Those were the kind of things in our community that were do's and don'ts. And I had some problems with trying to figure out if I was going to do a little dancing on the side and do a little preaching on the other side. After awhile, those that were going this way had to go, and those who were going the other way went that way. I kind of wanted to keep one foot in each camp: I wanted to be friends with the brothers, and I also wanted to preach. Finally, at seventeen, it just bubbled over. I said, "This is it, I've got to walk that walk." So I just changed courses. And all of that, it was trying to make absolutely sure that I followed the Bible line on some certain do's and don'ts.

T. Oscar Chappelle
Tulsa, Oklahoma

The Reverend T. Oscar Chappelle was born in Sapulpa, Oklahoma, on October 15, 1915, called in 1931 and ordained a Baptist minister in 1936. He received a BA from Bishop College and a BTh from the American Baptist Seminary (Tennessee). Until his death, he was pastor of Morning Star Baptist Church and President of the largest Black Baptist Congress in the United States, the Congress of the National Baptist Convention USA, Inc. Interview recorded June 21, 1989.

18

Young Preacher Influences Future Baptist Congress President

When I was eight years old, I head a young minister, who at that time was sixteen years old, preach. My father was a lawyer, and my mother was a school teacher. I was debating whether I wanted to go into education or go into law. After I heard this young man preach, he impressed me to the point that I began to think about it. I thought about it all those years. In fact, I told my mother, "I want to be a minister." I told the kids in school and they all laughed. At that time, being a minister wasn't popular. So that is my prior experience, see. Of course, I grew up in the church and I guess that would be about the principal thing to say about it. I didn't have no cataclysmic call —just always wanted to be a preacher. Never wanted to be anything but a minister.

Young Preacher Influences Future Baptist Congress President

    I was called to the ministry when I was a boy, on the eve of my fifteenth birthday. I finished high school at fifteen. I finished in June, and started preaching in October. I've been preaching since 1931—October 15, 1931. I was born in a small town called Sapulpa, Oklahoma—it's about fifteen miles from Tulsa. I finished high school in Tulsa and went to Bishop College. Well, I was a freshman in college. I was in the school of religion. I decided that I would go ahead and preach my first sermon. Well, I had an older minister, who encouraged me go on and preach my first sermon. So I preached it there at the Bethesda Baptist Church in Marshall, Texas. It was a sort of encouragement from all the folk around me to go into it. They said, "Well, if that's what you gonna be, go ahead and start."

    After Bishop College I went to the American Baptist Seminary. I got a BA degree in religion at Bishop College and a Bachelor of Theology at the seminary.

Arlene Churn
Camden, New Jersey

The Reverend Dr. Arlene Churn was born in Philadelphia, Pennsylvania, on December 20, 1940, called in 1945 and ordained a Baptist minister in 1960. She has a BS from Temple University, the BTh degree from the Philadelpia College of the Bible, and a Doctorate in Historical Education from Johns Hopkins University. She pastors the Cathedral of Faith Baptist Church in Camden, New Jersey. Interview recorded in September 1989.

19

Boy Preachers Yes, Girl Preachers No

My call to the ministry occurred October 16th, and we're going back forty-four years. I'll never forget it as long as I live. I was in elementary school, the Paul Lawrence Dunbar Elementary School, at Twelfth and Columbia Avenue in Philadelphia, Pennsylvania. I was seated on the second row in the fifth seat and it was two minutes before ten o'clock in the morning; that's how precise it was. And I think of myself in terms of the young child Samuel, because a voice came and I heard an audible expression. Yet I was conscious of the fact that it was not heard by anyone around me. I heard this voice call me by my name three times. It presented no element of fear at all. It was as if I knew that it was the voice of the supreme and divine Creator. The message that was given to me was (and I'll never forget it as long as I live), "Warn the people, and tell them that the day of God's wrath has come and you shall not be able to stand." The voice also said affliction was coming in the land and destruction, and that people were false pretenders and hypocrites professing to be one thing and they were something else.

I felt this wide space within me, and I heard myself respond as if it were going into an echo. I could hear the echo of my voice from within although my lips did not move, and I heard this within me saying, "Lord, I'm too little; I'm too weak; I don't have the strength." I heard my voice saying that. And the voice came back to me and said, "If you go and go willingly, I will give you the strength." And that was it. I got up and bolted out of the classroom. I ran out of the classroom and I ran home and I told my grandmother what had happened. She cried, and yet I could tell the combination of joy and fear, because I think that she saw in that moment a flash of what would lie ahead for me if, in fact, this was a call to the ministry.

She contacted our pastor, who is yet alive and recently retired, Reverend Austin Jefferson, Jr. of the Abyssinia Baptist Church in Philadelphia, and she took me to him that day. I shared with him what had happened, the experience that I had. He said, "Bring her to church Sunday," because I think it was such a convincing testimony and experience. He said, "I'm afraid to pass judgment." Of course, this was most unique in the Black church at that time—a child, although there were some child preachers that were very prominent: Howard Davis, he was a boy preacher, and Johnny Robinson from Philadelphia. They were outstanding boy preachers although they were several years my senior. But girl preachers in the Baptist church? Girl preachers proved that God has a sense of humor, I think.

I went to church that Sunday, and I can see it now—the little sailor dress, my little Mary Jane shoes and socks. I was so little. So they had to take a chair and put it behind the rostrum. Standing on the chair to reach the microphone, I told them at the conclusion of our morning worship of my experience, and the pastor said, "She has a story to tell. I don't know whether she can get it all out," almost just apologizing. And I remember thinking: "Oh, if he would just sit down, so I could tell it! Oh, if he would just sit down!" He was trying to prepare the people, I guess, for my saying nothing. I can remember what I told them of my experience. It was an explosion in the church, and Abyssinia is a very traditional Baptist worship center it was then. My grandmother and others were women of social prominence, and the church was not given to, in that day, a charismatic experience. So, for Abyssinia to explode like that was something.

From that moment the word spread. I guess people went home and told members of other churches. The first sermon I preached was on Matthew 27:22: *"And Pilate said unto them, 'What shall we do with Jesus which is called the Christ?' And they all said unto him, 'Let him be crucified.'"* I preached that the world was crucifying Jesus. That was my first sermon. And I have been uninterruptedly preaching from that day until this.

Caesar A. W. Clark
Dallas, Texas

The Reverend Caesar Arthur Walter Clark was born in Shreveport, Louisiana, on December 13, 1914, called in 1922-23 and ordained a Baptist minister in 1933. He did not receive the opportunity to finish high school. He pastors the Good Street Baptist Church in Dallas, Texas, and serves as Vice President-at-large of the largest Black Baptist Convention in the United States, the National Baptist Convention U. S. A., Inc. He is, without question, the leading Black Baptist revivalist in this country. Interview recorded April 26, 1989.

20

From a Seventh Grader to the Leading Revivalist

Well, I accepted Christ and was baptized in the month of August 1928, and I did what is traditionally known as one's trial sermon the fourth Sunday in April 1929. I have been a churchgoer and a lover of preachers and school teachers since early childhood. By being a regular churchgoer I came to know, respect and look up to preachers, and I still do. I think the most vivid thing or the most impressive I remember was my almost unbroken church attendance, and my having been influenced and swayed and moved and excited by the manner of the worship and by the power of the preaching. The preachers, as I look back on it, for that community, majored in the Word. They did not have much of what we have today. And by the same token, we do not have much of what they had then. They had one book and they majored in that book. Dr. William Hicks, one of the preachers of that day and time, used to tell us, "Read other books minorly but read the Bible majorly." I had the urge, that desire to preach, when I was some eight or nine years old. It is an urge, it's an inner urge that one has that is only satisfied when you yield to it.

I was born December 13, 1914, and I preached my first sermon in April 1929. There was no formal acknowledgment of it before then, but it was an atmosphere, an experience in which I lived and moved and had my spiritual being. In that particular section of the country in those days, "boy preachers" were not known. So it was a big step for me at that age to lay claim to having been called to preach. But my pastor accepted me and gave me an opportunity, and other pastors of that day, on the recommendation of my home church pastor, accepted and gave me an opportunity, as the old preachers would say in that day, to "exercise my gift."

I went to school in the church house, and on Sundays we went to church in the church house. I didn't get too much formal training. I never finished high school. In my native state we only had three months to go to school, and if the cotton was opened a little early we didn't have three months. So I only got to the seventh grade. I left home in my teens going to what was then Coleman College. That was at Gibson, Louisiana. At Gibson, Dr. Roy Mayfield and his wife Susie were our instructors. Among the things that I learned from Dr. Mayfield was that the first law of biblical interpretation is a correct reading of the passage, and that makes sense, because if you don't read it correctly you'll certainly not interpret it correctly.

I think every man called goes through a crisis period. When Moses was called, you know what crisis he went through. When Paul was called, you know what crisis he went through. Dr. E. L. Harris used to tell us that if a man can keep from preaching he ought not to preach, because if he can keep from preaching, that is a sign that he hadn't been called to preach. You don't preach because you want to; you preach because you can't help yourself.

Have you read of Jeremiah's frustration? He felt that God had let him down; he felt like he had gone out on a limb. He said, "I guess I'm through with it." But then when you hear from him again, he's on his mission, and he said the reason is that "Although I intended to go no further, the word was like fire." So you have that inner urge, it haunts you, and you only have a sense—a feeling—of satisfaction when you yield to it.

When I came to the pastorage of the Little Union Baptist

Church on Milan Street in Shreveport, I had been pastor for a number of churches in what we called "the country." In those days, if a man didn't have at least three churches, he was not considered as one of the leading preachers. Most of the men had four and some had five. I went through that period. At various times I served Magnolia Baptist Church at South Mansfield, Flower Hill Baptist Church at Grand Cane, Waterloo Number One and Two at Taylortown, Calvary at Benton, Pilgrim Rest on Phelps Lake, and some others. Finally, in 1936, I was called to Little Union Church, which was my first church in the city. After that, I was called to Paradise Baptist Church on Hollywood Avenue. Then, when I was called full-time to Little Union Paradise, I also went full-time.

During my years at the Little Union Baptist Church, I entered Bishop College then located at Marshall, Texas. I had no high school diploma, but Dr. Jessie J. MacNeil, Dean Elvin J. Banks, Dr. William R. Strassmer, and President Joseph J. Rose made it possible for me to take an examination which would be the equivalent of a high school diploma. With that I was admitted on a probationary period. That is how I got a chance to go to college.

My invitations to preach have carried me to the major, predominantly Black, pulpits of the nation. At a giant meeting of all the state conventions in Texas, held at the the Superdome or whatever, the correct name escapes me right now — this was held in Houston, Texas, and I was one of the preachers there. The attendance at that meeting was 41,000--plus people. I have also, by the generosity of the Good Street Baptist Church where I have been since September 1950, been able to preach in Africa, in Russia, in Rome; and I have had the opportunity to see Paris, London, Scotland, Switzerland, Germany, and, of course, the Holy Land. So that is, in brief, about the way that I have come.

Earl C. Cotton
Los Angeles, California

The Reverend Dr. Earl C. Cotton was born in Kilgore, Texas, on April 7, 1922, called from birth and ordained a Baptist minister in 1949. He received a BA and BD from Biola University, and an MA and DMin from Fuller Theological Seminary. He was the first African American to graduate with the Doctor of Ministry from Fuller. He pastors the Liberty Baptist Church in Los Angeles. Interview recorded June 19, 1989.

21

A Divine Seizure

My call to the gospel ministry is like a divine seizure or initiative. From the very day that I can remember, I have always known that the Lord had laid his hand upon me to preach the gospel. During those days, I developed a great love for preachers and preaching. From a child on, preachers were my idols, and everything that I did in life was directed towards preaching the gospel. I found myself, as a young child, imitating preachers, preaching to myself going through the woods, as I had to walk several miles to school.

I grew up as an orphan. My father passed away when I was four years old; my mother, when I was eleven. Therefore, I had no particular person to guide and direct me. I lived with some southern white people. They were Christians, and being in this Christian atmosphere, it kind of kept a sparkle of the Christian life moving in my direction.

I was able to live there and able to go to school for sometimes three months out of the year, and sometimes six months out of the year. The thing that motivated me to go to school was the very fact that the Lord had laid his hand upon me to preach the gospel. Most young men, when there was nobody to impel them to go to school, they dropped out of school.

Growing up in a rural area and knowing that the church, even in the rural area, wouldn't even call a pastor unless he had some formal training, I knew that if I was going to preach that I had to get some formal education.

So I endured much hardship even to get through high school. I worked at night. I had to drop out two or three times but I continued to manage a way to get back in school. And the only thing that really motivated me to go was that I knew that I had to preach the gospel, and in feeling that if I was going to preach the gospel I must have something to say. I felt like the so-called moan and sensationalism was not sufficient for God. It looked like in every direction that I went that God was moving me and preparing me for the ministry. The mark was upon me. Even when I went to the military service, most people I met said, "You should be preaching instead of being in a military uniform." Some of these people I'd never met and had never seen before.

So the divine seizure has always been upon me to preach the gospel. It seemed that God worked it out in my educational career. Because I had to work and go to school and drop out so many times, my grade point average didn't even qualify me to get into a regular college; neither did I have the money. But when I came out of the military service, I was eligible to go to school and even get paid to go, and even at that, my grade point average was low.

So when I answered the call and announced to my pastor that I was entering into the ministry, he recommended several schools to go to. One was Redmond University and the other was Bishop College. Living in Los Angeles, there was no way that I could get to those schools; so I entered into another field. I had worked in electronics in the military. I had developed a love for that, and I was going into electrical engineering. I went to that school and stayed in there three months. The power of the call was so pungent. After taking an examination one day—I did excellent on the final exam—I walked out of the school and never went back.

I went to the Veterans Administration and told them that I was changing and going to another school. They said, "Your change is quite diverse. You only have just once chance and if you don't stay with what you're going to now, you can't go back." I said, "I'm aware of that, and I know the risk that I'm taking but this is the way that I'm led to go." I went to the Bible Institute of Los Angeles. It was an unaccredited institution; and, so, they accepted me on probation. If you got through that institute on probation, you were qualified to get into the degree program. It was a requirement that you had to take Greek and Hebrew in the degree program.

So my grade point reached the point from the Institute that I qualified to get into the degree program. Then, while in the degree program, the Bible Institute instituted a college program—a bachelor of arts where you could attain a Bachelor of Arts degree. The school became fully accredited. I felt by that that God was working; otherwise, I never would have been able to get into an accredited institution. I had the ability, but not the opportunity. That's why my grade point was low.

I went through Biola College. I guess I was the first Black who went through there and through their seminary. I was honored by the school in 1970 as one of the outstanding alumni. From there, I went to Fuller Seminary in Pasadena, where their major was training scholars. I never dreamed that I would get into that institution. And I went through Fuller Seminary in Pasadena, which was I guess the second largest seminary in the United States of its time. I was the first American Black to graduate out of their doctoral program. So that's about it.

It had to be through divine revelation, because I couldn't be satisfied in doing anything else. My plan was to go into another field where I could earn a livelihood. Then after that I went to school to get a theological education, because knowing when you come out of a theological seminary, you have no assurance that you're going to get into a church or going to get into a teaching position or something of that nature. So I was using that as a backup, but God wouldn't even let me do that.

I was completely discontent in trying to pursue another field even on a temporary basis. And, so, I was led to put my full force toward preparation for the gospel ministry. Then when I got out I never had to look for another job. God had a place prepared for me as soon as I got out. I've never worked on another job, and the ministry is the only job that I had. That was an affirmation to me that that's where the Lord wanted me, and he put me under his employment and under his provision. He has not failed to provide.

"*In the earlier days of freedom almost every coloured man who learned to read would receive 'a call to preach' within a few days after he began reading. At my home in West Virginia the process of being called to the ministry was a very interesting one. Usually the call came when the individual was sitting in church. Without warning the one called would fall upon the floor as if struck by a bullet, and would lie there for hours, speechless and motionless. Then the news would spread all through the neighbourhood that this individual had received a 'call.' If he were inclined to resist the summons, he would fall or be made to fall a second or third time. In the end he always yielded to the call. While I wanted an education badly, I confess that in my youth I had a fear that when I had learned to read and write well I would receive one of these 'call;' but, for some reason, my call never came.*"

Booker T. Washington,
Up from Slavery: An Autobiography
(New York: *The Sun Dial Press, Inc., 1928*):82

Yvonne Delk
New York, New York

The Reverend Dr. Yvonne Delk was born in Norfolk, Virginia, on April 15, 1939, called in 1944 and ordained by the United Church of Christ in 1974. She has a BA from Norfolk State University, a MRE from Andover-Newton Theological Seminary and a DMin from New York Theological Seminary. She serves as an executive director for the United Church of Christ. Interview recorded December 19, 1989.

22

"God's Yes Was Louder than My No"

I think that there are three strong motives that helped to form what I came to understand as a call into ministry. The first is rooted in my family, and it was sort of nurtured even as I came into the world. In 1939 my mother was a member of Macedonia United Church of Christ, and my daddy was a deacon [there]. They had suffered the loss of a baby girl a year before that. They had one son, but they were so pleased when they discovered that they were pregnant again after they had that son, and rejoiced in the birth of that baby, only to discover about six months after its birth that the baby had developed pneumonia. My mother and father lost that baby. It was a devastating experience, and they wrestled so hard with that until my mother, at that time, nearly suffered a nervous breakdown. She says that what brought her back to herself was the realization that she was pregnant again. When she realized she was pregnant again, she went into our church, Macedonia, to give thanks for that. And in the process of giving thanks, she told me that she dedicated the baby that was growing in her back to God.

Now, when they told me that story, it already planted in me an image that my life, somehow, did not simply belong to me but that it belonged to God. Stories that parents tell you as you are a child growing up have a binding authority on the way in which you see life. When they told me that story as I was growing up, somehow inside of me, it already began to plant the seed that something special had to happen with my life.

The other reality was family. My father's mother and father were both ministers in the First United Holiness Church in America. My grandmother was a very powerful itinerant preacher. [She] moved around the U.S. preaching in churches, and they called her a traveling evangelist. Also, when I was [little] my father always said to me, "You look like your grandmother." The context of having him say that I looked like my grandmother and also having them dedicate my life to God at such an early age began to connect for me in a strong, positive way. Here was a grandmother that was already in ministry, and here I was having my life dedicated to God. So I felt that there was a call that was there, that was just rooted in those two events.

First, I was nurtured in a family whose stories about how I came into this world and whose connection to powerful women namely my grandmother and also my mother, made me feel that there was something special about my life. It was a plain family and it was a church-going family. The whole symbolism of the community of faith surrounding us was just so powerful. The spirit of being a part of the faithful community was sewn really strong in my family. That was the first beginning of my wrestling with call.

The second was really planted in that church that I grew up in. It was my church—Macedonia Congregational Christian Church. It was as much a part of my life as going to school, as living in the community that I lived in. It was the nurturing, supportive community that surrounded us. Mama and daddy wrestled with all the realities of racism and poverty and struggled day for day for day. On Sunday, they and my sisters and my brothers and I would move into that church. It was in that church and in that space that we were named in the context of the spirit. And no matter what we were wrestling with, I can still remember the powerful preached word of the minister who kept reminding us that we belonged to God. No matter the forces and powers and principalities that there were in the world, that were trying to name us in less-than-human ways, God's name took priority. And when God claimed us, and when God affirmed us as being somebody else, nobody else's name could take priority over that naming of us by God. It was in that church that we were named as somebodies, and where on Sunday I sang in the choir, ushered on the usher board and was a member of the church school.

Then, as I grew up, I began to teach in vacation Bible school and Sunday school, and I was a member of the Willing Workers. That community surrounded us and nurtured us. I can remember us going to prayer meeting on Wednesday nights, and mama would always say, "No matter happens to us, we can go into that space, that sacred space and give thanks to God for keeping our bodies and our minds and our spirits together." So, on Wednesdays when we went into the prayer meetings (we had to stand up, even as a child of about eight or nine), mama would say, "You always have something that you can be thankful for. So you can just thank God for helping you to be able to come out here and to praise his name. Or you can thank God for keeping your mind focused so that you can learn and grow as a person. You can always find something to thank God for."

Well, that community, that faithful community, was a powerful community on me. It was always reminding me that my life belonged to God and that I had to give something from my life back to God, because God had given so much. So, it was in that arena that I began to hear the call coming down, not just from mama and daddy telling us the stories about us, but also my grandmother. And it was in that faith community where the word was reminding me over and over again that God's gift of creation was life for me, and that I had to answer the question: "God has given you this life, now what are you going to give back to God?" I was wrestling in that setting with how to give my life back to God.

It was, therefore, in college—and I was in college from '57 to '61—that I began to wrestle with the whole liberation movement, or the Civil Rights movement, you might say, of our people. While I was putting the pieces togetherm it began to be affirmed by Martin King's leadership in Birmingham, Alabama. Then they asked students who were at Norfolk State at that time (Norfolk State University in Norfolk, Virginia) to go downtown and sit in and demonstrate. Suddenly, I began connecting the sense of fighting and struggling for our people's liberation and standing up against injustices, and all of those seeds began to come together for me at a time that a person came and said to me, "Yvonne, as you think about what you are going to do with your life, I have often thought that I would like to have you think about seminary." And suddenly when that person (the Reverend Purcell Austin, who was working then as minister of Christian education at the Convention of the South of which our church was a part) named that, all these other pieces seemed to come together. At first my response was, "No." I just couldn't see myself in seminary; yet, the pieces were there.

When I was in college, I was enrolled in a sociology degree program with a minor in psychology. So, I was feeling, like, if I could become a great sociologist or good sociologist I still could help people. I would still be working out of a faithful community. So when he [Austin] said, "Seminary," I said, "No," because I was thinking about going on to get a master's degree in sociology and finding a way that I could still go into our communities and help folks. I said no to it. It was frightening to me and I didn't know if I could be a minister of the gospel in spite of the fact that I had a grandmother who was an itinerant preacher. She still wasn't the role model that I wanted for myself at that point. I didn't see myself as being an itinerant preacher; so when he said seminary I said no. And I thought about that. I moved into my second year in college, and Purcell kept saying, "Yvonne, I hope you will just keep open, stay open to that."

Now, at this point in my life, I look at that as God's coming to me in a person who could help me to claim that call. That's how I understand it now. At any rate, Purcell was with me for three years that I was in college. He was just there, offering the idea. He kept the idea alive in my head even as I thought about going on to fulfill my degree in sociology. I was into my final year, my senior [year] in college, and that was the year that I had several opportunities. My professor of sociology had arranged for me to get a full scholarship to work on my masters in social work at the Atlanta University School of Social Work. I had been a student assistant to him; he had worked that out and here was the opportunity. I could leave college and go in with a degree, and with a scholarship that was already there to work on my masters in social work. I thought to myself, "Well, this is God's opening that door so I can just accept that and move on into that without wrestling with [it]."

Well, that final year Purcell came back to me again and said, "Yvonne, I'm saying one more time, I really want you to think about, just wrestle with, what you are going to do now." He said, "I know you've got the possibility to go ahead and complete your social work degree." But he said, "Think about this: how many young women do you think in this year will move on for a degree in social work? And how many young women do you think will offer themselves to prepare for ministry to the church?" And he said, "Think about what the church has meant to you and to all people, and think about what it will mean for you to move in terms of that degree in social work."

Well, I started wrestling. I wrestled, and for some reason, when he asked me to think about what the church had meant to us as a people, somehow [I started] to think about what that church had meant to us as a family, what it had meant to me to be able to be there and to be able to develop and grow and nurture myself; and the support that it was for mama and them. I thought about the civil rights struggle and our people, and the need to have strong institutions that were around them. They needed to have people who could commit themselves to that. And I started wrestling. For almost the final four months before graduation, I wrestled with that night and day, until finally I woke up one morning, and I went to mama and I said, "I've been wrestling and wrestling and wrestling." I said, "I know now that I've got to at least try. I've got to try. For some reason I can't put it down." Even though the scholarship was already there the door was already opened to take that degree in social work—I couldn't let it go, the image of my preparing for ministry in terms of seminary.

I remember I called Purcell and I said to him, "Purcell, I've been wrestling with this and wrestling with this, and I've decided that I am going to try." At that point, Andover Newton in Boston, Massachusetts (which is the seminary I attended, which was Purcell Austin's seminary—I mean, that's how I got connected to that) had already said that they had closed the registration on that incoming class, because they had been recruiting people for a year before that; and here I was almost a month now before graduation. I had wrestled with it four months. But now it is almost a month before I graduate, and here I've said to him, "I'm willing to look at it." Purcell got on the phone and called some folks over at Andover Newton. They sent papers back to me, and I filled out those papers and sent them back in. Even though they had closed off the registrations for the incoming class, they accepted that. They went into a faculty meeting. They debated and they talked about it, and then they decided that they would admit at least one additional student. So, within, I would say, three weeks after I had sent all that stuff in, I had the word back that there was a place for me in that incoming class at Andover Newton. When I looked at that, I also looked at that as another way in which another door was opening.

Ever since that time, I have felt myself to be on a journey continuing to respond to the call. So the call for me was not some [dramatic event]. I always thought it would be some very dramatic event that would be out of the natural with God's voice speaking, saying, "I want you to serve me." But then as I look at it, at all of those things that have happened to me, they were the way in which God came to me. God came to me through my mother and father who devoted and dedicated my life back to God and told me about that so that it kind of had a bonding authority. God came to me through my grandmother, who was a minister who moved around and helped me to have an understanding about how a woman could, in fact, respond to God's call. God's call came to me through that church, Macedonia Congregational Christian Church. But those folks there who were struggling, poor people who surrounded me with faith and power and spirit, they affirmed me in that whole liturgy of that church, Sunday after Sunday, as being God's person and invited me to give my life back to God.

I think God came to me for the civil rights struggle, which basically said that our people are still in bondage and people are still struggling. They are still wrestling, and we need to have persons who are willing to move into those arenas, where people are struggling against injustices, to offer a word of hope and to become a part of a catalyst of force that can help to change some of the conditions under which our people live. And then God came through a person who helped to put it together for me and helped me to claim that call, because I kept saying, "No, God, not me. One, I've got another door that's open. How will I do it? I'm female. How am I going to respond in the midst of a male-dominated world and all of the other pieces of it?" I mean, all of those things were in my head. No, no, no, no. I found all the reasons for no, but God's "Yes" was louder than my "No." God's "Yes" kept coming back to me and kept coming back to me.

Then, when I was able to respond to that yes, I moved myself to the seminary. The door just opened and it kept opening. So I knew, I know, without a shadow of a doubt that God was in that call, was in those moments. He was in those people, hoping to extend that call to me in the ministry.

Ronald English
Charleston, West Virginia

The Reverend Ronald English was born in Atlanta, Georgia, on February 20, 1944, called in 1967 and ordained a Baptist minister in 1968. He received a BA from Morehouse College and an MDiv from the Interdenominational Theological Center. He pastors the historic First Baptist Church in Charleston, West Virginia.

23

A Scary Question at Ordination

The call to the ministry has been something that I have had in terms of a burden and a blessing. I felt at least three calls. The first call was one that I felt at eighteen or nineteen when I was still a student. It was confused, because it was also during the time when I was very active in civil rights under the tutelage of Dr. King and being brought up in that church. I felt like there was something special that I was called to do, not knowing what it was. It was kind of confusing at first as to whether I was more admiring of Dr. King or feeling a real serious call into ministry. I naturally resisted that, as far as the call was concerned. I was thinking about Paul's situation, hearing voices and that kind of thing. I was working as a janitor at the church, and I used to make it my business to get through in the sanctuary real quick, because I thought that might be the place that God might call me to preach and I didn't want to hear that. I resisted even thinking about it, because the other thing was when you grow up in the church, the boys in the neighborhood are always saying, "I know you gonna be a preacher." The old ladies would say, "I'm praying for you to be a preacher." While you respect that, there is something that makes you resist that.

I think I came to the point to yielding in my third year at Morehouse, because I also had another influence. That was L. M. Tobin; he taught New Testament. In talking with him, he asked whether I had considered the ministry. I told him that I was struggling with that and his response was, "Yes, you do seem to be doing a lot of broken field running." He was asking, because at that time he was, recruiting fellows who would be eligible for the Rockefeller Foundation grant. His serious question, in the way that he put it, [got me thinking] whether it was not time to stop the broken field running. That was when I felt more like responding to what I felt was a serious call, my third year at Morehouse. It was a very highly active time for students, and my emulation and respect for Dr. King was still very much a part of this. I guess, also, the expectation of being a preacher had been there from four or five years old, when I would come home and imitate Daddy King's message on Sunday morning and being in the church. My mother, father, sister, grandmother, and great grandmother were in the congregation. From that time I had a sense of calling, but I had resisted it all the way up to my second year at Morehouse. I would describe that as the first call—the call to preach.

I did not feel a call to pastor until I was actually called to First Baptist Church, Charleston, West Virginia. Because at the time that I received the call, I was on the staff at [the Interdenominational Theological Center], where I had graduated, and I had primarily committed time to preaching as assistant at Ebenezer Baptist Church, Atlanta, thinking that I would want to make the academic community the basic residence, as far as how I would respond to the call to preach and call to ministry.

When the call came to First Baptist Church, I was excited about it, because it was the church of Mordechai Johnson, Vernon Johns. When I came, I was not anticipating coming to Charleston [as a pastor] by any means. In fact, the first time I got the call to come and preach, I was really thinking that I was coming to fill-in. I knew that the pastor was deceased, but I was not thinking about coming as a candidate. Then I was called back two other times when they asked if I would really consider coming. It was such a dramatic shift that my ex-wife was not one who anticipated that I would be in the pastorate. She was all right with me being in the academic community, but this call to Charleston was something that shocked her. Consequently, I really think that from that time it created a kind of situation where she could not adjust to being a pastor's wife as she had been preacher's wife.

So, then, the call to the pastorate was a little more traumatic. I had to deal with some images that I brought into the ministry—Daddy King being the primary one and Martin King, Jr.—in terms of the kind of style that I had been attracted to. Those images helped me and were blessings, but they were also burdens, because it meant that I was adopting their identity rather than struggling with my own. At the church, in their accepting me, I kind of worked with that for a while. But after a while, when the honeymoon is over and you get down to the reality of things, you discover it's not what you were, but it's what you are that makes people accept you. And the challenge of pastoring and abandoning some of the images that I had of Martin and Daddy King that I grew up with, and struggling with "Lord, what is it that I am supposed to do, what is it that I have been uniquely equipped to do?" was the struggle around that second call.

The third call I heard as a result of the divorce. It happened in 1983. But it came at a time in 1982 when things appeared to be working very well as far as the church was concerned, ministry was concerned and people kind of coming together. I guess that was a kind of settling-in time. But there remained a rift in my domestic situation. I guess I was really surprised at how wide it had gotten and my ex-wife's decision that divorce was her desire. It came at a kind of awkward time that I really had to argue with the Lord as to why so many things seemed to be working so well that I had finally settled in and felt that I was responding to what he wanted me to do. Then all of a sudden this happened. It was really nerve-shaking. I felt, at that particular moment, alone and abandoned by a sense of vocation that I had just recovered and by a calling that I just claimed.

And I think it was at that third place [I acquired] that sense of a calling in terms of personal integrity in spite of what kind of prejudices you might have, what kind of reputation you may be trying to get. I think that is where I came to a strong sense of personal integrity in responding to the call. In other words, I felt like the call had come, and it has taken three specific responses, three specific markers on my spiritual journey to respond to the call. It was not one that I did spontaneously; it was not something that I did knowing the moment, the time, the hearing of a voice or that kind of thing. It was a progressive urging that became clearer as a result of a variety of circumstances.

I recall another incident at the time of the ordination. There was an old preacher that I didn't expect to be there; he was from Memphis. On my council sat L. M. Tobin, Sam Williams, Dr. Benjamin Mays, Daddy King. At that time Martin had just died, though Martin's brother was there, A. D. King. So it was some heavyweights on that council, and they were asking me about my call. I began talking about how I had felt the call, but could not be precise in describing it. This old man from Memphis, Tennessee, looked me straight in the eye and said, "Son, do you know God?"

I had prepared myself to deal with the theology and the philosophy and those kind of issues that I felt this council were going to bring up, and this old man jumped up from nowhere and asked, Do I know God. That was scary, because I hadn't expected it and it was like a revelation that this is what it is all about; it doesn't have anything to do with philosophy and all that stuff you've got prepared.

I stumbled at that moment; I responded, "Yes," that I really felt convinced that he had called me to preach. But because it had felt so awkward, I found that at that moment when I got ready to leave, I broke down and cried because I felt like I had not convinced them as I wanted to convince them. And, also, that this old man had "peeped" my trump card.

I passed the council because they wanted to be encouraging and they wanted to be supporting. But that man's question has lingered in my head from that point on, and it always kind of brings me back to that personal thing of, "Do you know?" rather than who I have been inspired by, who I have modeled or who I have been attracted to in terms of an aspect of ministry." That old man's question is still one that challenges me right now.

Barbara Essek
New York, New York

The Reverend Barbara Essek was born in Demopolis, Alabama, on July 14, 1951, called in 1981 and ordained by the United Church of Christ in 1985. She received her BA and MA from Northwestern University, and her MDiv from Garrett Theological Seminary. She serves as the Secretary for Racial and Ethnic Educational Ministries in the United Church of Christ Church. Interview recorded December 6, 1989.

24
"Fear Not, I Have Chosen You..."

Okay, I probably need to go back: before I actually entered the seminary I had joined a large Black church in Chicago. Prior to that, I had not been in the church for about eight or nine months. When I joined the church, I was encouraged to become more involved in [it] and I started to go to Bible study classes and organizations in the church. The more I stayed at the church, the more my curiosity was aroused about theology and religion and so forth. I started to feel that there was something the Lord wanted me to do, but I wasn't going.

At that time, I was teaching high school in the public school system in Chicago and had thought about making a career change by taking courses at night in business. That was a lot of fun and it went very well. I had decided to pursue a master's degree in business administration at the University of North Carolina in Chapel Hill.

I quit my job, gave up my apartment, sold my car and moved to Chapel Hill. About two weeks into the program, I realized that I had made, what I considered at that time, to be a major mistake. I was not doing well in the program. I didn't feel good about being in that program and kind of knew intuitively that there was something more for me to do. So I made a point of continuing to go to church on Sunday, and I got together with friends of mine from Bible study and so forth.

Thanksgiving of 1980, I went to visit my cousin. They were having a pre-Thanksgiving worship service. I went and participated in that service. The minister got up to speak (he was what we call an "old-time preacher"—he was obviously not seminary trained and so forth). As he was preaching, I thought to myself, I could preach this sermon just as good as he could. As soon as I said that, the whole sanctuary filled up with a bright white light. I had an inkling that God was trying to tell me something, but I did not want to think that I was actually being called into the ministry. I didn't know any women in the ministry. I had no role models, no ministers in my family. I just felt that a call to the ministry was the furthest thing from my experience. So I kind of filed that away.

I continued with the program through the first and second semesters, and as time went on, it became increasingly clear to me that I was in the wrong program. I went into a very serious period of prayer. As a result of that prayer period, I decided to drop out of that program and return to Chicago. I returned to my home church. I wrote my pastor to put me to work, which he did. I worked with the youth fellowship and worked with the minister to start a young adult ministry. I felt so at peace doing the kind of work that I was doing—church, but I still did not believe that I was being called into the ministry.

At that point, I started to run out of money and I needed to look for a job. I had spent enough time in the MBA program to have a good fix on how to go about looking for positions. So I did my resume, got my basic black suit, and so forth. I continued to read my *Wall Street Journal* for annual reports of companies, and I started looking for a job. In the course of three months, I must have gone on maybe fifteen or twenty interviews, and in every interview I was either over-qualified, under-qualified, too tall, too short—there was always some reason why I was not hired. I began to think that maybe God was really saying something to me, and I needed to listen to what God was saying.

So, I went into a very, very serious period of prayer, because I was running out of money. I hadn't a job, I had no place to stay. I was living with my family and that was a difficult thing to do.

One evening in April, I had been praying very seriously to the point that I could hear. I knew at that point that I needed to feel clear about what I was experiencing. I prayed for a sign. As soon as I prayed that prayer, I saw in my mind's eye a scripture reference—Isaiah 41:10. I picked up my Bible and I turned to that scripture passage. The scripture said, *"Fear not, I have chosen you—this day have I chosen you. You will be my servant. I will be your God. I will hold you and take care of you . . ."* and so forth. I was so stunned at how appropriate that scripture was, I dropped my Bible and I was really in a state of shock. That experience was enough to convince me that I needed to talk to someone else about what was going on.

I made an appointment with my pastor. I went into to see him, and he looked at me and he said, "Why are your eyes so red?" I made some excuse about not being able to sleep and that kind of thing. He kept pressing me on what was going on. I said to him that I thought I'd been called into the ministry. I was expecting him to ask me a lot of questions about what made me think that and what had happened to lead me in that direction, and so forth. But his response was—the first thing he wanted to do was—to get me into seminary, "and then we'll put you in the in-care process for ordination," and so forth. I had to stop him, because I wanted him to tell me that I really had not been called. He was convinced that, indeed, I had been, and the only way that either of us could be sure was for me to initiate the process.

The next day, I called every seminary in the Chicago area and asked for a catalog and an application. During the [following] day I received the packet from Garrett Seminary, and I was very surprised that I would hear from them first, because Garrett is on the campus of Northwestern University, where I had done my undergraduate work about ten years prior to that. At that point, I had felt that I had done enough to answer this call and that I would then be free to go on and live the rest of my life. So I continued to look for a job and nothing was coming up. I did that until the very end of June. At that point, I called Garrett and set up an appointment with their admissions officer. I drove up to Evanston with my application in my hand, convinced that there was no way that I would be admitted to their program and if I had been admitted, I would not have been able to go because I had absolutely no money. By now I was down to fifty dollars. I get there at ten o'clock, I have an appointment with the woman. At 10:30 I am sitting in my car, and I am absolutely stunned, because within a thirty-minute time period, I had been admitted as a full-time student at Garrett and had been awarded a full tuition scholarship. I was really stunned and really felt that this door had been opened, and it would be foolish for me to deny it anymore.

So I went back to Chicago. Went back to my home church for Bible study class and wanted to share this information with my pastor. Usually after Bible study classes, he was surrounded by people who want to talk to him and he has all this stuff to do. This particular night, nobody stayed after class. He went into his office and he left the door open. I walked in and I looked at him and said to him, "You will not believe what happened." So I told him what happened, and he was very excited. I said to him, "I still can't go, because I don't even have enough money to commute from Chicago to Evanston." He then pulled out the Church's annual report and showed me an item that was entitled "Fund for Theological Education." There was enough money in that budget item for me to commute from Chicago to Evanston. He simply said, "When do you want the check?" At that point, I knew that my call was real; that God had opened the door and it was time for me to, more or less, put up or shut up. I decided I would pursue the seminary education.

When I returned home after talking with my pastor that evening, I received a call from Xerox Corporation. I had left my resume with the placement center at Northwestern, where I had done my undergraduate work. They wanted to know if I was interested in interviewing for a job. I said yes because I only had fifty dollars to my name, and I went in the next day for an interview. One of the things that I learned in the MBA program was that employers did not hire on the first interview. They always made you come back for at least one or two more interviews. I arrived at Xerox at 8:30 Thursday morning. I took a series of tests and did a round of interviews that afternoon with various people. Later, at about 4:15 in the afternoon I returned to the man who originally called me. He said to me, "Ms. Essek, we're not going to play around with you, we're prepared to offer you a position." We talked salary and were able to work that through, and I was to report to work on Monday morning. I left Xerox and went home and shared this information with my mother and father.

Friday morning, I called the admissions officer at Garrett and told her that I had been offered this incredible job with Xerox, and I was going to take the job and I would be starting Monday morning. She said to me, "I understand why you want to take the job, and I know that it sounds too good to be true, and it would be silly for you to turn it down; but do something for me." She asked me to pray about it over the weekend, and if the answer was to take the job, call her and she would accept that. On Saturday, Eve, a friend of mine called—a friend that I had not spoken with for at least a year and a half—and she said, "What's going on in your life?" I said, "Well, I thought about going to the seminary, but I got this offer with Xerox." She wanted to know how the seminary piece came up, knowing that I had been out of the church for a while. I had to tell the story of just feeling that I wasn't doing all that I should be doing and how exciting learning the Bible and about theology had been for me. I shared with her the sixth sense of the scripture reading. This friend of mine is not a particularly religious person, and she said to me, "You can always find another job. I think you ought to pursue the seminary thing especially since the doors have been opened." I just kind of fluffed it off—" Yeah, yeah, yeah, you don't understand. I don't have any money, and I really need to make some money and I can always go to the seminary." So we had that conversation. About four hours later another friend called that I had not talked with in about four years. We went to the same kind of catching up on each other's lives, and she, too, wanted to know how the seminary piece came up. I had to tell the story again, and as I told it, I felt a total affirmation that, yes, the seminary was the way to go. So, I decided that I would not take the job at Xerox and pursue the seminary education at Garrett.

Monday morning I got up. I went to Xerox. I went into the guy who was going to be my boss and I said to him, "I cannot take this job." He wanted to know if I needed more money, because they could give me more money. I told him that I would be going to the seminary because I was going into the ministry. He made some comments about how he had respected and admired my decision to do that, being that there were so few women—certainly so few black women—in the ministry. He agreed to hold the position open for me until the end of September, and that would have given me three weeks in the seminary. If the seminary experience was not working, [I could] call him, and I could go back to Xerox and take the job.

I started the seminary in September of '81. When I walked in the door that morning, there was a sense of peace and confidence that I had never felt before. I knew that that was where I belonged. I then went on to graduate and was ordained. And that's my story.

Cain Hope Felder
Washington, DC

The Reverend Dr. Cain Hope Felder was born in Aiken, South Carolina, on June 9, 1943, called as a young boy and ordained a United Methodist minister. He has a BA from Howard University, an MDiv from Union Theological Seminary and a PhD from Columbia University. He serves as Professor of New Testament at the Howard University School of Divinity. He is the author of *Troubling Biblical Waters* (Orbis Press, 1989) and editor of *Stony the Road We Trod: African American Biblical Interpretation* (Fortress Press, 1991), two books which have received wide acclaim. Interview recorded November 20, 1988.

25

The Troubler of Biblical Waters

My sense of call begins with my experience as a young boy in Boston where I was one of a very few members—if not the only member—of a fairly large inner-city Black family in Boston. I was just about the only one in my family to be exposed to the full range of services to be offered by the Morgan Memorial Church of All Nations, its settlement house and summer camps. This was the agency founded by Edgar Helms [that] emerged as Goodwill Industries of America. Also, Edgar Helms was important in establishing the Boston University School of Social Work. Because of the historical Methodist relationship, I'm United Methodist; there was a close relationship with the Church of All Nations and Boston University School of Social Work. In fact, it was routine for many BU School of Theology students to do their fieldwork or internship at one of the facilities at Morgan Memorial.

As a young fellow participating in the settlement house,

the church and so on, I came into contact with all of these seminarians. And I don't know why this was so, since I had several older brothers and a sister who did not participate as much in "Morgie" [Morgan Memorial] as I did. I seemed to be fortunate enough to be exposed to the different extension programs of this church. And what started to happen was that a number of Black, as well as White, seminarians and college students who were thinking about ministry or social work took an interest in me as a young fellow. And I think I stayed with the program [because of that]. I was very active in the Sunday school. I attended all of the summer camps where, again, I encountered these people. And the same thing with the settlement house. In each case I went very quickly from the status of being a recipient of these programs to becoming part of the staff. So, for example, I went from Sunday school pupil to Sunday school teacher, from camper to camp counselor, to camp leader to program director and, eventually, to assistant camp director of the whole camp when I was in college. Even though I was in college, we had staff members who were seminarians now working under me, because I was the fellow who made good in the community. I went from cub scout to cub scout master and boy scout to boy scout leader.

This became all the more significant because of a series of events. My mother was on Aid to Dependent Children. She had only completed the sixth grade in the South, but valued education, for some reason particularly for me. I developed, both with her as well as with the persons related to Morgan, a close relationship that went along nicely with my education. For example, until I was about eleven we were living in ghetto-type dwellings with rats, roaches, gang wars, people gambling on the street corners. With the redevelopment of Boston, many of the families were displaced as they tore up the old neighborhoods. My family moved out to an all-white neighborhood—and I went to the Champlain school. I was the only Black in my class. And to survive in that situation, my mother helped me to see a need to become sort of an over-achiever. That redounded to my benefit, because by the end of the year I was recommended to go to the Boston Latin School in the seventh grade. So I spent my time at the Boston Latin School. Again, I had moved from a recipient of services to an emerging leader.

I can't emphasize enough that in this whole set of events I had a number of persons that demonstrated, through deed and witness, the caring aspect of the gospel. These people showed that the gospel of Jesus could be embodied in specific acts of caring for persons such as myself. For, even as a small child, I had a child psychiatrist. Every Saturday, my mother would take me to him, Dr. Rose; I remember how he would pull on his ear lobe as he talked to me. Even then, I guess some thought I was a little disturbed fellow. I was very, very aggressive, a bully to some and so forth. So I had all of that operating, and I kind of suspect that some of the bully and aggressive attitude became rechanneled into what I perceive as a lot of natural points of leadership in multi-service agencies.

My mother tells me that at the age of ten I told her that when I grew up I wanted to be a police officer. I wanted to be a cop. Again, when I reflect upon it, I think it was because the predominant authority figure in the community was the police. And later, she said, this began to change, and I began talking more about being a teacher or social worker. In the midst of this, I was going around with my grandmother, as a child, to church services, and I experienced a series of spiritual events. I was baptized as a Baptist, a Pentecostal, a Methodist as I traveled with her to these different revivals. So I was constantly being baptized from one version of the faith to the next. And, I guess, I wound up settling for the denomination of these settlement houses, Morgan Memorial and these summer camps. I was very active with the Methodist youth fellowship in the Boston area. I ultimately rose to be the president of this group for the Boston area. It was at this point I began to talk more about social work and the ministry.

I also had two other families to take interest in me, one White and one Black. In fact I have dedicated my book to both of them, because they were like my pre-eminent figures in ministry. And as I look back, I developed a sense that I wanted to follow in the professional footsteps—not of a parent, because no one on either side of my family had even gone to college or been in the minisrty—of these two extensions of my family, seminal role models, White and Black, who demonstrated to me the Christian gospel not merely in terms of the pedagogy or the letter or doctrine, but who demonstrated basic acts of caring and becoming a person for others. Then, the notion was, "a man for others"—Jesus is a man for others and therefore his *agape* should become a living paradigm in our own lives. And I was captivated by that.

But when I went to college, I first declared a major in sociology, but I was not impressed with sociology. I didn't find it particularly challenging, and I didn't think it was very profound. So I discontinued sociology and became a philosophy major. After all, since I had attended Latin school, I wanted to play to my strength, so I wanted to carry a Latin and Greek minor. But in my mind this was quite [good] preparation for ministry —a Classics training for ministry, even though I didn't appear to be all that pious. I would go occasionally to a church service in the community. More regularly I would go to the university worship service. I became active with the Wesley Foundation on campus, the Student Christian Movement. Again, I did those things more out of a principle of continuity with my Methodist youth fellowship background at Morgan Memorial Church, [my] Boston experience, than any kind of conscious piety. I want to make that clear.

I was, however, a person that was keenly interested in alternate questions of value and meaning that were appropriated in both religious and philosophical texts. I was also interested in raising questions that were incidental to finding coherence vocationally in my own life.

When I graduated from college, that was a sort of crisis for a moment, because I was very much tempted to apply to law school. I was going to apply to Columbia University School of Law. For some reason, I wanted to go to New York. I did go to New York, but it was to Union Theological Seminary instead. It became a question of whether I wanted merely to make money or to make my self personally content vocationally. My final decision was based on a principle of continuity to what I thought really was my true interest and what would make me happy as a person. Then, for me it was no question, it was seminary, going into the ministry. At least, I was able to resolve what had become a real personal crisis.

At this point, I then had to make my decision quite public on campus. When I began doing so, many of my college friends, once they found out that I was going to seminary, were aghast because they had no idea that I was that serious about all of this. They thought it was quite a joke that I was going to seminary. Evidently, my high profile in fraternity life and campus politics obscured for them my involvement in campus ministry and chapel activities.

At Union Seminary in New York my first year was somewhat of a disappointment. I went to seminary with a strong background in the study of philosophy, Western classics, and religion. I had the expectation that my sense of vocation would be given more substance and clarity since I had made the basic decision that this was the context that I wanted to be in. But what I found was very little help in seminary in terms of assisting me to clarify my call to ministry. What I found instead was a Eurocentric academy, a thoroughly guild-oriented approach to the theological disciplines. In fact, I got a C in New Testament Introduction 101 because I just couldn't get ready for the way it was presented. That was the only C that I ever got on my whole transcript – and now I have a PhD in New Testament! I was just trying to cope with the way in which they were dissecting the difficulty of identifying anything that could be reliably attributed to the historical Jesus, or such questions posed by the Synoptic Problem.

Now I became exasperated, and had little patience or interest in dissecting the text and thereby seeming to murder it! Rather, I was concerned at the time with the broad questions of ministry. I would have been much more interested in questions of New Testament hermeneutics and applied theology.

I really found much of my formal study in the first year at Union Seminary more of an intellectual challenge than anything to do with my faith development, spiritual formation, or my sense of call. In fact, the one question that kept gnawing away at me was the reality of the wide chasm between Union Seminary and Columbia University, which really are in "Harlem Heights" despite the fact that the locale is now called Morningside Heights. There was also the wide chasm between both institutions and the larger Harlem section of New York City where I worked as a seminary intern. Here, in relatively the same community, there were two totally different worlds. I was studying religion at one and trying to make some sense of it in the absolute opposite of the realities in the drug culture and the poverty in greater Harlem. It was a very painful struggle for me during that first year—so much so, that I had again gone to a psychiatrist. But then it was fashionable, it was chic, and many of my fellow seminarians in the late 1960s would sit up in their dormintory rooms talking about their psychiatrist and that everybody was a little "off."

I made two major decisions at the end of my first year in seminary. One was to get married, and the other was to get out of the country. And the combined impact of getting married and going to England to study at Oxford for my middle year was very sobering in a variety of ways. That gave me a greater sense of vocational sobriety. I thought going to England would be another personal challenge, and it was in England that I was distracted quite a bit compared to my experience in New York, by the glaring discrepancies between my people and the great affluence of so many Whites and Jews. I was deeply troubled by the widespread signs of inner city pathology in particular and the growing tension between Whites and Blacks in general. All of these issues were constantly in the foreground of my mind in America. But then, when I went to England, I could suspend a lot of that and deal not so much with my own questions, but deal with the reality of the academic program presented to me.

Strangely enough, that was the year Dr. King was killed. During this period that yet another crisis hit me. I think this was the period of my real transformation: being in England and aching, my wife and I, aching over the reality that we were locked in over there while cities were burning over here. I think that at that point, a delegation from the ecumenical preachers association at Oxford came to our apartment on Banbury Road and asked us to lead a march in memory of Dr. King down the streets of Oxford. And that was a very mystical, euphoric experience for us, and was a major turning point for me, the death of Dr. King.

I realized that indeed I might have a major role as a black leader in religion. And, that my training could be a period of withdrawal for a significant return. I started thinking in these images. In fact, I took the diploma in theology at the end of that year, and we came back to Union. I immediately secured a job in the office of planning and strategy in the national board of missions as it was then called, within the United Methodist Church. That was a good orientation for me to study the policies and procedures of the denomination in terms of national mission, international mission, outreach and the like, and to study the founding documents of the emerging Black Caucus in the United Methodist Church.

As it happened, my student internship with the board of missions led directly to my ordination and my first full time job. I finished my MDiv work and was hired immediately as the first national director of the Black Caucus of the denomination. Having rallied to support the Black Manifesto, I moved to Atlanta and set up offices for Black Methodists for Church

Renewal. My call was never clearer as we worked untiringly to combat racism the church.

What began to happen to me was very much the result of reading Hermann Hesse and C.G. Jung. I ran across a little book called *A Study of Friends,* which was the study of the friendship between C.G. Jung and Hermann Hesse. In the process of talking about that friendship, the author reported that C.G. Jung defined vocation as "a high act of courage flung into the face of life." And I loved that, for it summarized what I took to be my call. That crystallized for me the element which would make a vocation most meaningful for me in ministry. I certainly did not want to become just another perfunctory, ecclesiastical functionary, a veritable priest to the status quo. On the contrary, I sought a ministry which would be troubling waters, raising questions, and being an an advocate of the underrepresented.

To me, "call" should be interpreted in the relation to the Greek word for church, "ekklesia," which literally means "called out of." In my view, this means a life of service on behalf of others as one is called out of mediocrity, called out of mere priestly functions and the oath of allegiance, the vow of obedience to the institutional church and its offices. It means, in truth, being called into the process of advocacy and ministry in the sense which requires courage and advocating matters of public policy. So, to me, my call was in this gradual unfolding of a sense of vocation as an act of summoning enough courage to represent the principles which I felt the gospel message does require. Therefore, whether I'm in the pastorate of a local church, in a professorship, or in some other form of ministry, I think that that has to be represented.

I must say, also, that my concrete models are persons who were much more than religious functionaries or those who merely made a business of religion. In fact, I have not always had that much respect for such persons. That is not the kind of ministry to which I have ever felt called. I have always felt called to answer one simple question: "How do we establish beachheads of caring and concern in a world that seems so unredeemed and so cruel to our people and other children of God?"

James A. Forbes
New York, New York

The Reverend Dr. James A. Forbes was born in Burgaw, North Carolina, on September 6, 1935, called in 1942-44 and ordained a Pentecostal minister in 1960. He received a BS from Howard University, a BD from Union Theological Seminary (New York) and a DMin from Colgate Rochester. He is the pastor of the historic Riverside Church in New York. In addition, he has served as a professor of Homiletics at Union Theological Seminary. He is the author of *The Holy Spirit and Preaching* (Abingdon, 1989). Interview recorded October 9, 1989.

26

When God Spoke through Tchaikovsky's Symphony # 4 in F Minor

My call to the ministry is a very unusual one, I think, in that I grew up in a family of preachers—father a preacher, grandmother a preacher, grandfather a preacher, a couple of aunts and uncles who were preachers. During my early years because of my enjoyment of the life of the church, everybody always assumed that I would be a preacher, like my father. As a high school lad, I began to assert my own determination to follow my own path and clearly not to be programmed by expectations. So I decided I wanted to be a doctor.

Early on in life, sometime between ages seven and nine, I found myself on my grandfather's farm out in the fields doing some kind of work, and heard in my own spirit the sense that one day I would be a representative of Christ in some way. So, that was a profound sense of having been selected for some kind of vocation, bearing witness to the Gospel. But, anyway, I went on and left that behind in my effort to become, maybe, my own man and decided I was going to medical school. First, therefore, I had to go to pre-med. So I entered a pre-med course at Howard University. While there at Howard, I was moving right along. I had majored in chemistry and hoped that finally I would get my degree of Bachelor of Science in chemistry.

From there, while at Howard, near the end of my junior year, it was the time when I began to think more clearly of what it was that I really wanted to do with my life. What was I called upon to do? And it seemed that during that period an unusual thing happened. First of all, I got a job over at the Frances Scott Key Hotel. While I was there, a man—I was serving as a bellhop and a man who was at the hotel at that time, I would take him to the seventh floor everyday—would get off the elevator on the seventh floor, turn around and say, "Young man, the Lord has a purpose for your life." He did this a number of days.

At about the same time, one of my friends from North Carolina came up to do a revival in Washington. I remember over at 1015 D Street, Reverend Equilla Lawson was his name. He preached on Isaiah. And he said in his sermon—you know, how Isaiah came to the place where he was somehow overwhelmed by the death of King Uzziah and had this vision in the temple and at a certain point the word was, "Whom shall I send and who shall go forth?" He had already said, Woe is me for I am undone." This expression he used to explain that there are some people who had made significant progress in life but they were still undone; that the Lord wasn't through with them and had other work for them to do. And it felt like those words had connected with my spirit.

Then I went home that night and tried to get myself freed up from the growing sense of urgency to be about some form of Christian vocations, and I put on the music of Tchaikovsky, the Symphony Number Four in F Minor, hoping that that would ease my mind. As I did that, it felt like—maybe some people don't know the music—it felt like the music conspired with God to help call me. For the music sounded like it was saying, "Jim Forbes, don't you know I've called you? Jim Forbes, don't you know I've called you? Yes, oh, yes, I have called you." It was very interesting how the music that I was using to escape from the call became the actual instrumentality by which I finally said yes, I would go on and accept the call to ministry.

Shortly after that experience, I went to inform my bishop that I had been called to the ministry. I told my parents and went on to finish my degree in chemistry but then shifted toward science for one year and then went to Union Theological Seminary in New York. Ever since that moment I have been involved in some phase of Christian ministry. I have felt throughout my ministry that it was destined that I would indeed be a person whose primary energies in life would be dedicated to Christian ministry.

Johnny Ford
Tuskegee, Alabama

The Reverend Johnny Ford was born in Tuskegee, Alabama, on August 23, 1942, called in 1975 and ordained in 1987. He has a BA from Knoxville College and an MPA from Auburn University. He is associate pastor of Mt. Olive Baptist Church in Tuskegee. In addition, he is the Mayor of Tuskegee. Interview recorded June 25, 1989.

27
The Preacher Who Is Also Mayor

I think, really, my call to the ministry occurred probably some fourteen years ago. At that time I was considering going into politics and, somehow, I just felt that it was not the time and did not respond to the call. But down through the years I've always had this deep yearning to be a spokesman for God. God has always been a source of strength for me.

Then in 1985, I had a chance to be a part of a group of twenty-five laypersons who visited Jordan and Israel, sponsored by several seminaries in the South. I had an opportunity to visit Jordan and Israel, places like Jerusalem and Bethlehem, and to walk in that land upon the hallowed and sacred grounds. I think one night, as we gathered there at a kibbutz on the Sea of Galilee (we were having a spiritual vesper and religious service) something struck me. I just got up and wandered away from the rest of the crowd. I just went down by the Sea of Galilee and, in a sense, I said to God—because all these years I had been fighting it and putting it off—I just finally said to the Lord, "If you want me to serve you, then that's what I want to do." I felt so relieved.

I returned back to the United States after that. We came back, and I remember in the report what they asked us to do following the trip I remember writing in my report that I [planned] to go into the ministry and accept my call. Max Miller—Dr. Max Miller, who is professor at Emory Univerisity—was probably the first one to know, because that was the first time I put it in writing. I remember, January 1, 1986, my father and I were riding down the road—Selma Highway as a matter of fact, old Highway 80—I was going to the Emancipation Program at a church there. Then I told my father about it—the call. And tears came down his eyes, and he was talking about how the Lord had been working on him, too.

So, about a week or so later I enrolled at Selma University School of Theology. I had begun my study of theology there. On April of that year, 1986, I was given an opportunity to speak before our church at Mount Ararat Missionary Baptist Church and gave my testimony there and indicated to the church about my calling. And the church and the acting pastor, the Reverend William Leonard, at that time, authorized us and issued a license for me to preach. A trial sermon was given about a month later. I began to actively work as an associate pastor there in Mount Ararat.

Then, finally, over the last couple of years I had been attending Selma University School of Theology. In November, 1987, I was finally ordained at Mount Ararat Missionary Baptist Church. Since that time I have been serving in my church, serving the Lord, serving God as a minister. But I will never forget that experience.

Ronald Fowler
Akron, Ohio

The Reverend Ronald Fowler was born in Cleveland, Ohio, on December 17, 1935, called in 1962 and ordained by the Church of God (Anderson) in 1964. He received a BS from Kent State University and an MDiv from Anderson University School of Theology. He pastors the Arlington Street Church of God in Akron. In addition, he serves as the chairman of the board of trustees of Anderson University. Interview recorded July 13, 1989.

28
God Called through a Little Boy without Shoes

My call to the ministry dates back to the year 1961. As a member of the Metropolitan Church of God in Detroit, Michigan, where my esteemed brother and mentor, Dr. James Massey, was a senior pastor there. I was very active in the life of that congregation, serving in the choir, serving in the youth department and really kind of applying my hands to whatever the church needed. I was a teacher in the Detroit public school system. I had developed a ministry to many of my students by bringing them from the east side of Detroit over to the west side to attend services.

Where I was teaching was in the heart of Detroit's poverty area in the grass-shed area. Those people who live in Detroit will know that. But it is interesting that the call began through, as I see it now, an incident in school. One of my students—his name was Mark, a young boy who was in the fifth grade that I was teaching—Mark, I noticed one day, had missed school every other day for two consecutive weeks. It didn't dawn on me until one day he came up to the desk—he brought me an apple that he literally was spit-shining, as I saw him from the window walking to school at the intersection. He would spit on the apple and shine it. Then he walked to school and gave me the apple. There was a close bond between Mark and me; but, nevertheless, when I noticed the attendance pattern, I asked him to come up to the desk to explain why he was absent every other day. He told me that he didn't have any shoes. It was in the winter time, and I said, "Mark, you have on shoes." He said, "Yes, I know, but I have to share these shoes with my brother." I didn't believe the story. So I thought to intimidate him, and to get the truth out I asked him a question. "Can I go home with you this evening and talk to your parents?" He said, "Fine." So I did.

I took him home. He lived in a flat upstairs, very dingy and very poor. Both parents were invalids. In talking to his mom, she apologized for the way the place looked and all of that, and then she said, "No, it's true. I'm sorry, Mr. Fowler, I can't afford to buy both of my boys shoes, because our allocation was not that much, and we have to pay the rent and buy some food. So I just couldn't do it, so I have to send him every other day." Well, I told her that I would find a way to address that need.

I went back to the school and talked to the principal, and he gave me umpteen forms to fill out; that would take probably up to three weeks to a month. And I went back to my room and I said, "Now wait a minute." I went to church, and it looked like everything I was hearing was in terms of, "Who cares?" The poor are being oppressed, mistreated, exploited; but it seemed like the bottom line was always, "But who cares?" And then passed the preacher's sermon from Isaiah dealing with his call, in which he raised the question, not so much a question but Isaiah's affirmation at the end, "Who will go for me?" and Isaiah responds, "Here, my Lord." And, Bill, I can't explain it, because I'd always tried to avoid any idea or thought about ministry. My daddy was pastor of this congregation for twenty-three years.

Well, his church was down on Roberts Street, and I succeeded him. But I always said there's no way I'd be a preacher: I didn't like the stress, I didn't like the pay, I didn't like the pressures. But he was a shepherd's shepherd, and I always said I wanted to be a part of the church. I had a romance with the church and even ministers, because there's nobody who stood taller in my eye than a preacher of the gospel because of my dad and others. So I wanted to be the preacher's right hand. I wouldn't mind driving him to the airport, driving him out of town; I wouldn't mind doing anything, but, Lord, I didn't want to be a minister. In fact, my wife asked me when I proposed to her, "Are you going to be a minister?" I told her, "Absolutely not." She responded back by saying, "Good, because I always said I'd never marry one." So that's the way we started.

I took a whole year, and I wouldn't tell anybody. I wouldn't tell my dad, because I knew he'd be so happy, that magnetism would be a pull on me and I didn't want that. I didn't even tell my pastor in Detroit; I didn't tell Dr. Massey either. I just walked with it for a year but I couldn't shake it. I'd go home after work, I'd do Bible study—I just lived in the book. In fact, my wife and I laughed today, because one day she came to me and said, "You keep studying like that, you're going to be a preacher." I laughed and said, "Well, you know what we said." She said, "That's right. You better not forget it!" So I knew then. I said, "Lord, if this thing is to be, you got a double problem. One, my own insecurities, and two, my wife's lack of affection for the ministry and being a preacher's wife."

I spent a year of privately thinking and praying, going to the altar and asking God for clarity, because I wasn't hearing bells ring and I wasn't going through what I heard from a lot of preachers that it was so definite with them. It was just a feeling, a sense that destiny was calling me to do something for which I felt so terribly inadequate. I wanted to work with young people—that was my deepest—and I enjoyed teaching, I enjoyed it to the highest. I should say that even my parents, they always said my oldest brother's going to be the preacher, anyway. And I always thought, "Yeah, Lord: That guy's got the gift of gab and everything else."

But what helped me to cross that impasse for some reason I could not shake Mark in my mind. I'd go to sleep and I'd start thinking about his future. Who's going to be there for Mark? Where is Mark's church in all of this? I got angry with the church, I got super-critical of the church. How in the world could a church allow a family to exist in that kind of poverty and not in some way try to better the lives of the people? And I sat down and wrote an article, and it was called "Vital Christianity"— because our national publication changed its name from *Gospel Trumpet* to *Vital Christianity*—and essentially it was a call to the church to unite the love of God and the love of people. To unite the love of God by the development of the mind with the love of God through the development of the heart. I was trying to bring together the social realities to which the gospel needs to speak as Jesus spoke so eloquently. Also with the spiritual dimension, inasmuch as our church has a holiness dimension, where we naturally have been cultivated in the whole life of piety, being faithful to God and the integrity of being. But, at the same time, I was seeing a dichotomy between our pronouncements and our practice, because we did not seem to have those social channels to which we could address the physical needs of people.

I thought I was being rather prophetic in our church and in writing this article, "Vital Christianity," and I gave it to Dr. Massey to read. He read it and in his typical fashion, he said, "Now, to whom are you writing this article?" I said, "Dr. Massey, for the church." He said, "It's written more for the academic community. I'd suggest that you'd like to rewrite it." I did, I went back and rewrote it and I brought it back to him, and he praised me for it again and made a few suggestions for clarity. I went back and rewrote it and sent it off to our national headquarters, who didn't know me from beans, and they published it. They published the article.

That did a lot for my own personal self-esteem, because I've always been a person who would rather be the cheerleader. Let me cheer the guy that's carrying the ball. Maybe it's also because of my high school experience. I played guard when I was in high school and made first string all-state here in Ohio, which back in the '50s was no small task, because guys came mighty big. But I enjoyed clearing the way and, I guess, I saw myself as a John the Baptist—just let me be that point man who kind of opened the way for somebody else to bring the ball on through, bring the gospel on through.

Finally, one day I was at our cabin, and my dad and I had been in the service; and we heard one of the young, aspiring ministers preach. He just blessed our hearts. I remember walking to our cabin, and there was a little, slight incline; and I said, "Dad, boy, that was a great service. I don't think I could ever preach like that. He's just so gifted." Dad was terribly wise, terribly wise. And we're walking up the hill and finally he said, "Son, he was awfully gifted, but so are you." And then he told me something I'll never forget. He said, "Remember now, there's a difference in those who are dash men and those who are marathon runners. In ministry we kind of need both, but you had better have some marathon grace in you if you're gonna pastor. You gotta go the long haul. It's not those who are the most eloquent that always succeed—many do, but not always. It's those who are the most faithful in serving others." I said,

"Dad, that's what I want to do is serve." And he said, "Well, just aim to be a marathon runner, and the Lord will make the way."

I asked him to pray for me, and I was rejoicing on the way back home. Then I told my wife, who was still in Detroit. I said, "Honey, I got something I want to talk about." She said, "I know it." And I said, "What do you think?" She said, "You're thinking about the ministry." I said, "That's right, but you know, I'm still not absolutely sure. But here's what I'm thinking, if it is true, then I need to go to seminary. It's not for everybody, but I definitely think it's for me, because I need the maturing and I need the discipline that goes with that I need to wrestle with some questions, and I think that's the best context for me to do that. If the the ministry is where God wants me, then he'll have to open up the doors. If he opens them by faith, can we walk through them?" And when she said, "Yes," I knew then that God had given me the first big impetus toward the ministry. I said, "You understand what that means?" because we had saved some money to buy our first house. I said, "We'll have to take that money." And she said, "That's okay, the Lord will give us more." I knew then that was a miracle, because I knew how bad my wife wanted to get a house, and I knew how desperately she did not want to be a minister's wife.

I resigned after the next year, and we moved to Anderson, Indiana, got an apartment across from the seminary, and I went to school full time. Those were vintage years. My New Testament professor, that was his first year there, was a great Greek scholar. He taught as one who didn't mind allowing the child in him to come out and celebrate the truths, and he'd get excited and happy and he excited us with his love of the Lord and love of scripture.

We went through some real tests, because my wife became very ill and I had to get a full-time job. I was trying to go to school full time, and she was working as a nurse, so then I had to get a full-time job. It was at a time when the factory was laying people off, so I got a part-time job down at the YMCA working as a masseur in the evenings and going to school full-time in the day. A man came in who was the president of Delco, and he looked at me and said, "Something's wrong, Ron, what's wrong?" I said, "Yeah, I've got to get a full-time job, and my wife is ill, and we have one child. I just don't know what I'm going to do because God sent me here to go to school, if I have to sacrifice anything. One of the reasons I've sacrificed trying to teach was because the

God Called through a Little Boy without Shoes

classes would be in the daytime and all my classes at the seminary were daytime, and we don't have any evening classes, so I've got to do something that will free me up to be in school." He said, "Well, you know we're not hiring, we're laying off right now." I said, "Yes, I know that." He said, "Well, I'll keep my eyes and ears open for you, though, down the road." I said, "I appreciate that."

The very next day I got a call from the employment office at Delco, and they said they understood I was looking for a job and would I mind taking a custodial job? I said, "Sir, I'll do anything if I can stay in school." He said, "Fine, we've got one shift that's 5:30 in the afternoon and you'll work till 1:00 in the morning." I said, "I'll take it," and I took it. They gave me hospitalization, gave me everything. Now, here people are on strike and I'm working, and I said, "That's an Ebenezer. That's another confirmation." And then the clincher—before, in fact. (I got out of sequence!)

Before I got the job at Delco, one of the businessmen who owned a gasoline station came in for a massage and we were talking. He always called me "preacher man," and he didn't go to church. He didn't go to church but he loved the young preachers that he came in contact with, that were connected with that school out there. Nevertheless, he went to church one Sunday and literally slept through the sermon. He said something woke him up, and he thought about the preacher was up there preaching, and he didn't know what he was preaching about. He only went because his wife kept nagging him. Something woke him up, and the thought hit him, "Clean out your freezer and give some of that food to that young preacher." And he said, "When I get home I'm going to clean out that freezer and I'm going to take some of that food over." Now he didn't know that my wife and I went to church that very Sunday. We didn't have one bit of food in the house. We never told one person, at church. I sang in the choir, she sang in the choir. We went; we had our daughter; we had a marvelous service.

The pastor at that church, who is now in charge of our Church of God internationally, was Dr. Ed Falks, and we just had a marvelous time. We went home. My wife said, "What are we going to do?" I said, "Honey, I don't know." I didn't want to call home, and I just said, "Why don't we just trust in the Lord? We've been trusting so far and he's met us at every road." She hadn't quite stopped work yet, but we paid my tuition with her money and that was it; we were broke. She set the table and found a teabag, and I said, "Well, honey, at least we've got some tea. Let's drink some." She came back to the table, and I knew, her confidence had fallen. I said, "God, what have I put my family in?"

We were getting ready to have prayer, and a knock came at that door. I got up and went, and it was Mr. Franken. He was standing there with this box; I've never seen a box like that—full of food. He said, "Preacher, can you use this? I was in church, and something woke me up and said, 'Clean out that freezer,' because I ordered this whole new beef to come, and I had no place to put it, and we just wondered if you could use all this?" Trembling, I took it and I said, "Thanks, sir. Thank you. Yes, we could use it, and I deeply appreciate it," and closed the door. My wife and I just couldn't get over it. It was an "Ebenezer," though. It was another confirmation that God is with us.

My call just evolved that way, to being crystallized in my own mind that God put that idea in my heart a few years back and asks the question of me, "Who cares?" I attempt to answer that and then follow his lead every step of the way. It was a venture of faith; and God just keeps on opening doors. I became convinced by the time I graduated and said, "Yeah, this is definitely where God wants me to be, and I will spend the rest of my life exploring in ministry as God has gifted me." Since then, I can look back now and see the hand of God was on me before I knew it.

As a child of eight years old—I think it was eight or seven—I was told by my parents. We lived up in Bedford, and at that time Bedford was country. There was a creek up there called Tinker's Creek, and we swam in Tinker's Creek. There was a place we swam there. One part of it was awfully deep, and water moccasins were in there and everything; but, hey, that was our swimming hole. And one of our neighbors, a friend of my parents, Mr. Wallace, invited me to go swimming with some of the other kids, and so my parents let me go. I normally stayed in the shallow end because I couldn't swim. Mr. Wallace wanted to take me across the creek on his back, and so I got on his back. He started across the creek, my feet were dragging the bottom; and I was just having fun, laughing. But when we got out there in the middle of that creek and I couldn't feel bottom, I panicked. I had my hand around his throat, and I just started choking him and he couldn't breathe. In order to breathe, he had to throw me off his back in the water. Naturally, I just sank, because I was a stocky guy, I just sank and came up. Everybody was screaming. My sister was on the bank and my brother, and they were screaming, "Somebody get him!" I went down and came up. I went down—in fact, I can see it to this day—three times. All of a sudden, when I went down I felt somebody's hand behind me, pushed me to the surface, and I shot up like a rocket and then this party grabbed me and pulled me to the shore where they had to pump me—I was full of water—and they pumped me out. I always wondered why did God do that? Why did he—and it was a young white girl that saved me and I always wondered—Why did God do that?

It was during the '60s—I'm in ministry now—and the tension between the Black community and the White community in this area is tense. I'm back here now, I'm serving as an associate under my father. This whole strip here is burning. This was our Hough in Akron, Ohio—Arlington Street. In fact, it used to be loaded with businesses on both sides. It was a thriving area. All those buildings, windows broken, buildings burning, and I was trying to come up and work with community leaders to try to bring some order. Suddenly it dawned on me, as my brothers were talking about the mistreatment, being Black and all that, yet I went back—the Lord led me through a flashback—and I remembered, Who was part of your rescue? It was a young White girl. She came to my rescue, and I always said, I owe her something, to be bigger than most, to rise above the tensions which often divide people, racism being one of them. I said, "Yes, God, I can see now why you were at work in my past. Before I even knew it, you had your hand on me, gave me an experience that would become a stellar moment for me, a reminder that I exist not just for Black people—I exist for people."

And I don't know, that has become very meaningful to me in becoming the bridge person that I've become in this community between Black and White, and now between Jews and Black communities, and trying to bring about at least better understandings and appreciation of our cultural and racial diversities. But I think God's hand was there all the time, bringing me to that point of realization that he wanted to use me precisely for what I'm doing right now.

Cheryl Townsend Gilkes
Waterville, Maine

The Reverend Dr. Cheryl Townsend Gilkes was born in Boston, Massachusetts, on November 2, 1947, called in 1981 and ordained a Baptist minister in 1986. She received her BA, MA, and PhD from Northeast University and a MDiv from Boston University. She is a professor of Black Studies and sociology at Colby College (Waterville) In addition, she serves as an associate minister at Union Baptist Church in Cambridge, Massachusetts. Interview recorded April 13, 1989.

29

"I Think I'm Going Crazy"

I must have gone and talked to my pastor in August of '81 about my call. I went to talk to him about the call that I got, then I answered, in May of '81. I didn't want to talk to my pastor. It took a little bit for me to go talk to him.

August. I didn't go talk to him right away. I had been struggling hard. I wasn't sure and it was—yeah, it's really hard to talk about it. I don't know why this is so hard. Well, I went to see him in August but I still wasn't ready. It wasn't until January '82 that I finally really said yes. It's a journey, it's not something where there's a voice and you just go. It doesn't work that way. Although, yeah, there was a voice, and yes, I heard my name called. And yes, I had to figure out what that meant. In fact, the first call that I got, I wasn't even in the church. I had left the church. I left the church when I was a freshman in college. I had grown up in church, and I was literally growing up in the church. I was baptized when I was eight years old, and I was very involved. I taught daily vacation Bible school. After I turned twelve, I was sort of allowed to do whatever I wanted to do. I went to prayer meeting. Since I took piano lessons as a kid, I used to play for prayer meetings on Thursday nights when I was in grammar school. Eighth grade, that's what I was doing on Thursday nights. And I was the only one who was on time. Well, seventh grade, I'm sorry, because I was twelve. I was the only one who was on time for prayer meeting. Finally, they got to the point where they didn't want me sitting out on the cold steps of the church waiting for them to get there. I was given a key to the church when I was twelve. I could get in and play the piano; I was the pianist for the prayer meeting. I think if I would have been a guy—with the kind of time I was keeping with the church, all the things that I was doing, all the various activities I was in—if I had been a guy, I think people would have said so and so is going to be a preacher.

My grandfather was a preacher. Oh, I didn't think about being a preacher. It had never occurred to me. I didn't even think about becoming a missionary, I never had that thought. My father was a deacon. My parents moved when I was at the end of my freshman year in high school. I found out from the man who was chairman of the deacon board up until right before I got ordained—I found out from him, that it was between him and my father,—that had my father not moved, my father would have been chairman of the deacon board instead of him. Because they all felt that my father should have been chairman. So, my father was very much involved there.

When I moved, I was just adamant that they had to keep commuting to Union Baptist Church. When I was in high school, as soon as school was over on Friday I got on the bus. I was still taking music lessons in Boston, and we rode an hour south of Boston. I would get on the bus with my little suitcase and go to my friend's house. We had another church [where] we went to prayer meeting sometimes on Friday nights, New Hope Baptist Church. My church was sort of "subdued." There were a couple of ladies that shouted twice a year, and that was about it, except on afternoon programs and when there was a gospel concert. So we used to go to prayer meeting on Friday night at New Hope Baptist Church. I'll never forget it, I remember more than one time when something happened. We then would come home and tell my mother. She would tell us, "That's the Holy Spirit and he will guide you." I grew up praying every night. I grew up immersed in the church.

I went to college, and the pastor of the church (the man who would be pastor) left. And there was a whole lot of accusations that were lies. I knew because these people they were accusing were my friends. I remember, I'll never forget the last

Sunday I went to church. I had my yellow, Sunday-go-to-meeting dress, my little black patent leather shoes and black patent leather bag. I had this peach print silk hat that was satin with a yellow print. I remember storming down the street and leaving the church. I was so mad about the situation. I just remember being angry. I was storming down the street saying, "The church is just another social institution just like any other social institution. The people are human." I was so angry at these people that I'd grown up with and loved all my life, could be so mean to this man—this man that I loved. I stopped going to church. A couple of times I visited an Episcopal church and visited a lot of other churches. But I eventually just stopped going to church. I stopped praying, and I stopped doing all the other stuff. That was in 1965-66. I didn't rejoin the church until 1978. That's how long I was gone. I started visiting again. I just sort of kept everything in effect. So that gives you the time that I was out of the church.

In the meantime, I finished school and started my graduate work in sociology. I found myself in a really strange situation, having grown up in the church, knowing how central the church is, being a sociologist, being with a lot of people who are religiously open to the people, and not comfortable with just dismissing the Black church the way folks were doing.

Several events happened during this time. It's hard to sort out exactly which happened first. I think one of the things that happened was my grandfather died. I think he died in February of '76. I'm not sure—it may have been '75. That funeral helped me to realize that what was very deep inside of me was still there. Grandad had been a general elder in the Pentecostal denomination called the House of God, which is the Church of the Living God.

Then, I was doing some stuff in sociology of mental health. One of the principal writers in that area is a man named R.D. Laing. So we went to hear R.D. Laing lecture one night. He was doing a series of lectures. Since one of my group was a friend of his, I got to meet the man afterwards. They had a discussion afterwards and these folk were getting up and talking about all these radical therapies. So, I'm listening to them talk about these radical therapies. I don't know if you've ever heard of the primal scream therapy. Well, this therapy, you pay good money, lots of money, to go to a man and learn how to do this thing called primal scream. They were talking about meditation therapy also.

I said, "This is interesting," and I listened to it.

I got a telephone call from someone who was trying to put together a special session, designed to study religion, at their 1976 meeting, which was going to be a bicentennial meeting. They wanted to have a meeting on the Black church. So I said that I was going to phone them. You know how you immediately respond to something, not from your head but from deep down in here? And I said, "Yeah, I'm giving the paper a title right now." "What is it?" "The Black Church is a Therapeutic Community." Boom! And that's how my paper got written. It was really weird. I wrote the paper, and somehow I'd gathered all this stuff. I taught this course called "The Sociology of Mental Health"—I think that's what it was called. So it gave me a chance to start putting all this stuff together, and I remember writing this paper, and all this stuff that had to do with my life. It just poured out. It was just me and the typewriter for two solid days. I wrote the basic draft of it in one sitting. It's in the *Journal of the Interdenominational Theological Center*, this paper. I mean, it took a couple of revisions, but the base, what was basically the paper, the outline and the headings [was there]. It just poured out. I remember I was in the house all by myself.

Right after I'd done the paper, the song, "Father, Open Our Eyes" came to me, and it was just me and the Lord all over the house. I hadn't shouted like that in years. Here I was trying to be a good agnostic, and it was just blowing all my attempts to be an agnostic. After all this, I was sitting in the house; I heard someone call my name. I looked around and I said, "Oh boy, I've been working too hard. I'm having an auditory hallucination." So I signed up to go see a psychologist. I went to therapy. Finally, one day, the guy asked me, he said, "Why do you come to see me?" I said, "What do you mean?" He said, "You're perfectly sane. There's nothing wrong with you." I said, "Well, okay, good." So that was the end of that. Plus, he was starting to have problems. He went crazy. Somehow we had gotten into some discussions of religion. I know now it was the Spirit. Remember, I didn't know at this point that what I was dealing with was God struggling to get me back on track.

I got to the point where I finally got back into the church. I would get up and do my testimony; I would tell people, I would say, "Look, I tried to walk away from God, but God refused to walk away from me." That's how I talked to people. In fact I'd just get up and say it in two lines and that's it. What happened was, the psychologist said, some stuff about prayer, but I said, "No, it's not." A part of me said that you cannot equate therapy and true prayer, because you're talking about communication with the divine. We're not just talking about getting one's head straight. Although prayer will get your head straight. But getting your head straight isn't necessarily prayer. I knew that. Here I am, I have no doctrinal commitments at this point. I am not in church, right? We are not dealing with that. We're dealing with this guy who's starting to lose it himself. My Blue Cross/Blue Shield ran out anyways, so we were not going back.

So then we did something else. I was also involved in a whole lot of political stuff. We started getting the pastor of the church I used to belong to involved. I had gone somewhere and he had participated or done something. So I suggested that they call him. We were looking for some clergy to support us. We were working on JoAnn Middle's case or some other case. I was a member of the National Alliance Against Racist and Political Repression, Angela [Davis's] group. I had been doing some stuff with Margaret Bruner and her lawyer, and so we were involved with that. We had organized this press conference, because we were bringing Jerry Paul to Boston to talk about this whole issue of legal oppression. We asked him to participate in the press conference, because we needed him. You know how political folks like get the clergy and how they exploit and use them. So I decided, gee, if we're going to pull him in like this, shouldn't we go visit his church? I mean, what's fair is fair. He helped support us; shouldn't we support him?

So I decided that to at least visit. And it must have been just before Easter; I think I even had an Easter dress. When I did political work, all I had were jeans and tee shirts. I was teaching sociology at college. I wore my corduroys and tee shirts and sweaters all the time. I lived in pants. I had this one cotton dress. And Easter Sunday, I said, Well, it's my Indonesian, cotton, boutique dress. Little Miss Hippy in Ebony came to church, and I ran into my "cousin." She had left the church too. She and I couldn't even get a seat inside the sanctuary. That's how crowded the church was. We came back to our own church, couldn't get a seat, right? We're sitting out there on the back bench in the hall. It was like, "You did wrong too? You left?" She left at the same time I did. You have to understand, she is co-pastor with her husband now at Ebenezer AME, in Fort Washington, Maryland. The fastest growing AME church in the country. And he left the church too. We all went through this. She and I always joke about that. We came back to church on the back bench, in the vestibule, on Easter Sunday morning. Talking about, "Yeah, I left because of the way they treated the [pastor]." "Yeah, I left too." "Okay girl, how have you been?" We did it in different ways, but we came back.

I started coming back, sporadically; it wasn't anything steady. I just started showing up every so often, and I'd listen to the sermon that this man was preaching [on] intellectual needs, etc. "Well, do you believe this?" It was a real intellectual battle. Every doctrinal point would come out in the sermon. I'm just sitting there, "Do you believe this? Well, yeah, okay, I guess I believe this." It was that very distant kind of thing. I got to the point, I would make a note of the biblical text of the sermon. I would go home; and some Sundays, sit down, open my Bible and read the text, and read around it. Sometimes I would get to reading, and I couldn't stop. Then it was just growing.

Now, this is going to sound crazy: re-joining the church came about because the church was celebrating its centennial. The father-in-law of my cousin and I had been seeing each other at sociology meetings all these years. So I wasn't totally cut off from my community. He was doing the canvas that was getting every member to contribute a hundred dollars to the centennial fund. He came up to me. I hadn't been coming to church. He said, "You know what?" I said, "What?" He said, "Your name's been taken off the membership rolls." He said, "How could you let this happen? I said, "Oh, really? Oh, okay." Which meant he was upset because I had my hundred dollars. He couldn't take it because I wasn't a member.

I had also just buried my great aunt. There were a whole series of folks who were important to me in the past. At that time I was going through changes spiritually [and] seeing the way God worked with people. It was just coming through in a variety of ways. I was teaching at Boston University by then. I had turned in the first draft of my dissertation it and had not been accepted. I had to revise my dissertation. That last Sunday in October, I just decided it was an intellectual decision that I should return to the church. I did. I marched down the aisle and rejoined. Folks were so glad to have me home. The mother of the church got up and made a motion for them to accept me by reinstatement; Mother McKenzie got up, and it was a homecoming. It was also a homecoming month. That way I could give him my hundred dollars. It sounds so crazy!

    I really began to pray in earnest. I just started growing. I had to finish my doctorate. It was one of these things where I gave it over to God, and God brought me here. I always call it my "Red Sea." I became friendly with one of the ministers. I became a friend to this woman who was in the ministry, and in the process became connected to the life of the church in a way that I had never been connected before. I also ended up becoming the church clerk. I can't remember how I did that. So I was really working hard on this stuff; doing a lot of the business for the church; also dealing with the craziness that was a part of the ministry, particularly all the problems that ministers sometimes have, which are considerable. I said, "Lord, why do I have to do all this? Why are you exposing me to this? What are you doing to me?" It wasn't shaking my faith; this time, it wasn't shaking my faith. It was not driving me away from the church the way it had done before. But, I'm still questioning it. I said, "God, what is going on here? I don't need to know all this. I don't need to know these people. Why can't I just be a nice unconscious church member like the rest of these folks here?" I was still reading more of my Bible, studying more and doing these kinds of things. I had weekends in the house. Times I had alone I would do Bible study. It would just seem like there's this incredible presence there. I didn't know what was going on. It was just a time of spiritual turmoil. In the meantime, the Lord gave me strength to work on this dissertation and get it done. In fact, we had an agreement, my friend and I. We were prayer partners. She was praying for me and my dissertation, and I was praying her through the ordination process. So this is what was going on. I had made a decision that as soon as the dissertation was done, I was going to join the choir.

    That was the way I was going to make my commitment. I'm still growing. I'm going to the altar praying. I started praying more at home. I was just growing spiritually. I got through the dissertation. God knows, and God really was with me. In fact, so much so, that after the defense, after they said, "Congratulations, doctor," the first thing I did was bow my head and thank the Lord. I just prayed right there in my thesis defense. I had no qualms whatsoever. You have to realize, in the process of doing my doctorate, I had devoted it to the service of the Lord. I already made that commitment. My father sits there, and the thesis was dismissed at something like 7:00 in the morning. I won't go into all the details, but the hand of God was involved in getting me over. That was clear. It was just parting the waters, taking me to him. That's why I call it my "Red Sea."

I joined the choir, and started going to engagements. It wasn't one of these choirs that was run almost like the military. My friend who was the minister, who had gotten ordained, was also the director. You know how choir directors can be, gospel choir directors, sanctified fascism. We had this thing for disciplining choirs.

I don't know when it was, but I guess [I got] post-dissertation depression. I came home one night, and I had just decided that I wanted to kill myself. It was a Friday night and I was so depressed. I don't know why. Had no reason to be depressed. It wasn't like I had no money. Wasn't like I had a major crisis going. I guess it must have been exhaustion or whatever people [attribute] these mental states to. I came home, and I decided to kill myself. I was going to cut my throat. I had decided, and then I remembered: "Oh my goodness, I had a singing engagement tonight. I can't do that." I promised I'd be there. So I went and got dressed, got my choir robe and stepped on out the door. I didn't want to be there, but I had to be there. That was the way I was. I'd said, "I'll do it, I'll be there." [My friend] preached this sermon. You know how folks say, "It was a Friday night"—it was a Friday night. We were at New Life AME Zion Church in Providence, Rhode Island. My pastor was preaching revival there. We had come down to lead the revival choir the last night. He preached this sermon out of Revelation. About the 144,000—you know, there was a number that could not be numbered—about every tongue, nation. And the title of the sermon was "I Want To Be in That Number."

Another story. When I was in high school, my folks moved. In the part of town where we moved, we were surrounded by Jehovah's Witnesses. The only people I had to hang around with who were anywhere near my age were Jehovah's Witnesses. My mother, being the good missionary Baptist that she was, would biblically de-brief me every time I came back in the house. When I came back, I said, "Mommy, they said that only 144,000 people are going to heaven." She sat me down. She showed me in Revelation, where it talked about the 12,000 of every tribe and then the number that no man could number. So my friend and I arranged a debate at her house. I came along with my big old King James and she sat down, and she started to talk about it. I said, "But look at this verse, it says . . ." And her father was also the assistant congregational servant, so he's like the assistant pastor of the Kingdom Hall. "It says here a number that no man can number". Her father came out, he said, "Why don't you all just agree to be friends? You don't need to debate any more." They cried uncle.

So, you have to understand, when [my friend the minister] hit that passage, that just broke open a whole big set of memories. All of a sudden I was with him in that sermon. When he started talking about Domitian and John—the struggle between them, in terms of who you are—the way he preached it, he reconstructed this conversation between Domitian and John. Domitian needed John to bow down, because he was the bishop of this incredible circle of churches. What he would do is make the rest of the folks fall in line behind this state civil religion of this emperor worship. He would say, "You are not my God, I will not bow down." So they tell me that I helped to preach the sermon. In the middle of the sermon, he just said, "Have you ever gone home and just wanted to give up?" That's when the Holy Ghost came down and took control. Just took total control. That was the real spiritual turning point for me, in terms of beginning to ask myself questions about, What does all this mean? What is God trying to say to me here? Why am I feeling this way? God, what is it you want me to do?

That fourth Sunday in May I woke up early. To show you how committed I was to the church, I didn't even need an alarm clock to get up on Sunday mornings. I was up and out the door. I remember that morning very well. Read my Bible, heard my name called and I woke up that morning. I recognized the voice. I knew. My friends tease me, people like Delores Williams. They said, "Only somebody from New England would have all these problems, because if you found this out, if you hear a voice like that, it's only going to be death or God. If he was alive to talk about it, it had to be the Lord. Right?" I didn't know.

I got up that morning and I had decided. It was African Liberation Day at St. Paul's AME Church, and I was going to go around the corner to church; but I figured since I was the assistant clerk (we had no clerk). . . I would not allow the people to elect me to be clerk, because I wanted them to get a full-time clerk, because I couldn't be a full-time clerk. But one of the things I did do as the clerk was all the resolutions of the funerals. Because since I was a college professor I had a flexible schedule,

I Think I'm Going Crazy

and other women who worked like nine to five couldn't go to funerals in the daytime or they couldn't go and talk to the relatives and do all the other stuff you need to do to get all this stuff together. Since there was no other clerk, I had to go there and get the notices ready. But since it was youth Sunday, it meant the kids were going to read the notices, and I was going to leave.

I started to go out the door and I said, "Oh, I've got to stay here, because if somebody joins the church, they won't have a clerk." I didn't want to stay. You know, it was one of these things where I really wanted to go around the corner. So I'm sitting there, and he's preaching out of Samuel, first Samuel, but the title of the sermon was "Youth: The Resource for the Future of the Church." So he wasn't preaching on Samuel's call. But you know how what Renita [Weems] said last night about something happened in the middle of the sermon that had nothing to do with the sermon. And he's telling the story about Samuel, and he said, "The voice called. Samuel said, 'Hush, hush, somebody's calling my name.'" I almost went under the bench, and that just threw me into a crisis like you would not believe. It was one of these things where I just screamed and wanted to crawl under the bench there and hide. No, not me, right?

And then a whole bunch of folks joined the church that morning; so it was a good thing I was there, because they wouldn't have had any clerk. Two of his own kids joined the church. I remember the little four-year-old came tip-toeing in the office with his older brother and said, "Chaplain, I want to join church this morning. Do you know, if you get baptized you have to put your face under water? Do I have to put my face under water?" And he believed in Jesus; he was a four-year-old. He had his little confession of faith but when they told him he had to put his face in the water, he turned right around and went right back out of the office. He went, "Later for baptism."

So, I said, "Oh, no." In fact, I was in such a crisis I didn't even wait until service was over. Soon as my work was done, I went downstairs and hid in the office. The assistant pastor came in and asked me, "What's wrong?" I said, "Nothing." He said, "You're lying. Something's wrong. What's wrong?" And I just burst into tears and left. I couldn't talk. And didn't that Negro call me up at two o'clock in the morning, because he was so worried? I guess I was so upset that he could not sleep, worrying about me. So I told him, "Nothing's wrong." I was lying! Okay, he called me up. The next day, thank God, was a holiday. This was Memorial Day weekend. I could stay in the house all day; I could stay in the house and pray and cry. I couldn't face anybody, couldn't see anybody.

I finally went to my office. And by this time, BU was in its summer session, and I had to teach on Tuesday afternoon. We're not into Tuesday, and I am still in crisis. It was like I was praying. I was like, "How am I going to get through this class?" And it was one of these things where I had to wear dark glasses, because I had been crying so. I had to wear dark glasses to teach my class, because I couldn't let anybody see these two big bags under my eyes. I had to sort of teach the class by rote and go right back to the office, because those were the first other human beings I had been around since Sunday morning; and I couldn't handle it.

I'm just sitting in the office, crying, "I have to talk to somebody. Who do I call? I'm going to call my friend Fluker." As soon as I said that, peace like a river just descended. It was like the Spirit said, "Yes." And I picked up the phone and called Fluker, and I said, "I've got to talk to you." "What is it?" "I think I'm going crazy." He said, "Cheryl," (he was staying at somebody's house) "let me call you right back. I have to go in my room and get dressed." I know what the Negro had to go do, he had to go pray. You don't know Walter Fluker, do you? He's on the faculty at Vanderbilt with Renita [Weems]. He was up there in Boston; he was doing his doctorate at BU, and he and I were good friends. He and I went to dinner and talked. I had no peace until I picked up that phone and called him, and I had gone through all these names; and I'm like, "How am I ? How do I?"

You know, there were other things that were happening to me. This is a summary, because there was a whole spiritual journey in terms of prayer life, in terms of learning to cope with everyday situations, in terms of dealing with other people's situations. And you find yourself doing this stuff, even talking to students. I was starting to get students who were in the ministry and helping them. I mean, all this stuff that was happening to me and I'm saying, "God, why am I having to cope with all this stuff?" Because I really did not want to know about the backstage of the ministry; I really didn't need to know that. I didn't like having all my idols, you know, having their feet of clay all being exposed and stuff like that. I just couldn't cope. But I was getting students and being challenged to guide and direct them. And part of what I do in terms of interpreting Afro-Christian tradition comes out of these kinds of demands.

I had one student who's from Mississippi. I'll never forget him. He was involved with some white evangelicals in the air force base that he was at, and he was going to go to seminary; he was called to the ministry. He was going to go to seminary and go home and teach the folk back in Mississippi and Memphis how to worship God properly, that kind of thing.

I still hadn't talked to Mel, I just was not ready to talk to my pastor at all. I mean, I still hadn't accepted, but at least I had talked to somebody. Fluker calmed me down and talked to me about "what the call was not," and so I took some time to reflect and study. I mean, I really got serious on the biblical stuff. All of these things in terms of encouraging people to go to graduate school, and getting their MDiv—all of my arguments came back to haunt me. I had gotten my doctorate and so I had to do that.

So, that's essentially it. I finally talked to my pastor about getting my MDiv in May of that same year.

"Unmistakably some men are called to enter the Gospel ministry, and in a manner so vividly clear and impressive as to leave no doubt. At least this was true in my case. I had long meditated quite a different career. But my 'call' came with such compelling urge, found no peace until, with my whole heart, I surrendered to it and embraced it with joyous fear."

Reverdy C. Ransom,
The Pilgrimage of Harriet Ransom's Son
(Nashville: Sunday School Union, [circa 1880's]): 37

Sterling Glover
Cleveland, Ohio

The Reverend Sterling Glover was born in New Jersey on August 3, 1925, called before birth and ordained a Baptist minister in 1950. He a BA from Rutgers and a ThM from the American Divinity School (in New York). He pastors the Emmanuel Baptist Church in Cleveland. Interview recorded July 19, 1989.

30

"You Are No Longer to Work with the Dead, but with the Living Dead"

The best place for me to start is that I was born into a Christian family. My father before me was a minister of the gospel of Jesus Christ, and he never encouraged me to become a minister. He would always say that he wanted me to do whatever I was led to do. All he wanted me to do was to bring the appetite for education, and he would foot the bill for it. Early on, there was that initiative and incentive from the family to aspire to be the best possible person whatever I decided I wanted to do. You cannot do that unless you are adequately trained.

So, early on, I began to talk about being a business person. I'd seen a lot of the difficulties that my father had with [the church] membership, because he used to take me around with him when I was very, very young. In fact, I was still wearing knee pants, as they called them. He would take me around to visit with him as he visited people's homes on Saturday. I would rather do that than to play ball with my brothers, and I was an excellent athlete. That kind of orientation really had something to do with my desire not to be a preacher. You start out by rebelling against what is naturally yours by design.

I would have to be a mortician, because there was a Black mortician in our little town in New Jersey that my father had a lot of interest in. Also, because that town had never seen a black or Afro-American mortician. Everybody gave their bodies to a White fellow by the name of Shorter. Mr. Shorter buried everybody in that town. Finally, when this Black fellow, tall, young, handsome came to town, my dad took an interest in him. We lived right around the corner from his funeral home. I used to go down and watch him clean up. One day, he asked me, "Hey fellow, may I put this here?" I said, "Help yourself," just like that. Every day I'd go by and watch what he was doing. So, he said to me one day, "You seem like you're interested in what I'm doing here." "I am." I was about fourteen then. He said, "Come around anytime you want," just like that. So I'd go around there after school. He was really struggling. Ultimately, my father saw to it that he got his very first Black case. For months, he had to go out and work on the local garbage truck to make a living for himself and his family, because Black folk would not give him a body. He was too young. He was Black, and he couldn't do it. So my dad prevailed upon this one family; that sort of broke the ice. He began to get other jobs. One summer, off from school, I went down and he said, "Come on in." I went in; I had already been exposed to chemistry. I smelled the embalming fluid. I said, "Oh, I know what that is." "What is that?" "That's formaldehyde." "What do you know about formaldehyde?" I began to tell him about the qualities of formaldehyde and my experience in the lab with frogs, snakes, and all that kind of stuff. He said, "I'll tell you what, Sterling, you can help me. You just come in here on Saturday and sweep and set the chairs up for a service and that sort of stuff." General caretaker, that's how it started.

Every evening when I could, every Saturday, he took an interest in me. After I finished high school, in fact, during my high school years, I became so good at working with him that he set up an apprenticeship for me. I went through a three year apprenticeship for the state of New Jersey. I got very good at it, to the point where he wrote a letter to the high school principal indicating that I had already selected my career. He said he would appreciate the school releasing me from my studies when we had a funeral service so I could work with him. To that, the principal said, "Well, if Sterling has made up his mind that's what he wants to do, and if he maintains a good average, then we will give him release time." That was unheard of back then. Then he had a tailor design a suit for me, just like he wore, striped trousers and a dark coat with a braid on it. It was sharp. Without any hesitation, whenever I had a service, I would go into the office and tell the principal that I would have to be excused at twelve o'clock, because most services at that time were at one o'clock in the afternoon. I had that privilege. I maintained my average, and I graduated on time [and with a] proper grade average without any problem.

I said, "This is it. I'm going to be a mortician." I was good, believe me. So I went into the Air Force, came out, went right back with him. It just so happened that after many moons, while I was embalming, something spoke to my mind. It said, "You no longer are to work with the dead, but with the living dead." That was the exact quotation to my mind.

I said, "Oh!" Just like that. Then I told him about it, his name was Carney Bragg. He said, "I always knew it. I knew you would never make a good undertaker even though you have the craft, the skill. There are certain things you do not like. You don't like to miss church on Sunday." I would actually pray that I wouldn't have to be bothered on a Sunday. What were we there for? I had stayed up all night, Saturday night, working on cases so I could be free Sunday morning to go to Sunday school and church.

It was at that point in my life that I began to restructure my thinking. I left the funeral home, still in rebellion to that inner drive. I was good in accounting. I said, "I know what I'll do. I'll see if I can't be an accountant or something." So, there was a Black firm, a fellow who owned the trucking company, White Trucking and Transfer Company. He needed a clerical worker. He needed a bookkeeper. He needed a good dispatcher. I had never done that. I said, "I'll do it."

He accepted me in his family, so to speak. I spent about three years working with him. I got to the place where I could read the rates. He had a White fellow who was a graduate of Rutgers University as his rate man. He told this fellow, "I want you to show Sterling everything." Well, this White fellow rebelled against that. "A Black," he said, "He can't learn it. He has to go to Rutgers. He's got to stay at least two years to learn this." But to his chagrin, I could read, I could conceptualize, and I could analyze. I got to the place where I could read tariffs, New England tariffs. We were hauling heavy freight, steel wire, stuff like that. I would come up with a rate, and my boss said, "Don't use that rate. I want Mr. Connors to check it." Mr. Connors would come in, he'd check the rate and say, "Where'd you get it from?" I said, "I got it off the tariff." He'd say, "You just can't do it. You've got to read the supplements." I said, "I read the supplements. The supplements indicated no increase or no decrease." He would turn red. So, finally, he said, "On the business that I bring in, I don't want you to come up with the rate. I will come up with the rate. You just do the typing of the bill."

On my own I would still run the tariffs and find his material, and he was handling *Redbook* and *Reader's Digest* in just mass volumes. And so I'd come up with the rate, put it in pencil, and he'd look it up and, by golly, I was right! Maybe every now and then I would miss one, but overall—without that formal training anyway—was right.

I would leave the office and go out in the garage and close the door and begin preaching to the trucks. I would just go berserk in there. Just like I would preach to the cadavers when I was embalming. When I was embalming, I would say, "You have lived for nothing." Some that I knew who were beggars, bums, for example—I would cry and it wasn't from the astringency of the embalming fluid. I said, "You have lived for nothing, man. You're going to hell." I would actually cry. I did the same thing in the garage. I would preach to the trucks and the mechanic would hear me. I didn't care. The boss would come out and he would hear me. I didn't know I was that loud. He would call—he nicknamed me Roger, for whatever reason—he'd say, "Roger! Come in here." I said, "Yes, Mr. White." He said, "What are you doing in there preaching? I heard you." I said, "Well, you didn't hear me." He said, "Yes, I did." This fellow was a member of Bethany Baptist Church, a sound Christian fellow. And he said to me, "Roger, you're supposed to be a preacher." I said, "No, not me. No."

That went on for about three or four years. One day, it was emphatically made clear to me, "This is what you are to be!" So, I go back to Rutgers; I begin to study philosophy. Then I told my father. He said, "I knew it all along." I said, "Dad, why didn't you say so?" He said, "I wanted you to make sure that this is what you are to be about. Only then will you be successful at it."

That's how my call came. I completely turned my back on the other professions, being an accountant and being a mortician. I went full-time in study. My dad took me to his board of deacons. They had been looking for it all along. They set a time for me to give my trial sermon as they called it. The night that I had to give it, I was as nervous as a cat. I was trying to eat my supper and I was trembling, and my mother scolded me. She said, "What's wrong with you? Eat your supper." Dad said, "Leave him alone."

I went on to the church, and I preached on that passage where Jesus responded to the call of Mary and Martha, and Thomas said to his fellow brethren, "Let us also go with him, that we might die with him." I talked about going with Jesus. That was my first sermon. I look at it every now and then and say, "How in the world did I deliver such, so that people accepted it?"

From that time on, it's just been an adventure, a romance with the word of God. I went on and I got my bachelor's. I then went on to American Seminary College and Divinity School where I got my master's in theology. Now I'm considered a theologian-in-residence here at the church. That's my official title, not just a pastor. If one is to have the last word on what the Bible means, I have that here in this congregation. So here I am.

I pastored my first church while I was going to college and finishing up. They were very kind to me. It was a $25 a week church. I wrote my thesis on my experiences I had with my membership. That's what it has been for me.

I thoroughly enjoy scholarship. I enjoy being able to interpret Scripture. The Lord has afforded me with illumination that is not found in theological writing. I have had the responsibility to teach other preachers right here in this town and across the state for eighteen years. I was the dean of Christian education. I conducted classes across the state in various churches and so on. So that's where I am now. This is my second church. I pledge to be here for the rest of my life.

"When called of God, on a particular occasion, to a definite work, I said, 'No, Lord, not me.' Day by day I was more impressed that God would have me work in his vineyard. I thought it could not be that I was called to preach—I, so weak and ignorant....

I took all my doubts and fears to the Lord in prayer, when, what seemed to be an angel, made his appearance. In his hand was a scroll, on which were these words: 'Thee have I chosen to preach my Gospel without delay.' The moment my eyes saw it, it appeared to be printed on my heart. The angel was gone in an instant, and I, in agony, cried out, 'Lord, I cannot do it!' It was eleven o'clock in the morning, yet everything grew dark as night. The darkness was so great that I feared to stir.

At last 'Mam' Riley entered. As she did so, the room grew lighter, and I arose from my knees.

From that day my appetite failed me and sleep fled from my eyes. I seemed as one tormented. I prayed, but felt no better....

One night as I lay weeping and beseeching the dear Lord to remove this burden from me, there appeared the same angel that came to me before, and on his breast were these words: 'You are lost unless you obey God's righteous commands.'

I had always been opposed to the preaching of women, and had spoken against it, though, I acknowledge, without foundation. This rose before me like a mountain, and when I thought for the difficulties they had to enounter, both from professors and no-professors, I shrank back and cried, 'Lord, I cannot go!'

Nearly two months from the time I first saw the angel, I said that I would do anything or go anywhere for God, if it were made plain to me. He took me at my word, and sent the angel again with this message: 'You have I chosen to go in my name and warn the people of their sins.' I bowed my head and said, 'I will go, Lord.'"

> Julia A. J. Foote, A.M.E. Zion preacher, from the 1879 edition of her *A Brand Plucked from the Fire* in *Sisters of the Spirit: Three Black Women's Autobiographies of the Nineteenth Century* (Bloomington: Indiana University Press, 1986): 200-202.

Cynthia Hale
Atlanta, Georgia

The Reverend Dr. Cynthia Hale was born in Roanoke, Virginia, on October 27, 1952, called in 1975 and ordained by the Disciples of Christ (Christian Church) in 1979. She has a BA from Hollins College, (Virginia) an MDiv from Duke University's Divinity School and a DMin from United Theological Seminary, Dayton Ohio. She is pastor of the Ray of Hope Christian Church in Decatur, Georgia. Interview recorded June 22, 1989.

31

When Her Father Said, "I Won't Support You if You Go to Seminary"

Well, I guess I need to begin by talking about my upbringing because—well, this isn't anything different—I was raised in a Christian home, a Christian family and church. I'm a member of the Christian Church (Disciples of Christ), and so I was raised in the Christian Church in Roanoke, Virginia. At the age of eight years old, I became a Christian, and that was somewhat unique in the sense that it didn't happen in my church. A neighbor of mine, Blanche Craig, took me to into a child evangelism program where they talked about the love of God and taught us the scriptures. I mean, really, a detailed Bible study approach for children. And as they taught the story, I remember this particular day, they taught us the scripture John 3:16, *For God so loved the world.* I asked Mrs. Craig if God's love was like my daddy's love—I'm the firstborn, and he's real special to me; [we're] real, real special to each other; and my dad's a tremendous provider and just a good person and everything—and I said, "Is God's love like daddy's love?" Mrs. Craig, knowing my father, said, "Yes." So, when they asked us if we wanted to accept Christ, then immediately I said, "Yes, I want to do that" and knew that that was real. It was a tremendous experience for me as a young child, and then I just began to study the scriptures, continued to go to this Bible study to become much more active in my church, studying the scriptures. My mother started to have a Bible study for children in our home. Then, as a teenager I grew up in that. When I went to high school, during that period, we were called "Jesus freaks," because I was just really turned on about the Lord. But the other interesting side is the fact that I had a well-rounded life, enjoyed partying and games and things like that. So there was that interesting mixture of the sacred and the secular, and just a well-rounded upbringing.

I think it was because of this mixture and the fact that I was so involved in all aspects of life, that I sort of missed any sense of a call or even thinking about going into ministry. And the other interesting fact for me is that I was during this time a biblical literalist, and I didn't believe that God called women to preach. So I was struggling with any sense of being used; if God didn't call women, how I would be used? I knew that I loved God, knew that I wanted to be whatever he wanted me to be, but just did not sense that I would be called into ministry. But others saw that in me, so that when I went to college I majored in music, and I thought about teaching music or performing. I was struggling with those two. Then my pastor—well, actually the chaplain at Hollins College where I attended college—suggested to me that God was calling me into the ministry that I had the gifts and graces for ministry. Then my pastor, Alvin Jackson, at my local congregation confirmed that. I told them they were crazy, because God didn't call women to preach. In fact, the chaplain there was going on sabbatical and they were interviewing women to take his place. I was on the committee, and I was very clear about the fact that no woman will ever preach to me. Then a year later, within my own spirit, I sensed God's call upon my life and not knowing what to do with that, I went back to my chaplain and my pastor and I said, "What do I do?" And they said, "Go to seminary." And I said, "Seminary?"

So what I did was to take a year off after college. I graduated and just took a year off and worked as a head resident at my college, just to sort of think and pray about it. I guess you could say I wasn't all that comfortable with it, so I was trying to find something else to do. But during that year, I really prayed about it and decided that I would do whatever God said. So I just really felt led to go to seminary. I applied to Duke Divinity School and was accepted there. It was during my first week of seminary that it became crystal clear that this was the place for me. I'd never been so happy and so fulfilled. The other peace that confirmed it for me (and my parents said this was how they knew) was that I never was a serious person about anything. I mean, I was just sort of into everything and enthusiastic about life, just joyful and happy and crazy, but not serious. I was serious about Christ but I was just kind of flighty. But when I got to seminary, I settled down and I took my studies seriously for the first time in my life. I went into that experience with a reckless abandonment; and I felt the sense of God's leading in my life, because little by little all the pieces started to fall into place. This whole thing about my questioning whether or not I was called to preach, and then by this time others questioning me . My father said, "You can't go to seminary. You need to go take this job in a bank and be prosperous," that kind of thing. He said, "I won't support you." And I said, "I'm going anyway, because God has called me." I went to seminary out of sheer obedience to God. When I did that, my father came back and was tremendously supportive.

    The men on campus said, "God didn't call you to preach." Gardner Taylor came to our campus to do a series of preaching lectures—sermons and lectures—and we had a meeting with him. He was asking the guys, "Hey, what did God call you to do?" And they said, "God called us to preach, Doc." And then he said, "Well, what did he call you to do?" talking to me. And the guys answered for me by saying, "Well, she says God called her to preach, but you know God doesn't call women to preach." He said, "Miss Cynthia, did God call you to preach?" Timidly I responded, "Yes." He looked at me and said, "Well, Miss Cynthia, don't worry about what others say, because if God called you to preach, God doesn't waste his material."

    Shortly after that, a friend of mine, John Borens, invited me to come be his associate in Pittsboro, North Carolina. It was there that I learned, in this little country church with a little prayer band of women, how to preach in the Black tradition. You know what I mean? You had to preach down there! It was that kind of affirmation and others that came that really gave me a sense that God was indeed calling me to preach. Over and over again, the word just became crystal clear, the call became crystal clear to me.

As I've entered each of my ministries, first as a federal prison chaplain in an all-male institution—there, again, the question, "Did God call a woman?"—and just having tremendous success there in terms of my walking with those men and being present for them. Then the question came again when I came to Atlanta to start a congregation, "Does God call a woman?" There, again, having people respond to my ministry. So that's my call, and that's where I come from.

Cornelius Henderson
Atlanta, Georgia

The Reverend Cornelius Henderson was born in Portordale, Georgia, on September 12, 1934, called in 1953 and ordained a United Methodist elder in 1959. He received a BA from Clark College (Georgia), a BD from Gammon Theological Seminary and a STM from Gammon Interdenominational Theological Center. He is District Superintendent of the Atlanta-Emory District, the only Black Superintendent in Georgia. Interview recorded June 22, 1989.

32

From a Physical Education or Music Major to District Superintendent

I finished high school in 1952, and rather than attend Clark College, a United Methodist institution of higher learning here in Atlanta, I decided to matriculate at Fort Valley State College, Fort Valley, Georgia—the principal reason being two of my older brothers had attended Clark and neither had graduated. Hence, I felt a change of scenery would be productive for me in pursuing an undergraduate degree. Fort Valley State College at that time was one of three black state operated institutions of higher learning, the other two being Albany State and Savannah State.

In 1952, when I arrived on the campus, much to my chagrin, there was not a major in physical education. Because of limited athletic equipment and space, etcetera, they did not even have an accredited, regulation-size gymnasium, so that our basketball games at that time had to be played in Macon, some twenty-four miles away. My second choice was that of music; so I sought to pursue a career in music with a concentration in voice. At the end of my first year in music, I still felt a tremendous sense of restlessness and started chatting with some of the student and faculty leaders, some of whom felt I might have had some of the gifts and graces that a minister possessed.

I'd heard since my childhood days that ministers were called. My interpretation of that call was based upon what they had said, time and time again—that God literally, vocally called them to preach. Some mornings I recall getting up early, going into the men's room, raising the window and listening for God to literally call my name, "Cornelius Henderson, I want you to preach." That did not happen. Had it happened, I probably would have been dead of a heart attack. I would have been, I'm sure, at least shocked into something perhaps far more catastrophic than anything I've ever imagined.

But I did chat with some of the more seasoned ministers on the campus about my restlessness and my inquiry and my seeking and probing, and I recall very vividly how one minister, who was an older student, told me that God called men (at that time men) for ministry in different ways. If God ever called, I would get the message. I pursued that advice, listened to it, appreciated it, and was greatly influenced by it, and kind of made nearly a full-time vocation of going to church. I went to every church in Fort Valley that Black people could attend at that time, including the Seventh Day Adventist Church. I was offered a full scholarship if I would withdraw from Fort Valley State and go to Oakwood College in Huntsville, Alabama, an institution operated by the Seventh Day Adventists. I was grateful for the offer and continued to attend that church on Saturdays, but on Sundays would attend the CME Church, the AME Church and the Baptist Church and sometimes the Episcopal Church in front of the campus, still working on putting some flesh on the call to preach.

I also became very familiar with the president of the institution at that time, Dr. Cornelius V. Troop, a great churchman, a Baptist—Trinity Baptist Church in Fort Valley—Sunday school teacher, a tremendous organ player who sang in the college quartet when he matriculated at Morris Brown. He was kind enough to allow me to make some trips with him to drive for him as he would speak at various functions, including high school commencements and baccalaureates. It was during that period of being close to the president of that institution that I really felt God had a special work for me to do, and that that work would be within the context of the Christian ministry.

At the end of my sophomore year, I was introduced to Dr. James Phillip Brawley, then president of Clark College, an outstanding United Methodist layman. My third grade elementary school teacher, Mrs. Sarah Frances Thompson Hardiman, felt that if I intended to go into the ministry, I would need to be in a church-related institution, and she made the necessary contacts with the president of Clark. I was given an opportunity to visit with him in his office on the campus. Subsequently, on a visit to his home, I met Mrs. Brawley. He normally kept one student in his home, but he said after our first meeting that he would consider taking two. So from that point on, the rest of my undergraduate career was on another kind of level. I did not have to worry about any financial obligations—all books, tuition, food, clothing, housing, all of the financial resources were available to me. And I was never treated as a servant, never had to wear a white, starched jacket as the millionaires and the philanthropists and trustees would [who come] to the campus and to Dr. Brawley's home; I was always treated as a son. When this layman of the church, this outstanding churchman and great educator, started taking an interest in me, a country boy from Covington, Georgia, whose dad could barely read and write his name, my life took on new meaning. I met people like Dr. James Thomas of the board of higher education in ministry of our church in Nashville [and] Dr. Ernest Dixon of the same national board. Both men are now bishops in the church. Bishop Thomas recently retired from East Ohio and now is working out of Perkins SMU in Dallas. Bishop Dixon is now the bishop in San Antonio, Texas. So my life continued along a certain kind of track.

I was elected, after a few months on the campus, president of the student government association, which was unheard of—a transfer student, preministerial student, living with the president, tied to the administration and a country boy and all of that. Things continued to unfold for us. Upon graduating, in just two years—even though I transferred from a state institution to a private school and lost some hours in the process—I was still able to graduate on time and on schedule I enrolled in seminary, and that now has been some thirty-six years ago.

There have been times, understandably so, when I have questioned the authenticity and the veracity and the completeness of that call. I still think that God calls men and women to ministry, various levels or lanes of ministry, that God's call is not necessarily ever totally consummated, that he continues to call us and to remind us of that call and that calling. To this day, I still feel that as being in process.

If I think about it, seeds were planted back almost to my early childhood development. Charlayne Hunter, the first Black female graduate of the University of Georgia, who is now a TV reporter—Charlayne's daddy was an AME chaplain, a minister of an AME church, and I lived next door to his parsonage. When I was two and one-half, three years old, he started planting seeds in my mind about ministry, as I think about it. In high school, ministers would often make similar kinds of comments, Sunday school superintendents, school teachers, etcetera. I think that Christian men and women have a very definite role to play in helping to crystallize a person's call. God still does the calling in his own way and in his own time; but I think that Christian men and women, anointed men and women, can and often do play a major role in the crystallization process of that call, the refinement of the same, and the enablement process of the same.

Edward V. Hill
Los Angeles, California

The Reverend Edward V. Hill was born in Columbus, Texas, on November 11, 1933, called to preach in 1944 and ordained in 1954. He received a BS from Prairie View A & M College (Texas). He pastors the Mount Zion Missionary Baptist Church in Los Angeles, California. He is one of the leading evangelists in this country. Interview recorded June 21, 1989.

33

"Are You Ready to Preach?"

I was born in Columbus, Texas. My mother moved to San Antonio with four children (when I was a year and a half), because my father would not support us and Columbus was not a place where you could get support. She moved right next door to a lady by the name of Mrs. Moore. Mrs. Moore had a sister, Mrs. Langram, who lived twenty-nine miles outside of San Antonio, out in the country. She and her husband came to visit Mrs. Moore, because Mrs. Moore was ill.

One day, she saw my sister and me playing in the yard about age four and wanted to know "Who are these children?" Mrs. Moore told her, "Those are Mrs. Hill's children. She has four of them, but she has to work."

Mr. and Mrs. Langram waited until my mother came home that evening and said, "Can we help you with these children? We live in the country, and we have plenty." Though mother was only making about $12 to $16 a week with four children, and there was no aid for dependent children or anything like that, she explained that she would not give her children away. The Langrams said, "We're not asking you to give your children away. We come to town every other week to see our sister, and we'll just take them to the country and care for them to help you out." In those days, they didn't have any welfare or aid for dependent children. In that my mother didn't have any other good choice, she agreed.

So, my sister and I moved out into the country with the Langrams to this place where the Langrams said they had plenty. This plenty turned out to be a two-room log cabin, wild squirrels, wild rabbit, wild hickory nuts, wild grapes, wild duberries, mulberries and peanuts. There was a cow, so we had milk.

The agreement with mother was that she wanted both of us at six years old to come back to San Antonio and go to school, since San Antonio had good schools. My sister hated the country and left, but I loved it. And at six, when mother tried to get me to come back to town, I ran off trying to find the country. So mother decided to let me stay with the Langrams.

Sweet Home, Texas, was a community of about ten miles by ten miles that was basically all owned by Negroes. It was one of the largest rural communities owned by Negroes in the South. We had our church, our schools, and our co-ops: a molasses co-op, a chicken co-op, and others. Two or three hundred people were involved. Our church was a historic church down in south Texas. So, I was nurtured in a very strict Baptist Christian religious community where everybody could whip you and correct you. My school principal was superintendent of our Sunday school, and one of our teachers played the piano for the church. In the Sweet Home community, when you applied for a job to teach, the first question asked was, "Are you going to play the piano, teach in the Sunday School or whatever?"

I was called the semi-orphan of the community. I ate at everybody's house all over the community. I was into everything, the junior choir, junior usher board, junior everything. I made fires for my school. We had four rooms and teachers gave me fifty cents a week to have their fires red-hot by eight o'clock. Each day by eight o'clock, I had already milked three cows and had the fires red hot. A neighbor, Hicks Thomas, gave me $1.25 a week, plus milk to take home, to milk three cows twice a day. So I was kind of everybody's boy. I was into everything. I led the choirs, led this and led that.

When I was eleven years old, papa and I were home alone—mama was in town with her sister Mrs. Moore—when I woke up, I found papa dead. That left mama and me. Therefore, it was just a matter of time before I would have to stop school, because there was no welfare, no SSI, and she wasn't old enough to receive any old age pension. And even if that had been the case, she would have gotten only about $50 per month. So we had to make it by shaking peanuts and raising a pig to kill, picking cotton, preserving some things and me working wherever I could work.

While I was still eleven years old, what I perceived to be the Holy Spirit of God came upon me while walking down Grandma Jody's lane. And, he communicated to me that I was to preach the Gospel. It was a fearful experience. So, I tried to pay no attention to it. I tried to ignore it. But it consumed every thought of mine. I tried to get rid of it just by becoming very active in the church. At the age of fourteen, as testament of how active I was, I made the motion to dismiss all the deacons of our church. I taught Sunday School. I did a lot as a child. I had the gift of talking and I used it.

The unction, and I use that word as the inner stirring, the inner compelling daily thought, was to preach. I finally got rid of it by promising the Lord that if he would see me through high school, I would preach. After that, the Spirit of the Lord did not bother me too much about preaching.

Now, the reason I did that was because I knew the possibilities of me finishing high school were nil. I wasn't going to finish high school. There were a few people who finished high school, but, I was large and when you were large, you normally went to the tenth grade, then you had to stop and go to work.

The next time, the Spirit of the Lord came upon me strongly. And, I don't know if I can explain it beyond that. The Spirit of the Lord came upon me and spoke to my spirit, not audibly, but I mean, came upon me. I was walking down the road from the school to the log cabin, which was about three quarters of a mile, with my high school diploma. I was valedictorian; I was president of my class. I was the highest academic student; I was the only graduate in my class; they had a whole commencement just for me. Then, the Spirit of the Lord came upon me and said, "Okay, are you ready to preach?"

Incidentally, I had been very active as a youth. Every time the church doors opened, I was there, prayer meeting, everything. I was the only kid in the building, everybody else was grown. I would sit down on the front row helping the old folks sing and pray. I would start shouting and praising God at fifteen years old. But then the Spirit of the Lord came upon me and asked me, "Are you ready to preach?" I didn't expect it, because

I was very active—4H Club President, speaking, testifying, and youth speaker. So, I thought I had gotten away without preaching.

But again the Spirit of the Lord came upon me and said, "Are you ready to preach?" I said, "No, Lord, no, Lord, I can't preach because I don't have a college education." I knew the need for educated preachers. Fortunately, in my section of the country, we had some of the best in the world. Texas preachers, period! And especially those down around Austin and San Antonio were the most learned and renowned preachers anywhere. The Jacksons, Miles, Hardmans, Rectors, these were worldwide evangelists. Therefore, we felt if I were to preach, I needed a college education. So, I said, "Lord, I will preach if you get me in college." Well, it was another lie. I didn't plan to preach anymore then than I did after high school.

Through a series of acts of God and faith, my mama sent me to Prairie View A & M University with my ticket, five dollars and my clothing in a little suitcase that I tied up with a rope. Her closing words were, "I will be praying for you. Now, you just go on, and somehow you are going to get in and you are going to do all right." When I got to Prairie View, I only had $1.92 in my pocket, for I had splurged on the way.

I went on to the office where there was a sign up that said, "$83.00, money order, cashier's check or cash." Though I had only $1.92, I got in line. Soon there were only two people between me and the clerk and the devil came upon me with a fearful fright. He said, "Now what are you doing here? How are you going to get in? Where is the $83 coming from? This is real, this is not prayer meeting at Sweet Home." But I could hear Mama saying, "I will be praying for you."

Soon, there was only one girl in line ahead of me. She paid her money, but she hesitated, folded her receipt, and put her money away. Then I was next. At that moment, Dr. Drew came up and put his hand on me and said, "Are you Ed Hill?" I said, "Yes." He said, "Get out of line." I panicked. I thought he wasn't going to let me in the school. I said, "Oh, please don't take me out of line. I want to go to school, I'll work hard, I'll get a job if you just let me in." He said, "Get out of line." I said, "Sir, please." He said, "Son, we have been looking for you. We have a four-year scholarship that will pay all of your tuition, all of your room and board, and give you $35 a month to spend." And that's how I got in school.

Then, after getting in school, the Spirit of the Lord came upon me and said, "Are you now going to preach?" I not only told the Lord that I wasn't ready to preach, I told Him that I hadn't ever planned to, and that I didn't want to be a preacher. All the preachers I knew were very poor, with the exception of a few. We paid them off (preachers) in our community with eggs and bacon and chickens and peanuts. They used to call the roll, the church dues was two bits, and people would say, "A dozen eggs, or a slab of bacon." A slab of bacon was worth $1. You could pay for the whole month with a slab of bacon, that's how we paid the preacher. I didn't want this. I wanted to be somebody. I wanted to help my people. I wanted to have money. I wanted to go places. And I didn't see these potentials in preaching. I explained to the Lord that I was in school now. I had this four-year scholarship and I was going to finish and go on to be a lawyer.

Within thirty days, I had lost my scholarship. I had been in jail. I did things in thirty days I never thought about doing in all the years I was coming up. But then, I cried unto the Lord and he heard my cry. I asked him for one favor, "If I must preach, then let me preach." I can count upon my fingers the times that I have not been able to preach due to illness, and I can't remember a week that I haven't had from one to five invitations from college on.

I preached on the college campus on Tuesday nights for the Baptist student union because the director was sick. There would be anywhere from 900 to 1,800 students, including the president and teachers. My English teacher would have a fit every time I would open my mouth. But the people came out to hear this freshman. I only spent four weekends on the college campus in four years, because I was preaching all around the country. I lost my scholarship, but I made my way through school. People loved me and gave me money. The president of the National Baptist Convention supported me. The Negro pastors in Texas and other places gave me support. And I've been preaching ever since.

Three things I have never lost, [in] all I've been through. Foremost is, the desire to preach. That which I have desired to preach has always been around the subject, How to accept Jesus Christ as your Savior. My preaching—and teaching—has not been legalistic or moralistic or helping Black people to overcome. I've just been preaching the Gospel to everybody. I don't preach much more than the simple story about Jesus Christ. I've never been to seminary. I've taught in them; I've lectured in them; I've had visiting professorships. I do not speak Greek or Hebrew. I just preach the simple story of the death, burial and resurrection.

I don't know of a major denomination and few major churches in the United States that I have not either preached at or have been invited to preach at. Last year, I received 843 invitations and I could only accept forty. This year, I'll receive around 600. I'm already into 1992 and 1993.

I'm just simple a teacher, just a preacher. I'm not a Gardner Taylor or those that have exposed themselves to higher learning. Maybe I should have, but I never had the time. I was called to pastor before I finished college. I was twenty years old and pastored the second oldest church in Fifth Ward, Houston, Texas, the Mount Moriah Missionary Baptist Church. It had in its membership forty-one public school teachers, four principals, doctors, lawyers—and I was still a student at Prairie View A & M College.

I now thank God for making me a preacher of the Gospel of Jesus Christ.

Samuel Hines
Fort Washington, Virginia

The Reverend Samuel Hines was born in Savanna-La-Mar, Jamaica, West Indies, called in 1946 and ordained by the Church of God (Anderson) in 1952. He has a BTh from Jamaica Bible College and a BRE from Detroit Bible College. He pastors the Third Street Church of God in Washington, D. C. Interview recorded June 16, 1989.

34

"Nobody with Your Color Eyes Can Be a Preacher"

I should say, by way of introduction, that I am a second generation preacher. My father was a preacher before me and pastored in the Caribbean—several islands of the Caribbean. Well, I should say perhaps, [in] that he prefers it, being his ministry—he was a Salvation Army officer. That's what he was. Then he came in touch with the Church of God while he was in Trinidad and felt called to transfer his credentials there. He came back home to Jamaica in about the year 1916, having been widowed while he was in the eastern Caribbean and having brought with him one son. While in 1918 he married Miss Espidell Smith, who had done not too many errors previously and graduated from Tuskegee where Dr. Massey is now. She and her sister had gone to Tuskegee, in 1908, I think it was, and graduated in 1912 or something like that. So they were home, and she met my dad and married him and so on.

I was born then in Savanna-La-Mar, Westmoreland, on the Island of Jamaica, and grew up there. I grew up in an unusual home where spirituality was as normal as our physical being. My dad was a man who lived by faith and lived a very transparent life, which was reflected in the glory of God. He was a man who had an unusual ministry to people. He was a very quiet unassuming man, but one who was very relevant to people's needs. He was a good preacher, a proclaimer of the word. But more than that, he was a terrific pastor. I was more impressed by his pastoral ministry than anything else because the way people gravitated to him for service. He was a servant leader way back then. Although he never claimed this for himself, everybody gave it to him. He had a wonderful healing ministry. I never saw him conduct a healing service in his life, but I did see people come to his door every day with illnesses and ask for his help and his prayer. He would pray for them, and I saw them healed. I could go on with that.

We were extremely poor, and the ministry gave him no financial rewards. I found that quite a turn-off, myself. And I swore I would never have anything to do with the ministry because of that. But on the other hand, I saw what it had been to live by faith and to see miracles. I used to tell folks, it used to take at least three miracles a day to keep me alive: one for breakfast, one for lunch, and one for dinner. And they all took place on a daily basis. So I grew up that way.

My father also was a very ecumenical person in his ministry. I still marvel, back there at that time, when sectarianism was the thing of the day, how he managed to do what he did in his home town with that church; how he kind of became the dean of the preachers of town because he was the oldest. On a Thursday afternoon I would see his living room—five, six, seven, eight, nine, ten pastors from that little town who would come to him and sit with him, and he would expound scriptures and explain and answer questions. They had this on a weekly basis. I was very impressed by this. I was very impressed that it sometimes included even the Roman Catholic priest who lived right across the street from us. So I grew up in that ecumenical atmosphere, the big missionary services. I saw all the churches close on Sunday night, and everybody would go to the church that was having the missionary for the month. So I saw that. They had big united services all through the year. I was very impressed with them.

My father also was a very sensitive man about dealing with the poor, maybe because he was so poor himself. He established some contact with some wealthy people in London, and they cared for him. Every year they saw that he was provided with resources to administer to the poor. For instance, one man's father gave him a cow each year, which was butchered and served out as meat for the poor. Indian families gave him things of rice, bales of rice that he gave out to the poor. The shopkeepers gave him flour and canned goods and whatnot. Now you have to remember I'm talking about the 1930s and early '40s in Jamaica. So I saw that in action. We were obviously a mission church connected to the Church of God USA through its missionary ward. So, frequently we had visits from the missionaries. Yes, I saw that model of ministry, which I suppose almost unconsciously impressed me as a boy.

Then I graduated from high school. In my last year of high school, I got severely ill. It was the last year of World War II, 1945. As the boys came back from the War, they brought some virus or something with them, and epidemics spread all over the island. People were dying like flies. Whatever it was, I developed it. I was confined to bed and had to take a real look at myself; because that was my last year in Jamaica. Of course, our high school experience is very different from here. High school was a privilege reserved for the privileged. You had to get scholarships. I happened to get scholarships; that's why I got a high school education. I couldn't afford one, but I got scholarships. And here I was at the end of it. We had to take a big exam; and it depends on your ability to pass an exam, which of all things came from England, set by Cambridge. It was called a Senior Cambridge Exam. If you passed that, you graduated or else you were flunking. So here was I, my last year getting ready for that exam, and I got ill. I remember this prayer very specially. I prayed to God, saying, "Lord, if you just enable me to get out of this bed, and take the exam and get through, I'll give you my life with whatever you want it to do." That was a real prayer with an earnest boy of sixteen years old. It was an earnest prayer, and I really meant it.

Well, the Lord touched me, I believe; and I got out of bed, and I went, weak and feeble, prayerful to the exam. Of course, you don't know the results right away. I took the exam in December, and you didn't know the results until May. So you went back to school for another semester or another quarter, anyway, hoping the results would arrive. I'll never forget the twenty-fourth of May, which in those days was called Empire Day. That's the day when we colonials celebrated the glory of the

Empire, and we sang all these wonderful songs about Britain and her authority, power, and molded it as we were made to do as faithful colonials. I remember that day when I was at a colonial party at the school, and the word came that the results were out. The results had arrived from Cambridge. Somebody from the school's office had come to me and told me I had passed the exam. That was a glorious celebration for me. I went and told my dad, and my dad reminded me. He said, "Now, son, remember what you told me you told the Lord when you were sick. You told the Lord that if he healed you and raised you up and made you pass the exam, you would make yourself available to the Lord." So, I said, "Yes, sir. I remember that." So my next move was, "What to do?"

I was a high school graduate. I didn't know college was so expensive. They were just beginning the West Indies University; it was very expensive, and you had to have resources to go there. I didn't have any of those. So I went to work with the government. I got a job 130 miles away from my home in Kingston, Jamaica. I got in a very pagan community up there. They were ungodly people, but it was a good job. My parents were very upset that I was going so far away from home. My mother felt surely that I would get seduced into the ways of the world and the sin and the devil and the flesh. That would be the end of me. I was going to the big, bad city of Kingston. Anyway I was eager to get away; so I did.

I went to Kingston, and I got this job. As I recall it, two things happened. I got invited on Saturday night to go to Youth for Christ. It was a big movement in the islands. It met every Saturday night at a church hall downtown. It drew young people from every possible walk of life and denomination. I just got turned on by Youth for Christ. I was musical. I had a singing voice in those days, so I became a soloist for Youth for Christ on Saturday nights. I became, afterwards, the song director for Youth for Christ. I really found it a lot more exciting than my local church which I was attending—a local Church of God congregation which I was attending in Kingston. But I hadn't experienced that eccentricity in my call.

I was going one night to Youth for Christ—a little country boy from South Lamar, a small town boy and a real novice to big city life. This was my first experience. I went to Youth for Christ Collegiate Hall and a woman meets me, stops me in my tracks; and, as I learned, the word was she had propositioned me. I discovered for the first time in my life what a prostitute was. Here was a young woman all dressed up accordingly and painted up offering me her body. And I want to tell you that was a shocker! I had never confronted anything like that in my life! Well, I knew enough to resist her and tell her that I was a Christian, and I was going to Youth for Christ. I don't think she was much impressed with that; but she didn't bother me, and I went to Youth for Christ. I was really upset through the whole meeting. I was nervous. I couldn't believe I actually came that close to a woman of the streets. I was, as I said, just over sixteen, not quite seventeen years of age. And, so, I went in to this meeting, came back out and who did I meet when I came back out? The same lady. She was there and she was telling me what a good time she could give me. She was telling me how she liked the color of my eyes and she was really going to town on me. Right there and then I could almost hear my mother's voice saying, "You're going to go to the bad city and get seduced and become worldly and ungodly and forget your promise to God." I could actually hear her saying these things, like before I had left. So I resisted this prostitute and went home.

That night when I got home—I stayed at my sister's house—I prayed about the whole experience. It was the first time when I really felt the different call to ministry. Because during the course of praying for that woman and that situation, I developed a real concern for who's witnessing to such people. Who is taking them the good news? I didn't preach to her at all. I just told her I was a Christian and I wasn't interested in her offer. I did not share the gospel with her in any way. So I developed a gift for what I had not done. I hadn't shared the gospel. I couldn't understand why I didn't, so I really began to develop a real call to administer to help this kind of people. I was dead scared that I didn't want to get too close to that kind of person.

So I went back to my job the following Monday morning, and from that time on, my job lost its joy. I remember getting my pay after that and saying to my friend, "You know, I don't even enjoy getting my pay." He said, "C'mon, man, all of us look forward to pay day." I said, "No, I think I should be doing something else." He said, "Like what?" I didn't tell him, because I knew he would laugh me into the ground. But as time went on and the more I went to church, it was strange enough that lady never approached me again, because I saw her several times. I began to pray and pray more to help me to know what my ministry is in regard to such people. What was I talking about?

I would go to work, and finally I went to my pastor and I told him what was happening to me. He suggested I pray about it. He suggested that maybe I was experiencing a call to what is called "full-time ministry." Had I ever considered that? I said, "Yes," I had considered that and decided against it. But that is what I wanted to do then. I would prefer to train in some other field and then make myself available to the church as a layperson. I told him my dad was a preacher. I thought one of us was enough in that calling. But the more I thought about it, the more concern I began to develop for people, and particularly for those like that prostitute lady who seemed to be so mixed up in her purpose in life. I wanted to help them.

I became involved in Youth for Christ teams after that, that would go out and witness on the streets. I began to find that very enriching, very stimulating, and very soul-satisfying. I began to develop quite some skill in doing that. That was surprising to me. So as I developed the concern and the interest and the skill and the opportunities kept multiplying, I decided one weekend that this was it. I had to go talk to my dad. I talked to him about it. So I took the train and traveled 100 some miles and then caught a van from their home. I sat down with my dad, who was a very saintly, godly, almost mystical man and told him my story. I expected him to jump up and be very excited about it. But he didn't seem to be. He said, "Son, are you sure this is what you want to do?" I said, "I don't know, this is why I am here." He said, "Well, I'll give you the advice somebody else gave a young man one time; I'm going to give it to you." I said, "What is it?" "Stay out of the ministry until you can stay out no longer." I thought, "Thank you, very much. That's an awful lot of help for somebody who is trying to find himself." He said, "Really, I'm serious about that. I don't want you making any game of the ministry. I don't want you to enter on any emotional basis. I don't want you to enter because I'm a preacher. I don't want you to follow in my steps." He said, "I want you to enter the ministry when you feel a sense of calling that you cannot resist." He said, "If you can resist it, stay out." I said, "Okay, but how will I know if I have a calling that I cannot resist?" He says, "You will have so strong a desire and a hunger that you will not even do anything else and be happy and satisfied." I said, "Oh, thank you."

So I went and talked to my aunt about it. She laughed me

Nobody with Your Color Eyes Can Be a Preacher

to scorn. She said, "You've got to be kidding." She said two things: "Nobody with your color eyes can be a preacher. That would turn off anybody. Your eyes would turn off anybody. You will have the girls thinking about something else and not the ministry." This is my aunt telling me this. "Secondly, you laugh and act like a jackass. You're always laughing. Preachers are very serious people. So on those two notes alone, I would cancel you out." I thought, "Boy, I'm getting a lot of strokes here at home among my people."

I went back to Kingston, and maybe I was just sentimental, silly, foolish; and I went back to my job. But I tell you the honest truth, there were young men there who were so happy about their jobs and so excited on pay day and I had none of that joy. One weekend when I got my pay, I took it home to pay my sister for her board and lodging. I told her what was happening to me. She said, "Why don't you just listen if the Lord is talking to you." I said, "This is what I'm going to pay you." She said, "You don't look happy." I told her I was very miserable. She asked why and I told her. She said, "Well, you know it is very obvious that God is calling you to the ministry. Why don't you just say 'yes' and just do it and stop being miserable?" So I did what my dad had told me and what my aunt had told me. Go in, talk to the people in school. We had a theological school there in Jamaica. It was the Bible College. I went to talk to the president of the Bible College, and he just quickly asked me how old I was. I told him seventeen. He said, "Oh, no, you're just a boy. You're too young. You usually don't know what you want to do with your life yet." He said, "Go on and work a little bit more, and maybe you may want to do a general education course some place. Then you may want to see what you want to do."

So I went back to my job, and the more I worked there, the more miserable I got. One day when I got my paycheck, I just wrote a resignation and handed it to the supervisor. He said, "What is this all about?" "I am resigning." "What are you going to do?" "I think I am going to go into the ministry. " "What ministry?" "The preaching ministry." "What church?" I told him. He said, "You've got to be crazy. Those people don't pay preachers, they starve." I said, "I know that, my father was one." "And you still want to do that?" "Well, I want to do whatever God wants me to do." He said, "My son," and he opened his desk, "this has just come to my desk—my endorsement for your promotion." "You have a future with the government. Out of all the youngsters around here, you have been singled out for promotion, and that's just another step. In a few years from now you'll be laughing. "Don't throw this away." He said, "I'm a Christian, too; I believe in God. You'll be as good a Christian as anyone, but don't throw away your job. Preachers are starving and leaving the ministry because of it." I said, "Well." He said, "No, take it back—take back your resignation. Don't quit. Keep it and if later on you want to, bring it back then." "No, sir, I want to take it now." "Where are you going?" "I don't know, but I want to give my resignation now."

So I gave him my resignation, and then he called for me in the next week or so, and he told me how silly I was, you know, and all that and that I would be back. My job would still be there when I came back. I should feel free to come and see him. So I went back to the school and tried to apply again, and they gave me the same pitch that I was too young. Anyway, I sat there and I pleaded with them, and I prayed, and I pushed myself until they finally decided to take me on probation the next January. So I had a few weeks that I was footloose and fancy free.

Then I went into training for four years—four long, tedious years. Many times during those four years I had second thoughts, by the way, as to whether I should have gone back to my job, because I wasn't awfully turned on by all the courses that were being offered. In these Bible colleges you learned more about the Bible than the Bible itself; you know what I mean? You learned all this criticism and stuff, and I began to get very discouraged with that, and I told my preacher friends; and they said, "Oh, that's only a state. You'll pass it." But I began to get interested. They sent me to the Baptist school where I got my first instructions in New Testament Greek, and that turned me on. I got really turned on by New Testament Greek, and a new world had opened up to me in the New Testament. So, I spent four years there.

Well, towards the end of the third year, I left school because my father was ill, and I went home to be his helper. So they would send me the courses, and I would come back and take the exams and study and take exams and so on. Did that right until my mother died; went to help my father and my mother died. I remember the last thing she said to me. She said, "Son, God had his hand on you. Never let God down." And I promised her I wouldn't. And then she said a funny thing next. She said, "Wear a hat." I looked over at her, I'm roaring; I didn't wear hats.

So my mother died. I went to try to find hats to wear to keep my mother's request and to keep true to the Lord.

So I did that and went back to school and finished, graduated and came out of that institution, felt I was well trained to enter the ministry. I couldn't find a church; nobody wanted me. Of course, as the man had told me before, I was too young. I was twenty-one years of age when I graduated, and nobody wanted a twenty-one year-old pastor. Those were not days when you had pastors and associate pastors and assistant pastors; you just had a pastor. So they wanted me to preach, but they didn't want me to pastor. I traveled around for six months in Jamaica, preaching up the mountains and down the valleys, and walking through the rivers and so on and getting no stipend and getting yams and potatoes as my reward for preaching, and bringing the yams and potatoes home to my sister, and my sister saying, "Well, for God's sake, preach all you want, but bring no more yams, no potatoes here."

That was how that went, and I did that. I pastored in Jamaica for a few years. It so happened, eventually I got the largest congregation, largest Church of God congregation in the country. I was over twenty-one years of age, bit off more than I could chew, felt very cocky and confident I could do it. I had been ready to change the world upside down, and after three years or so felt totally frustrated and decided I made a mistake—that I should not have been a minister at all. So I resigned my congregation, much to the chagrin of most of my friends and last time, of my father, by the way. My father who had retired and had come to live with me as pastor. He lived with me at the parsonage. I was ordained by him who was a member of the committee of seven; I think it was. They ordained me on Sunday, April 20, 1952. Little did I know that that was the last time my father would appear in public. Having laid hands on me that evening, he went home to the parsonage which was right across the street, took ill, and the next Sunday evening, the 27th of April at the same time he ordained me, he died.

I want you to know, when he died, that was like closing the chapter for me; because I was a young fellow, single. I was in this huge church, but I had my dad for my backup. If I couldn't solve a problem, the senior elder was right there with me. If I had a question, I could go to him, I could send people to him. He up and died, and I thought it was very unfair of the Lord to do that, to take my resource away. So I resigned from the church right after that or a few months later. Oh, I had some real problems of my own, and I resigned. I went to England and decided I would get some education. The first four years, perhaps, were not sufficient to qualify me. That's why I got frustrated, I thought.

I went to London, and I registered at London University for a while and began to do some work there and began to do some work by correspondence also from Woodsy Hall (as they called it then), attached to Cambridge. I had an exhilarating academic experience. But beyond that, the main thing was that I had an opportunity to hear what I call the world's best preachers, and to me that's when my ministry took shape. I heard Jones, who was still in my mind the world's best expositor. I got the tail-end of W. E. Sangster's ministry. I didn't like it. I thought that Sangster was a much better writer than a preacher. By the time I heard him, he was telling funny stories in the pulpit and making people laugh; and I thought that was a clownish thing to do. But I was glad that I got him at the tail-end of his ministry. His books were much better than his sermon, by the way. But he was good to hear.

I also got to hear Leslie Weatherhead. That was an exhilarating experience. I would hear him when I was in a certain frame of mind. I would go to City Temple and hear Leslie Weatherhead preach. You know, he had this big clinic, psychological clinic, attached to his church and he'd pull out a case from his clinic. I'd never heard any human being do a prayer like he did—never in my life. It was a pilgrimage to just follow him in his prayer group. Of course, to hear him expound the scriptures, the theological plus, the psychological insights and with his particular clinical healing, was a mind-boggling experience.

I had a chance to hear Graham Scroggie at the end of his career. I heard the best sermon I've ever heard of a prodigal son preached by Graham Scroggie when he was too old to stand up; and he sat down in the pulpit and preached the most moving and eloquent, impacting sermon I've ever heard–the "Sermon of the Mount." Then at that time, Steve Malford was then at Richmond, London—somewhere outside of London—and his Sunday healing services had grown so much as to have been taken as theater, and I would go up there some Sunday evenings and hear him. I don't know of anybody who could expound a passage like he can.

So I claimed that no school in London or here or anywhere did for me what those experiences did, those exposures did. That was where, I think, I reclaimed my call or my call reclaimed me. I don't know which one of us grabbed each other. I had to work a job in England to earn my way through, and I worked. Suddenly, a friend in Toledo invited me to come to America to preach for him. That was what I did. While I was in England, the Baptist Society of London, for some reason, somebody heard I was there and sent me a preaching itinerary. So I was stomping for the Baptists every weekend all across the country. The only thing was, they didn't promote me correctly. And most places I went were shocked because they thought I was an Englishman returning as a missionary from Jamaica, and they couldn't understand where I came from. But my call, I think, was reclaimed and refurbished there.

By the time I came to America, I was sort of back on track. I must say this one thing. I had decided, when I went to England, not to go into ministry, to go into medicine. I said I would go into medicine, and then I would be a good Christian doctor. Because I had put on my high school—formally, I applied. What do you want to be? I put "a missionary doctor." So I thought it was my chance to do that, and I applied to some medical school in London and got accepted. I was going to start there when a friend from America, who was a radio broadcast speaker, appeared at my door in 1954 or '55, and he said, "Sam, I hear that you are changing tracks, changing occupations." By the way, he was one of those who laid hands on me in Jamaica at the ordination. He said, "That's not what you said when we ordained you in Jamaica." I said, "Yes, that was then, but things have changed." He said, "Well, I just came to you for one reason. The Lord just sent me to you for one reason." I said, "For what?" He said, "A message for you." "What is the message?" "Very simple. The Lord told me to tell you that the calling of God is without repentance." "You're quoting the scripture." "Yes." "Well, explain that to me. I don't know what that means." "Yes, you do." "No, what does it mean?" "Sam, the Lord did not tell me to explain it to you. He just told me to give it to you. If you want an explanation, go to the morgue!" "Thank you, very much, Doctor." And that was the end of his conversation with me.

That, I think, is what really bugged me back into track: "The calling of God is without repentance." So I went and researched that scripture myself and gave up and decided that

God had not changed his mind about my calling even if I was trying to change my mind. So it was that I should get back and do what the Lord had told me to do. That's why I accepted the invitation to go to the United States and preach. That was it. Once I did that, I had bitten on the bait, and I couldn't get unhooked after that. I have been going like blazes ever since. I have been to Jamaica; I have preached in Detroit, pastored in Detroit. Massey and I did a flip for about three years, three or four years. He went to Jamaica, the same school as I had been trained in; he took over the presidency of that school. I went to Detroit and pastored his church while he was there, and he pastored my local congregation while he was president of the school. That was from '63 to '67. Then I went back to Jamaica (thought I was finished with that), and the Washington church called me, here. And I've been in Washington since 1969. So, in the rough, that's the story.

Jim Holly
Detroit, Michigan

The Reverend Dr. Jim Holly was born in Philadelphia, Pennsylvania, on December 5, 1943, called in 1949-50 and ordained a Baptist minister. He received a BS and MS from Tennessee State University and a PhD from Wayne State University. He pastors the Little Rock Baptist Church in Detroit. Interview recorded in April, 1989.

35

"The Calling Came as a Fact That I Was Raised by God"

You know, the thing about it is—first of all, I was called into the ministry not so much by loud noises, I guess, or even a strong inspiration. When I was growing up as a kid, I had always worked in the church. We were very poor in West Virginia: we only had one church, one store, one school. And so, I guess, the church was sort of like an option, in terms of just being in the house. It was sort of localized. I always enjoyed it.

When I got into my teens and went to high school, I still worked in the church constantly. It always had a tremendous influence on my life. It just seemed like it was mandatory to go. Not until my junior year in college did I really feel a call. I went to the pastor, and I told him, "I just feel like I am supposed to preach." Of course, in those days, when you talked about being called into the ministry, if they did not see it, you didn't have it. You almost had to prove it. I really didn't know what to do. The guy was A.M. Walker, who was my pastor at Mt. Nebo Baptist Church, in a little place called Mount Pleasant, Tennessee, a population of maybe sixty thousand people. Very small church, but a very spiritual and meaningful church. I was always impressed with him. Someone was always writing a speech for me to say on men's day or Christmas or Easter. Someone was always doing something, and whenever they would do it for me to say, it was a key. As a young man, I always seemed to put a little extra in it, I guess.

When I got to my junior year in college, I just felt a tremendous need that I would not be satisfied doing anything else but preaching. It is something I really can't explain. I wanted to be a lawyer; I was going to Howard University Law School. That was my intention; I was majoring in pre-law. I guess, to sort of give God's stamp of approval on it or to substantiate the call, it was that every door was closed.

When I finished college, I finished with a 3.5 average. I was an excellent student teacher, which means any school should have recruited me. I had credentials to go to Howard, but I didn't have any money. There was no scholarship money for anything. The only door that was open was a scholarship to the University of Chicago for seminary. That was the only door—every [other] door closed.

So, really, I guess, what I am saying is that God had directed my life, all of my life. I did not grow up with parents; I grew up with an elderly lady that was my grandmother. So all of my life the direction was very clear. Doors closed, a door opened. It was like that all my life. Getting into the ministry was no different. It was basically no different. There is an open and shut case, so to speak. I did not, like some people say, wake up in the middle of the night and hear a voice or anything; it was just a strong urge. It was an unction that "If I didn't do it, I would not be satisfied as a person." It is true, because I have done other things. I have been vice-president of college, I have taught school. I have done so many things, but when I felt like there was an interference between that and my ministry, I have always put it out.

I don't know if that answers or explains it, because I don't even think about it that much anymore as I did when someone would ask, How did you get into the ministry? The calling came as a fact that I was raised by God. I was not raised by parents. I did not have a grandmother that was very active or very strong church lady. So God became a very real person to me. He was not someone way out somewhere. He was a real person. For example, when I wanted to do things, I would ask God, because I didn't have a father. And it would come to fruition. I wanted a job—I remember very clearly—I was nine years old. It was a job I wanted, and I got that job at nine—janitoring the school that I went to. It was a one-room school, one teacher, six grades, one classroom, potbelly stove concept. That's the only way I can explain it. I never thought about it; I really thought I had something really significant to say until I started talking about it.

Susan Newman Hopkins
New York, New York

The Reverend Susan Newman Hopkins was born in Washington, DC, June 14, 1957, called in 1976 and ordained a Baptist minister in 1983. She has a BA from George Washington University (DC) and a Master of Divinity degree from Howard University's Divinity School. She is the Co-ordinator for Church-College Relations in the United Church of Christ. Interview recorded August 14, 1989.

36
"Who in the World Would Marry a Woman Preacher?"

My full name is Susan Mary Delora Newman Hopkins, but I just dropped all that when I got married—I couldn't sign all of that. I'm thirty-two years old, and I accepted the call to the ministry Palm Sunday, 1976. I'm a native of Washington, DC, and I grew up there. When I was thirteen, I made the conscious effort, accepted Christ as my Saviour, and was baptized and joined the church.

Shortly after that, really about two or three years after that, I told my pastor one Sunday that I wanted to be the speaker for youth Sunday. Every third Sunday was youth Sunday, and our pastor never liked to preach, anyway. He used to let the choir sing. For the hymnal preparation he would say, "Well, we will have a sermon and song," and he'd sit down and not preach. So it was youth Sunday coming up, and I told him that I had something, a message that the Lord had given me that I wanted to give on youth Sunday. I was president of the youth council, youth ushers, youth choir, and all-around member of my church, so he said, "Well, Susan, you haven't said that God called you, so I want you to write your speech out and read it." So the next Sunday, I did.

I remember it was from the Gospel of Matthew, part of Jesus' Sermon on the Mount, where it said at the end, "Be perfect as your Heavenly Father is perfect." My title was "Be Like Your

Heavenly Father." I was about fifteen at the time, and when I finished, deacons came and shook my hand. They said, "Girl, you preach better than the pastor." That was my last Sunday at that church. I grew up in that church since I was two years old, and I was baptized there, but I was saved in the preaching of a visiting evangelist, a woman who came to do a revival that week. Nothing the pastor ever said, ever moved me. It was my Sunday school teacher, Miss Powell, who I had from youth, who was my nurturer biblically. I wanted to start a Bible class at that church. The pastor didn't want it. He said people didn't want to come out during the week and blah, blah, blah. So I just went on to another church, and I joined Mt. Sinai Baptist Church in November of '75, and Reverend David Derm was the pastor—great preacher, great Bible teacher.

I was sitting in his Bible class, and Reverend Derm would quote a scripture, name a text and ask for someone to get it. The first one who got it was supposed to read it. Well, every time he would say, "Someone get me Matthew 5:29 through 50," or whatever, I would know most of the Bible by heart, and I would just start reciting what it is, and everybody kept looking—Reverend Derm kept looking—and so they started calling me the "living Bible." The pastor would be preaching Sunday morning, and he would say, "Susan, what does it say, Second Timothy 3:39?" I'm sitting in the front row of church, and I would quote it up to him, and he'd say, "That's what I'm talking about," and he'd go on and preach.

So that was fall of '75, spring of '76, and all I was, was an undergraduate at college at George Washington University in Washington. I had a double major in speech communication and broadcasting, and I was going to have a career in journalism. I sang with the James Cleveland Gospel Music Workshop Choir of America, the DC Chapter, and I was in a Bible class every Thursday night taught by the same evangelist who preached the night that I got saved. She was a member of the Workshop Choir working at Mt. Sinai.

Reverend Derm started doing revivals a lot the spring of '76, and whenever he had to be away, he would ask me to teach his Bible class. The Wednesday night Bible class had about 200 people in it. As time went on, the group I sang with, a small group named Exodus I, we had to sing at a little storefront church on George Avenue, NW. I had never been there before. We sang, about eight of us. My friends had been telling me, "You know, I think God's calling you to preach." Family, people had been saying that. I said, "God didn't call me to do nothing." I would almost get belligerent about it. I taught a Bible class at George Washington University every week; I even got an award. I got the GW Outstanding Contribution Award for teaching my Bible class, and they gave it to me at the graduation in '77. I was the only person to walk up on the stage with the president. People conferred their degrees from their seats, but they gave me an award for teaching my Bible class. So all this was behind me, the nudges.

So this Sunday night, Palm Sunday night, sitting in the back of this storefront church, this guest preacher was up there preaching, and his text was from Galatians, talking about "Redeeming the time wisely, knowing that the will of God is for you." And like any other good Christian, I'm sitting there waiting to be fed from the word; and he said, "God has called many of us to do things, and we refuse to accept God's instructions for our lives." So I got a little antsy. My friends were looking down the pew at me. I turned my back to them so they couldn't see me. And you know how you listen to a sermon and you're thinking in your mind how this applies to you? And I thought to myself, "Well, I know this is not about the calling to preach, because I know God hasn't called me to do that. I'm too young for that." I think I was about eighteen at the time. As soon as I thought that, the preacher said, "You know, it doesn't matter how young you are, God has something for your life whatever it is. I was in Texas and a little seven-year-old boy was preaching a revival, thousand of souls came to Jesus." I thought then, "Well, fine, that's good for that little boy, but I don't know that much about the Bible. I know enough to teach it, but I could never call myself a preacher." And the man said, "If you don't know the word of God, the Holy Spirit will teach you." It was back and forth. And I'm sitting there thinking, "Well, that's fine, but I'm not sure about this thing about women being ministers. I don't know but one or two. And he said, "If you're a woman, God can use you. The first one who ran to tell the Easter Sunday morning message was Mary Magdalene."

By the time this brother got finished preaching this sermon, I was crying; I was almost on the floor. I was just, "All right, Lord. All right, Lord." So that was Palm Sunday, and that whole week I thought I had the Lord fixed then, because I said, "That's all well and good, but I cannot be disobedient to my parents." And my father was dead by this time, and it was just my mother, and I'm the baby—there's my older sister and myself and I'm the only one at home. I said, "No way my mama's gonna let me be out in the street at night preaching revivals and running around like a preacher." So I said, "Okay, I'm eighteen years old, living at home. Lord, if my mother says it's all right, then I'll do it." So I just waited and said, "Lord, you let me know the opportune time to ask her."

Somewhere during that week, I was looking at movies—you know how during Holy Week they show all these religious movies. I was looking at some story about Esther, and when it went off, the Holy Spirit said, "Now." I said, "Lord, it's two o'clock in the morning. You don't wake my mother after ten o'clock for anything. She'll be angry, and something like this—no way!" The Lord said, "Now." So I went in the other room, I woke Mom up, and I said, "Mom, I have something I want to tell you. Do not interrupt me until I finish." I took a deep breath, and I just spilled it all out, the whole thing, that the Lord had called me to preach and I felt very strongly that this is what God wanted me to do. She didn't interrupt me. When I finished, I looked at her and she had tears in her eyes, and she said, "Baby, I'll be praying for you. I'm so happy." I said, "That's not fair, God! You were supposed to use my mother to say no!" I was looking for a way out.

And then I just kind of argued. I said, "Well, Lord, who in the world would marry a woman preacher?" All I wanted to do was graduate. When I graduated from high school, I just wanted to get married, have children—2.2 children. I love ironing men's shirts; it's a challenge for me to get all those cat whiskers out. I wanted to be a homebody, maybe a wife with some Christian magazine as a journalist or something. But I didn't have a boyfriend; I had all these scholarships for college. I was the valedictorian in my high school, so I went to college. I thought, well, I'll meet somebody in college.

So here I am in college, accepting the call to ministry. I still didn't have a boyfriend, so I said, "Okay." The Lord said, "I have somebody for you. You just go preach." The Saturday before Easter Sunday, I called pastor and I said, "I need to talk to you." He said, "Well, we're here running around getting ready for Easter Sunday service. Come see me." I walked in his office and said, "Reverend Derm, the Lord has called me to preach and I've accepted the call." He said, "Susan, is that all you're bothering me about? I knew that the first day I saw you. Everybody knows it but you. It's been written all over you. We'll be working with you and praying with you, and I'm really happy. We'll set a date for your trial sermon."

That was Easter Sunday, and somebody was before me. Another guy had already come in before me, so I preached my trial sermon September 5, 1976. Being in Washington, DC, it's the most backwards city, I think, next to the State of Texas when it comes to women in ministry. In the Baptist Ministers Conference, you can be excommunicated from the conference if you ordain a woman or anything like that. It's all right to license us, just don't ordain us, you see.

So, according to the rules, you have to have two-thirds vote of the members present at a business meeting after your trial sermon. Well, my trial sermon, the church was packed. I remember, when I finished preaching, pastor was just supposed to do the benediction, and they were going to have the church meeting during the week. Pastor stood up and he said, "I'm ready to take the vote now. All those in favor? I have a motion." Deacon moved it, and it was seconded, and it was a 100 percent unanimous vote that I showed gifts that God had called me to preach, and they licensed me. That was when I was licensed, September sixth. But, unfortunately, my pastor, I guess, his hope was that I would just be satisfied with leading worship on women's day and maybe preaching eight o'clock service twice a year—hoping that God really was not calling me to the ministry, but had some evangelistic fire in me or something.

When I went to seminary and I had to do field education, I had to be at a church where I could participate in leading worship and different areas of ministry from the pulpit on Sunday morning. Women were not in our pulpit unless it was women's day, and that's only if you were asked. I remember when women's day rolled around. We had fourteen ministers on staff, and when the ministers met we had our time to air our grievances about things. I asked the pastor what direction were the role of the sisters in the ministry going, because by this time there were three of us. After me, there was one woman who was older licensed as a preacher, but they just called her deaconess, and she just served as a deaconess. She never preached or anything until I came. He said, "Well, what do you mean?" I said, "Well, for instance, communion Sunday, all the ministers go around at the three o'clock communion service and give the right hand of fellowship to the new members. The women sit back in the congregation, and the men go in the pulpit. The men sit behind the communion table; the men assist you." And there were three of the brothers up there who had just graduated from high school, were thinking about going to college and were thinking about going to seminary—the three of them had been in my Bible class for two years, you see. The only difference was that I had training, and they were male.

I couldn't understand the difference—why they were up there, and I had to sit in the congregation. He said, "Well, the church is not ready for this," and he went on. Well, women's day rolled around, and they asked me to sit in the pulpit, and I said very nicely, "No, thank you. If I can't sit in the pulpit and lead worship because it's a day the Lord has made, I don't think I should be here just to go in the pulpit once a year." And I was so ungrateful, you see.

We've never really reconciled that, but I had to go on. I mean, I have remained friendly—we've remained friendly. When I got married, he performed my wedding and things like that. But accepting the calling was not something I looked for. I fought it; I ran from it; I offered every kind of excuse. I mean, I was giving tricks: "Lord, do this. Okay, now do this." And every time it would happen. But I wouldn't trade it for anything. I guess, to me, it reminds me so much of when women describe labor when they're having a child. They talk about how the nine months are so uncomfortable, and they're wallowing around, and they're fat and out of shape, and they have morning sickness or evening sickness and then labor. It hurts, and it's so painful; yet and still, they say they wouldn't trade it for this loving child they have. So, for everything that I have gone through, I wouldn't trade it.

I've had friends, colleagues, people to tell me that I'm influenced by the devil, because I accepted the call to the ministry and women aren't supposed to do that. But one of my friends who is a pastor, who is straddling the fence—he's uncertain about women, whether to license or not—I gave him a button that says, "Ordain women or stop baptizing them." Because my feeling is, if you believe that the Holy Spirit and the gospel of Jesus Christ is powerful enough to convert someone's soul, but is not powerful enough to call them into service of that Spirit, there's a problem.

The thing that he doesn't realize is that he preached a sermon one Sunday when I was visiting his church that clinched it for me, that I even stopped arguing about it. I mean, I just go ahead and do my ministry and just let folk catch up. He preached from Mark [where] Jesus said, "My father said if you deny me here, that I will not own you there." And the Lord is the only one I have to answer to. I can see Jesus saying to me—you know when I have to stand before the Lord and answer for the works done in this body, and the Lord says—"Susan, I called you to preach and you became a housemaker. Housemaking is wonderful, but I had something else for you to do. Why didn't you do it?" I said, "Well, Lord, they told me I couldn't because I was a woman." God said, "Don't you know I made you? I knew you were a woman. I knew that when I called you." I said, "Lord, they told me I couldn't do it because I was Black, because I was too young." God said, "I made you Black, I called you at that age, I made you a woman. I needed someone with everything you had." When he preached that, I said, "He doesn't even know he clinched it for me."

Thomas L. Hoyt, Jr.
Hartford, Conneticut

Dr. Thomas L. Hoyt, Jr., was born in Fayette, Alabama, on March 14, 1941, called in 1958 and ordained by the Christian Methodist Episcopal church in 1961. He received a BA from Lane College (Tennessee), an MDiv from the Interdenominational Theological Center (Atlanta), an STM from Union Theological Seminary (New York) and a PhD from Duke University. He is Professor of New Testament at Hartford Seminary. He is a contributor to *Stony the Road We Trod: African American Biblical Interpretation*. He serves on the faith and order commissions of both the World and National Council of Churches (vice-chair of the latter). Interview recorded November 11, 1988.

37

Considered Most Likely to Be Bishop in High School

My call comes out of the context of being born in Alabama, and nurtured in a family in which my father was a minister in the CME church for about forty years. And, in the context of that ministry, I was nurtured in the parsonage. The parsonage spoke to me in terms of a life of discipline and in terms of a life of being with people constantly, and a life of being nurtured in the church, especially with prayer meetings and being involved. Everytime the church door opened, I was there. I was a part of the children's choir and served on the usher board. I recall singing in that Sunbeam Choir so vividly, on Sunday mornings.

But being nurtured in the church, as I was, I have never known any other way of life but church work. Now, that means that the church is very strong in my upbringing and nurturing families. My mother is a very quiet, intuitive person, and having that kind of response to all kinds of situations, she's always a calm, cool, but very caring person. This was in contrast, at some times, to my father, who was very rigid in discipline, and at the same time a person of conviction, especially coming out of the fundamentalist bag at some points. The fundamentalist bag, "This is the way its supposed to be, right and wrong, and you shouldn't deviate from those patterns." That meant you don't go to dances, you don't shoot marbles, you don't even listen to the radio on Sunday or look at the television on Sunday, you don't cook on Sunday, you cook on Saturday nights. Someone said to me, "It's a wonder that you wanted to become a minister after coming out of that kind of context."

My concern was that, at that point, I always felt very close to the church in relationship to that process, even though there [were] some rigidities that I did not like. So the family was very strong for me. The faith aspect was very strong for me. I was converted in terms of making a decision for Christ when I was about eight years old. Now, my conversion experience was not catastrophic in terms of falling on the floor, wailing and all of that. But my conversion experience was something that I remember very well, because this man was preaching at the revival, and I was sitting on the ancient seat of mercy—the mourner's bench. And on the mourner's bench I sat there for about two nights, and they were praying for me. And, one night—I don't know what night it was, I'm not like some of the people who can say, I remember it was on a Thursday evening—I don't know what night it was, but I do know that it was an experience that I will never forget.

I can see myself now sitting on the front seat. The man was preaching about Jesus Christ and the crucifixion, and I was deeply convicted, at that time, to give myself to Christ. I started crying, and I felt this sense of warmth that I could not express. I had never felt that way altogether before, but I had that sense at that point. At the same time, I go back to that event in my life when I go through some difficulties. I return to that event when I begin to question if I am in the right relationship with God. That event always comes back to me. I asked my mother, specifically, about that event, that evening when I got home. I said, "What is that that burns inside? I don't know what it is." She said, "Well, that's always a feeling that you have that maybe reassures you that you are in relationship with God." So then, I got the faith, feeling and family that was very strong in my life.

So, it was a step-by-step process. I went from conversion to working it out in terms of being with my playmates in school and high school. They started calling me preacher, even in school. They started saying, "Rev." I had a teacher in elementary school who would make us wear ties all the time, and I got in a habit of doing that, wearing ties and being very neat. So, when I got to high school I kept wearing ties and people would always say, "Here comes the preacher." I think it became a nurturing process even in the school situation.

When I was seventeen years old, I accepted the call to preach. And I felt that the call to preach, at that point, was something that I had been nurtured in. It was always an urge to deal with freedom and liberation for people. That whole freedom aspect when you talk about the family, the feeling and the faith and understanding of freedom, talk about making people have some sense of justice in relationship to Black people. That has always been a strong urge in me.

I think the urge to help somebody was a part of my call. And the urge to deal with liberation in relationship to our people is the sense of my call. I have never dichotomized between my faith and the call to help people survive in this present time. Those things need to work together. Without the faith, I don't think I would deal with the freedom, and I would not be sustained over the long haul. Even when I was called, I felt that I was called to be a person that dealt with the ecumenical work as well. I even prayed that I would make a contribution in terms of the universal church and be involved in helping churches to come to the reality of working together. And at the same time, helping people to see how churches could be a corporate unity for dealing with liberation and justice issues. I didn't just start with that, because even in my high school career and college, I was involved in some justice issues; and that was working out what I considered to be my call to the ministry.

So, if I had to summarize my call, I would say that, yes, I had an urge to serve, that's the feeling level. I had an urge to deal with liberation of people, and that's a feeling level as well. I had a nurturing family that was full of love and concern, and a father who was a minister, who was a role model at that point. I had a prayer life that kept nurturing me in that faith that I had. I had a loving mother, and that was very helpful to deal with who I am. I had a school system that put me under the purview of people giving my name identity as a minister. Even in high school they said, "You are going to be a bishop." I had an interview in the paper when I was a senior in high school, and they put a robe on me and put it in a cartoon kind of caption with a title that said, "Young man wants to be minister and become bishop." I still have that in my scrapbook, but I was just in high school then.

Those kind of energies are part of the outworking of your call. I don't think I could go on with the call unless I had the sanction of the church itself. That's why I think the ordination is to say that the church recognizes what you have already received. But it gives the opportunity for others to be a witness to your spirit, that you are in the right place. And so that is what I consider the churches role to be in my life in the sense of the call—that is it gives sanction to what I have already felt is an urge in me, and it becomes corporate then. Those are the factors then that I would consider to be a part of my call.

Alvin O'Neil Jackson
Memphis, Tennessee

Reverend Alvin O'Neil Jackson was born in Laurel, Mississippi July 10, 1950, called in 1971 and ordained Disciples of Christ (Christian Church) in 1973. He received the BA degree from Butler University (IN), and the Master of Divinity degree from Duke University. He pastors the Mississippi Boulevard Christian Church in Memphis. This interview was recorded August 14, 1989.

38

Influenced By An Old Testament Professor

I grew up in the Delta of Mississippi, in a small rural community by the name of Indianola and completed my elementary and secondary education there. My folks became members of the Disciples of Christ. They were raised in the Baptist church, but they went to one of the small mission schools in southern Mississippi that was sponsored by the Disciples of Christ. They went to high school and college there. That began their affiliation with the Disciples of Christ. So I grew up in the Disciples of Christ. Of course, it's a predominantly White denomination—about 1.2 million and only about 40,000 blacks.

Growing up in it, I was active in the church there in Indianola with the youth group. We only had church one Sunday out of the month. Our pastoral day was on the third Sunday of each month. So on the other Sundays I would visit. The first Sunday I would go to the Baptist church, second Sunday to the Methodist church and fourth Sunday the Sanctified church—Church of God in Christ.

During my high school days ministry was the farthest thing from my mind. Although I was active in the church, I thought I wanted to go into law. I was moving in that direction even my first year in college That was during the time of the Civil

Rights Movement, the freedom rides and all that in Mississippi. I wanted to go off and go into law and come back; and a couple of us was going to come back and turn Mississippi around. At the time, I thought I wanted to get as far away from that climate in Mississippi. as I could get. So I went to a small school in southern California; it was one of our Church's schools, Chatman college.

I got out there, and all of my course work the first couple of years was moving toward a career in law. But I took an Old Testament class that was taught by a man named Willis Fisher who had cancer in the throat. He was retired and about 70 years old. He was teaching Old Testament, and I took the introductory course to Old Testament and was really impressed. That was my first exposure to any structured Bible study. I took that class and took another one the next semester on the eight century prophets. And in dealing with the call of those prophets–Jeremiah, Amos, and Hosea–getting into their call as prophets really started me to thinking about ministry.

Dr. Fisher's life was key. Because, my whole exposure to ministry had been my pastor there in Indianola who I only saw one Sunday out of the month, and the other ministers who also were circuit preachers who would come a Sunday or two out of the month. I would go to hear these other preachers preach, although I was not required to go; but there was something about it that was really fascinating to me. But, as I spent time with Dr. Fisher–I took every class he taught I just felt God leading–me in the direction of ministry. I started my junior year taking more and more religion classes; and finally my second semester of my junior year I acknowledged my call to ministry. That was in 1971 that I acknowleged the call. I started later that year working with a congregation up in Los Angeles. (Chatman college was in Orange County about 40 miles south of L.A.). So I started working with their youth group. I started doing youth ministries. As I got into it, there was all kinds of confirmation along the way that ministry was where the Lord was leading me. There was not a dramatic moment that I can point to, but it was just a growing awareness, a growing consciousness that that was what the Lord was calling me to do. I acknowledged the call my second semester in 1971. And it was not until 1973 that I was ordained to ministry. I had completed college, and I went and accepted a church in Roanoke, Virginia; I was ordained in October, 1973.

"One day while in the field plowing I heard a voice. I jumped because I thought it was my master coming to scold and whip me for plowing up some more corn. I looked but saw no one. Again the voice called, 'Morte! Morte!' With this I stopped, dropped the plow, and started running, but the voice kept on speaking to me... You are a chosen vessel unto the Lord. Be upright before me, and I will guide you unto all truth. My grace is sufficient for you. Go, and I am with you. Preach the gospel, and I will preach with you. You are henceforth the salt of the earth."

I am blessed but you are damned,
in Clifton H. Johnson, ed.,
God Struck Me Dead: Religious Conversion Experiences and Autobiographies of Ex-slaves
(Philadelphia: Pilgrim Press, 1969): 15.

Joseph Harrison Jackson
Chicago, Illinois

Reverend Joseph Harrison Jackson was born in Rudyard, Mississippi at the close of the 19th century, called at the turn of the century when he was eight years old and ordained Baptist sometime later in Jackson, Miss. He received the BA degree from Jackson State University and the MA from Creighton University. Until his recent death, he pastored the Olivet Baptist Church in Chicago. Considered by some to be the most dominant president of the National Baptist Convention, U. S. A., Inc.; he held that position for the longest period of time in the organization's history–1953-1982. This interview was recorded December 6, 1989.

39

The Most Dominant President of a Baptist Convention in the 20th Century

My belief in God as an object, a creator, a redeemer and a director of human life came to my attention as a child. Listening to the voices of preachers and their preachings I knew that they were not learned men, but they were men and women with a certainty that God existed and that He was in communication with all mankind. He had included me as one of the persons to be trained, to be used and to be redeemed as one of the sons of God, to tell the outside world what God, the Father, had entrusted to me. I have gone through life believing in this reality–believing in this creator and this redeemer and believing that, in him and through him, life and the souls of men are saved.

By his authority and his mercy I was redeemed and

selected to be one of his servants. I came to this conviction of reality believing that he was and is as a rock of my being and as a Savior of my soul. I received from Him a church, a certainty, a belief, a message that directed me to rise from my weakness, in view of my strengths, in my life to God. God was in reach. God was consecrated; and God was moved to inspire my life, my mind, my body, my soul. And the call of God to me through Jesus Christ was a message and a directive for me to come closer to Him to serve Him as His messenger, as my Savior.

Through the years of light and darkness, through peace and storm this high power and all the forces of righteousness have never deserted me. I come to this hour believing and blessed with a certainty of his presence and of his willingness to pardon my sins and to forgive the sins of all mankind who listen to him. My call as a preacher then was a certainty, but I had to place it in the Man of salvation and I have privy for my own communion. It was this certainty and his presence and the glory of his cleansing that made of me a living servant of His, but as a man, it was me until this hour.

I don't recall, with exactness, my age at the time I was called. All I know is I had an awareness and a certainty of a plan that was greater than myself. I was more than 8 years old, however, when that certainty came, when I was able to listen to Bible stories and religious talk from my mother and father. This was part of a nurturing process, because my encounters with God came to me through parents, preachers, deacons and other Christian leaders. After the revival meeting in a little country church called Little Hope Baptist Church in Mississippi. And my accepting the challenge or the calling to pastor following this. I became keenly aware of the fact that I had been selected by the spirit of God as one of those to be witnesses of Him and be a preacher of his gospel. I was preaching long before I was certified by my church.

Suzan D. Johnson
New York, New York

Reverend Suzan D. Johnson was born in New York City January 28, 1957, called in 1970 and ordained Baptist in 1982. She received the BS degree from Emerson College (Boston), the MA degree from Columbia Teacher's College, the Master of Divinity degree from Union Theological Seminary and the Doctor of Ministry degree from United Theological Seminary (Dayton). She pastors the Mariner's Temple Baptist Church in Manhattan. She is the author of *Wise Women Bearing Gifts* (Judson, 1988). This interview was recorded August 14, 1989.

40

When God Spoke in a New York Traffic Jam

I was called to the ministry at an early age. I sensed it around the age of 13. My mother is Presbyterian, my father is Baptist, and as most children, we went to church more with my mother. So we were raised Presbyterian and confirmed in that faith. But we also walked to the non-black church, my father's church, when we finished. Two Presbyterian services, two Sunday schools, and then we'd walk up to a Baptist church to meet my father. So the church — I either had to love it or deny it. I chose the first. In that Presbyterian church I was always very attracted to the minister, and then, in terms of the role of the minister, in terms of leadership. And around 16, I began doing some things in the church in terms of the youth department, planning youth services. I played the piano. I was always the one people gravitated towards. Around 13 we used to spend summers (before we started work) working a job with my grandmother(my maternal grandmother in Concord, North

Carolina). Around the age of 11, 12, 13, somewhere in there, I met Dr. Katie Kennedy who was the first woman ordained in the Presbyterian church. She was from Cannopolis which was the neighboring town. Both towns, I think, had more than 20,000 residents. But, she had already entered the ministry. She was maybe 6 or 7 years my senior. So she was my first role model of a woman in ministry. Although I never really talked about it very much, I hinted at it here and there. And so I went to college in Boston, Emerson College, in 1974. I transferred there from Fisk. At Emerson I was introduced to the St. Paul AME church which is in Cambridge, Massachusetts, where I'm ending up going back to now. It was there that I met Reverend John Bryant and Cecelia Bryant and that was the first time in my life that I saw black women active in the leadership of a church. Because there were many called women in that congregation. And so I was still in the choir, and I still did not publicly talk about a call. I was very vividly dealing with it. I remember writing letters to my friends in the summer saying that I was thinking about going to seminary after college, and trying to get a reaction from people in terms of how they would feel about that, because we were certainly black social middle class. Even though the church was something everybody in our circle did, nobody in our circle was a minister. So I was trying to get a reaction. Everybody was planning for their children to become doctors, lawyers and Indian chiefs. I was trying to feel people out. But I knew, very clearly, that God was dealing with my life; and I didn't know how to express that publicly. I certainly had no support base for it in New York City, because nobody talked about it.

    I entered a career of communications. I was a TV producer, which was what I prepared for in college; and I was very successful. I was up and down the East Coast. Every nine or ten months or so I got the itch to move, because I was never satisfied in those markets. When I landed in Washington in 1987 with my first full-time TV job, I started taking courses at Howard Divinity School while working. And again, I still had not publicly expressed a call, but was really trying to: Number 1–See if God was really moving on my life to be a leader in a church, or if it was just something I just had a real zeal for the Lord, and maybe would be a good committed Christian.

    I moved a couple of other times until I was back in Boston and then to Miami. Finally in Miami, I was so unfulfilled even though, I was making, perhaps, top dollar in terms of what–

producers make in the country. I was in demand, because there were very few black producers. I could really write my ticket to any market. I wrestled just about every day about what God would have me to do in this life. I was clear that working at that TV station every day, where others made the decisions on my life and where there was clearly a white male-dominated network, was not the answer—not for me, anyways. Some do very well in that.

I just packed up. I did not have a job, and I said this is not it. I had an insatiable desire to do more for the Lord. I was always attracted to black concerns and Christian concerns. That was just kind of the theme of my life.

I came back and got a job at Bronx Lebanon Hospital as a public relations spokesperson, back in New York City. I entered Union Seminary, full-time, while I was doing this job full-time. In my second year, I'll never forget the day—I hope I won't—I had a final exam with James Forbes, who was my preaching instructor. At the same time it was a day that a major story broke at the hospital, and being the spokesperson, I was supposed to be the one that not only contacted the media, but also made remarks on behalf of the hospital. I was caught in a traffic jam, and I couldn't get to either one. I was stuck. It was about five minutes from my house, five minutes for the hospital, ten minutes from school, and I was literally stuck. It was at that point that it was, as though the Lord said to me, "Make your choice. You know which one you're going to do." I was trying to do the communications piece and the church piece, back and forth; It was like, "Make your choice."

In that frustrating moment, when traffic finally broke and I had not gotten to the hospital, I stopped and pulled over at a telephone and asked my secretary to let them know I could not make it. I would explain later, but I couldn't get there. I literally couldn't. Then I prayed on it that night. I wrote my letter of resignation the next day. I remember my blood pressure was just high; I just hated the feeling that I had. I was so frustrated. I wrote my letter of resignation that I had made my choice to enter seminary full-time and not work any longer; and that I would be leaving the hospital. Of course, family and close friends, although they knew the Lord had a call and was working on my life, they thought I was crazy; because I was giving up a very lucrative, very stable, very visible kind of position. They said, "Are you sure?" I stepped out totally on faith; I mean I had no job. But it was my last year at seminary, and I started working in the American Baptist Church's office of Metropolitan New York. And in that setting I met every preacher in New York and I started filling in for them for vacation relief and preaching and those kinds of things. Three months before I graduated from seminary, the church where I'm at called me as a seminarian with no experience. I realized, totally, that God's hand was on my life. Everything that I thought was lucrative before, God restored to me—the kind of living I desired. He's given me, for the first time in my life, the fulfillment that I've been searching for.

When I got to Mariner's Temple, the answer was clear. At that time the church was $6,000 in debt. They couldn't afford to pay me; they wrote the checks but I couldn't cash them. So there was no money; but I saw the challenge, the mission. There were fifteen people in a sanctuary that holds about 1000. The church was slated to be closed. That was the plan. I was sent there sort of as the one to give the final benediction. We gave this woman a chance; we gave her a church and then it closed.

The Lord had another plan, and it totally reverted. From day one the church grew. I remember the feeling, even with the lack of funds and even with the lack of numbers and even with all this empty space to fill, for the first time I felt the marriage of work—heaven and earth were connecting. My life and God's were mixing. Everything that I had done in my life prior to that prepared me for this ministry. I'm in a multi-ethnic setting. I'm in New York City, a female, at a time that's breaking some barriers. And all of the things that I had done were breaking barriers, whether that was ethnically, racially, class-wise; everything I had done in terms of studying abroad was that multi-ethnic preparation I needed. Everything that I had done in terms of communication skills prepared me for the times of visibility the church was going to have.

So, when you realize it, I think that even when you can't articulate what the call is—because it's something that you're going through, you really don't know. When you try to communicate what that is—that you've had glimpses of it all your life, but you didn't know where that was leading until you got to the point that you really said, yes—then it all makes sense.

I think that there's a period when you get one answer, but I think the call even continues after you say "Yes." I believe once you're faithful and you're committed and you're totally in God's light and will, that there are new callings and new charges and new missions and new planes that you get to go to. You don't always know where that is. You sense the change, like this is the period in my life very much that I know a change is happening. I don't know where I'm going. Harvard is one of the answers. I wrestled for a year before this offer came to me, but I knew something different was going to happen in my ministry. But where that's going to take me and why in this time, I don't know. I know on the other side of it God's got an answer that will make it all clear to me.

I think that there's a call, and then there's more calling, if you're really in God's will. You wrestle at various stages. There are moments of comfort, and you say, "I'm in the right place at the right time, and I know what I'm doing." There are moments of total discomfort, where you're saying, "God's moving me and I'm not always sure I want to go." I think it's a lot of Jacob's kind of wrestling. But, also, with the promise and the certainty that knowing that because God called you, that he's going to send you somewhere where he needs you, where you're going to be able to handle it; because everything he's done in your life is preparation for where he's going to send you.

I'm probably not one of the more seasoned ones, but I'm now, with seven years, more seasoned than I was before. So it's awesome, because there are lots of different kinds of callings I feel on my life. One is because of this ministry, this pastorate I have. I'm now like a role model, a mentor for a lot of women in ministry, which is something that I never anticipated; it adds a new kind of pressure and new kind of weight to your life. Women's issues now grip me in a different way. I'm more sensitive about things about women. Before it was like, when I came into it, I was like, totally, "I'm not a feminist. I'm just going to be a pastor just like everyone else." But you can't deny the female part of it, that there is a difference, and you're treated differently. My church is filled with women who are not able to exercise their gifts in other places. So they show up on my doorstep. I have a waiting list of people who want to intern with me. For a moment, you're flattered that they want to do that, but the real side of it is that they're not able to do it somewhere else; that's why they're there. So it puts you in a new position: you see things differently, you see things more sensitively. And that's a calling on my life.

I taught in a seminary totally on a fluke last year—at Union Theological Seminary. Someone recommended me, and I said I'd try it for a year. That experience, seeing poor, perhaps poorer students, in the Union Theological experience who work all day and they have to come to school all night, because they can't afford to give up their jobs... You see that and you become more sensitive to those kinds of needs, needs of the oppressed, the so-called underclass.

Then, when you're pastoring, and you're in a community now for seven years, I can't think my life is going to be like television: I'll stay here for a couple of years; I'll move on. Now it's seven years, and I'm not feeling that urge like I used to. And I'm maturing. In the daily life, you see people who are seriously economically deprived, socially and culturally deprived, who are serious victims of the system. You see them, sometimes so overwhelmed by it all, they can't even articulate the depth of their pain, and so they just cry. You've got to interpret what that crying means. It's sad.

You see life differently, and the call grips you even more. I think that part of the call is how much you're really going to surrender. When you enter it, you say yes. But you're still guarded, and you're trying to be in control of God's ministry for you. The more you stay in it, the less control you have, and the more God has. You say, "Gosh, this thing is really real, and I'm in it."

I guess where I am in my life at this particular point is just trying to figure out, "Is this it for the rest of my life? Is this what I'm going to be in?" Because, thirty-two is the age where people are making serious career decisions. You've tried a few things in your twenties. But [in your] thirties, people kind of expect you to decide where you're going to be, at least for the next five or ten years. So I wrestled with that. My friends, who are not ministers, are in the fast lane, and they're bringing in megabucks. They're Wall Streeters; they're in a number of things. Sometimes that does become attractive, and you wonder if you made the right choice. Sometimes you say, "Should I have given up television?" But then the other side is, . . . like yesterday, I preached and I was with my people, and I knew I was in the right place. So the money didn't matter and other things didn't matter, and you knew you were really helping some people who loved you and who you learned to love. So you wrestle.

My sense is that some area of ministry is going to be what I'm going to be doing the rest of my life. Whether it's the pastoral ministry, I'm not sure. I'm not sure anymore. I've been good at it and I've enjoyed it. But there are some other callings on my life. The year at Harvard will give me a chance, a sabbatical, to reflect, be away from the day-to-day demands which are intensive, particularly in a growing congregation where there was no support whatsoever. The only resources we had were the people. When you have that kind of intense ministry, you need a little break from it to reflect upon who you are, and why God put you there, and what are you to do next. This year will be a year of many questions and, I hope, some answers. Next year at this time, I'm sure I'll be in a very different place in terms of my thinking and my feelings and how I've grown. So that's where I am. This program at United Theological Seminary, Dayton, Ohio, I also see very much as a gift from God. I'm the only woman in my section of the Proctor fellows out of, I think they announced, seventeen of us. I'm sitting at the table, sitting at the feet of those who have been pastoring and preaching as long as I have been alive, many of them. So for me it's an honor. I just want to learn, be around them and listen to them. Some things are coming out of this experience that also effect your calling. My preaching is stronger, because I'm around preachers who preach, who know how to preach; and just listening to them, I get some things, and I take that.

I think the call is complex and multi-faceted, and it's inspiring and intriguing, and it's exciting. At the same time, it's frightening and it's awesome because you realize that once in your life, it feels like it's not your own anymore. That's awesome. That's all I have to say in terms of my experience.

William Johnson
North Benton, Ohio

The Reverend William Johnson was born in Youngstown, Ohio, on November 24, 1942, called in 1979 and ordained a Baptist minister in 1981. He received a BA from Youngstown State University and an MA from Ashland Theological Seminary. He is the associate pastor at Christian Love Missionary Baptist Church in Canton, Ohio. Interview recorded May 23, 1989.

41

"It Was like My Body Was on Fire"

I first received my calling one Sunday morning. I was in church. I was sitting down. I was just simply praising the Lord to myself. If I recall correctly, I was saying, "Thank you, Jesus." At that time, it was as if I felt a bolt of lighting hit me. It was a power that I had never experienced before. I felt myself tumbling to the ground; and as I lay on the ground, I heard this very strong voice speak to me. This voice said, " Know my word. Don't worry and I will lead you, and I will guide you, and at the proper time, you will bring forth my word." I was, at that time, somewhat awed at the experience. It was an experience that is hard to put into words. It was like my body was on fire. I was going through this feeling of elation, just enjoying and basking in what I was feeling and knowing that some higher power had spoken to me. However, after that, when I got up off the floor, I found myself really questioning what had transpired—the experience that I had gone through.

So I found myself going to the pastor of the church and other ministers and persons, and asking if maybe God had given them some insight as to what he had spoken to me. And everyone that I had asked obviously said, "No." After that, about two weeks later, I had a similar experience. There were people being prayed for, and I was in the group praying for the people. All of a sudden, I felt this overwhelming power come over me again; I found myself on the floor, and there was a voice. The same strong voice spoke to me again. It said to me, "I don't care if I never give anyone the revelation that I have given you. I told you to know my word and at the proper time you will go forth with my word." With that experience I got up off the floor, knowing within myself that I would have to know the word of God. That I, from that point on, would have to live for Jesus and to preach His word or die. It was just that powerful in me.

Some years ago, it had been prophesied—I was at a meeting, and this minister said that one day I would preach the word of God. At that time, I was outside of the believing community. I was purely a spectator, even though I was raised in the church. I said to myself, at that time, that this individual was just purely saying this for show, trying to make an impression upon someone else. A lot of things that they told me I would go through, I sort of shrugged off; but when I did get into the ministry, these thoughts came back, and I had the opportunity to share with this individual the validity and truth of what had transpired so many years ago. Basically I would say that was it.

Henry Wise Jones
Cincinnati, Ohio

The Reverend Henry Wise Jones was born in Lexington, Kentucky on July 28, 1941, called in 1965 and ordained aBaptist minister in 1967. He has a BA from Kentucky State University and an MDiv from Southern Baptist Seminary (Louisville). He pastors the Mt. Zion Baptist Church in Cincinnati. Interview recorded July 7, 1989.

42

Two Similar Accidents— Is God Speaking to Me?

My call to the ministry dates back to the early part of the '60s. I was in college and realized that the ministry was pulling heavily upon my heart, but I did not feel at the time that I was quite ready. There were at least two significant things that occurred which sort of concretized and solidified in my own mind the fact that this is what the Lord wanted me to do.

The first instance occurred when I was riding with some friends of mine. I was a passenger in the back seat of the car coming from Frankfort, Kentucky. I noticed a car that was trailing us for several miles, and when we topped the hill making our descent, the car behind us came around us, hit us from the rear, then hit us again from the side. The car in which we were traveling ricocheted in the highway at the very foot of the hill— there was nothing but rock wall on either side. We hit the wall head-on at about sixty-five miles an hour. I just knew, at that point, that all of us, no doubt, would get killed. Fortunately, I survived it with just a dislocated hip, but the driver was killed on the point of impact.

About a year later, on the same highway, I was driving along with a brother of mine, Clayton. We were going to Frankfort this time, from Lexington. I had passed the car in front of me, and then there was yet a second car in front of the car I was passing that decided, at the last minute, to turn off the highway into a little private drive, which caused a tremendous impact. I was thrown out of the car onto the highway and, frankly speaking, don't even recall hitting the ground. The only thing I remembered was standing on my feet in a moment's time. I just received a few bruises on my arms and legs. My brother, fortunately, was able to grab the wheel and bring the car under control. Those two accidents, almost a year to the date on the same highway, sort of provided the force for me to relinquish and go ahead and accept the call.

Between those times, the first and the second accident, I was wrestling, I was restless, couldn't sleep under normal conditions, always tossing and turning. It was not until I actually announced and accepted the call that things seemed to just look up. Everything just started moving very, very, very nicely. It's just been a forward movement since that time. It seems the Lord was putting me, really, to the test. I was trying to deny the call, and at the same time I was involved in what you might call the "approach-avoidance conflict:" I wanted to and I didn't want to. But ultimately I yielded, and I'm glad I did.

Odell Jones
Detroit, Michigan

The Reverend Dr. Odell Jones was born in Stevens, Arkansas on November 21, 1932, called in 1941 and ordained a Baptist minister in 1956. He received a BA from Arkansas Baptist College, a BD from Virginia Union University and a DMin from Drew University. He pastors Pleasant Grove Baptist Church in Detroit. Interview recorded April 25, 1989.

43

"I Would Not Be a Boy Preacher"

I feel that I was called into the ministry at the same time I was converted. I was nine years old, attending revival in my own church, the Baptist Church in Magnolia, Arkansas. The great late Dr. M. K. Curry was the evangelist. I remember when I accepted Christ that the Lord called me into the ministry, and I agreed to it, but I would not be a boy preacher. I told the Lord that I wanted to preach and I would be glad to preach when I had something to preach.

So, although being converted at nine, I continued my regular education. When I finished high school, I went away in service. I recall when I had about nine months to go in the service, I went to my CEO and told him I wanted to get out to go to college. He asked me why, and I told him I was preparing for the ministry, for which I had been called ever since I was nine. He [said], "Okay, Odell, you will be the first one to get an early discharge," and I enrolled at Arkansas Baptist College. After enrolling there, I met Dr. M. W. Williams, who was the dean, and

Dr. Alfred Bradford, who was the dean of religion. We'd talk about the ministry and the work of the ministry. Then I talked with Dr. Proctor, who came there from Virginia Union, and he told me that I should prepare myself, that after graduation from Arkansas Baptist, I would go to the seminary at Virginia Union. And because Arkansas Baptist College was an accredited college, I prepared myself by taking the courses that were required at Virginia Union. So, I really finished Baptist College with a major in social science and a minor in history and religion.

Then I went on to Virginia Union, and prepared myself; and after that, I went back to Arkansas Baptist and worked as dean of religion and stayed there for five years. Then Louis Johnson came and asked me if I was going to stay in the institutional ministry, and I told him, "No, I came there to stay for five years and this was my fifth year." He told me about this church here (Detroit) and made contact with this church, and this is where I've been. After graduating from Arkansas Baptist, I also graduated from Virginia Union, then I attended Southwestern Baptist Theological Seminary in Fort Worth. In fact, I was the first black student permitted to stay on the campus at Southwestern, and I needed nine hours to finish there when I came here. Then I went to Drew in Madison, New Jersey, where I got my Doctor of Ministry.

My calling was that there was an inner voice or inner urge or inner dissatisfaction with doing anything else except the ministry. I knew that I was called; I just wanted to be prepared for the task.

William Augustus Jones, Jr.
Brooklyn, New York

The Reverend Dr William Augustus Jones, Jr., was born in Louisville, Kentucky on June 24, 1934, called in 1956 and ordained a Baptist minister in 1959. He has a BA from the University of Kentucky, a BD from Crozer Theological Seminary and a D Min from Colgate Rochester. He pastors the Bethany Baptist Church in Brooklyn, New York. He is a former president of the Progressive Baptist Convention. He is the author of *God in the Ghetto* (P.N.B.C. Publishing House, 1978) and *Responsible Preaching* (Aaron Press, 1989). Interview recorded June 7, 1989.

44

"I Was Down in the Motor Pool Preaching to Trucks"

At the outset, I probably should inform you that preaching was something that I had promised myself and others I would never do. Although I was born the son and grandson of very successful preachers and pastors, and though I had great respect for preaching, I just knew that it could not and would not happen to me. When I was commissioned an army officer at the age of nineteen in the Corps of Engineers, I decided that I would make a career of the military. I knew that I would be a brigadier general by thirty-five at least. That was it. I was not to preach, and I just knew that.

During my third year in the military, when I was commanding the company at Fort Knox in Kentucky, there came the beginning of a time period when I instinctively found myself in constant search of worship services where I could hear some preaching. I'd get off duty at Fort Knox, get in my car and drive into Louisville, just ride through the streets looking for a church where something was going on, anxious to hear some preaching. Almost every weekend, I was in Lexington where my father pastored the largest black church there, Pleasant Green Baptist Church. I was there every weekend. I would go to ministers' conferences; I read everything that I could find in my father's library dealing with preachers and preaching. And this thing became compulsive. Even though my father noticed what was happening, he played it rather cool; he said later that he would never be personally instrumental in alerting anybody to the call, but he knew that I would come to him eventually to deal with the matter.

But, I suppose, the real turning point—if you could call it that—came one day when I found myself in my company motor pool at Fort Knox, preaching to the trucks. I was down in the motor pool actually preaching to the trucks—the trucks were my congregation. The very next Sunday, I was in my home church, Pleasant Green in Lexington. I had to be there that weekend, because I knew what I had to do; and when the invitation was extended following the sermon, I came down the aisle, and I had on my pinks and greens (my dress military officer's uniform). I came down the aisle, and I told my father that I wanted to make a statement. I announced then that I knew the Lord had laid his hand on me, and that I had to preach. I remember him asking me, "How soon would you be ready to preach your trial sermon?" I said, "Well, I'm ready now." And he scheduled it for about nine days later, on a Tuesday night. I preached my trial sermon that Tuesday night; the place was crowded. I went back to Fort Knox on Wednesday and filed for separation from the military. That was in June, and I closed out my military career on June 30th. Everything happened very expeditiously.

I came out and, well, the rest is history. I will never look back. That was it, in essence. It "came upon me"—I was never aware of any gradual urge to do it. It was an overwhelming thing. I did not seek to run from it. I accepted it for what it was. As I said, I've never looked back, and I've never—I've doubted God on occasion—doubted the authenticity of my calling.

About twelve years before I got converted I was in a crap game out on the Harding Pike. I'll never forget it as long as I live. I and three or four others were gambling. I had the dice in my hands. A voice spoke to me, and it spoke three times. Every time it got nearer and nearer, until it seemed right over the top of my head.... In 1906 I prayed for six months. God showed me what I was to do, and to my complaint that I was from a poor tribe and had no learning and had not had the advantages of other people he answered in a voice, 'I am wisdom and possess all knowledge. I ordain you to preach."

> My jaws became unlocked, in Clifton H. Johnson, ed., *God Struck Me Dead: Religious Conversion Experiences and Autobiographies of Ex-slaves* (Philadelphia: Pilgrim Press, 1969): 22-23.

Arthur E. Kemp
Akron, Ohio

The Reverend Dr. Arthur E. Kemp was born in Hickory, North Carolina on November 21, 1929, called in 1952 and ordained a Baptist minister in 1963. He received a BA from Capital University (OH), an MA and a DMin from Ashland Theological Seminary. He pastors Mt. Olive Baptist Church in Akron, OH. Interview recorded in February 16, 1986.

45
Rebellious Soldier in Two Armies: Man's and God's

I guess to get at the very rudiments of my call experience I have to tell you what it was not. As a child of about eight years old, I accepted Christ as my personal Saviour in response to the appeal of the superintendent of the Baptist young people's union in Hickory, North Carolina. The superintendent taught a lesson—I don't recall which part of the Scripture it was from—but he asked us if we believed what he had just said about the Lord Jesus Christ. And I acknowledged that I did believe that. Then he asked me if I would I make a decision for Christ and come to him to give my life to him. Not fully understanding what that meant, I did respond. The only thing I knew at that time was I believed what he said about Jesus being God's Son, that he had died on the cross, that he had been crucified and raised again from the dead on the morning of the Sunday that we now call Easter.

From that point on, persons in my family had predicted that I was going to be a preacher I had a head like a preacher, I looked like a preacher, I acted like a preacher. Somewhat different than the other kids, I guest I had spent a lot of time reading the Sunday School books, but it had never occurred to me that I would be a preacher. I certainly did not want to be [one]. That did not seem to be the kind of direction that I would want my life to go in.

So we moved. We were living in Washington, DC, but I had moved back to North Carolina with my family when I accepted Christ as my Saviour. Well, we moved back to Washington DC. I was raised on up there through the public school system. And I graduated from high school.

But, I had led such a sheltered life in the home of a mother who was, as far back as I can remember, president of the missionary society and whose father was chairman of the deacon board in the Baptist church. That really precluded my having a lot of experience in the kinds of things that people of the world do—the parties, the dancing and all of that, the free and open life. Ours was a very sheltered life. I am one of seven children and we were all brought up under that same regimen.

Once I had turned eighteen and graduated from high school, I was forced by economics to get out in the world and make my own living. I had decided to turn down a four-year scholarship to Howard University, because I did not want to go to a black school. The alternative was to go to a white school, in order for me to do that I'd have to work and save the money. I took a job in the federal government in Washington with the avowed intent and purpose to save enough money to go to Ohio State University. I don't even know why I picked that one, but I wanted to go to Ohio State. And I was kind of torn between Sociology and going into the medical profession, kind of torn between the two. I hadn't really made up my mind.

There wasn't enough money. Well, by the time I started saving enough money, my youngest sister, who is the youngest under me, was coming out of Dunbar High School in Washington and money was needed in order for her to go to school. So, I took the money that I had been saving up to send her to Ohio State, which means that I didn't start my college level training until twelve years after I graduated in '48. I moved to Columbus, Ohio and started at Ohio State in the Summer session, 1960. It had still never crossed my mind again to take seriously the things that the people had said about my becoming a preacher.

But an odd thing happened—now remember I brought you up to 1960 where I've started at Ohio State as a 30 year old freshman. But an odd thing happened in 1952, eight years earlier. I was in the United States Army, the signal core station at Fort Monmouth, New Jersey. And, because of a high aptitude on a test given by the military, I was put into a special demonstration outfit. The purpose of the outfit was to master the latest communication equipment, to master the implementation of that equipment. This was a team that they called the Army-Navy ground core, twenty-six demonstration team, a really elite group. There were only twenty-six men in the unit: two officers, two captains and twenty-four enlisted men. Our job was to take this newly developed equipment there at the signal core engineering laboratories in New Jersey—Fort Monmouth, New Jersey—and go around the country, and for that matter all over the world, wherever there were US military establishments and demonstrate this equipment. It was the latest technology.

Then, in 1952 my mother had a heart attack and the Red Cross arranged for me to come home to be with her while she was recovering. In the meanwhile, this special outfit that I was in shipped out to Canada on a field trip and they would be gone for six months. When I got back from looking after my mother, my slot had been filled by my backup man. I couldn't join the team. Then, they put me in the supply room of the supply sergeant, handing out fatigues and that kind of stuff.

So I became really really embittered with the United States Army, and at that point I started to rebel against them. I had just re-enlisted for a six year period, but I was so bent out of shape by being pulled off that team and not allowed to go join it in Canada, that I started to take my revenge out, as it were, against the Army. So I refused to suit up in military clothes. I just started wearing civilian clothes. I wouldn't do anything. I wouldn't take orders from anybody and naturally that brought me into disfavor with my commanding officers. They put me on company punishments and I broke that, they court marshalled me and I disregarded that. So ultimately the company commander said, "This was one of the best soldiers I had and all of a sudden he's gone off the deep end, maybe something has happened to him, maybe he's cracked up." So he remanded me to the custody of the military hospital there at Fort Monmouth, New Jersey.

But before I got to the hospital, the commanding general had me to come in for a personal consultation with him because I was trying to get out of the Army. And as a way to do that I had written a letter to the Communist Youth Party, seeking admission. And that raised quite a stir among the intelligence officers on the post, because the signal core engineering laboratories of which I was a part was a highly secretive arm of the military. So, the general had called me up and wanted to interrogate me to see whether or not I was communist or exactly what was going on. When the determination was made that I wasn't communist, then he concluded that I must be crazy. So he called a doctor, a psychiatrist from the military hospital, to give me a personal examination.

It was during the period of the examination during my hospitalization that Captain Freeman determined that there was nothing wrong with me mentally or psychologically. But he determined that I was having the same problem he had, because when they forced him to go into the Army, he had to give up a $300,000 a year New York practice and he was bitter with the Army because of that. And, he detected right away that my bitterness with the Army made for the anomalous behavior. He confided in me that as soon as he could, he was going to fix the papers so that I could be discharged.

I was there in the hospital in a private room. On one occasion when I had been reading whatever I could get my hands on, I heard a voice, a voice of a male. Now you have to understand that the room I was in was a single hospital room, and because it was in the psychiatric ward the doors were locked. It had a glass peephole, as it were, and there was nobody in the rooms on either side of me, and the halls were padded with carpet and soundproof tile on the ceiling. There were no radios in the wing. I heard a voice saying to me "Go feed my sheep." And I looked around and I was really kind of befuddled and wondering who had said it. The first thing I did was got up and went to the door to look out the window, to see if there was anybody out there that was talking to me. As I left the door to go back to sit down on the bed where I had been lying down, in an interval of about five minutes, exactly the same statement occurred again, "Go feed my sheep." And by now I'm really having some apprehension. I know I keep hearing somebody talking to me and when I check back at the door a second time, I didn't hear any movement out there and I didn't see anybody. And it was nearly an half an hour later that I heard the the same voice the third time, "I said, Go feed my sheep." And I was restless all of that night.

I was scheduled to see Dr. Freeman that next morning. I was quick to share with him what had happened, and he wanted to go back over some of the files to see whether or not there had been any history of hallucination in my own psychological profile. And, there was not, because I had never had the experience. I just basically dealt in reality. I knew what I saw and believed what I heard and felt and touched and smelled to be real phenomenon. It had not been a case where I had been given to hallucination.

The Irresistible Urge To Preach

And at the same of the call, I guess an impacting, almost as a heavy weight occurred that I could not get out of my mind this voice saying "Go feed my sheep." There was a sense that I had to respond to that, a sense that I had to obey that. Those words made a lot of sense to me, because I had read that those were the words that Jesus had said to Simon Peter, after Christ had been crucified, raised from the dead and was preparing to ascend into heaven again. That's precisely what he told Peter.

When it sometime later dawned on me that that would have been a call for me to go into a preaching ministry, then I determined that I was not going to do that. Because preaching was the furthest thing from my mind. I was going to make sure that I would not preach (this is still 1952), because I had been taught that if you are going to be a vessel for God you've got to be a fit vessel and you got to have good behavior, good morals, and good ethics.

So, I determined that I was going to be the worst possible human being that you could be, to make myself unfit to be a minister of the gospel. And then I started. I wasn't drinking then, but I started drinking. I had been gambling occasionally, but I became an avid gambler. And subsequently drove getaway cars for thieves. While I did not ever use narcotics, I participated in those kinds of things—money-raising ventures if you will, criminal money raising ventures that would get money for those persons. It was a gang of five; they did use narcotics. I would assist them, not only in getting the money to get the narcotics but on the occasion where they would need a fix of heroin so badly —and I'm talking about mainlining now—I even held the arms of the person while they would make the tourniquet and make the injection. They were flagellating so wildly that they couldn't do it themselves. They were sticking the needle all over their arms and everywhere. Well, in short I had prostitutes working for me. I had just become a dyed-in-the wool rascal through and through with the avowed intention and purpose that I was never ever going to respond to that call in that hospital room, "Go feed my sheep." And oddly enough, virtually everything I touched was successful, even though it was criminal. I made a lot of money. I spent it as fast as I made it and had a good time.

In 1959 I left Washington, DC and moved to Columbus, Ohio. I was going to spend ten days with my mother and father in Columbus, Ohio and then go out to make a new life for myself out in Los Angeles, California. Because, in Washington, I had done what the old folks used to say, I had run out. I had really hit the pits. I had lost self-respect. I was really in the gutter—a street person, sleeping in fourth-rate hotels that now I wouldn't even ... I don't like dogs but I wouldn't even keep a dog in some of the places that I stayed in when I was going through that particular period in my life.

In 1959 I put all that behind me. On January 10, 1959 I left Washington, DC. (January 11, I'm sorry.) It was January 10 when I had my final drunk in Washington. I sobered up enough on the eleventh to leave Washington, DC and come to Columbus, Ohio. When my parents came home from church that day, they were shocked to see this little old man, as my mother described me, sitting on her front porch all bearded and bedraggled and little knowing that it was her son Arthur, her youngest son, until she got close enough to see me.

But after a good shave and a bath, I was recognizable again and it was a good family reunion. And my mother and dad began to, as I stayed there for a while, ask me to stay longer than the ten days. You know, they were getting older and they kind of needed somebody to look after them. And besides, I didn't know anybody in Los Angeles. So they put that kind of parental beg on me and I stayed there. My mother asked me if I would go to church with her sometime and I did a couple of times. Then after that, I guess after the first month, maybe into the second month, I was going to church on Sunday, she asked me one Wednesday night if I would go to pray meeting with her. And I did.

While there in prayer meeting—this was in the third month that I was there, in March of 1959—I was sitting in prayer meeting and prayer meeting was almost over, everybody had prayed around and it was just about the time that the pastor would usually make his closing commentary and pronounce the benediction and we would all go home. There would have been twenty to twenty-five persons in that prayer meeting. And, just before he got up to make his remarks, I had a sudden flush of heaviness to impact on my heart, just as though I was carrying the weight of the world around me, and I broke out in uncontrollable sobbing. And nobody could understand what was going on and the pastor, Rev. L. H. Johnson, who is now deceased, said "I know what's wrong with him. I know what's wrong with him, he hasn't told me but I know what's wrong with him." And when I got to the point that I could stop crying well enough to make audible words, the first words that came out of my mouth was, "I've got to preach, I've got to preach, I've got to preach." And he said, "I know it, and you're not going to have any peace until you do." And it was at that point, eight years after the hospital incident, that I made the determination that I would not ever again spend a moment of my life outside of the call of Christ to be a preacher of the gospel.

And from there its been a kind of historical thing where I learned under Pastor Johnson's tutelage in church. And, subsequently in 1960, I went to Ohio State, again in sociology. And I really didn't like Ohio State because it was too big. So I transferred to Capital University, where I took the Bachelor in Religion after nearly fourteen years of on and off courses because I had subsequently married and had a son and was not able to go to school full-time, because working at Westinghouse with very little seniority I'd get bumped a lot from job to job. So it was kind of tough, trying to hang onto a job and go to school. So it took me twelve years to get the bachelor's degree on a part-time status.

And after that, after getting the bachelor degree in Religion, I took a pastorate in a country church down in Ohio for three years. Commuting sixty-five miles one way became too much after a period of time. So I stopped and went back to school. This time [I was] working on a masters in criminology. I did all of the course work and got to the point of writing the thesis for that.

It was at that point, then, that I had received the call to come to pastor the Mt. Olive Baptist Church in Akron, Ohio in 1978. I responded to that call by the church to come and pastor Mt. Olive, where I have been happily engaged every since. In the meanwhile, once coming to Akron, I started attending Ashland Seminary where I took the masters in religion, then ultimately the Doctor of Ministry at Ashland Seminary. So, there you have the call experience of Arthur Kemp.

There is no question in my mind as to what I heard. It was male, it was a voice, it was audible. Now, the question that I have always raised for myself, since there was nobody else in the room with me and there was nobody to witness what I had heard, [is], Did I in fact experience the auditory phenomenon of hearing the voice, or was it something that was subconsciously or psychologically placed on my mind, within my mind?

Walter Kimbrough
Atlanta, Georgia

The Reverend Walter Kimbrough was born in Atlanta, Georgia, on July 30, 1940, called in 1962 and ordained a United Methodist elder in 1968. He has a BA from Morris Brown University and an MDiv from the Interdenominational Theological Center. He pastors the Ben Hill United Methodist Church in surburban Atlanta. Interview recorded June 23, 1989.

46

"God, If You Want Me to Preach, Wake Me Up at 3:00 or 4:00 o'Clock in the Morning"

My call is a process. I did not accept what people perceived to be the call. I grew up in a Baptist church, and people would say or make comments like, "You gonna preach, I know that. You've got the marks in your forehead." I'm not sure what that meant. Wasn't sure then and I'm not sure what it meant now either. I'm not sure what they saw, nor am I sure that they knew what they were talking about. But, academically unlearned to people said that "You're going to preach."

I remember the time I wanted to be the president of the junior choir. The director of the choir, [the] adult sponsor, wouldn't let me, because I hadn't even joined the church. They began to push me about joining the church. "You're a good boy, why don't you join the church?" And I would not join the church even before the call, because I grew up under the philosophy that in order to join the church you had to be born again. That was defined to me as meaning that nobody will have to tell you when you've been born again. You'll know it, because you'll be able to tell a difference in your life. And I had not experienced that difference in my life. No spiritual reawakening or awakening of any kind.

So, I did not join the church until I was under the persuasion that something had transpired in my life. Nor did, by the same token, I accept as a call what people said to me. In other words, I did not want to preach. I suppose one of the reasons I did not want to preach was because I was scared. I thought it would be so tough to get up before the same people Sunday after Sunday after Sunday and to have something prophetically to say to the people who would come to that particular place for worship, looking with expectant hearts to receive the word from the Lord. I thought it was so tough and I was, frankly, scared.

My call came with the intensification of the feeling in my own life that that was what I was to do. The intensification of the feeling of call was on an escalating plane. It did not lighten up, it got stronger and stronger—worse and worse, if you will. Until I came to the point that I had better encounter God about it, so I prayed. And my prayer simply was, "God, if you want me to preach, I'll tell you what I want you to do. I want to wake up in the morning about three or four o'clock. I want to think about preaching, I want to go back to sleep, right away." And the catch to it is that whenever I'd wake up between three or four o'clock in the morning, I couldn't go back to sleep. You're just there laying awake. So, I wanted to wake up, I wanted to think about preaching, having a sense of awareness and then I want to go right back to sleep, that was it. So that would be the total picture, the total episode. I'd wake up, I'd think about preaching and I'd go back to sleep.

So, that was, like, on a Sunday I prayed that, and Sunday night nothing happened. Monday morning, I celebrated because nothing happened. Monday night, I went to bed, I was a little leery; but Tuesday morning, I got up and I celebrated because nothing happened. Then Tuesday night came and I went to bed, I woke up about three or four o'clock in the morning, and I thought about preaching and I went right back to sleep. Then I said, "What the heck." I said, "I'm not going to fight it any more." Then I told my pastor about it. I didn't catch up with him until that Thursday. I told him on Thursday. Thursday morning I shared with him and from that point it was like a burden just kind of rolled away. So, rather than the apprehension, the fear and the rejection, was total acceptance and harmony and peace in my life. Which for me was kind of the affirmation that this is what I wanted to do and had to do and be about. So, that's kind of the way I see and sense my call into ministry.

Bernice King
Atlanta, Georgia

The Reverend Bernice King was born in Atlanta, Georgia, on March 28, 1963, called in 1980 and licensed in 1988. She earned a BA from Spelman College and the dual Master of Divinity-Juris Doctorate from Emory University. She is the youngest daughter of Dr. Martin Luther King, Jr. Interview recorded June 23, 1989.

47

One Regret: Daddy King Wasn't There

I received my call into the ministry at seventeen. At that time, I didn't feel worthy of it. And I struggled with what a call even meant. The reason I, at that time, knew that it was a call, was because of some things that had been taking place in my life.

My calling has essentially been unfolding by some sort of evolving process, probably from my mother's womb. And I did think that part of it had a great deal to do with my father's life—and also his death.

I was sixteen when I first realized that my father was gone. I mean, I knew it prior to that, but that's when I came to a full realization of his assassination and what it meant and what he represented. And I was viewing the film *From Montgomery to Memphis* with the youth movement at Ebenezer. And then in the film there's a funeral scene, and at that point I broke down in tears. And that lasted for about two hours. And all kinds of questions came to my mind. Why? What did I do? Why can't I have my daddy? You know, even to the extent of, What did he do?

And I found myself becoming very angered at this with God. And . . . about to result to turn away from the church. That's all my life, that's all I knew was the church—the central part of my life. I think because of that, the resistance wasn't great enough for me to totally turn away. As a result, there was somewhat of a spiritual tugging in me a year later, at seventeen, that kind of began to unfold this old mystery about being in the ministry. It was frightening, you know? I was only seventeen, I was a female. The only thing I knew about ministry was people being up in the pulpit and preaching, because I didn't have some of the personal experiences with my father that my other siblings had. So, I never really knew what a preacher was. I mean, I had a relationship, semi-relationship, with my grandfather. But all I knew was I saw him preach; I didn't know all the other facts.

So, at that time, I kind of kept it low-key. I shared it with my mother and siblings, and I shared it with another minister. I guess at that point I began to explore the possibility of what it meant to be in the ministry as a female—a black female—as one who has been affected by a lot of tragedies that has resulted in a lot of anger toward God. And as the daughter of a minister—a prominent minister—and granddaughter, and what all that meant.

It was maybe a few years later, I was sitting in church and Pastor Roberts was preaching a sermon—I don't even remember the name of it. The thing that stood out in the sermon for me was, he was talking about ministers and a call to the ministry and how so many people, you know, they just up and go. He said, you know, sometimes there's two calls. The first calling is a call to get prepared. The second calling is "go," in a sense. At that point, I felt a little more comfortable in my calling. I felt that initial, as I call it, calling was to prepare myself. Because I'm one, at this point in my life, who believes that even though you're called, I think there's a period when you have to purify yourself. I don't mean become perfect. But that you have to examine and explore and try to discover more about yourself—those deficiencies and weaknesses and strengths and all the things you have to offer and what you don't have to offer—and to be able to embrace that and accept that before you actually get into the ministry. Because you have to deal with a flock of people. It's like you're responsible for so many people. And if you don't know yourself, it's kind of difficult to even try to begin to be servant to other people.

One Regret: Daddy King Wasn't There

And so I spent the period, I guess, from seventeen to twenty-five, when I publicly [accepted the call] in my trial sermon—I spent that period preparing myself. On the way, of course, was the education, theology school, and I'm not yet finished with theology school. I'm like five hours away from finishing. I began to work on some personal things, like looking at who I was before that. It was just—I was just existing; I had no consciousness about what Bernice is or who Bernice is as a human being. I mean, I could feel things, but what does all of this represent, and what was my relationship to God, to the church, to the world and even to myself? And that has been the process that I have been going through since the age of seventeen.

At twenty-five, when I did finally, publicly accept it, it was at a point when I realized that a lot of things about me, about my relationship with God, about my relationship to other human beings and everything—and even though I don't have the answers in terms of how to go about this and how to—it's coming into a certain consciousness. So that I can embrace certain things and not run away from them and reject them. [At that point] I felt I was prepared to then be a servant in the ministry. That's essentially how it happened for me.

There was no in-breaking, no audible voice, even though sometimes there is. I guess, there's one in all of us, a little voice somewhere, maybe on the other side, talking to us that kind of lets us know what we're not to do. And I guess also that was a time for me when I had to really accept the fact that it was a call, to verify that. You know, just going to the ministry, for me it's not—it's sacred. It's not like I'll be a businesswoman today, and tomorrow I'll be something else. It's like marriage. It's an eternal commitment, a lifelong commitment. And so I felt that a call like that was important enough for me to explore, to prepare and to get ready.

Carolyn Knight
New York, New York

The Reverend Carolyn Knight was born in Denver, Colorado, on August 7, 1956, called before birth and ordained a Baptist minister in 1978. She received a BA from Bishop College and an MDiv and STM from Union Theological Seminary. She is pastor of the Philadelphia Baptist Church of Christ in Harlem. Interview recorded June 9, 1989.

48

"I Don't Come from a Lineage of Preachers"

I don't come from a lineage of preachers, although there are preachers in my family. They are so far and few. I have a cousin who is in the ministry as I am, and that makes us the only modern-day preachers in our family, although, historically, there have been some preachers. I know without question that I am the first woman to preach. I've always had a simple call to ministry, particularly to preaching. I think at a very early age, I was attracted to the pulpit and to the beauty, the poetry of literature, of sacred literature, especially as it comes out in sermons.

I entered this profession in 1974. It was after hearing another woman, who was denied access to the pulpit, preach from the floor—preach a sermon in every sense of the word —that I began to reflect again on my own ministry, my own call to ministry.

I have always found along the way the little ones who have been ready to assist. I have found men and women who were both intellectually and emotionally maturing to the fact that God could call and could use women.

I believe I was sixteen when I preached my trial sermon. I took my text from James. It was the first chapter, when he says, "Count it all joy when you suffer various trials," so forth and so on. The title of that sermon was "Hello, Trouble, Come in and Sit Down." I never shall forget it. I don't know that it was an invitation to difficulties and obstacles that would be encountered along this journey. But that was the text that I chose. I preached that sermon at the Gilead Baptist Church in Denver, Colorado. I remember very vividly and very clearly, the night that sermon was to be delivered, going over to an empty church and preaching the sermon word-for-word, as if the house was filled. Then, after having preached that sermon in the emptiness of that sanctuary, sitting down and having a long conversation with God about this journey upon which I was about to embark. I just felt that night, that August night—I believe it was a Thursday, if I recall, it was Thursday—having the keen assurance that he would be with me.

Ever since then I've never wavered from this path. I hear a lot of my brothers and sisters who walk this way, say that they could do other things, that they could be in business, be in politics. I really can't. I can't do anything else. For better or for worse. God has laid this thing on me so strongly that I don't have any other path to walk, have a desire to walk. I'm in this thing, I'm in this ministry. I have been preaching this gospel with some success, and as much success as I anticipate in the future. I don't believe that I have begun to preach. I'm still learning the craft, still perfecting the craft, still refining the craft. It has been a glorious pilgrimage, so far. I say that with all the blessings and all the curses of the good and the bad that have attended unto this journey. I say that confident of what Romans the eighth chapter says, "All things are working together for good." I believe that all things, all things, are working together for good. The good and the bad, they're working together for my good, because of my love for the Lord and the fact that he has called me according to his purpose.

So, I continue to preach. I preach now because I have organized the Philadelphia Baptist Church of Christ in Harlem, which is about fifteen months old. I now enjoy the pleasure of preaching every Sunday. Sermon preparation is an arduous task for me. It takes for me a lot of blood, sweat and tears to prepare a sermon. But I enjoy what has been prepared. I enjoy the labor of sitting down with the Bible and drawing out from the text that which God has for his people. I'm convinced that preaching is not only a fine art, but I believe that it's the only way that we're going to save ourselves—through strong, eloquent preaching like we had in the earlier generations. That kept the family intact, that admonished young people to go to school, that championed social and political causes. It was strong preaching. In my preaching and in my ministry, my goal, my challenge is to recapture that type of preaching that sets souls on fire, spiritually, morally and intellectually. To recapture that kind of preaching. That challenge men and women to elevate their sights and to live higher.

I listened to the old preachers [like] Gardner Taylor. I just loved his picturesque language, the way he could, he can still, paint the picture as if it's just before you [as a] master artist would. Just a clean white canvas. He gets through to you. You see it clearly and not only do you see it, but you want to do it. I believe it is that type of preaching that will get us off of drugs and back into the halls of education. I believe it's that type of preaching that will challenge our young people to want to go back to our Black institutions that made our foreparents—Spellman, Hampton. I believe that it was a preacher that inspired me, all along the journey. When I think about whether those fine men have been preachers, lives of preachers and the living of preachers and the words of preachers. They have inspired me to be all that I want to be. So, in my ministry, that's what I try to recapture. If I can get just one young person, I feel that it will be all worthwhile.

"*I* had just turned my twelfth year the previous March. I not only know the day, the time and place where Christ saved me, but I know that it was there at that place in the same hour that He confirmed what I had already known. For never has there been a day in my conscious memory that I did not know that God had chosen me to preach the Gospel of His precious Son.... Indeed its roots antidate either my memory or consciousness.... According to the testimony of my mother, the impression behind it began during the period of my gestation... My mother received the conviction while bearing me that she would bring forth a boy who was to be 'my preacher.' Whereupon she then and there gave me to the Lord. From this she never retreated nor would she let me forget. And strangely enough, I knew myself all along that I must preach."

W. H. R. Powell,
Illustrations from a Supervised Life
(Philadelphia: The Continental Press, 1968): 29, 49.

Ann Farrar Lightner
Baltimore, Maryland

The Reverend Ann Farrar Lightner was born in Raleigh, North Carolina, on March 22, 1945, called in 1981 and ordained an African Methodist Episcopal elder in 1986. She received a BS from Boston University, and a MTh from St. Mary's Seminary (Baltimore). She pastors the Mt. Calvary AME church in suburban Baltimore. Interview recorded June 15, 1989.

49

"I Never Wanted to Be a Preacher"

I was raised in the AME Zion Church in Raleigh, North Carolina, so I had basically been a church person all of my life. Then, as I grew older, I got married and left home and then got divorced and went to Boston, which was where my real religious experience started.

I was a student at Boston University and joined St. Paul AME Church [where] now Bishop John and Cecelia were ministering. That was when I gave my heart to the Lord. I had grown up in the church, but it was like "going to church" and I never really had any personal experiences with the Lord. So it was while I was at St. Paul, that I gave my heart to the Lord and really began striving to be a Christian and to live like a Christian. So that was, like, in the last three years that I was in Boston. Then, when I finished Boston University, I accepted a job in Washington and the Bryants were then in Baltimore. So, some of us in Washington started coming to Baltimore to church because we just couldn't find what we wanted in these other churches over there. So we just started commuting back and forth from Washington to Baltimore.

It was during that period that I just began to grow in the

Lord. It wasn't really something that I was aware of. I was active in the church. I was active from the beginning when I joined St. Paul. I was there for, like, three services a day, prayer meetings, Bible study, the whole nine yards. I just jumped in with both feet. Then, when I came to this area and started going to Bethel, you know, I just continued in that realm, studying, and Reverend Bryant appointed me as director of the youth department of Bethel. I did that for, like, eight years before I accepted the call to preach. Teaching Sunday School but basically just wanting to do all of it and wanting to be really involved and to really study and learn and try and be who the Lord wanted me to be.

It was about after eight years of that I accepted to call to preaching in 1981. So I guess it was in December and it really never came to me. I mean, I never really knew what was going on until, I guess, about mid-year in 1980-81 that the Lord was speaking to my heart about preaching. It was like I just could not do enough. I didn't realize that the Lord was calling me to preach. It was just that I was so active and so busy and so caught up in this thing even more so than I realized. My testimonies had become sermons and I didn't realize that. You know, to have a testimony always [meant I] had something to say for the Lord. I would stand up and people would tease me and say, "You know, when are you going to accept your call?" And I would say, "The Lord didn't call me to preach." Because during that time, so many people were coming forth at Bethel. I mean the Bryants probably told you, they got a hundred children in ministry.

While I was doing all this work and all this ministry and stuff in terms of Sunday School and directing the YPD and that kind of thing, I never realized or even thought or had any idea that I was going to be a preacher. I never wanted it. It just never dawned on me. So as time went on, the Lord began to speak to my heart and it was like I started having—these visions. It was like this girl in the Sunday school teachers you know, there were a group of Sunday school teachers—and she said to me, "Ann, I had this dream about you and you were in this big coliseum and you were preaching to all these people." I said, "Girl, you are crazy." That was like a year before it started coming to me.

When it started happening, it was like I would have these visions. I would be listening to radio and it was like I would, like, transform and whoever was preaching on the radio wasn't them, it was me. I would see myself before all these people, preaching the word of God. I would try to block it out, you know, like, Who wants to hear you? This is ego, and all this stuff. I didn't know if it was me or if it was the Lord, and it scared the living daylights out of me. But I couldn't get away from it. It was like every time I turned the radio on, Bill, it was like before long it was not that person anymore, it was me. I would go to bed and I would dream, and in my dreams I would be before these people speaking. It was like I wouldn't necessarily know what I said when I woke up or where I had been, but it would always be before this larger congregation of people and I would have been preaching. After a while, I just kept trying to ignore it. I kept trying to block it out. I just did not want this thing to be real, because I never wanted to be a preacher. So, finally, it just kept on, and kept on and kept on and I called Reverend Bryant one day.

I was working as a sales representative at the Baltimore Convention Center. I called him and I said, "Reverend Bryant, I need to talk to you about something, but I don't want to talk to you about it because I am not sure about what it is." He said, "Well, you're not going to tell me what it is?" I said, "Just pray for me." I said, "I don't know how it can happen and I don't know how it can be, if what I'm thinking is happening is happening," and he just kind of chuckled. He said, "All right, I'll tell you what, I'll be praying with you, but know this, if the Lord is directing you into something, he will work it out. He will make every way plain and you'll be clear about it. So just pray about it and let me know when you want to talk to me." I said, "Okay." It seemed like after that it just got more intense. I mean, I could not get this thing out of my head. It was like [being] outside of yourself and you are not in control. All I could see was me preaching to these people ... and I mean I had no peace. It was like everything on the radio was me and all I listened to was Christian stations, teaching and preaching and that kind of thing. I couldn't get away from it.

Then, when people started saying, "When are going to accept the call?" I'd say, "The Lord hasn't called me to preach." I mean I would get angry about it. Like "Mind your business and leave me alone," that kind of thing. So, finally, it just got so intense I said, I'm going to talk to my pastor. Before that, Reverend Bryant said one night as he's done it many times and it never crossed my mind to go down . . . he said at Vashti's [McKenzie] trial sermon, it was at Vashti's trial sermon Reverend Bryant said, "If there goes here [anyone who feels] that the Lord may be calling them to preach, I want you to come and not accept the call to preach but just come and pray about [it]." Bill before I knew it, I don't know how I got from my seat to the altar, I was at the altar. Now I'm known as the biggest crybaby in church. I mean they will tell you, they laugh at Lightner. You've got a handkerchief today. I mean I will walk into church and they start singing the doxology and I'd just be gone.

So, I was at this altar praying about this thing, and at that point I knew I could not run from it. I knew that it was clearly the Lord and it was not me. So, after that, I called Reverend Bryant up and I told him, "I need to make an appointment to come talk with you." So when I went, I told him, "I think the Lord is calling me to preach." He said, "Oh, yeah?" "Yeah." "Tell me how it manifested itself." I told him just like I told you. I said, "Reverend Bryant, I can't get this vision—every time I look up I'm preaching. You know I can't get enough of the word. I can't get enough worship." I mean, Bill, I would be at church eight o'clock service, eleven o'clock service. Reverend Bryant would go somewhere and we'd preach at 3:30, come back at six o'clock at Bethel—Sunday school, then Bible study during the week, prayer meeting on Friday night. I just could not get enough. I didn't know what was going on. I told him that I kept having these visions that I was preaching and I couldn't get it out of my mind.

So, he said, "Have you accepted it?" And I said, "Well, at this point I realize that that's what's happening but I don't know what to do." "Well, you either say yes or no." "Well, I can't say no. Because it is haunting me. But I don't know what to do." "You do what the Lord is calling you to do." "But I can't do it." "If you're going do it you know you're not going to do it, the Lord is going to do it." "Reverend Bryant, I never wanted to be a preacher." "Well, I'll tell you what. I'll give you a trial sermon date if you want it." "Right now?" "Yes." "But you make people wait." "Not when I already know." I said, "What?" "Not when I already know. I've been knowing this." Well, then I was floored. I said, "Well why didn't you tell me. He said, "It wasn't my place to tell you. The Lord had to show you." And that was like three months—two or three months before.

He went to his book and he said, "I'll give you December fourth." That was my trial sermon date. And he said, "But you watch the Lord in this. You'll know if it's God. He'll put everything in place." I said, "Reverend Bryant, I've got a son. I don't have any money to go to school. I've got to support my son. I need to go to seminary," and dah-dah-dah. He said, "Don't worry about all that. If it is God, you go ahead and do what he is calling you to do and He'll put everything in place."

Before I preached my trial sermon, it was like the Lord opened the door for me to go to seminary. The Lord had already made every way for me to take care of my son even when I was in school. My son was on campus with me. But it was just like parting the Red Sea. There was never any obstacles to my preaching his word. It was just like, well, there it is, you've accepted it now and everything just opened it. I preached my trial sermon. In fact, I enrolled in seminary before the trial sermon because seminary started in September, now that I think about it. How did I get in seminary before I . . . ? Maybe I was just taking courses beforehand because I was doing everything. I was doing everything.

I must have been taking courses, because when I preached my trial sermon I was already in seminary. When I went before the examiners board in my first year classes—in my second year classes, I had finished seminary. So, as a result of that, before my third year, Reverend Bryant told Bishop Brook and Bishop Adams that he had two people in the class who were just getting into the examiners board but who had finished seminary and would he skip us so that we could go into—skip the second year and go into the third year or something like that. Anyway, they did all of that, which accelerated my time.

I got ordained my deacon orders. We get two ordinations in AME church. I got my deacon orders on a Thursday, and on that Friday night Bishop Adams sent me to pastor. Then two and a half years later, he moved me into Carlson to this church. I got my final orders in '84 . . . no, '86. Yes, I was at one church two and one half years and he moved to the other church, and I've been there almost three years. I mean it just all happened so fast that it really just blew my mind.

For the AME church it really blew my mind, because there were not a lot of women pastoring. Women were not being moved. The Bishops were afraid that the people were not going to accept women as pastors. I promise you that I have never had a problem. I mean, it's just like wherever I went the people were just hungry. They just—it's like they didn't know if I was male or female, Jew or Greek, they just accepted me as their pastor. There have been isolated incidents in this last church. I had one lady who was determined that she was not going to have any pastor other than the one who had been there fourteen years before me, but even after that she came around and changed her whole story. That's basically how it happened. It just happened.

God knows I don't know how it happened. I woke up one morning, this was all during this time when I was struggling. I was dreaming, here I was preaching again. Preaching in my dreams and I woke up singing "Tell Them"—it's a song you might have heard. I think the Wymans or somebody sing it. It says, "Tell them even if they don't believe you, tell them even if they don't receive you, tell them for me. Tell them that I love them." It was like that was the seal for me. Because I actually woke up and it was like I was still in a trance, but I was actually sitting up in my bed singing this song when I came to myself and I just said, "Well, Lord, I surrender. I mean it was like all the while I was struggling—see, there were lots of things going on.

People were saying that all these preachers just coming forth because of John and Cecelia, you know, they just come in because they saw somebody [else] come in. Well, by the time I came, I think I was, like, number forty-three or forty something like that. I didn't want people saying this about me—you know, that I was just doing this out of a trend or whatever. But I knew in my heart that it was the Lord. Still for a while, I just kept resisting it and not wanting to believe it, but then after it all just came together and when I woke up singing that song it was just like the seal. Then when I went to Reverend Bryant and he said that he had known all along, that really just blew my mind. That's my story. That's just how it happened.

Vashti M. McKenzie
Baltimore, Maryland

The Reverend Vashti M. McKenzie was born in Baltimore, Maryland, on May 28, 1947, called in 1981 and ordained an African Methodist Episcopal elder in 1986. She has a BA from the University of Maryland and an MDiv degree from Howard University's Divinity School. She pastors the Oak Street AME Church in Baltimore. Interview recorded June 15, 1989.

50

From a Broadcasting Career to Preaching

Well, if you had asked me about the call to preach maybe about seven years ago, I would have said it began eight years ago or nine years ago. But having been in the ministry now eight years, eight or nine years—well, almost a decade—I can tell you now that the call to the ministry began as a girl growing up in church. I can't remember a time when I was not in church. I remember wanting to sing on the junior choir and I couldn't read, I was not old enough to read. So I would come to choir rehearsal and I would memorize the songs. I wanted to sing on the choir, and I look back on it and I see just wanting to be close in that worship experience and the presence of God. I would go to choir rehearsal, memorize all the songs that they were going to sing on Sunday, and the older choir members would turn to the proper page for me and put the book in my hands each Sunday to sing, through vacation Bible school, and all of that.

At that particular time only men, only boys, were allowed to serve the altar. I thought it was unfair that only the boys could carry the cross, carry the Bible, be a part of the procession. I wanted to serve on the altar, too. But, of course, that wasn't a part of our tradition at the time.

And, going through college years, the regular adolescence, [I was] still not recognizing that pull, that closeness to Christ, that presence of God and serving him other than doing. As an adult at Bethel Church, which is my home church—John and Cecelia Bryant are my parents—walking into the door of that church for the first time, I felt such an extraordinary pull that I had never experienced in my religious life up until that point. I couldn't find anybody who could explain what was happening to me at that time. I really couldn't until later, of course, when all of it became clear. But God just made it so in my life that in order for me to live out my faith would be to preach the gospel and then later to serve as a pastor. He cuts off all of your options, makes it very clear, very plain that the only thing that he wants you to do and that you can do is to preach the gospel; there is no peace in any other line. Now, when God is pressing you in this manner, of course, all of us think, "Who? Why me at this time?" I had been married for ten, twelve years, settled [with], a house, a husband, a career in broadcasting—program director of a radio station. Now why the call to the ministry? If God wanted me in the ministry, why didn't he call me when I was in college and go straight through seminary? Why now? Why now? And it was just very clear that God called me as a woman, as a mother, and as a wife; that all of these gifts and all the experiences that I had up to that point would be beneficial for whatever use in his ministry. And it's true. All of those things—wife, mother, all of the other vocational experiences—have become quite significant in my pastoral ministry and in my preaching ministry. God has used all of those aspects.

I knew God wanted me to do something other than where I was. Where I was at the time is—you're talking about 1978—I was program director of a gospel radio station in Washington, DC, and it seemed to me that, as God begins to pull — that what I was doing was not enough for him as far as the ministry is concerned. One night in studying the Bible, God brought me right on through to Acts, the sixth chapter, verses one through six, and those were, I guess you would call, my "call scriptures"—the call-to-action scriptures. Then the other particular point is in the scriptures where God tells us to wait on our ministry and that we are to minister out of the power . . . as far as those who are called to prophesy, go ahead and prophesy in faith and so forth and so on. And that, I guess, you would call my "call scripture."

Going to church and being uncomfortable, uncomfortable in that present state. I mean, it's a decided consciousness of disobedience if you did not. Knowing that every time when people asked you to say something, it was as if you were preaching, and finding that you are not able to say anything else but. In my capacity at the radio station, there were many times when I was asked to emcee a gospel concert. But all of a sudden somewhere in the middle of the gospel concert, as you're taking out one group and bringing in another, all of a sudden you are proclaiming the gospel, and it's nothing you intended, it's nothing you planned. It's just that you open your mouth and there it is. Then others, of course, coming and they are affirming what God is already doing on the inside of you, making it clear. So, finally, one time I said, "Lord, this is it. I mean, there's no halfways. We're not going to 'Maybe, maybe not/is He, is He not.' We're just not going to go through that anymore. I mean, just make it clear to me exactly what your calling needs to do." It's like laying out the fleece. This is it.

So, of course, I'm on my way to church . . . sitting as far away as I could, and the word is being preached, and at the end of the sermon then Reverend Bryant says, "Turn to the person who is next to you and ask them if they're in Christ, and if they're not in Christ then you witness to them." Of course, I turned to this sister and I began to witness to her and to share with her, and said, "Do you want me to walk you down?" And I helped walk her down and led her down and off she went. She went in, but when she came out it wasn't a she, it was a he. And he took off his wig and said that, "I came here dressed as a woman but I'm going out as a man." And, you know, I was through. I was just thoroughly through. I was just totally undone. Then a sister who was on the other side of the balcony who was watching us as we were encountering, who had seen the whole thing, came over—both of us could have fallen out of the balcony at any moment, I mean, we were shouting and praising God so much—but it was just that thorough; it was just that clear. So I went home and I said, "No, God. You really can't mean this." Through a process of fasting and praying and fasting and praying and God just pressing in on you, then he just tells you, "You were called to preach. You were called to pastor," and that's it. Period.

Of course, at that time, you're talking about in a very turbulent time in the church where men and women are grappling, "Are women called to preach? Are women called to pastor?" And I sat in a convocation in 1978, it was a Baptist woman conducting a workshop on black women in the ministry, and she wrote a sentence across the blackboard that just really pierced through my confusion. She wrote, "God does call women to preach. I know because God called me." That just, boom, reverberated right in my heart, and then finally I said, "Yes, Lord. Yes, Lord. Yes, Lord." I'll just never forget that. It was in November that I walked down the aisle and finally told my pastor that I'm accepting my call to preach and I've got to be about my Master's business, my Father's business, and that is to preach the gospel.

Then after that, I experienced such a peace I had never experienced. It seems like for the whole year and a half it was like a fighting and struggling, waking up every morning and saying, "Who's going to win today? Who's going to win out?" After that I never had such a peace. I mean, it was just like, whew! I was just at peace with the world, at peace with God, at peace with myself. I mean, just the whole future became clear. Then the turbulence of the past was just the bridge that you came over. That was it. I mean, lightning didn't strike, a voice didn't come out and say, "You are called to preach my gospel." I mean, it didn't happen. God didn't write across my house, "You are called to preach." But he just makes it clear on the inside of your heart that you will not be happy, you will not be satisfied, you won't do anything unless you preach my gospel. And that's it.

James Earl Massey
Tuskegee, Alabama

The Reverend Dr. James Earl Massey was born in Detroit, Michigan, on January 4, 1930, called in 1946 and ordained by the Church of God (Anderson). He received a BTh and BRE from Detroit Bible College and an MA from Oberlin College. His honorary doctorates are numerous. When interviewed, he was Dean of Chapel at Tuskegee Institute, but is now Dean of the School of Religion at Anderson University in Indiana. He has served as a distinguished professor of New Testament and Homiletics and is considered to be one of the leading homiletitians of our time. Among his many publications is *Designing the Sermon* (Abingdon, 1983). Interview recorded July 5, 1989.

51

Called While Reading a Score of Chopin

When I was called to the ministry, I was a teenager attending Cass Technical High School in Detroit, Michigan. At the time I was in high school, I was also studying to be a concert pianist and was having classes at the Detroit Conservatory of Music. I was in the music department at Cass Technical High School, and the two institutions were preparing me for a professional life as a career pianist. It had been my custom to take my music with me all the time and when I had a spare moment to sit, whether in church or wherever I might be, and study scores and memorize them.

One Sunday morning, I was sitting in church reading the score of Chopin and while I was reading, the service was progressing and my mind left the score and became enamored with the ingredients of worship. In an almost transfixed state, I heard a voice insinuating itself in my consciousness, saying, "I want you to preach." It was as strange to me as the sounds which came to

Isaiah when he experienced the temple theophany, but it was just as definite. I was seventeen years old at the time and I have never forgotten that moment. I have never doubted the call. I have never had a reason to reinterpret what happened to me because the voice was so clear. The meaning was so forceful and the bidding was so insistent that I have never had reason or temptation to doubt.

Since that time when I was seventeen, I have known what I am to do. I had a strange struggle thereafter, though, because there were times when I wondered how my music would fit into my new experience of call. But I found, as the years wore on, that I could use music as a creative outlet for my spirit and sometimes use my music to pray to God. That was when I would play Bach preludes. I would address them to God in privacy and play to him. Now in the years that have ensued, when I am overburdened or when I am waiting on something, I resort to the piano and I relax myself before the Lord using the musical scales that I amassed in those years when I was studying piano. I would have to confess, though, that for a time, I hungered for the piano more than I did the pulpit. But in time, that hunger abated and my interest in the pulpit became keener than it was in the piano.

I used to practice the piano five and six hours in a day. Then I transferred that time to the study of the word and, before I was nineteen, I had mastered the New Testament in my memory. In fact—I need to say this with some humility—I had mastered scripture at the point of memorizing it so that if anyone was quoting from any portion of it, I could tell them where they were reading, often chapter and verse and even finish out the section that they were about to read, so hungry was my spirit for the word of God. So it was my transfer of my interest in the piano to the business of the pulpit that helped my concentration and, given a good memory by the Lord, I had very little trouble in getting into the book that would form my basis for sermonizing.

I am glad the call came early to me, because it grabbed me when I was in my formative state. It grabbed me when my interest was keen in things of the Lord. Since that time that interest has continued and even intensified. But mastering scripture at such an early age, between seventeen and nineteen years of age, it gave me the foundation for the studies that I would pursue when I would go to seminary. The languages—all three of them: Hebrew, Greek, Aramaic—all of them came with such depth of interest on my part that my knowledge of English helped me in relating what I was studying in the other languages. Now, whenever I need something in preparing a sermon, I can just draw from my memory but always recheck it against the Greek or the Hebrew, or the Aramaic. And it is interesting how much that early study of the word has sensitized me to Biblical faith, helped my understanding of Biblical ethics, and given me a kind of guarantor against many of the fads and currents of our time for there is so much abroad in our day that has no Biblical ethical basis. I am able to spot it very quickly. Not that I am so intent on what the Bible says that I do not seek to relate it to my time in a contemporaneous fashion, but it is that the Biblical point of view has so informed my thinking that I critique everything that I see in order to test it by the Biblical mandate as I would understand it.

In my own handling of the ministry, it is the centrality of the word that makes the difference for me rather than pleasing the group or moving the crowd, or anything of a more personal nature such as success or fame. I do not claim that my call is exactly like anyone else's, but I do think it has the earmarks of what elements of the call [were] to certain of the prophets. If my reading of their literature is correct, Jeremiah heard from the Lord at a very early age. Samuel heard from the Lord at a very early age, as well as others. I can look back on that time when I am going through rough periods and remember that I am not in this for myself. I'm not in this by myself. I am in it because the Lord ushered me into this by his own sovereignty. If he gives me health and strength, I want to continue it until I die. It has been a great and glorious journey. There have been twists and turns along the way. It has been uphill quite often. Never a smooth journey, ever, but always meaningful and never monotonous.

Carey McCreary
Cleveland, Ohio

The Reverend Dr. Carey McCreary was born in McWilliams, Alabama, on April 16, 1917, called to preach in 1922, and ordained a Baptist minister in 1957. He finished high school in Pensacola, Florida and received the honorary Doctor of Divinity from Florida State Christian College, Ft. Lauderdale. He pastors the New Mount Zion Baptist Church in Cleveland, Ohio. Interview recorded August, 13, 1985.

52

Betwixt and Between: Blinded at High Noon

Well, Doc, I knew that I was going to preach all of my life. From the time—you heard me say—that I preached my little sermon out there around five years old. I guess I was about five or six years old, somewhere in that neighborhood. I knew that I was going to preach the gospel just as sure as I could look at the sun. But I didn't know when. I didn't have anybody to guide me. But I knew it.

Now this was before I became a Christian. Deep down in my heart I knew it, and I don't know how I knew it. But I did. Without a shadow of a doubt, I knew I was going to preach one day. I think the reason that I got much older before I started preaching, I guess, was because I didn't have anyone to guide me. I was by myself and most of the folks around me were doing a lot of sinning, like dancing, and I was in the bunch with them, but this never left me—that feeling of preaching the gospel.

When I was about twelve, maybe thirteen years old, we went to a party. I guess we had about six miles to walk through the woods on a moon-shining night. We had an old guy with us.

He was blind, but he could go almost as good as you could go, he loved to sing the blues. I never will forget it. I started singing the blues that night and something told me not to never sing the blues like that anymore. And I never did. Something went through my heart while I was singing, and I mean, you talking about singing, I sung with all I had, singing the blues. I'll never forget this: something told me not to do it, not to put all I had into something like that. I had put everything into it, you know. And, I don't know why, I never understood why, but I felt sorry that I did it. You know, singing the blues with those guys, because I knew I had to preach one day. And the words told me to hush, and not to sing it like that and put the feeling I had into it. That bothered me a long time.

Well, I was preaching all the time after that. I just started preaching. I'd go off to myself and get in my car and just drive along and preach. The last time I preached that way was just before I left home to come to Cleveland. I went out, nobody was at the house, and I backed my car into the driveway and I really went to it. I was in my twenties then.

But I had been preaching all the time and having visions all of my life. Like I said earlier, all of my life I knew one day I was going to preach the gospel. I don't know how I knew it. I knew just as good as I'm riding in this car with you. But after I preached that sermon, every now and then it would come to me that the Lord didn't want me.

After I got older I went to thinking about money, cars and land. I was saying inside myself I have made it over, I won't have to do it now. Now that's when God is about to get you. Yessir, when I came to Cleveland it worked so fast. I came to Cleveland in April or May, 1956, and I started preaching in September.

Now, this is what happened. I got to the place that I didn't want to be around anybody doing or saying anything wrong. I would even go up into the room and shut the door. I just got sick of it. I started to reading and praying. I started having visions at night. I sat down and told Bobbie (my cousin that I was living with) that I was called to preach. She said, "Cous[in], you mean the Lord done called." I said, "Cous, he done called me to preach. I've got to do it."

Then I got a job in the building trades. One day I finished one job and left to go downtown. Now this is when it got on me real rough. When I got to that place downtown I walked inside, and I turned blind, but not completely blind. I could see folks, you know, moving around, but I felt like I was about to fall. A fellow came over to me and asked me if I was a preacher. I don't know what made him do that. And I didn't know what to say. Man, I hated to say yes and I hated to say no. So I said, "Yes and no." That man said, "What kind of talk is that?" Then I tried to explain it to him to the best of my knowledge.

Doc, I heard a voice saying, "I want you to leave here and go tell your pastor that you have been called to preach." I went home, pulled those clothes off, and I went on down to the church and knocked on the back door. Rev. Fuller opened that door and a voice said to me, "Look at the clock." And that's something I've never understood yet: why that voice told me to look at the clock. But when he opened that door and the Spirit said to me, "Look at the clock," that clock was straight up twelve o'clock. I told him with tears in my eyes what happened. As I was telling Rev. Fuller what the Spirit told me—"I was downtown looking for a job and the Spirit told me to come and tell you I was called to preach"—he said, "Well that's one thing you got to be sure of."

Then I said, "Well, maybe I won't have to do it", because he didn't seem to believe me. And since Bobbie had told me what a great man Rev. Fuller was I felt that whatever he said had to be right. I said, "Rev. Fuller, I want to ask you to do something for me. Will you pray for me?" He said, "Yes." He laid his hand on my head and he prayed. And I said then, since that man prayed for me I won't have to do it, you know, the way Bobbie had talked about him. He's close to the Lord and the Lord will hear him and I won't have to do it. But, Doc, that thing looked like it was getting tighter and tighter. And it got so tight my plate would talk to me, my pillow would talk to me.

I'd have my plate, sitting there looking at it, and I was about to put my food on it and it would tell me, "You got to preach, you got to preach." Boy, I tell you the truth, I would get so sick in my stomach. I would hear it so often that I'd try to get mad with it. And when I'd lay down at night, my pillow would tell me, "You got to preach." Sometimes it would say, "You must preach." Boy, you talking about being sick.

Then I started having visions. One of the visions I had just before I was called to preach seemed like I was in Jerusalem. I'm not saying that's where it was, but it seemed like a place like that. It was a big pasture that had a tall fence and inside that pasture was a river, a small river. The river became narrow at places, but it would widen at other places and then get narrow again. Doc, it was so many folks trapped in that place. It was so many of God's children trapped in that river. And there was what looked like, to me, a bob-tailed horse inside that pasture. And the Lord told me that I had to get those children out of the river, but I had to get into the river because that horse would get me too. I was outside the fence. But I had to get inside that fence and get to this river before that horse would get me. And it looked to me like it was as fast as lightning. It could be here and over there at the same time.

The Lord told me, "You've got to get in there." And he said, "Your oldest brother is in there, way up at the other end and he's trapped too." When he started that way, I opened that gate and I shot out there, and about the time I jumped in he just missed me. I didn't get them all of them out, but I showed a bunch of them how to get out and what to do. I'd get one out at the time. And you would have to do it that way because when you got in that small place, he could get you. Only way he'd miss you is, you'd have to get in that place where it was wider and you could go to the other side.

And, Doc, after I got them out, I went on up to where it looked like the sun was shining. I walked on up and it looked like a field of straw, but when you got up there it was a highway. I asked a man that was standing there to "tell me where this highway goes." He said, "This way will carry you to hell, and this way will carry you to heaven." That was the prettiest highway I've ever seen in my life. The sun was shining, and it looked just like gold. You know, while I was in Israel I looked for that place. I looked for it. The only place I found looked something like it was over there at Caesarea Phillipi back out there in that field. I saw a spot that looked kind of like it. Now, that dream was three hours and a half long.

That one was before I received my call. Then I had another vision right after then when I was called to the church. That's when he showed me all these folks. I've had plenty dreams about my calling, but these are some which really shook me up. These folks were all around me; that was before I started preaching. God gave me that Bible and that was another long vision, dream. Sometimes those dreams would last two and three hours, and when I'd wake up I'd be so tired. I would be given out doing what I was supposed to be doing in the dream. And when I'd wake up, it would be so clear. I can see the day when God handed me that Bible, just like it was done this morning. He said,

Betwixt and Between: Blinded at High Noon

"These folks are waiting for you." Yessir.

Now, that Sunday night after I went to Rev. Fuller and I asked him about what the Spirit told me when I was downtown... Rev. Fuller told me to meet him a couple times, but we didn't get together. So, finally, he asked me to come to his house. I went down to his house. He told me, "Now you got to be sure that the Lord called you to preach." In the way he talked to me and what the folks had told me about him, I felt like whatever he told me, that would be what God wanted. So I talked with him and he carried me through some scripture that I didn't know too much about. Then he said, if I had been called I would have known that scripture. So I said to myself, all right, maybe it's not so.

Well, I felt kind of good because I thought I didn't have to preach. He told me to "Get on your knees and talk to the Lord about it." I got on my knees that night, and I asked the Lord if he had called me to the ministry. I wanted to know. And, Doc, I woke up; I think it was about the crack of day and I felt pretty nice about it because I hadn't felt anything and I didn't see anything in a dream. I don't know whether I went half way back to sleep or what. But the Holy Spirit jumped on me and it felt like to me it was going to choke me to death. It was so hard until I scared my wife. I scared her so that she jumped out of the bed, and it grabbed me and held me down and it almost killed me. I had woke up and the Lord hadn't called me. I was a little disappointed, but I was partly glad too, because I felt I wasn't gonna do it. So I was betwixt and between. I was kind of worried that I misled myself. Then I said, well, I won't have to do it now nor what I had gone through with hearing these voices talking about "preach the gospel, preach the gospel." Then I said, well, it could have just been something else.

But, man, after that experience [with the Holy Spirit], I said then, and I've said to everybody else, "If the Lord told you to do something, you do it and don't ask anybody else nothing. But be sure the Lord told you." That man [Rev. Fuller] almost messed me up, you know, with doubt. But the Spirit of the Lord got on me and gave me confidence to know not to fool with nobody when the Lord tells you to do something. Go ahead on and do it. And I have said that many times. I just want to be sure the Lord said so and ain't nobody can tell me nothing. And I'm not going to man for any advice. I'll do what the Lord says. Of course, I was young, you know, and I didn't have nobody to guide me. That's why I was trying to get someone to guide me and tell me what to do. But I found out if God tells you to do, just go ahead on and do it. He will fix a way for you to do it if he tells you to do it.

Now, this is the next thing I thought. I would try to get out of it because, you know, dedicating your life and living the type of life expected of a minister, you wonder if you will make it with all you have to give up. But at the same time, it looks like the clock keeps rolling for you to get going. And with me, I was in a strange place and fooling with these old preachers up here. I didn't get any encouragement and it was a hard thing. But that spirit will keep rolling inside of you, and then you've got to do it.

After that, it looked like I was gonna preach, because this pastor I was under set up a time for me to deliver my first sermon; then I started getting sick. My stomach got to the place I couldn't eat. And I was so sick at the stomach that medicine didn't do me any good. But when I preached my trial sermon, all that left me. That left me. I felt better than I ever did in my life.

I figure that's the reason I always try to treat everybody so kind in the ministry, because I was treated so badly. A man in the ministry needs a lot of encouragement. Someone needs to tell him what he's got to go through and how he ought to be schooled. Because if he is not schooled, brother, he's got to go through the pits of hell. You need that schooling to help you, and you need somebody behind you to tell you to go ahead. But you know a lot of guys, especially if he's got a good voice, he thinks he's got it made. But, you see, from now on you got to study. And right now I study more than I ever studied in my life. Sometimes, I go over to the church and I study all day if I can get that chance, and I love to do it. You see, that's what God's word will do for you, it make you love to do it.

Now one last thing. With my call, the Lord gave me a gift of seeing things. I can see death on people. The first one that I remember, or at least paying any attention to it, because I've been seeing it for a long time. But I never paid too much attention to it, because I felt it was just me. But in my pastoring in New Mount Zion, I started watching my members very closely. And the first one I saw was Sister Brake. When she got ill I went over to her house and I sat down, and I looked at her and I knew she wasn't gonna get well. And while I was looking at her, although she was talking like she was well, I could see in her face that she was sick, real sick, and within a few minutes she had a stroke and after that she died.

Then, one Sunday morning in Sunday school, I left my

study and went down in the basement into your classroom. And when I opened the door I looked at Deacon Brake, and I saw death in his face. He was sitting there like he was happy [spiritually] with the teaching that you were doing, but I saw in his face that he was sick unto death. And I sat down beside him and I kept my eyes on him, and in a few minutes he fell down on the floor. He didn't die there on the spot, but after that he died.

One Sunday evening Deacon Collins got up in the choirstand and said, "I want to sing a song for Rev. and Sis McCreary." As I looked around at him, I could see death on him. After he finished his song and made one step out of the pulpit, he fell. When he hit the floor, I knew he wouldn't make it.

Another time I was sitting in the pulpit and I looked at Deacon Jones. Deacon Jones was sitting across from the pulpit on the first seat, and I looked down on the right side of his face and I saw death on him. And I told Deacon Means and I told you that I saw death on Deacon Jones's face. I didn't know how long he was going to live, but I wanted you all to know I had seen it. Deacon Means couldn't believe it because Deacon Jones seemed to be in good health. But we buried him two or three weeks ago.

One time I was fortunate enough to eat dinner with Deacon Woodard. He asked my wife and I to come over to his house and eat Thanksgiving dinner with his family. After we ate he said to me, "Reverend, let's go into the living room." We went in and sat down, and he started talking to me about life and what he had done for his wife. And he said to me, "Reverend, you know, after I'm gone my wife won't find nobody else like me. I gave her everything she asked me for." When he said that, I looked up in his face and he was looking out through the window and I saw death on him. Well, I didn't believe it because he seemed to be so well and so young. A week from that day he died. Yes, I can by God's help—nothing I know—but I can see it, when death is on someone.

Also, I can tell when someone is going to be seriously sick. He has a different look than the ones who are going to die. I don't see death on them. Rev. Turner preached for me on Sunday and when we came out, I was sitting down in the pulpit when I looked across and I saw his wife. When I looked in her face, I saw that she was going to be sick. And I told my wife on the way home that Mrs. Turner was going to be sick, serious sick unto death, but she wouldn't die. The next week I met Rev. Turner and he said, "My wife is so sick, it seems like I'm gonna lose her." I said, "Well, Rev. Turner, I wanted to tell you, but I don't know how to. I don't know how to deal with these things when I see these different things."

I can sit down and talk with a person, and just look in their face and I can tell whether they are going to be serious sick or die. If it's close around me I can see it. I saw Bobbie's illness before she got ill. I saw it.

When I first came to Cleveland, Mr. Coleman, Annie Mae Coleman's husband, had two fine eyes, he thought. And I looked in his face and I told Bobbie, "You know what I see?" She said, "What?" I said, "Coleman is going to be blind in one eye." She said, "Ahh, cous." I said, "Well, you just watch." About two and one-half years later, he was stone blind in one eye. Yes, I can see these things. I've seen many things in New Mount Zion just looking at a person. And whatever I see, it will happen.

I saw the trouble you were going to have with your eyes when you first came to join the church. You were about nine years old then, but I didn't want to tell you, and I don't think I ever told you, but I saw it. I told your mother about it. I said, he's gonna have trouble with his eyes. But after you started going to the doctor and taking care of it, then it was no use of me to tell you, but I saw it. I told your mother that she was going to have trouble with her eyes. And when I first met her, I told her, "You suffer with headaches." And she said, "Yeah, how did you know that?" And I said, "I know it."

I pay more attention to my members, but, if anybody is around me I can see it. Now, I'll tell you something about the preacher in Akron, your friend. When I first saw his wife, I knew she was going to get sick. I started to tell him about her, but I hated to do this. I wanted to tell him not to take her on that trip, but I just didn't know how to do it. I saw that when I first met her, that she was going to be serious sick. I certainly did. Now, I'll tell you something about him. He has a hand of healing and he doesn't even know it. Yessir, he has it. But, he has never paid any attention to it. But, in that fellow's right hand, God has given him a hand of laying it on folks, and they will feel better or get well.

And I'm going to tell you something I want you to watch. This little boy in the church [gesturing] is going to have a hearing problem. I don't know when it's going to be, but it's going to be. He won't hear good out of one of his ears. I've seen that for a long time.

I'll tell you something else I want you to watch. This woman [unnamed—since it is still future] will eventually be serious sick in her stomach. It will eventually come. Yessir, I can see all these things. If it's trouble around, especially in health, I can see it.

I can see all these things. It's nothing of my makeup. It's just when I look at you I can see it. And I can get it also when you shake hands with me. I can tell certain things that way. I see a lot of things that I don't tell folks because I don't want to frighten anybody. And many things I see I just watch it myself in order to be sure that I'm right, because I don't want to tell anybody something wrong. Yessir.

Leroy McCreary
Berea, Ohio

The Reverend Leroy McCreary was born in Mobile, Alabama, on December 5, 1946, called in 1969 and ordained a Baptist minister in 1970. He received a BS from Cleveland State University, an MSW from Case Western Reserve University and an MA from Ashland Theological Seminary. He pastors the People's Community Church in Berea. This interview was recorded February 22, 1985.

53

The Presence of God in the Wind

I am going to speak for the first time in any detail with anyone other than my former pastor [and cousin], Rev. Cary McCreary, about my call to the ministry, And I say for the first time, because I have not for many, many years—in fact, some sixteen years—revisited in my own mind from beginning to end my call into the ministry.

In fact, as I sit here now giving this preface to my detailed review of my call, I cannot remember having taken a very careful and detailed view of my call to the ministry. My call to the ministry occurred in 1969. I can remember very clearly that God was moving in my life. Let me be clear about that statement. I felt that God's presence was with me daily during this time period.

I had a sense of his presence doing my walk. Even [in] the wind that blew against me as I walked across the parking lot at my job. I sensed his presence. This was a presence of such intensity that I had never experienced before. It was pleasant, it provided me with a sense of confidence and of direction that I had never before experienced. I also sensed his presence in the work I was doing at the church at that time.

I don't remember the name of the group that I was working with in the church at that time. But I do remember I was working with a group of young men. We were interested in bringing other people into the church. And I remember a strong sense of direction to encourage others to come to the Lord. I remember walking the streets and knocking on doors and inviting people to come. I did this with a number of other young men in the church.

In addition to that, I also felt his presence in many quiet places that I would go to. Perhaps the most vivid of those quiet places was when I went to "a remote place in a remote building" at my job. I was working as a male clerk at the time. I went there and while sitting there I prayed. And—it was if I had dosed off to sleep while sitting there—I dreamed and I saw a face with a beard that I can never forget. It was a calming feeling, of course. It was like I was in a trance.

After that experience I got up, went back to my job, worked the rest of the day [and] I went home. I don't specifically remember the sequence, but it was sometime later that I either in reading the paper and in listening to the radio, or watching television, or hearing someone tell me, that [I learned] there was an evangelist who was going to be at the public auditorium and this was on a week night. This was a fairly well-known evangelist to some people. I had never heard of him.

However, for one reason or another, I was intrigued by the publicity about this evangelist, and as best I can recall, he had some role in helping those who felt that they had gotten a call or that they were getting a call to understand it.

So, I alone drove to the public auditorium, went in to that service that evening. I listened as this man preached, I don't remember his name, and he preached with great fervency. He was, as I look back now, a very emotional preacher, and at the end of his service, he invited people who felt that God was dealing in their lives to come up and to meet him upon the stage.

I went on stage with many others who walked up there that night. And he talked and he said, "if God has called you, you should go to work for him." I left, in fact I never did shake his hand, I saw him from a distance on the stage. I left and returned home and continued to feel in my heart that God had called me to preach, that he wanted me to do something for him.

And it was some time after that, and it was a short time after that I, went to my aunt with whom I was living. And I said to her that God has called me to preach. She expressed some surprise and shock, and I told her he had and she said to me,

"Well you better go and see Rev. Cary McCreary," who was my cousin, whose church she and I were both members in good standing [of]. I went to him.

However, I do need to backtrack for a minute. Just before going to her, my aunt, I believe . . . I spoke to a minister, a minister who someone had told me was very good in helping young men get started in the ministry, whose church was on east 79th or 89th and Wade Park. It's a Methodist church. I called there and made an appointment with him. And I went there and told him that I had been called to preach. And he told me the first step in getting started is to go see my pastor.

It was after that I met with him after having talked with my aunt. I went to Rev. McCreary and I told him. It was on a Saturday morning, as best as I can recall, and I told him I had been called to preach, and I was shocked at how easily he accepted my confession that I had been called to preach.

I had anticipated some difficulty there. I did not think that he would accept it as easily as he did. I had some reluctance in going to him initially. But I felt at ease in talking to him about my call. I remember him asking me if I was sure that I had been called, and I told him I was sure that God had spoken to me and wanted me to preach.

He said, Well, we will set a date for you to give your trial sermon. It wasn't very long after that, perhaps several weeks, something like the fourth Sunday, at which time it had been publicized to the other churches and to the members that I would be giving my trial sermon, which I did. And the church was full when I gave my trial sermon, and I have been preaching since that time.

The testimony that I have just given is one that I have not given [before] in the sequence, and in the order, and in the detail that I have just given. I am giving it after some sixteen years of being in the ministry. I have never written down in detail my call, how it occurred. I have not analyzed it, but I have accepted the experience I have described to you thus far as having been my call from God to preach.

Since that time, I have held that conviction, and even though at present I pastor a church and also hold a full-time job, I still see my ministry as the fulfillment of the call I received from God in 1969. This ends my description of my call to the ministry.

Samuel B. McKinney
Seattle, Washington

The Reverend Dr. Samuel Berry McKinney was born in Flint, Michigan, on December 28, 1926, called in 1949 and ordained a Baptist minister in 1951. He has a BA from Morehouse, and a BD and DMin from Colgate Rochester. He pastors Mt. Zion Baptist Church in Seattle. He co-authored *Church Administration in the Black Perspective* (Judson, 1976). Interview recorded June 21, 1989.

54

"I Didn't Call You to Be Your Father's Clone"

I'm Samuel Berry McKinney, pastor of the Mount Zion Baptist Church in Seattle, Washington, since the first Sunday in February of 1958. And on September forth of this year, I was in the ministry preaching forty years. My call to the ministry is not as dramatic as some of another era and another generation, where people saw something in the sky [or ask themselves] Why did I hear a series of voices? I was not dangling overhead or over held with a spider thread. Nothing that dramatic.

I am a third-generation Baptist preacher in the family. My mother used to say . . . my father was a preacher, and she married a minister, and her son, her second son, was a minister. I am third-generation. Born and raised in a Christian ministerial home. My father, the pastor of the Antioch Baptist Church in Cleveland, Ohio, for thirty-four and a half years. When I was born, he was pastoring the Michigan Olive Baptist Church in Flint, Michigan. So I have an uncle here in Nashville who was married to one of my mother's sisters who was a minister, so I have been surrounded by the ministry and the church all of my life.

I've had some good exposures. I can't say that my father was the typical or stereotypical minister of his time, because he was college and seminary trained, Morehouse, etcetera. So, I grew up in an environment of the trained clergy. And I have to be careful that my ministry doesn't become what some would call name-dropping: mentioning of prominent names that I have had contact with. However, I would not be honest without recognizing some of these persons that have had some bearing on my life. Because our home, our home was open. That was before the time when Black folks could stay in hotels. So people stayed in the home. Our dining room table was the place for a lot of ministers when they came to Cleveland, Ohio. And we would break bread at our table. So, as the old folks would say, "from the earliest of my existence" I've been exposed to the ministry.

And coming up in a home of a trained and prepared minister, maybe I made some assumptions. I did make some assumptions in my youth, but as my mother's sister who lived with us would say, I don't want to sound elitist. That both of your parents had advanced degrees before you were born, had finished college, I just assumed that I would do the same. Many of the ministers that we were exposed to as children were of similar backgrounds. My father was a minister who recognized that to whom much was given, much was required. So he did not look upon his advanced training as a badge of distinction, but saw it has a hand of mercy that had been extended to him. Because he was the son a Georgia sharecropper. My father was eighteen years old in the fifth grade when he went to the old Atlanta Baptist College, which later became Morehouse, and he was there for ten years, from 1910 to 1920, when he finished at the age of twenty-eight from college. Went there in the fifth grade and came out ten years later from college. My mother had the distinction of being one of the few women who actually graduated from Morehouse, because Spelman at that time was unaccredited.

So, I was involved in this and exposed to it. Also, my father's church was also a place in the Cleveland community where mass meetings, rallies, civil rights meetings in the 1930s and 40s were held. So, as a child I heard people like A. Philip Randolph and other outstanding black leaders. That made an impression on me. That's where Wings Over Jordan started.

"I Didn't Call You to Be Your Father's Clone"

The group had started off in the late 1930s as Wings Over Cleveland, and soon went over a nationwide broadcast and was heard all over the country. It sort of disbanded after WW II. The first nationwide broadcast was from our church. So I had exposure as a child to the religious life, our home, our church. Although I found out later that it was not the typical story. When WW II came along, my brother was a little older and he went into service. So I spent quite a bit of time going around with my father, following and listening to him. And he would take stands on issues that were of significance. My father was quite an exponent of the social gospel, having received such emphasis at Morehouse, and was on record around Cleveland speaking out against injustice and trying to help our folks improve their lot. So we had those kind of sermons.

So, I had an interest in the ministry. By going around with him I was a minister's child. We had to go to church. So minister's kids did get exposed to certain processes and procedures that other kids did not, and ended up being presidents of organizations and groups, ecclesiastical associations, NAACP and things like that.

When I went to college, I turned eighteen. I went to see Dr. Benjamin Mays and told him that I had been called to preach. And he asked me, "Now, has the Lord called you or Uncle Sam?" And, I said, "You know, Doc, it was simultaneous." He said, "Well, I think you ought to go ahead into the military, a little military service might help you." So I went on into the army and was there for seven months and came back to Morehouse. I knew then that I was going to end up in the ministry. But I did not want to make any pitch about it. In fact, on the campus the fellows accused me of persecuting preachers. I guess I was kind of hard on what was called the "jackleg" type. So, since I've been in the ministry I've been teased by some of the fellows I used to give a fit to. One fellow said, "He was hard on jacklegs in college." I said, "I still am hard on jacklegs."

I had started in a pre-law course, so when I got out of the Army, only having been in the Army for a shortened period of time, I thought I would return to college on the GI Bill. I did not have the luxury of changing my major to something else. So I had to sit down and plot out my course to finish my pre-law. The thing that was more interesting, however, was that to re-enter Morehouse on the GI Bill, you had to take a series of psychological exams. And, once those were approved, they would judge whether you should go there to school. I put down law, the ministry and public service. According to the results of this exam, I would have done well in law and public service. The examiner said, "But you forget about that ministry." I said, "Why?" He said, "According to this exam, you have a low sense of values."

I returned to school, went to two Summer school terms and came out in June 1949. And, when I graduated, I had been accepted in two or three law schools, but I knew I wasn't going and I was very put out with my father. During my senior year, we had a food strike on the campus and I was accused of being one of the ring leaders and I was. Mrs. Mays sent a letter to my mother, telling her what a fine Christian lady she was to have such a contentious, obnoxious son. And she gave me a copy that I found in my mailbox. I went to her and talked to her about it. And some other students asked, "Why didn't you write my mother?" She said, "Well, I don't know your mother." Then, I got a telegram from my father which said, "Cease leadership in strike and prepare to come home." So I got on the phone, and that was the first time that we nearly came head-to-head on anything. I told him, "First, what makes you think that I the head of this thing?" because we were trying to hide the leadership and we would put folks out front so they couldn't pinpoint who was leading. Even though we tried, it didn't always work. He said, "Don't you know that if there was a plot in Geaorgia to blow up the capital, you would be in on it?" So, that was his assessment. He said, "Don't you know that I could talk to Dr. Mays and he would put you out of that school?" I said, "Yes, I know that." "But what makes you think I'm coming home?" He said, "But where are you going to go? I'll call all of your aunts and uncles and all your relatives." I said, "This is a bigger world than that. And furthermore, you are not paying for this education. Uncle Sam is paying for this." My mother got on the phone and tried to cool us down. It went on from there to "the straw that broke the camel's back."

The Morehouse Glee Club sang in my father's church; the glee clubs would travel around, and they would put you up in homes and the church would give you breakfast and dinner. We were eating a meal and I guess we were saying the grace, and he eased up behind me. And I saw him standing there. After we finished saying grace, he put his hand on my shoulder and said, "Now start a strike here and see how far you get." That was a put-down in front of my peers, and I got, and I got, all kind of teasing behind that. So, I said this is it, I won't be going home. I didn't tell him that, but I did say to my mother, "I won't be back." She said, "Where are you going?" I said, "I don't know yet, but I want you to know."

And then I was about to graduate and they were making plans to come to my commencement. I had the attitude that I could care less. Then, my mother was on her way to a tea one Sunday afternoon. The city used to have streetcars with little islands where you would get off and then you would have to cross the street. She stepped off the streetcar island and a car coming out of nowhere hit her. She was banged up a little bit and they took her to the hospital and then released her. She wrote me and told me that she would not be coming to my commencement, and begged me to please come home. And, really, I didn't have anywhere else to go.

So I went home. And I guess my father wanted to assert his authority, so he made my brother, who was fifteen months older than I am, and twin sisters, who are five years younger, and myself go to prayer meeting. I really didn't want to go, but my sisters who were graduating said, "Ah, come on." I didn't want to get anything started, so I went on. There was a fellow there that I had not seen before. Since I had been in and out of town, a lot of people joined the church that I did not know. This fellow told the story about a man that had been called to preach. It was very obvious that he was talking about himself. So, after I listened to him, I went home and said, "Now, Lord, I have finished college and I'm not going to law school. If you want me you had better tell me something. I need to know. I need to know something. I don't know how you do this. I've heard all these stories about how it's done to other folks, but you need to do something for me."

Well, that summer, I really had no work and that was a summer in which there was no work. I just attended our fortieth class reunion of Morehouse last May, and a number of us were sitting around sharing experiences of what we have done since we graduated. One fellow said, "You know, there were several fellows who weren't preaching in college, like myself." All of us referred to the summer without jobs and how rough it was, and somebody said, "No wonder so many of you fellows started preaching. You couldn't find employment that summer."

My father would never say he made a mistake or that he was wrong, but he would try to soften things up. So he made some work. So, I was around the church working and it was lunch time and everybody else was out. I was in the office and the phone rang. It was a white minister who wanted to speak to the fellow who use to assist my father when he was a student at Oberlin Seminary. I told him that he was back in Texas. He said that he wanted him to come out and speak one Sunday while he was on vacation. I said, "Sorry he's gone. What about me," I said, "I'm a preacher." He said, "No, I remember you when you were active in the BYPU," etc. So, he twisted my arm. It was on the west side of town.

In the meantime, that started me to thinking about seminary. I said, "Lord, if you really want me to do this, I'm going to see if any doors open. So, I wrote to the dean of the school of religion at Oberlin and made an appointment to go down there to see him on Saturday. This was after I had spoken at that church. I went down there to see the dean and he had a copy of my grades. He said they were good but that I had waited too late. He said I could enter in January. So I said, "Well, put me down for that."

On my way back, I didn't go back the main road. I went a back road and it took me right past the church that I had just spoken at. The minister was out in the yard. He said, "Oh, you like the West Side?" I said, "Not particularly. And, he said, "Well, what are you doing over here?" I told him that I had been to Oberlin to see if I could get in school but I have to wait until January. That next Monday I happened to be downtown. I ran into another white minister who was on the Cleveland Baptist Association, which was part of the American Baptist [association]. I just happen to pass the office and he came up to me and said, "Have you been trying to go to seminary? I told him that I had been to Oberlin but that it had not worked out. He said, "Would you be willing to go to CRDS?" I said, "What's that?" He said, "Colgate Rochester." I said, "Oh, yes. Do you think they will take me at this late date?" He said, "Well, I'm leaving this afternoon and I'm going to stop in Rochester" — he used to pastor there, and I'll talk to the president. In the meantime, why don't you get your records straight?" So while I was downtown, I went and got there address and I sent everything to Colgate Rochester with a special delivery stamp. That Thursday, I got a letter from the president, telling me that the minister had been by and that they would be glad to have me, but of course that would be contingent upon grades, etc. But if I was accepted, I would be hearing from the dean. The next day I heard from the dean, who said that I was accepted.

I didn't have any money. My GI bill had run out. One of the requirements was that you had to be licensed and all that. When I got the letter, I was suppose to take this young lady to the ballgame. But I called and cancelled it. She got a little mad, but I told her, "Well, if you want to see me, you come to church tonight." She said, "For what?" I said, "Just be there." My father was reading the paper. When I put the phone down, he said, "Why you going to church tonight, that's prayer meeting?" I said, "I want to raise a question to the church." He said "What?" I said, "Preach my trial sermon." So that's all I said. My mother was in the kitchen. She dropped what she was doing and came in there. My mother's oldest sister, who lived there with us, came in. They said, we're glad we knew you were wrestling with something this summer, now maybe we can get some peace around this house. My brother went upstairs and got on the phone and [started] calling folks, saying, "He's done it now. He couldn't find a job, so he starting preaching."

So, I read and interpreted all of that, and I subsequently learned as a result of that and other things that the way the Lord moves in my life is by opening doors and making opportunities possible. I saw that as a definitive call. So I went to church that night to tell my story, and I really didn't get a chance to say but one or two words and the old ladies started hollering and so on. Then, the phone lines got busy and my father set the date. And he established the first Sunday in September, the fourth 1949.

I was waiting to go to church that Sunday, and before church started, this old lady named Mother Taylor, she was about a hundred and three when she died, called—she would start talking, and soon as someone picked up the phone and I just happened to pick it up this time—and said, "Send somebody down here to the project to pick me up. I want to go to church tonight. I want to see that boy just standing up in the pulpit. I know he ain't got nothing to say, I just want to see him up there."

Well, that church was jammed packed that night. This was going to be the biggest show in town. All ages and generations were there. Parents and little children alike dragged out there because they didn't have babysitters, because they wanted to see this. After I had finished and it was very well received, my father told me, "We had the same text." His trial sermon, just like mine, was based on the temptation of Jesus, but he didn't tell me that beforehand. Because before that, he had asked me if I had a scripture and he put it in the bulletin. Of course we handled it differently, but it was the same text, and I had gone to the same school and was going to the same seminary as he did.

So, I went on to Rochester, although I had to work that summer. Right after WW II they had on the GI bill what they called the 52-20 club. If you couldn't find work, you were entitled to 52 weeks at $20 each, which was a lot of money then. Well, I applied for that unemployment, but I didn't get it. After I got to school, it came in one lump sum and that was a blessing. After the offering that the church gave me to send me up to school, that was all the money I had. I had used up my GI bill. I got to Rochester, I was late. The dean said I was the last person to go through there on a complete tuition, room and board scholarship with everything taken care of. One of the fellows who was already there, who knew about it, said to me, "Now the only way you can maintain this is don't buy a car"—I was there from 1949 to 1952—"and don't put any money in the Rochester Bank." I went through there in three years. I worked in the dinning room, my first year in the kitchen. The last two years I sold the meal tickets and collected the money. And they gave me $3.50 a week.

I assisted in a church my last two years. I guess I was looking for reinforcements for the call. Have I made the right decision? Right after I finished my first year, a well-known sociologist who had taught at Morehouse and Atlanta University was on our campus, and he invited me and some other fellows to spend the summer working for him. He had a grant from the National Baptist, Southern Baptist and American Baptist dealing with the educational background of Negro Baptist ministers.

So, we all gathered in Philadelphia and went over our forms. One of the questions was, "Tell us about your call." That helped me a lot. And we got all types of interesting and bizarre answers. Although we got the bizarre, the dramatic, and so on, but by and large what I heard was people saying it was an inner urge that [they] couldn't throw off. There was a compulsion, some[thing] propelling [them] to function and respond in a certain way. And at some point in time, they were dealing with an inner voice or opening of doors, the provision of opportunities that had not been there. One told me that in was in the "blueprint of eternity that he preach"; others talked like Jeremiah; some of them quoted various verses of the Bible that you were called before you were born in your mother's womb. But by and large it was not the dramatic experience, but a growing sense and awareness that this you had to do. One fellow said, "If you don't do it, you are going to end up on God's chain gang."

So, I have shared with you some of the details of [my call]. It was something I knew very early in life. One of the things that kept me from it—made me not acknowledge it sooner—was my father, a very high, loyal, principled figure who was so much up there that I kept saying, I can't be like he is. So the Lord and I had to untangle the idea that I'm not calling you to be his clone, but I'm calling you to give what you have to offer. So, I told him, "All right, then, so long as we understand." That's basically it.

Marvin A. McMickle
Cleveland, Ohio

The Reverend Dr. Marvin A. McMickle was born in Chicago, Illinois on December 16, 1948, called to preach in 1963-65 and ordained a Baptist minister in 1973. He received a BA from Aurora College (Illinois), an MDiv from Union Theological Seminary (New York) and a DMin from Princeton Theological Seminary. He pastors the Antioch Baptist Church in Cleveland. Interview recorded November 17, 1988.

55

When a White Candle Turned Red

As best as I can remember—I reviewed this with a Bible study class just the other day—my call became apparent to me in my middle teens. I didn't accept it at that point, but it first began to dawn on me that that's where the Lord was leading me. It happened at a Summer church camp in 1963, '64 or '65. I don't recall the precise year. The camp director was in charge of the closing devotion on a Friday night at the end of the week when the camp setting was over. And [he] gave the campers one of two options as an act of consecration. One act was to consecrate oneself to Christian living [with] no particular vocational connection, just that you wanted to live as a Christian and that sort of thing. If that were the case, he asked us to come up and take a white candle, light it, hold it and that was a kind of light against the darkness symbol. And then to a second group of people he said, "And if you would like to commit to full-time Christian vocation, ministry, missionary, Christian education, using whatever you think your talent is and whatever your inclinations are, you come up and get a red candle and do the same thing, but stand somewhere else and light your candle." And they were talking to us in different groups based upon our response.

So, I took a white candle, because that's all I ever intended to do was to try to live right. I had never thought about anything beyond that. We were then told that we could keep the candles as a memento of the week. Of course, those who had taken the red candles would have cherished it more than those of us who took a white candle. I put my candle under my pillow as we all did for lack of any other place to store it. The next morning, it was red. Now, a number of questions went through one's mind. Did somebody in the night come under my pillow and for some reason change my candle? Had I taken the wrong candle all along and never realized it? Had the candle miraculously changed colors, you know, through some process?

I don't know to this day. Nobody ever came forward. If it's a practical joke, somebody will tell you twenty years later, "Oh, by the way, you are in the wrong vocation, because I'm the one who changed your candle." But nobody ever told me that they were responsible for it. I was never able to resolve that. I told the camp director the next morning what had happened, and he had no solution except to say, "You know, maybe the Lord is saying something that none of us understand right now." That obviously was not a sufficient enough act to persuade me to do anything, except be more open to what may be happening around me.

That was sort of the beginning of my thought about the vocation. How did this candle turn colors? I did nothing else with it until the Civil Rights movement. It was really during the 1966 Chicago campaign, when Martin Luther King came to Chicago, that two things came together: my own continuing struggle with vocation dating back to this camp meeting, and my own relationship with him, seeing in him a model for Christian ministry that was different from any I'd ever seen before.

So, it was then in 1966 that I began to think more assuredly about this as a vocation. And, I went to a small Christian college in Aurora, Illinois to persue it academically. Still, I really hadn't become fully persuaded what form it would take, but was now fairly sure that this was going to be something to take seriously. However, I had already made my own mind up about what my vocation was going to be. I was first going to be an architect, but all opportunities to pursue that seemed not to be forthcoming. I had a job as a printer, working in a print shop. There [was an] early ample income in relationship to that, but there was this inward sense that this wasn't it. And that's when

I was going off to college in 1966.

What finally began to nail this down for me was that every other thing that I tried to become interested in academically and vocationally was a dead-end street. The only opportunities that were being afforded me in terms of chances to exercise natural gifts and talents were in relationship to those gifts and talents that could best be applied in this field. What I began to deal with then was a series of confirmations and a series of dead-end streets. Anything that I wanted to do, everytime I seemed to say, "All right, Lord, I'll try this one more time." I was asked to speak in the chapel, unheard of for a freshman student. Success! All the academic work that I was doing, all of the things that I thought I really wanted to focus on, wasn't gelling. But in religion and philosophy it was as if I was seeing things that I didn't even know was there in terms of concepts and ideas and information.

So, for me, it was a long, prolonged series of my trial and error in trying to pick my own vocation, and the Lord opening up over a long period of time more and more, larger and larger, areas of opportunities, which, when I chose to say yes to them, almost always yielded further confirmation. That this is really what you are built to do, what you are meant to do and what you ought to do.

Then it ceased to be a question of Christian vocation and it became a question of form. By the time I got to my last year in college and into seminary, the question was, Academic or pastoring? So that the question about shall I be in some church-related role went away at a moment that I can't tell you. I'm going to be doing something that involves all of these books. Now, what am I going to do with it, you see? Well, all of my first instincts were purely academic. I'm going to teach Old Testament. So, I decided to just pursue that and I took Hebrew, took Greek, Akkadian, took Aramaic, took all that stuff. Got through the MDiv and got through the first two years of the PhD at Columbia.

I got an invitation to pastor a church. Now, I had been on the staff at Abyssinia [New York, under Sam Proctor], but that was just, first it was field work, then it was just extra money, but I wasn't doing it because it was my career. Because I would go to Abyssinia to grade papers in Old Testament as a tutor. So it was clear to me what I was doing. But, suddenly, my primary professor moved to California, my secondary professor retired, and I'm left with no department. And on my desk [is] a letter to become the pastor of a church, a position that I had not sought at all. It was not anything that I had asked for, I hadn't sent a resumé in, and when they had phoned me, I said, "No, I'm not interested, I'm going to be teaching Old Testament this time next year."

And, here again, the thing that I was trying to accomplish in my own life, the bottom fell completely out of it. The thing that I was not the least bit in pursuit of was laying on my desk, no effort on my own. And, then what happened was the moment I said yes to full-time pastoral ministry, opportunities, I mean opportunities to do academic work on the side have just come to me. If that's what you want to do also, that's not a problem, but that's not what you are going to do primarily. So that the moment I got that straight in my own mind, it's been pretty much a straight road ever since.

And now, more than twenty years later, I've seen the pattern. It was always a narrowing of options from the whole down to the church-related work, finally down to this particular pattern, which I now call full-time pastoral work augmented by a variety of academic involvements as this schedule will allow. So, I didn't have a moment in time that I can point to. I know that some people do, but I didn't have a moment in time where everything gelled.

As much as there was a moment, [it was] this candle when it entered my mind and got my attention. Then crossroads—through the influence of Martin Luther King when I was a high school senior and had a day job in the print shop where after I would leave school and go and work a few hours all that summer in 1966. And his influence on a whole generation of us who went into Christian vocation, not quite knowing anything but that he was [a model]. Many said that's a thing to look into.

So, I decided to be in the printing business and go to college to study religion and philosophy, that kind of thing. In college I knew that I was going to go into some kind of church-related field. In seminary I had decided that that church-related field was going to be either seminary or university professor.

It was not until I had finished all of the academic requirements for a PhD, everything except the dissertation, that the entire body of that whole enterprise collapsed. But I was left with this question. All right, shall I go out and round up some professors and piece together the remainder of the program, or am I just not understanding what God is saying? How many times does he have to say this before I accept what he is saying? So, that's basically the moment that it was clear to me that the pastoral ministry was where I was being directed, and, so long as I was willing to do that, he would take care of any other interest. And, he has. My interest in civil rights has been satisfied. I've had opportunities to serve with the NAACP branches, I'm being asked right now to run for president of the Cleveland branch, NAACP. Well, I didn't ask for that. I didn't say I wanted to be president. Somebody came to me and said, "Would you run?" It's that kind of thing. Anything that I try to make out is a disaster. When I let the Lord surprise me, wonderful things occur, so long as I sit here and do this [pastoral ministry]. So, there it is.

Ella P. Mitchell
Atlanta, Georgia

The Reverend Dr. Ella Pearson Mitchell was born in Charleston, South Carolina, on October 18,1917, called to preach in 1938, ordained as a Presbyterian in 1943 and as a Baptist in 1978. She has a BA from Talledega College, an MA from Union Theological Seminary(New York) and a DMin from the Claremount School of Religion. She holds a joint appointment with her husband Henry H. Mitchell III at Interdenominational Theological Center. She has edited three books all published by Judson Press: *Those Preachin' Women I and II* (1985) and *Women: To Preach or not to Preach* (1991). Interview recorded in spring 1986.

56

"In the Same Year That Mama Died, I Also Saw the Lord"

My father, a Presbyterian minister in Charleston, South Carolina, served Olivet Presbyterian Church. When he came to the church, he was the first of Black pastors for that congregation. He was a single man and he married my mother. I was literally born in the church. Through my childhood I enjoyed church work very much. I have averaged some Sundays as much as six services, from Presbyterian to Catholic. I played music for a number of the churches. My father allowed me to work in his church becasue he served another church in Mt. Pleasant, South Carolina. So I got a chance to really enjoy actually serving in the pulpit, handling the worship services and at times actually giving the message. I visited him when he went on Sunday afternoons into the homes of the congregations, especially the older folks. I would go with him to serve communion.

During the summers of my high school years, I served as vesper speaker for a number of the youth conferences. And when I went to Talladega College for my undergraduate work,

I declared religion as my major. President Gallager did not have a religion major in the curriculum. In my senior year, Joe W. Nicholson and Benjamin Mays, who were co-authors of *The Negro Church*, came to our campus. I got a chance to take all of my courses in religion, some of them privately as directed studies. But I did major in religion and graduated with a major in religion.

I served as a Sunday school missionary, and I taught in high school for my sister—high school English. Meanwhile, I was speaking in churches, going from one conference and one meeting to another. I felt very much the call to ministry. I grew up in it, and felt nurtured by my father and very much encouraged by him. All the while my mother was just dying inside, and when I went to seminary she just about flipped. And I said to her, after all Jesus was in the teaching ministry and that is what I'm interested in, the teaching ministry. I really did not convince mother too much. She wasn't happy that I would go to seminary and studied.

I went to Union Seminary in New York City. There, fortunately, I met Henry Mitchell and we sort of grew along together. He encouraged me, never saying to me you should go on and say you are called to preach. Because, I never really felt called to preach. Even today I don't have a definition of preaching as over against teaching. I think that they are just so close together, that there's such a fine line. I believe Jesus was in the teaching ministry. I'm convinced now that we weren't ready for a thing like the teaching ministry. I don't know any church who performs ordination for the teaching ministry, but that was where I was. And that is where I am even today.

During my seminary years, I served as student assistant to the pastor at the St. James Presbyterian Church in New York City. Interestingly enough, Henry and I applied for the same student job the same night, and I was awarded the job. I think one of the reasons, was that my predecessor in that position was my cousin, Robert P. Johnson, my first cousin. The other thing that might have influenced their selecting me was that I was the daughter of a Presbyterian minister. And it was a Presbyterian church. I served as worship leader in most of the services. I did the messages for the evening service on many occasions. The interesting thing about it was that even when there were visiting ministers, in the evening service I had the responsibility as worship leader.

There were only a handful, literally a handful of women in seminary at that time, 1941. I had applied to Yale Divinity School and was discouraged by the administration there because there were no fieldwork opportunities for black women in New England at that time—1941 was very early in the game. So they suggested that I go to Union in New York City, where there were more opportunities and a wider receptivity of women in ministry or potential women in ministry.

After seminary I was invited to join the staff at the Church of the Master with James Robinson, later of Operation Crossroads Africa. There, I served as minister of Christian Education. I did some preaching, but most of my responsibility was in the teaching ministry.

After Henry and I were married in 1944, we went to North Carolina first, then to California. Most of that time, I was in counseling roles with students who were at North Carolina College for Negroes. We sang with the college choir, the community chorus and the White Rock choir, so that we spent a lot time singing that year. It was just beautiful. Later, when we moved to California after the birth of our son, Hank, the first people that invited me to do anything in church ministry were the Unitarians. Interestingly enough, our pediatrician was a Unitarian, so was his wife, and they found out that I had studied with Sophie Lyons Fahs, who was at that time the editor of the Beacon Press and they used me a great deal. It was not until later that the Baptists started using me.

Then, I went on the faculty of the Berkley Baptist Divinity School in the field of religious education. During that time, I really preached all over the state, most of the time on women's day. I did not call it preaching, I would give the women's day message—the women's day message, youth day message or some other message. It was never a sermon. In Henry's pastorates, I served most of the time in Christian education roles and at times in music roles. But it was always in the church. I did love the church. I still love the church and I always wanted to be in the church.

Later, I think perhaps because of the influence of the women's liberation movement, activity in the National Council of Churches, activity on the board of publication in the American Baptist Churches, I was used often to teach and preach. It was then that I felt I wanted to be ordained. What a struggle. I had been licensed in 1943 in the Presbyterian church where I worked in New York City. And I had all kinds of opportunities for service. I tried to get ordination to the teaching ministry and over a period of time was delayed, one year and then a period of time later. If I had asked for ordination earlier, which I never really felt led to do because Henry had baptized me in the Baptist church by immersion, I could have been ordained. I'm sure.

Then mama passed and I kept pushing and I kept pushing. Elliot Mason set the time for ordination and then advised Henry that he was led by the Holy Spirit not to do it. He called Henry to say he was sorry but the Holy Ghost had told him not to do it. So I didn't receive ordination from him, but on the very same day, J. Alfred Smith, Sr., said, "I'll ordain you." He did it in October 1978. He set up the time, and invited outstanding national figures that he knew to participate.

In the year mother died, I also saw the Lord. That's right. Henry tells the story all the time, "In the year mama died, I also saw the Lord." I don't think my sisters were excited about it at all as I had hoped they would be. Henry's folks were much more responsive to my going into ministry, that is to actually declaring it. In fact, Elbert, Henry's younger brother, and Sherry, the whole family was there for the ordination. My sisters sent telegrams and things like that. And, even Darlene, my younger sister, has heard me preach only a few times.

"That call didn't come all at once, in any single place or at any one time. It built as an ever-deepening experience that I could not deny, even though I was so young, so unprepared to understand all of this. When I was ten, there was a certainty growing in me."

The Rev. Martin Luther King, Sr.,
Daddy King: An Autobiography
(New York: William Morrow and Company, Inc.,1980): 28

Henry H. Mitchell III
Atlanta, Georgia

The Reverend Dr. Henry H. Mitchell III was born in Columbus, Ohio, on September 10, 1919, called in 1937 and ordained a Baptist minister in 1944. He received a BA from Lincoln College, an MA from California State University, an MDiv from Union Theological Seminary and a ThD from Claremont School of Theology. He has held numerous teaching posts throughout the country and inaugurated the Black Church Studies program (first in the country) at Colgate Rochester. Presently he serves as Professor of Homiletics at Interdenominational Theological Center. Among his many books are: *Black Belief, Soul Theology* (Harper & Row), *Celebration and Experience in Preaching* (Abingdon, 1990) and *Black Preaching: The Recovery of a Powerful Art* (Abingdon, 1990). Interview recorded in spring 1986.

57

Has Anyone Written More on Black Preaching?

To start with, my parents are both children of Baptist preachers. And both of these Baptist preachers, born in the mid-nineteenth century, were named William Henry after William Henry Harrison, the great Indian fighter. And, both of them got so sick of everybody being named William, they both—completely independently, because one was in California and one was in Virginia—dropped the William and kept the Henry. My grandfather Mitchell left Canada—his mother was an escaped slave [who had] escaped to Canada, he was born up there. He left Canada and went with his mother and stepfather to California, and then from there back east to Lincoln University to college. In his class there were sixteen men. Of the sixteen, twelve were name William. And of the twelve, ten were named William

Henry. So, he dropped the William for obvious reasons. Now, both of them were Baptist preachers, both of them were carpenters by trade. And my mother and father, my father being H.H. Mitchell's oldest son, named his first child after his father and his deceased brother, so I became H. H. Mitchell III. But I was Henry after two Baptist preachers. And all the time I was a child, well, my mother taught me to recite a lot of scripture. I could stand up and recite the same passages that I would do now, for instance, at a funeral. I could stand up when I was five years old in little pistol britches, we called them, little shorts and say, "Let not your heart be troubled; ye believe in God, believe also in me." I could have led the funeral in then. So, everybody had me pegged for a preacher.

[But] I swore and be-doggone if I was gonna be any preacher. "No way José, will I be a preacher." Both of these grandfathers, well, they just didn't have anything, financially speaking. In their eighties, my mother's father was on what they called old age pension, but it wasn't, it was a form of welfare. He didn't have any vested rights in any plan. My father's father didn't have anything that I can remember, except the same sort of thing. And I grew up in the Depression, a little bit aware of things material, because they weren't there. So I just didn't want to be no preacher. And I didn't see a lot of things about a lot of preachers that made me want to be a preacher. My grandfathers I respected, they were men of great principles, they didn't play games (and that's one of the reasons they didn't have anything). So I swore I never be a preacher, and somebody was always bugging me about it. But I was always staunchly denying it. Now, I give my parents credit, they didn't meddle. They didn't have anything at all to say about it. At least not that I knew of, they didn't try to make any direct assault on me in that regard.

Now, I was fairly articulate. I was a little tiny guy, I finished high school weighing 112 pounds. But, I got something of a reputation as a speaker, even as a little fellow. And this also added to the thing, and I was president of the youth group when I was a junior in high school. I guess I should go back, though. Into my life in the early thirties came another preacher, his name was E.W. Moore. He was a big, athletic-type man, in his early seventies as I recall. He had been pastor of the church at a previous point, during WW I, and he had hired my mother as church social worker. We were very close to him and he came back and visited the town, and I remember he bought me my first baseball glove or bat or something. I think it was the bat, that's what it was. You see he was my hero. Then he came to town as pastor, and at one point when I was only twelve years old, he had me and others of my age leading adult prayer meeting. He was some kind of genius at getting kids involved in serious religion. So, at about that time I started praying, "Lord, what will thou have me to do?" with pretty clear notions even at the age of twelve that "You know what you are supposed to do, idiot." Just about time that I was really ready to surrender, there were some unfortunate things happened. Somebody accused this seventy year-old preacher of some sort of moral mistake, and they actually asked him out of the pulpit, voted him out of the pulpit. And I was so crushed by all of that, I said, "Later for that, I'll never be caught fooling with this business. These people are too hard on these preachers." So, as I said, I was about twelve years old.

Now, I finished high school in January, 1937, at the tender age of seventeen. I got a job working for a farm implement company. This was something of a miracle, because nobody got jobs then, and certainly not seventeen year-old boys, with no more weight or muscle than I had. But my father had been kind to the boss in this company. When my father went to see if he had a job, he said, "I haven't got one, but for your son I'll make a job." So I got this job where I was janitor, and a number of other things—warehouseman, sometimes I was a packer and shipper, I was a mechanic's helper, all of that. When there was nothing to do, the boss to cover up for the fact that he didn't need me would send me to some obscure corner in the warehouse and put me to bolting spade lugs on tractor wheels. And the idea was that he still needed me because he was stockpiling tractor wheels which came in from the factory without the spade lugs, but which had to be delivered with the spade lugs on. I'm sure he had far more stockpiled wheels than he would ever need, but this was his way of covering.

And all of this becomes significant for my call, because it meant that days on end I would be in this obscure corner of the warehouse with nobody else anywhere around and my mind, therefore, [was] left to its own designs. The result was that with my job requiring no thinking whatsoever, just pushing a wrench and picking up bolts, my mind wandered far and wide. I discovered that some huge percentage of my time my mind would wander into the church. I would see visions of myself involved, in fact a great deal of the time I was involved in Africa, which had been my mother's dream. Wherever I was, I was in a church leading a choir, sometimes even preaching. It was very, very obvious to me that this was very big in my deepest consciousness. I wasn't too long figuring out that I was back where I started at age twelve. And of course, I tried to fight it off, because I didn't want it and had no interest whatsoever in being a minister.

But the more I tried to fight it off, the more it just haunted me and dominated all of that free-association time. I was so glad to get out of that warehouse and go somewhere and work where I could talk to people and get all of that out of my mind because it became a terribly worrisome kind of fixation. Well, to make the story no longer, I finally just decided that, well, I can't even sleep, it's gotten this bad. I might as well give up. And, in prayer I surrendered. It was not a very humble surrender, it was almost as if I was saying in modern-day terminology, "Okay, I'll preach your old gospel if you'll get off of my back." I had also a stipulation: "But you understand that if I do preach it, I refuse to be a stereotypical chicken-eating, Cadillac-driving, whatever, whatever, preacher. And, I want to do something different and really creative if I'm gonna be a preacher."

Well, I guess it can be said now, after forty-seven years of preaching that the Lord honored that part of the commitment, because I haven't done anything like anybody I ever knew did it. In fact, I have done a little of everything. I was going to be an engineer and I've used all of that as a church executive. I studied Spanish in order to do engineering in South America, because Black people were not allowed to practice engineering in this country at that time. And I have since been the missionary director in bilingual work in northern California, preaching and presiding and negotiating in Spanish. Its been a very, very interesting and abundant life.

Nothing that I learned when I was in rebellion has actually been lost in ministry. Even such strange things have happened as this when I first went to northern California, I was responsible for Black churches. And, this because a lot of Blacks, thousands of Blacks had moved into California during the war, and there simply hadn't been the resources, material resources or organizational resources to absorb that many people. So I was organizing churches, I got involved in drawing plans, just like I started out as an engineer. And all of this, they found out I spoke Spanish, and I became the director of Spanish work, I'd preach in Spanish, and all that. Very interesting kind of life, but during that period—I held that job incidentally for fourteen years, and when I left it, my English major in college had been used as editor of the American Baptist magazine for that area for years. I was replaced by an editor, I was replaced by a bilingual missionary executive, I was replaced by a church extension person because I had been building churches in White communities anticipating population growth and all of that, as well as doing the Black work that I had been called to do originally. So I was actually replaced by three and one-half people.

But while I was in that business, I said to the Lord one day, not desperately seriously, "When you get me out of this business here, I wouldn't mind if you put me in a church in the Los Angeles area. Now, I don't want to be in Los Angeles, I want to be out in the suburbs. I don't like big cities." And, I named two churches, one in Santa Monica, and one in Pasadena.

It's rather awesome to contemplate that when I left that executive job, I spent seven years in a church in Fresno, of which my grandfather had one time been pastor; and when I left there, I went straight to the Santa Monica church that I had mentioned in prayer twenty years before (or whatever years it was) stayed there briefly, and was called to a professorship at Colgate-Rochester. And when it was obvious that my health wasn't right and I should go back to California in all probability, the church where I engaged in an unofficial candidacy was the other church that I mentioned in Pasadena. And I was not in good enough health to make a very good impression. The very next time afterward, however, the chairman of the deacon board said to me, "Doctor, if you had preached like you preached today, the day you came from New York and preached here we never would have let you get away." It's awesome in that respect.

I also said even when in seminary, "If you don't mind, Lord, I'd like to serve churches and so forth and when I'm fifty years old, I'd like to go on a theological faculty. Now I don't know where I was going to go on the faculty with, but I assumed that by that time I would know enough to have something to say in a theological institution. And, out of the clear blue sky, I got a summons to a full professorship from zero.

I left Santa Monica after three years to be the Martin Luther King Professor of Black Studies at Colgate-Rochester Divinity School. I got there January first and I turned fifty September 10th. That again is one of those awesome things. I was desperately serious. My whole life has been a matter of saying, "Now, Lord, whatever you want me to do, that's the main thing. I just want to find out what you want me to do." But my own casual yearnings were honored beyond my fondest expectation, and in the case of the theological education, there is no question in my mind in the sense that my yearnings about it may have come from the Lord in the first place.

So, the call has unfolded in an astounding variety of ways, with me using the engineering day and night as a church extension director, using the Spanish, using the English major in college as the editor of a magazine. Just everything that I ever had has fitted into ministry. Now in theological education, my experiential data base is such that I can counsel students on almost anything you can think of, because I even defended churches in zoning petitions and never lost a case to a lawyer yet. So, it's been an amazingly varied kind of career.

Eugene Morgan
Akron, Ohio

The Reverend Eugene Morgan was born in Mobile, Alabama, on November 24, 1918, called in 1945 and ordained by the African Methodist Episcopal Zion church in 1948. He has a BA from Dillard University, and the BD from Hood Theological Seminary. Before his recent death he pastored the Wesley Temple AME Zion church in Akron. Interview recorded July 15, 1989.

58

"I Made a Bargain with God"

I think it's important that I was born in Mobile, Alabama. Alabama happens to be a very strong section of the nation in terms of the AME Zion Church—it's the African Methodist Episcopal Zion Church. My father was a pastor in the AME Zion Church and his father was a pastor in the AME Zion Church.

However, living in Mobile, where I graduated from high school, I opted to go to Dillard University in New Orleans rather than Livingston College, which is our AME Zion school in Salisbury, North Carolina. I think it was good for me, because it broadened my perspective in terms of my associations with people of other religions, of which I was not very conscious at that time, as well as people with backgrounds very much different from mine. At that time Dillard University was a new school, two years old, and came about as the result of the merger of Straight College and New Orleans University, one of which was Congregational and the other was Methodist, as I recall.

When I graduated from Dillard University, my father at that time was pastoring in North Carolina. So I went to North Carolina with my parents. First of all, it was during the days of the depression, and the imminent onset of World War II, so I really didn't have anything available to me. I took a job in a bank as a janitor. My job was on a split shift: in the early morning from 6:00 to 10:00 I was a janitor, then from 4:00 to 6:00 in the afternoon I was the elevator operator at the same bank. I did that for a while. Then I got a job with the *Norfolk Journal and Guide*, which was the Black newspaper. I tried that, and I didn't like that. I got a job then with the North Carolina Mutual Insurance Company. I had a very good debit that was given to me by the manager, who happened to be the chairman of trustee board of my father's church, [he] gave me this good debit. I had a tendency to reap the benefits of the premiums to which I was entitled. [I imagine] that debit would not bring about any new business, so the manager was very sympathetic, and he told me, "Well, in this business you have to sell new business. Everybody from the president of this company on down has to get out there and bring in new business. You're just carrying the benefits of the debit that another man had worked hard to build for you." Then, when I found out it was that much effort had to be put into insurance, I didn't particularly like it. I said, "That's not for me."

I had always said I didn't want to be a preacher; I had been a preacher's son. I had lived in parsonages all my life. In this parsonage, the sink would be too low, the next parsonage the sink would be too high, and the next parsonage might not even have a sink. So I just didn't want to get into that.

Anyway, I got this job, eventually, teaching elementary school down in North Carolina. I didn't like that either. I thought maybe I had found my niche, but I didn't like that because, at that time, school systems were segregated. And there must have been a thousand people ahead of me, in the push or administrative jobs, principles or what have you. I figured it would take me sixty years to get through that crowd to get a position that would mean anything to me.

I was still trying to find something else to do. Then two strange things happened. Some of my buddies and I were riding one night in a car, and we crossed the railroad tracks. Just as we crossed the railroad tracks the train struck the car. It pushed us about a block down the tracks. We all got out of there without any serious injuries. But then, within about three months, a train was crossing another set of tracks and my buddy and his girl and I and my girl were in the car, and my buddy struck that train. None of us got hurt, but the flagman on the train broke both of his legs and we got into a little trouble over that. So I asked the Lord if he was trying to tell me something.

I guess the response I got from the Lord was that I'd better settle down and do what the Lord wanted me to do, and that was preach. I'd been in the church all my life, I'd been Sunday school superintendent, director of the choir and all of that, but I just didn't want to preach. So then I told the Lord, I made a bargain with the Lord and said, "I'll tell you what, I'll go to the seminary and I'll study religion, and I will become very proficient in the discipline of religion. Then I will be a teacher at the seminary or college campus." I don't recall if the Lord even answered, but I kept my part of the bargain.

I quit teaching; I went to the seminary and I was totally encouraged to seek a career in religious teaching because I got good grades in the seminary. The dean of the seminary at that time indicated to me that I had been able to compile an academic record at that seminary, Hood Seminary, better than any other student previously that had been there. So, I don't know whether I felt good about that or whether it boosted my ego or what it did. But I decided, well, if that's the case, I'll go on to further studies. I made application to Union Seminary in New York and I made application to the Oberlin Graduate School of Theology in Ohio.

Immediately upon graduation at Hood Seminary in North Carolina, I enrolled in a summer session of Union Theological Seminary. There, again, I made very good grades. But I enjoyed more going to baseball games in New York, because that was the first year that Jackie Robinson played baseball with the Brooklyn Dodgers. I spent quite a deal of time watching baseball. That was enjoyable, but I also found out that New York was not the place for serious study for me. It was too big, too many distractions.

So, at the end of the summer session, I took Oberlin up on the offer that they had made. They were going to give me full tuition, and they were going to give me room and board for the hours that I worked in the dining hall and what they called "answering bells" (that was [being] the phone operator in the dormitory). So I took them up on that and I went to Oberlin. I had to go to Oberlin in order to confirm, I guess, the basic bachelor degree that I got in theology from Hood Seminary, which was unaccredited. So in order to get an accredited degree, I went to Oberlin and finished my work there.

I then decided that maybe I wanted to pursue an STM, a master's in sacred theology and I started. But by that time, the bishop of the Ohio Conference suggested to me that maybe I

"I Made a Bargain with God"

could help in Cleveland at St. Paul AME Zion Church, because the minister was getting old, and to work that in with my work at Oberlin. I agreed to that. But in the process of working with the church in Cleveland, I had a strange feeling that maybe that's what the Lord wanted me to do. Maybe he didn't want me to teach. He wanted me to be directly involved with people and I did not want to do that. I had been involved with people all my life as a son of a preacher living in the parsonages and all, so, anyway, I felt a peculiar satisfaction with that.

They sent me to a place on the north side of Pittsburgh that had about six members, and I felt very strange. I had a college degree, I had a degree from Hood Seminary, a degree from Oberlin, and at that point I also had a wife and a little boy, and I had a membership of six. But I thought, well, maybe this is what the Lord wants me to do, so I'll stay with it. So I was there for two years and then I was sent to Sewickley, Pennsylvania, for two years, and then I was sent to Akron, Ohio. And that's where I've been ever since.

I remember at the Ohio Pastors Convocation some years ago, we were standing out in the lobby between sessions and we were talking. This was an interracial group of preachers; I don't remember its constituency, but they were interracial. And we were discussing our call into the ministry, why we were there at that particular point, at that time. And my answer to them was, that I really didn't know why I was there because I had no intention of being here in this place today. This was a good ten years after I received the call to the ministry. But at that point, I still didn't know why I was there, other than that this, obviously, is what the Lord wanted me to do in the first place.

So, I have taken this in stride—that I am simply doing work the Lord had wanted me to do. And, although I have tried my best to deny this call to the ministry, I guess that's what the Lord wants me to do. I can say this, subsequent to that, and this now is in the neighborhood of about forty years that I've been an active pastor, I still have a feeling of uneasiness when ever I get into the pulpit. It's an awesome task, an awesome responsibility. A lot of my colleagues or my friends take a great deal of pride in their ability to move a congregation by preaching, and they have developed various styles of preaching. I still look upon it as something that I really don't want to do even now, but the Lord wants me to do that so I approach it that way: this is something the Lord wants you to do.

It's not any easier now than it was when I started. It is still a very difficult responsibility. I suppose when you have to preach to the same people, as I have done for thirty-five years, Sunday after Sunday after Sunday, it becomes even more awesome. But I have and I've experienced it, and I feel very satisfied in the fact that I think I have received a call from God to do this, and that God in turn has blessed me that I have been able to do it. I think I indicated to you earlier that about a year ago I was stricken with cancer of the esophagus, and cancer itself is bad enough, but if it's in the esophagus it means that you might face the rest of your life not being able to talk even, much less preach. But the Lord has been very good to me so that I don't have the physical strength at one time, but I'm able to communicate and continue this ministry, and I'm very thankful. That's about it.

Otis Moss, Jr.
Cleveland, Ohio

The Reverend Dr. Otis Moss, Jr., was born in LaGrange, Georgia, on February 26, 1935, called around age five or six, was publicly acknowledged the call at seventeen, and ordained a Baptist minister in 1953. He received a BA from Morehouse College, (Atlanta) a BD from Morehouse School of Religion and a DMin from at United Theological Seminary, Dayton, Ohio. He pastors Olivet Institutional Baptist Church in Cleveland. Interview recorded February 25, 1986.

59

The Urge to Preach

My call to the Christian ministry is possibly less complicated than the experiences of some of my colleagues, both elders and peers. I cannot remember when I did not carry in the inner core of my being the urge to preach. I can recall vividly a dream concerning the ministry at the age of four or five. It has been a consciousness, an inner consciousness throughout my life. However, I did not always acknowledge that. This inner awareness, urge, grew stronger as the years passed. And its acknowledgement was not made public until I reached the age of seventeen.

There were, from time to time, conversations that touched on this with persons, a few people, whose confidence I shared and whose sensitivity to my own growth and development established a special kind of communication. But even in those conservations there was not a total acknowledgement, but simply a welcomed discussion of ministry as a possibility. And, to some extent, even an indirect admission that this was the dominant purpose of my life.

But at the age of seventeen, I sat down in counsel with a minister and said to him what my overriding urge was. And I suppose at that point it had reached a critical level in my own development, to the extent that I could no longer keep it as a private awareness.

When I shared this with a minister, who is [presently] a pastor in Pensacola, Florida, Rev. R. L. Hill, he was extremely sensitive, prayerful and understanding, and his counsel I value until this day. For he said that a call to the ministry is also a call to preparation. And one should accept that responsibility as inseparable from the call itself.

I have remembered that to this day and try to pass it on to others who come to me for similar counsel. In terms of God's designation of me as an instrument for the preaching of the gospel, the proclamation of the gospel of Jesus Christ, there has never been any doubt. Maybe, at times, questions as to my own worthiness, or my adequate preparation for the task or for the challenges that [are] involved in the responsibilities of the ministry. But in terms of God's designation through his own use of an individual, there is no doubt and there has been no doubt.

That essentially is my experience as far as the call to the ministry. I have taken on since that time, I think, a better grasp of an interpretation of that call and sought to pass it on to others. Because I believe one should preach because you cannot help it. If you could be just as fulfilled, just as satisfied, just as comfortable doing something else, then you ought to do something else. But I think one should be in the ministry because there is no way on earth to fulfill the will of God and the purpose of God for you, except through that calling.

Andrew K. Newberry
Akron, Ohio

The Reverend Andrew Kevin Newberry was born in Cincinnati, Ohio, on July 30, 1956, called in 1967, and ordained by the African Methodist Episcopal Church in 1982. He has a BA from Wilberforce and an MDiv from Payne Theological Seminary. He pastors the St. Paul AME Church in Akron. Interview recorded July 13, 1989.

60

The Influence of Being a Preacher's Kid

My name is Andrew Kevin Newberry. I am presently the pastor of St. Paul African Methodist Episcopal Church. I was reared in an AME parsonage, my father being a minister, and knowing nothing but the ministry all my life, there was a considerable amount of influence that being a PK [preacher's kid] had on my desire to become a minister. My calling would not be, *per se*, the dramatic, one-night event. I would say it was more or less a series of experiential things that took place over the years that led me into that desire to be a preacher.

The earliest things that I remember about those experiences came in Sunday school and in church as I listened to my father preach. I felt my heart strangely warm; not in the sense of my heart, but just exhilarating feelings of satisfaction with what was being said, relating to some of the ideas [pictorially] in my head that my daddy was saying about faith and about Christ, watching what would take place in the lives of those who would come to the worship experience. [All of this] had a great deal of impact, I think, on me. On Sunday mornings sometimes dad would have a what we called testimony service, which was somewhat unique in our church experience, and it would be in place not prior to the service but in place of the sermon. The testimonies that were given always seemed to touch and set the entire church on fire, so to speak, as people would cry and would talk about how good God has been or how he has blessed them, healed them or something. That had a lot to do with the experiences that led up to my accepting the responsibility of the ministry.

My grandmother, who lives in Cleveland today, always prayed and let us know somewhat of the history of the ministerial roots in our family and how she felt there was nothing more important than answering the call to the ministry. She's a very spiritual person, my grandmother, who helped to put in my mind the idea that serving God in the form of a minister or parish minister is a very high calling and something that I could really be proud of.

Being a PK, I was expected to do certain things, especially in the young people's department of the church that at least demonstrated that we were children of a minister. That expectancy from the family and that help that they gave in pushing us out to the forefront in Bible class, Sunday school, etc., and plays and all of that also helped, because some of those experiences became experiences that were not just, you know, the routinized response—we had to go because they made us go —but some of them became soul-stirring experiences.

Bishop Bearden had a lot to do with my calling. I remember that he came over to our house—in answer to the call—he came over for dinner and he spoke to us, my brother and myself, about the ministry and about the need for young people to give themselves to the Lord in this noble task. Some of the things that I recall him talking about . . . [he] was just a very impressive person to us as youngsters. He helped to play a role in the answer to the call.

But now, as I mentioned earlier, I did not have the one-night experience, but it was a gradual growing process. I was asked a number of times, and maybe sometimes too much, about following in my father's footsteps in the ministry. And perhaps that served in my formative years to almost cow or keep me from coming right out and saying, "I'm going to pastor. I'm going into the ministry." A fellow tells us all the time, Major Dickens—in fact, every time I go home to preach now, he'll come up and say—he says that I came up to him when I was just knee high to a grasshopper and said, "Brother Dickens, I'm going to be your pastor one day." Whenever I see him, he makes mention of that, that I told him when I was a kid. Maybe in an indirect way, that had something to, in a subliminal way, much of the senior and the adult group as I was coming up, they always touched the—how can I say it—those strings of ministry in one way or the other, since, you know, my father was the pastor and my mother was the first lady of the church.

After high school and after doing everything that I could possibly do—well, no I can't say everything, but a lot of things that we felt would make us acceptable as regular people rather than PKs—near my junior year, I was ready more or less to accept fully the call into the ministry. While in college I attended a number of churches, many of which had considerable impact on my life. I remember going with friends to church and feeling the power of God tug and pull at me, almost as if it was a human pull. Within the context of that worship experience I found myself asking, "What is it that I can do for the Lord who has obviously done so much for me?"

In addition, some of the influences critical in my mind have to do with a story my grandmother told about my father. She said, before he was born other relatives had prayed for the first-born to be a preacher. Likewise, before I was born prayers had been lifted on my behalf by my father. He shared with me that he named me Andrew after the biblical Andrew who brought his brother to Jesus; I could as well bring people to Jesus.

After reflection and meditation about these influences and especially the gospel messages, I became convinced that my life belongs to God and the ministry that is set before me. I felt, "Woe is me if I preach not the gospel."

Ernest W. Newman
Nashville, Tennessee

Bishop Ernest W. Newman was born in Kingstree, South Carolina, on April 9, 1928, called from birth and ordained a United Methodist elder in 1956. He received an AB from Clafflin College and a BD degree from Gammon Theological Seminary. He is Bishop of the Nashville area. Interview recorded June 23, 1989.

61

"I Had No Choice"

I am from a large family of preachers. There seems to be—especially in South Carolina, which is my home state—a number of clergy families to a large degree responsible for replenishing preachers in South Carolina. Kind of a family conference tradition, seemingly. My father was a Methodist preacher. My grandfather was a Methodist preacher. I am one of seven boys and out of the seven boys, six of us went into the ministry.

Now going back, my father was a Methodist preacher and at the age of sixteen when I completed high school, I had a sense of call. Of course, it's been pretty much understood as far as my entire life up until that time, that I was going into the ministry. I did not see any other profession or calling as to what would be my life's commitment. So, at the age of sixteen, I received a local preacher's license by the charge conference that my father was pastor of at that time. Then after completing high school, at the age of sixteen, then I entered Clafflin College in Orangeburg, South Carolina, which is one of our eleven black colleges supported by the United Methodist Church.

Upon my completion of my college work, or even during the time I was in college, I did some preaching for different pastors across the state of South Carolina. Then, on completion of my college work, my father was desperately ill at that time and I did not find it possible to continue my education to the old seminary.

Upon his death, shortly after I got out of college, I was asked by the district superintendent to carry on his work where he was pastor. I completed one year of the tenure that was his. Then, at the end of that year, I asked to be moved and assumed a pastorate of two other congregations in South Carolina. After two years, pastoring these two churches, I felt that it was necessary for me to ask for another move because I wanted to have rural pastoral experience. I was in what was considered a county-seat town, and I wanted something that would give me a different exposure to the ministry.

I became pastor of two little churches in South Carolina, stayed at these churches for approximately a year and a half and then transferred from South Carolina Conference to Florida Conference. And from transferring to Florida I still liked my theological education. And after—I say, about eight months, I guess, I went back to school in Atlanta at Gammon, where I did my theological work which I completed. Went back to Florida and pastored in Florida, of course, then the remainder of my Florida ministry.

While in Florida I pastored what was at that time one of our most historic black churches, Ebenezer Church in Jacksonville. After seven years I became a district superintendent of a merged Florida Conference in 1971, and became the first black district superintendent in Florida. After six years, which is a tenure, after six years, I became pastor of the a United Methodist Church out of Fort Lauderdale, Florida. All of my congregation [was] 2,200 members and I pastored there for five years. Then from there to the Conference Council on Ministries, where I served as associate director of the Conference Council for a year. Then went back to the position of district superintendent of Florida and at the end of a year and a half, then was elected to the Bishopric, out of the Florida Conference.

Upon my election to this position, I was assigned then to the Nashville area comprising of two annual conferences—well, yes, two annual conferences, the Tennessee Conference and the Memphis Conference. And that's where I am now after five years in the Nashville area.

My call to the ministry was almost a kind of thing that I

considered I had no choice. I had been born and brought up in the Methodist Church and the family of preachers. I just assumed that on the day of my own knowledge of ministry that this would be my calling. So, my call to some extent comes out, I guess, of a family tradition. And it was not a matter of any time that I considered I wouldn't do anything else. It was a life commitment.

So, my call, I don't think is any unique . . . it's not unique to any extent of any other person's call, call and a commitment. I feel that there is the call and you make the commitment to it and dedicate your life to it. I did not see any spectacular vision of some kind or some unknown mysterious voice that came to me. I did not see that. I saw mine as a family tradition, heritage. A desire to be a participant in working with people, looking at their concerns, developing a ministry that would respond to their concerns. Let's say it was social and at the same time it was a commitment, and out of this commitment a dedication. I tie the call and history together. And this has been my response to the call to the ministry.

Henry J. Payden
Cleveland, Ohio

The Reverend Henry J. Payden was born in Columbus, Ohio, on April 3, 1923, called in 1946 and ordained a Baptist minister in 1948. He has a BA from Westminster College (Pennsylvania) and an MA from Ashland Theological Seminary. He pastors the Holy Trinity Baptist Church in Cleveland. Interview recorded July 14, 1989.

62

Awakened by the Hand of God

The call to the gospel ministry has many aspects to many people, and I'm sure that no two will be the same. Mine is a very odd one. I, first of all, feel that I was called at the age of thirteen. At the age of thirteen, I found that I really felt one day literally a hand upon my shoulder. I was lying down, and lying there I... being a child, I was supposed to be practicing my piano lessons but I fell asleep, and in the process of my sleep, from which I had awakened really, I felt this hand. I got up from the couch that I was lying on to look around, and I saw nothing and no one. My father was not there. Then, when he did come home, I told him about this particular experience.

Well, as time intervened, I went into further vocal music study, and then I went into boxing. My father was definitely against the boxing but, his being an old baseball player, he couldn't deny me some kind of athletics. I went into boxing at the age of fourteen and I fought for six years. I also taught boxing somewhat in the army. That's going ahead in my story a little bit. But I was always against going into the ministry, because I felt that my temper would not adjust to that kind of profession. I had seen so much coming from my father, things that he had to encounter, that I just felt it was not for me. I listened to a little, short man talk to my dad once about the sermon he preached on adultery. I wasn't there at the time (I was in the army), but the fellow walked up and told my dad he must have been talking about him, that he was personalizing his sermon to him. My father, being a 6' 2" individual as you can see by this picture—he's not a pushover and was quite strong and a very loving personality—he just pushed the man aside and walked on. The fellow was relatively short, maybe about five feet. And my father didn't say anything, just went on about his business. Now, had I been there, the way that he spoke to my father, I would have punched him out. This is not the attitude, for we're not supposed to be brawlers, so the Book says, nor contentious, etc. The Lord can't use a man like that effectively.

So, I thought of those things, I thought of many things that I saw my father have to endure, and he wasn't making a lot of money but he was happy—dad was very happy. He worked as a chauffeur and as a pastor until his last years when he got out of the chauffering—he was doing both. As time intervened, I went into music, studying at Capital, came out of it and went into the armed services, volunteered. After coming out of the service, I went into Wings Over Jordan. My father had told my mom that when I came out of the service, I would be preaching, but he didn't share it with me. His reason was that he didn't want to call me, he wanted the Lord to do it. I never knew this until after I acknowledged my call to my father.

Going into Wings Over Jordan, we traveled all over. As you know, it's an international choir. You're acquainted with Wings Over Jordan, aren't you? I traveled with them for about a year, and then after that I became married. I was featured soloist with Wings Over Jordan for a year or a little over, and then I went on and was married. At that point, I started working for CTS—Cleveland Transit System, which now is RTA. Working for CTS, I was going to school also at Cleveland Bible College, which is now Malone College in Canton. Cleveland Bible College was at 30th and Euclid. So I went there for three years, and I was called to a church in New Castle, Pennsylvania, St. Paul's Baptist Church on West North Street. I went there and stayed for two and one-half years. That was a great challenge. I asked the Lord to send me to a place where I could get some experience and, rest assured, the latter prevailed.

I also was able to go to Girard College, which was an extension of Westminster in Girard, Ohio, and I was able to get my bachelor's. From there I was able to give a concert there and sort of supplement the funds, which they were paying me $35 a week in my first church, then they would pound you. But my call came to me definitely as I was driving CTS down Superior Avenue, and I had just been burdened with seeing all the way from the St. Clair station down around through 125th and all those other streets into Superior, and when I left 105th Street, tears just overwhelmed me. I mean, I thought I was maybe going to have to stop the bus, the streetcar—it was really a PCC car. Remember those modern streetcars they had? My eyes were just filled with water. I said to the Lord at 103rd and Superior, "Yes, Lord, I will." I couldn't get away from it. I did everything I possibly could.

I had an opportunity to go to New York, I had an opportunity to go into college. A fellow came and talked to my father and said, "If you will just send him, we will pay all of his expenses and he won't have to worry about a thing." Julliard School of Art, the music school—the guy was from there, he was going to take me. I told my father I didn't want to go. Here was all my expenses paid, a great opportunity for a musical future, and I said, "No."

I must admit to you the government paid my way in school. I have not regretted one minute the change from the music profession into the gospel ministry. I have had my down moments, I've even had my "out" moments, but I have never yet felt that God was not with me. My faith has not diminished. The first Psalm is one of my favorites. So as a result of the call, it's not something I'm guessing about or have ever guessed about. I have known that the divine hand was upon me and that the oil has been poured upon my head. I have an anointing. I don't doubt my anointing. God has overly blessed his work through me, so I have no doubts in that area. I have been called, I know I'm born again, I know that my Redeemer lives for he lives within me and I live within him. We have an interchanging residence and I'm proud of it. I'm glad to be his.

Roderick Pounds
Akron, Ohio

The Reverend Roderick Pounds was born in Columbus, Ohio, on July 5, 1958, called in 1979 and ordained a Baptist minister in 1981. He received a BA from the University of Akron. He pastors the United Baptist Church in Akron. Interview recorded July 13, 1989.

63

An Overwhelming Burden

In light of the call in my own life, I'll never forget the time. It occurred in 1981 during the month of March particularly, though I cannot remember the exact date. It was a Wednesday evening and I'll never forget the night. The particular night in which the call occurred and my emotional state was accompanied with tears and a sense of fulfillment as if I had finally got in touch with God. I was to embark upon what precisely God had destined for me to do. I think previously I had been going through some re-evaluation in terms of my own personal life. I had just came home from college from Ohio University. I was majoring in architecture. And I was so bothered socially, although academically I did well. I was troubled socially. I had problems with the social life and with dancing and partying. I imagine and I am assuming that I had reached—well, I did reach a point of moral consciousness, a strong moral consciousness. I was thinking that out perhaps a year prior to that night—really re-evaluating myself morally and socially and asking questions about God and about life, very vague and general issues about morality. The state of affairs and I had been going through that for quite some time, about a year. As a matter of fact, it was so drastic and so intense that my friends were uncomfortable with me. They'd always bring up the issue, So what about life? Or what about truth? Why should we go skating, and things like that. So I spent a year of contemplation in terms of just what was happening around me.

That particular night, nothing I think abnormal I can recall happening. What I can recall, that is really clear in my mind, was a strong emotional sort of outburst that I experienced. I know I was upstairs. I just got home from work, at which time was architectural engineering. As a matter of fact, I was doing some drafting work at Western Electric, to be precise. It was on my way up the ladder of corporate, at the corporate ladder there, and I went home and I went instead to tie into some of my friends after work. I was really uncomfortable, as if all that I had been thinking about the year before had reached an apex. Perhaps I was my most uncomfortable that night and I went to bed very uncomfortable and with the sense of yearning to really want to discover just what my purpose was. It is as if I was calling out at God, too, because I wanted to know what he wanted me to do about all these things that I had been thinking about. I was sort of calling at him also.

So that night I just went to bed with those thoughts over and over going over in my mind, and certainly I became flustered and I was in tears. I was just profusely crying and smiling at the same time. I immediately began to just pray because I was just so uncomfortable and I felt so awkward and a little frightened. I couldn't shake myself from the impulses inside. I just—I was moved. The burden that got placed on my heart revealed truth. I had not really known my Bible then. I had been in church all of my life. I come from a rich tradition in preaching in my family. My grandfather, uncles and a long line of Harristons. This is the family that I come from, which is pretty popular nationally. I knew that that's what I was to do in life is to preach. I also recognized that a part of my fright and anxiety—I realized how limited I really was, academically, and educationally just in terms of interpreting God's word. And I felt a little fear and trepidation from that perspective. But I knew this is what I was called to do and therefore I just left school.

At that time I was back at Ohio State, still pursuing an architectural career and drafting career. I quit the next day. I left and changed schools and I went to Franklin University for the next semester, majored in something that I thought was closer to truth—sociology and philosophy. And at which time, I pursued that. I quit my job. About two weeks later, I just went full time into my schooling. I got married about six months after I preached my first sermon. That's how it went for me.

Later, as I think about the call and as I have been relating it to other people, I associate it with an overwhelming desire, an overwhelming burden sort of desire. And I had that desire. And that basically depicts what happened that night. I felt the impulse inwardly and I ran down stairs and relayed it to my mom, at which time she relayed it to my pastor, who was then my grandfather. From there it was just a matter of church formality and preaching that first initial sermon.

Samuel D. Proctor
New York, New York

The Reverend Dr. Samuel DeWitt Proctor was born in Norfolk, Virginia, on July 13, 1921, called in 1939 and ordained a Baptist minister in 1943. He has a BA from Virginia Union University, a BD from Crozer Theological Seminary and a ThD from Boston University. He has taught at numerous universities and seminaries. He presently teaches at Rutgers University and United Theological Seminary. He is pastor emeritus of the historic Abyssinia Baptist Church in Manhattan. He has authored many works, among them *My Spiritual Odyssey* and *Preaching about Crisis in the Community* (Westminster, 1988). Interview recorded June 6, 1989.

64

Isolation, Separation, and Confrontation with the Brutality of Fraternities

My call story begins with the fact that there never was a time in my life when I was not a part of the church. My family was very church-oriented; my father was a leader and an active member in the Ninth Street Baptist Church of Norfolk. So getting to know Bible stories and sermon themes and things like that was something that I didn't have to get accustomed to later on. That was part of my youth. Then I had a very high opinion of the clergy. We always had an educated minister at our church. We never had any scandal of any kind. Our pastors were leading people in town and they were highly respected people. Ninth Street Church had a long tradition of going out after that kind of pastor, outstanding preachers. It was a small church, but had a very strong budget, very well-employed congregation of people. Therefore, I did not have to overcome any negative images of ministry. There are a lot of young people today who say that they would have to think about going into ministry because of their poor opinion of several ministers. I didn't.

In college I was involved in music, playing in a dance songstrip, played in the band and I was a music major. College bandmaster, that was my image of where I belonged in life. If I had a second choice, maybe I wanted to be a lawyer; and I had a good biology teacher, so if I had a third choice, I wanted to be a High School biology teacher. But mostly I wanted to be a Kappa and I wanted to have the girls to like me, and those other things were secondary. My first two years of college I was very young, sixteen my freshman year and seventeen my sophomore year. I really ought to have been home somewhere, but I was up there with the big boys since I had finished high school at fifteen and was thrown right in it.

It was not a tramautic experience, because I was around a lot of home boys. My uncle was on the faculty of Virginia State College, my uncle was a PhD from Michigan and he watched over me. But I did not have any very well-defined career goals. Then something happened. I was initiated into the fraternity, and it was so brutal. And I can just say that with a ton of exclamation points behind it: it was absolutely brutal. Fellows had to be hospitalized. It was not so much the fellows on the campus, but old alumni, who [were] not doing well in their career at all but just hanging around drinking, would come back to the campus to help brutalize. One cannot believe the things they did to us. They would wake us up at two or three o'clock in the morning and make us come down to the fraternity room. I remember one time I stood up and a guy hit me as hard as he could with that paddle for thirty-one times. I was so bruised I couldn't sit down for two or three days. Then that night they were back at it, banging on me again. And we [were] captured by the great desire to be in the fraternity. (And, incidentally, that's going on today. And almost every one of our black fraternities has a serious lawsuit against them, right now. In fact, I would not be surprised if all of them would not be bankrupt in two or three years, because if they lose these lawsuits they are going to go under. This brutality has returned to the campuses and if you look at any of the journals of any of the fraternities, there is a long list of the chapters that are on probation for violating the hazing regulations.)

I found that so repulsive. It just violated everything I believed in about brotherhood, buddyhood and everything. The anger and rage in me was furious. My dearest, closest friends had no idea how that upset me. I thought I was going to have a crack-up because I was in this so [far] and didn't know what to do about [it]. And I was young, I was seventeen years old. So in the spring initiation of 1939 I informed the head of our fraternity that if it went on again, I was going to report it to the authorities of the fraternity and the authorities of the college. And they told me that I would get killed if I did. Then, I told the heads of the other three fraternities that I was going to do that. It was a one-man crusade and everybody told me that I had better back away from it. I don't know what got into me to make me want to do that, but I did.

And in the middle of the initiation period of that spring, I found out from all of the guys who was on probation—we called it probation, it's pledge line now—that they were doing the same thing and worse. One morning about 6:30 I got up and went to see Dean Johnson who was at Virginia State College and told him everything that I knew about the initiation. Dean Johnson called a meeting of all the fraternities and sororities at 1:00 o'clock after lunch that day, and told them that everybody that had to be initiated that night before the sun went down. Everybody. And some them hadn't been on the line but two days, some had been out there for three days. And they had kept us out there for three or four weeks at a time. They were as angry as they could possibly be. They were upset, girls and boys. Nobody spoke to me. My roommate said nothing to me. I thought they were going to get me. My uncle was upset. And later he was the grand pole mark of the Kappa fraternity. I said the grand pole mark. I don't mean one of the lieutenants. He was the grand dragon. He was an old Michigan man, [an] Ann Arbor track star back there in the days of Jesse Owens.

So, he and my aunt [thought] that I was having a crackup or something. They couldn't imagine anybody being sane and doing that sort of thing. So they put me in the infirmary. The infirmary was regarded as sacrosanct in those days and nobody would go in there and invade the nurse's infirmary. The nurse was a big mean fat lady and nobody would mess with her. I guess she gave me some kind of tranquilizer, I don't know. I felt like a fool because nothing was wrong with me. I knew exactly what I was doing. But that experience imposed a lot of solitude, a lot of isolation on me. And when they let me out, I decided I would concretize the whole thing. I stopped going to the college chaplain anymore, because the college chaplain was ashamed of the gospel. He mumbled and he did not affirm it strongly. He acted like he didn't care if you bought it or not. He was going to get paid anyway. The college chaplain made about as poor of a representative of a preacher of the gospel as I have ever heard. Highly educated, Yale Divinity school, we heard all about that, but other than that, just a nice guy. So I went downtown in Petersburg. The first day I walked down there becasue I had heard that there was a good preacher down there name John Brown, a little short fellow who was a West Indian and who had gone to school over here and was a good pastor.

And man, in the Spring of '39 around Easter time, it wasn't Easter Sunday, but it was leading up to it—he preached a sermon on courage. His text was "As I was with Moses, so I will be with thee: I will not fail thee nor forsake thee. Be strong and of a good courage; be not afraid, neither be thou dismayed, for the Lord thy God is with thee whithersoever thou goest." And those words was just etched right in my mind. I had heard it before, but it never had such poignancy as it had then. Because I was in the throes of this experience of having turned in all the fraternities for initiation violations.

I had never joined church, because joining church was a little too perfunctory. I was a part of it, but baptizing was not my cup of tea and, as independent as I was in my thinking, I didn't see the necessity for all that water and all that confusion and all those ugly robes and things. I just thought it was too literal of a thing to have to do. I didn't want to be bothered with it. We never had revivals in our church—they didn't allow that, they were too high for that. But we graduated into baptism out of Sunday school. They called it decision day, and everybody was supposed to join the church. But I never did go up there. I would just sit there and watch the rest of them. And on baptizing Sunday, they all looked silly to me going down there. It looked like an unnecessary ritual. However, I learned later it was symbolism that I could appreciate more, and I baptize people all the time now. In our church, right now I still have some prejudice against the idea of making a Methodist or Presbyterian or whatever get baptized. If Roman Catholics join our church we ask them to accept baptism because their philosophy is so different; we think they need any symbol they can get to understand things differently. That's the only trouble I ever had in Abyssinia in seventeen years—wasn't trouble really. In a church meeting we had a long debate with some of those hard-shelled Baptists saying, "You know the only way to be saved you know, dah- dah- dah- dah . . . ," throwing all those scriptures around. But everytime they had one, I had others that matched it: "The thief wasn't baptized on the cross, you know, dah-dah- dah-dah."

Anyway, I said I love the Lord and if this is what you are supposed to do, I'll go ahead and do it. So I went through that exercise. And the next Sunday there I was this tall fellow with all the little children who had to be baptized.

However, let me say this: that the call to preach, to be a minister, I think, was the outcome of the privacy, the isolation, separation that was imposed upon me in the throes of that decision to stand up against those fraternities. And when I came out of it, I began to relate my life to all of the ministers that had been in my family that I had forgotten about. And I found myself in kind of a train of procession with them. My great grandfather. My mother's uncle. These were very fine men, well-educated and weren't involved in a lot of scandal. People respected them very highly.

Then D.C. Rice became the pastor of our church. And he was such a sparkling preacher and so commited. And his wife was just a lovely person. At the end of that school year, the war was on. I decided that since I wasn't certain about my career, I didn't want to sit around there and get drafted when I turned eighteen. I was going to turn eighteen in the summer. I took an examination and went into the naval apprentice school right over here in Norfolk. They were not letting any Black kids in there. But Roosevelt had given an order to change it, and I took the exam and I got a chance to get an apprenticeship. I thought that would be a good thing. I'd make a lot of money, buy me a Chevrolet car and look pretty. I had a taste of college and I was really turning in a secular direction in my mind. But I was still going through the devotions of the church and thinking about the ministry. There was a kind of conflict there. And it was sort of like the devil was after my soul, especially turning that age and having a chance to make a lot of money during war in the shipyard and starting off driving a car and things like that. Just trying to be a man. Never was engaged in whole lot of alcohol and sex and things like that, but that was more of a matter of a cultural taboo than anything else. It was absolutely against anybody's rule to get a girl pregnant. You might as well go out and shoot yourself if you did that. In my family they didn't allow that. We didn't know anything about an abortion nor where you would go to get one. We didn't know anything about it at all. We would hang around these girls and fool around with them, but at the critical moment you backed away because all you saw was yourself being scandalized for being a teenage daddy. We knew what happened to other teenage daddies around there. People looked upon them like they were trash. And the girls all left town. It was like they died, you never saw them again.

So, that was a rough time. But I got hooked up at the church with Rice. Rice's sermons preached me into a real conversion experience. Rice's sermons called me to consider the ministry as a life career. Out of all that chaos and all that turbulence at that time, his well-prepared orderly sermons just march through my mind like a steady phalanx. They just made me feel that there was the place where my life energies ought to be. I never saw a barn on fire. I never saw a drowning man, none of those things. Mine was an urban experience—arising out of college conflict and arising out of seeing myself as a shipman in the navy yard and driving six grown men back and forth to work in my daddy's car every morning and hearing their conversation. I knew that they way they live and what they did and how they talked and what they used their lives for was not what I thought I ought to be doing.

So I resigned the apprenticeship. Nobody could understand it. "As hard as it is for a Black man to get in a program like this, you mean you are going to quit?" But I resigned. I took the little bit of money that I had saved ($300-400) and went back to college. And it was a different experience. For one thing, at Virginia State College we were in brand new buildings. But back at Virginia Union the buildings were nearly a hundred years old [with] plaster falling. I never dreamed that one day I would be the president of that place and I would have to put that plaster up.

They put me on the top floor, because I was late applying and late sending in my deposit and they were late telling me. But when I got there, I found these wonderful professors who made such a strong impression on me. I made A's under all of them. Never hardly made a B. Made a B in Greek or something like that, but the rest of it, I lapped it up. I was so voracious and I was so hungry, so predatory to know.

I tell you what happened. They bumped me back to twenty-four credit hours. I had sixty-two, just to show you how sloppily the administration operated. One old man there who thought he was a great saint, he really was a kind of dumb dude. He took all my credits from me and left me with twenty-four hours that made me a second semester freshman. He was the vice-president, dean, registrar, he was everything. In the chapel I had to sit with the freshmen. Everybody there from Norfolk knew I had been in college for two years, so it looked like I had flunked everything. What a horrible thing to do to a young person. So I made all A's, all A's that first semester, then I could take twenty hours. Took twenty hours and made A's again. Went to Summer school and worked like a dog and lost about thirty pounds, because I had to work for my summer school bill. I took an extra course in Latin. The man made me work in his yard, in his garden for that and I never felt so much like a slave in all my life. Every hour of Latin he taught me, he wanted an hour of work in his garden. He didn't have a garden any bigger than this [hotel] room but he had me doing something out there. He would stand out there over me and watch me. He was a Black man with light skin and green eyes. And I was sitting there just like a slave.

And I hated that man, if it was hate. I don't know what it was, God just has to forgive me. But he had the mentality of a White slavemaster. And by the way he wouldn't go to the Black church where there were dark-skinned people. I use to drive him also. I would have to drive him from Richmond to Washington so he could go to the yellow folk's church. He went up there to that little church, the church where only fair-skinned people went. And when I went up there with him, he told me, "Now you go take the car wherever you want to go, and then come back and pick me up." He didn't invite me to go in there with him. And I was a student of the ministry and he knew it. But his idea of ministry and that in my theme this morning, [was] about respectability—what a deceiving thing that is. Respectability, it's an almost sinful thing. And he was a person who was all for respectability. Didn't smoke. His use of grammar was impeccable. But he was a slum landlord who hated dark-skinned people. The only God he had was getting the ending on the Greek verbs straight. If you got that straight you were Kingdon-bound, but if you messed up on that you were hell-bound. I ran into him and he made a believer out of me. Boy, you talk about Phariseeism, I found out what that was all about.

But anyway, my call, you see, was as a result of Brown and Rice, Brown in Petersburg and Rice in Norfolk. But I think preachers need to understand also that a call, no matter what they read in the Bible about Jeremiah's call and Paul's call, it is really a process. It is not a one-shot thing, I think. Once you get that urge and that commitment, it has to be fortified and solidified. A lot of folks went as far as I went, then backed away and moved on to something else, dropped it. But at Virginia Union it was fortified. Those wonderful people made it so clear. Then, I got to be a campus politician and started making speeches and people thought I did it well, and all of that added to my image that maybe the Lord would use my life.

So, I never turned back. After college, I went on to seminary. If anything was going to turn me back, it was when I ran into Crozer and those guys began to pull the New Testament apart. The Bible I took with me to seminary got cut up like a razor blade ripping it up, and I had to put it back together myself. Going through that experience confirmed me more in ministry than anything. Now there was a chance to go into sociology or labor relations or something else because of what they did to me in the seminary. God will have to forgive those fellows for they way they ruined a lot of lives. A lot of white boys just dropped right out, never did preach anymore. A fellow that was head of Psychology [at the] University of Pittsburgh, he quit, didn't want to hear anymore about it; Ebersole, head of Sociology, University of Tennessee — they were my classmates. Boy, they drove them right out of the ministry. The first day in class the professor said, "We're going to study the New Testament like any other kind of literature, and I want you to know the only thing we can know about Jesus is 'that the child grew'." That's where he landed. We came out of there after that first lecture and old Woodrow Hastes — he's the pastor now of a big Congregational church in Miami, great big thing, he's got all these millionaires coming to church — old Hastes said to me, he said, "Sam, I feel like Mary at the tomb." I said, "What is that, Hastes?" He said, "They've taken away my Lord and I know not where they've laid him."

But Fosdick brought me through. Harry Fosdick on the radio church of the air. At 2:00 o'clock every Sunday, no matter where I was, I raced to get back to my dormitory so I could hear Fosdick. He always opened that service, "Behold, I stand at the door and knock, sayeth the Lord, If any man would hear my voice and open the door, I will come in." His voice, his style of preaching, he always used [the] dialectical method, although I never heard him say that or never read that he said it. But that's what he did. He always had a strong antithesis, that brought you right into the room with it. When you listened to his antithesis you knew something was coming in the thesis just after that. He set you up. You follow me what I mean? And his antithesis was so real, so real. And he swept every corner clean in presenting to you what the situation is, and you could almost feel him put his clutch and change the gear—but, notwithstanding, nevertheless, on the other hand. I hear those connectives right now: "But come further," "but looking deeper into the matter." He would always bring you to that point, and you would rise right out of your chair and say, "Have mercy, Jesus." And when he went from there—the real to the ideal, the error to the truth, the vacuum to the fulfillment—he really did a job on your mind.

Fellows tease me today about being dialectical in all my sermons; everything I do I go about it that way, because I just habituated to him. I think it is the most honest way to present the gospel of the Lord Jesus Christ. That is to say, lay out the situation to which you want it applied, lay it out, make it clear and then, in your thesis, do the application. And then go to court and challenge yourself with the most radical questions you can think of, then answer the questions. And when you get through, you've got a sermon. I've been teaching that at Princeton, Boston University, Union in New York. Everytime they ask me to teach a class in preaching, I do the same thing. And they are all very grateful. Now, you always have somebody who will say, "I don't want to be monolithic." But, its not monolithic. It's not monolithic.

You can do anything with that structure. You can preach devotional sermons, exegetical sermons, anything. Because, I don't care what you are preaching about, you have a thesis. I don't care what you're preaching about, you have a thesis. You may not tell anybody what it is, but there is something that made you stand up to preach. You have a thesis. And all I ask you to do is serve it. You've got a thesis, please walk me through the antithesis so I can join up with you. Tell me where you were, before you got to that. Tell me what called you to that. You follow me? Now this morning I want to preach about Christian ethics versus Christian respectability. That's my theme. "Sam, what brought you to this point?" Because I have seen so many churches and ministers forsake the strength of the gospel to simply become apostles of respectability. Do you hear me? You see? And, if Jesus ever walked through there it would scare the daylights out of him. They've got themselves anesthetized in respectability. Something bland and average, the cutting edge of the gospel, this and that.

    I had a deacon to tell me, about four or five weeks ago during a crisis at the church . . . he said, "Now, [I don't know] how you feel about it, but I go along with Jesus on a lot of things." He "goes along with Jesus on a lot of things." What did he mean by that? Now he is the chairman of the deacon board of the church. "I go along with Jesus on a lot of things," that's what he said. Now, he might have slipped up and said it, but he sure did say it. He wanted to start a dog fight in the deacon board about some other matter. So I said, "You've got to go read the gospel of Matthew, go slowly through that fifth, sixth and seventh chapter, go very slowly, because that's the key to the whole thing. That's the mind of Christ now, the Sermon on the Mount. "I read that," he said, "I go along with Jesus on a lot of things." Now that's the end of my story about that call business.

On my first night alone in the parsonage, I was awakened by the telephone.... 'There is a patient here who is dying. He's asking for a minister. Are you a minister?' In one kaleidoscopic moment I was back again at an old crossroad. A decision of vocation was to be made here, and I felt again the ambivalence of my life and my calling. Finally, I answered. 'Yes, I am a minister....'"

The ceremony of ordination was held at eight o'clock in the evening, and the moment of transcendent glory was for me the laying on of hands, which I had so strongly resisted. During the performance of this ancient and beautiful ritual 'the heavens opened and the spirit descended like a dove.' Ever since, when it seems that I am deserted by the Voice that called me forth, I know that if I can find my way back to that moment, the clouds will lift and the path before me will once again be clear and beckoning."

Howard Thurman,
With Head and Heart: The Autobiography of Howard Thurman
(New York: Harcourt Brace Jovanovich, Publishers, 1979): 3, 58.

Frank M. Reid III
Baltimore, Maryland

The Reverend Dr. Frank M. Reid III was born in Chicago, Illinois, called in 1971 and ordained an African Methodist Episcopal elder in 1975. He received a BA from Yale University, MDiv from Howard University's Divinity School and a DMin from United Theological Seminary. He pastors the Bethel AME church in Baltimore. Interview recorded August 14, 1989.

65

"Called from My Mother's Womb"

My father always said, with a smile, that I was called from my mother's womb. What he meant by that is that five generations on my paternal side of the family had been AME ministers. His father, my grandfather, was an AME bishop; my daddy is an AME bishop, and so he told me, very early in age, that I was just trapped. It was something that I fought. When I was about eleven, when folk would ask, "What do you want to be," I wasn't sure what I wanted to be; but I was sure what I didn't want to be: I didn't want to be a preacher.

But I knew at about twelve that that was the life—using adult terms, looking back now—that there was a call upon my life. I enjoyed being around the church, I enjoyed going with my father to visit the sick, to go do revival services and sit in the meetings. I enjoyed it. But I didn't want to do it, because everybody else in my family had done it. So there was this period of rebellion that lasted quite awhile, even until my freshman year at Yale. At which point, I was visiting a young lady I was seeing. That year Curtis Mayfield's second album (second solo album) came out, and he had on there a song, a Carpenters' song entitled "We've Only Just Begun." We were sitting downstairs eating breakfast with her mother. I said to her, "You know, that would make a wonderful sermon." I began to outline the sermon. This is about 1971. I knew in the Methodist system that we had what you call the trial sermon—then and there, that very morning, I called my father, "Listen, I want you to preach my trial sermon. I believe this is what I am supposed to do. And if it's not, after I do it, I'll know it. This is what a trial sermon is for."

Of course, he was very happy—any father would be. I preached the sermon, and I knew from the moment I stood up. It was just confirmed for me. Now, what led me there at the end of my freshman year was the fact that the one thing I knew I wanted to do was to serve Black people. I was clear on that. The period in which we were in school up at Yale, the Black Panthers were there to try—Bobby Seale's trial was going on. I knew that I wanted to serve Black people, and I went saying I wanted to be a lawyer. Much on my mind at that time was a William Kunstler-type of attorney, serving the people and taking cases popular or unpopular, depending on your viewpoint—political cases.

Then, as you remember, '69-'70 was a rich period of time for Black theological writers. I was an African-American studies major. In fact, at Yale you had to have two majors to be in the African-American studies department: you had to have a major in African-American studies and then in another area of concentration. Mine was history.

So (James) Cone's book and (Gayraud) Wilmore's book came out at about that time. As I began to read those books and really get into my interest of African-American religious history, I saw whatever was wrong with the church and whatever Malcolm, and later the Panthers, were saying about the church: that in fact the greatest history of service to our people was the Black church. As I began to look at some of the Black graduates of Yale who, many of them, had also come in wanting to do great things for their people, when I began to look at them and talk with them as they came back, I saw that most of them started out with the greatest of intentions but they ended up actually working not for the community. They were working outside the community to maintain a lifestyle that they wanted. I wasn't critical of that lifestyle, but I wanted to serve.

All of this was when "We've Only Just Begun" hit. When the song hit, that song just crystallized it for me. I did not hear any bells, I did not see any visions. It was as if my life story and history had led up to the moment of that song which clicked, "Yeah, this is it." The sermon was received very well; I never turned back from the call. I did not become a holier-than-thou student, I just knew that I wanted to go to seminary. I knew I wanted to be a pastor. Did not attend church much when I was in New Haven. Did my dissertation, my senior dissertation, under Al Raboteau on the "Spirituals and the Foundation for Black Theology." So, all of my studies and interests peaked towards that. That, basically, was the story of my calling, how I became involved in the process of ministry.

As Wilmore talks about the need for a second conversion in his introduction to his new book, there was a second part of the call that helped—I might call it that—which is good Methodist theology, which really formed my ministry. That was when I graduated. I went with my father to preach for Reverend, now Bishop, John Bryant. I was scheduled to go get accepted at Yale Seminary. I had a full scholarship. I had a year of undergraduate education and was president of the Black Student Alliance, so I had a good relationship with the president of the University. I was going to have a good job but I went up (I preached at eight, my father preached at eleven), and I had never seen anything like this church before. There were African-American artwork murals on the walls. There was a red and black flag. There were young Black people from all of the institutions in the area, be it BU, Harvard Business School, Harvard Law School. It was coming out of my traditional AME background, it was just wild. I walked up and I joined the church, and then decided that I would catch the train from New Haven to Cambridge. New Haven was in the Boston area, and I would be up there at least two or three times a week.

Then Bishop John [Bryant] said, "I could get you into either Harvard or BU; where do you want to?" I was clear that wherever I went to seminary at that time, if it was going to be a White seminary, what I needed was hands-on experience and mentoring by somebody who had the type of ministry and ministry of liberation empowerment that I was hungry to see put into place. I saw that there. While "We've Only Just Begun" was the moment of the answering of that call, St. Paul (Cambridge) was a refining of that calling, a development of that call.

So often, after this part of the story, often when I think about my calling, I wonder why I didn't see all the visions that other folk talk about. For a while I said, "Well, maybe something is wrong with me." But then as I look back over it, I see that God calls often through the events of your life and everybody doesn't have a Damascus Road. I think one of the things that would be exciting about your book, to me, will be to look at the other stories and see how many actual Damascus Road, knocked-off-the-horse experiences that people had. I did not have that experience and because of our tradition, or what I read about tradition in the seminary, what the older preachers kept saying to me as I listened as a young boy . . . I felt something was wrong with me in my call, was too intellectual. But then, when I thought back to what my daddy used to say to me as a youngster — "You were called in your mother's womb — then I kind of believed that, not because of just the Biblical implications, but because I see now that my call was something that I had to be aware of, but was always there. That's basically the story.

W. Franklyn Richardson
Mt. Vernon, New York

The Reverend William Franklyn Richardson was born in Philadelphia, Pennsylvania, on June 14, 1949, called in 1967 and ordained a Baptist minister in 1969. He has a BA from Virginia Union University and an MA degree from Yale University Divinity School. He pastors Grace Baptist Church in Mt. Vernon New York. In addition, he serves as the General Secretary (the second ranking officer) of the largest Black Baptist Convention in the United States, the National Baptist Convention USA, Inc. Interview recorded December 13, 1989.

66

Called in the Midst of a Medical Mishap

My call to the ministry came, I think, subconsciously and consciously. I suppose that I will never be able to measure the impact of the fact that my grandfather before me was a Methodist minister, the powerful influence of his ministry to a young boy of five, six, or even before that. How I used to visit his church in the summer time and how the preacher in my growing-up was held in such high esteem. Those things working together probably made a real positive impression on me of what a minister was.

I am sure that that fact voided, later on, [my] making some conscious decisions about ministry. How, nevertheless, as I continued to develop my own ministry and my own life in middle school, more and more in the context of my growing-up, people would also make reference to the fact that they thought I would be a preacher. I don't know how much that impacted me. Nevertheless, as I got towards my teens (I think I was complimented about it when I was younger), when I got toward my teen years, I was less excited about their saying that about me. I think I developed a rebellion on being a minister, because for me as a teenager or as a younger person, adolescent, the prospect of being a minister was a dull and unexciting prospect. It was not something that a young person really wanted to be, because it suggested a lifestyle. In a young person's mind, the lifestyle is less attractive, less full of excitement. So I began to rebel against that notion; what I began to do was look for other options for career.

It was in high school that I got employed after school. I worked at the West Park Hospital. Somewhere along that thing, maybe over a two, three year period where I worked, I began to articulate the desire to be a doctor. I worked the laboratory in pathology and also became, ultimately, an orderly and head of the orderly department. The medical board was impressed with that and the hospital. They said that would (they made an official vote), Dr. Weinstein said that they would support me to be a doctor. I began to talk about that. However, I think, all the time I was fighting the notion to be a preacher.

The thing that happened next was in 1966-'65, November of '65—I had an appendectomy. In the process of the appendectomy, something went wrong with the spinal tap—disrupted my nerve system. In the uncertainty and the anxiety of it all, I acknowledged to myself that the Lord wanted me to preach; but I did not want to preach. So, I prayed to the Lord and promised the Lord that I would preach. I promised the Lord I would preach. I did say to myself that when that was over that I was going to be a minister—that was, when I got out of the hospital. This is at about sixteen years old. I withdrew that and continued to pursue being a doctor.

I worked in the summers and occasionally for my uncle, who was a big funeral director in Philadelphia. I would direct funerals. It was on this one particular night that I was directing a funeral. I went into the church, and there were three young ministers down front directing the service. It was that night that something in me surrendered, saying, "You should be doing what they're doing. You are running away from God." That night I surrendered. I went home and read my Bible. I called my pastor and told him that I wanted to accept my call to ministry and that I had been called. It did not seem to be a shock to him.

All the time I was president of the youth department. I was very active in the church, so it wasn't any shock to him. So he set up a call, I mean a trial sermon, and I went through the trial sermon and then went to Virginia Union that next fall. This was right after graduation from high school.

In June of '66 I graduated from high school, but it was in May of '67 that I preached my trial sermon in West Virginia—September of '67. So, for me, I think that it was always there, but, for me, I did not want to accept it. I remember part of my dialog with the Lord when I decided to switch from medicine. I said—this might not have been theologically or even ethically proper I remember talking to the Lord very distinctly and saying, "Lord, I don't want to be—if I want to be a pastor, I want to be a successful pastor — I don't want to be marginal. I don't want my ministry to be any less than what my medical career would have been."

I can say now, twenty years removed from that decision, maybe twenty-three years, that the Lord has honored that simple request that I made earlier, that he would vow my life to be—that my ministry career would be greater than what it would have been if I had been a medical doctor. And in every way, in financial ways, in recognition and fulfillment, it has been all of that. So, my call was a gradual call but it started, I guess, very long ago. It was not something that I immediately wanted to accept. I wrestled with it, not really wanting to do that.

Joseph L. Roberts
Atlanta, Georgia

The Reverend Joseph Roberts was born in Chicago, Illinois, in February 1935 and ordained a Presbyterian minister in 1959. He earned a BA from Union Theological Seminary and a ThM from Princeton Theological Seminary. He pastors the historic Ebenezer Baptist Church in Atlanta. Interview recorded May 9, 1989.

67

Rebellion of an AME Preacher's Kid

I grew up in an African Methodist Episcopal minister and his wife's home, coming out of three generations of African Methodist Episcopal folk. So there was a certain extent in which, I feel, that I was almost always, in part, a child of the church. I knew nothing other than that. I went through the natural rebellion that a person will go through in my teenage years, feeling that if I wanted to do anything, it would not be in the ministry.

I was bothered by the poverty of ministry, the lack of material acquisitions, as was evident in my father's life. I was bothered by the solicitous nature and stance (which I felt was demeaning) that was laid upon him not only as he had to deal with trustees who would determine what kind of furniture we had in "their house," not our house but the house that was theirs—the parsonage. They would often feel that it was quite appropriate for them to work for White people and to have White people give me something. Then they'd use it and pass it on to the preacher, so that it had gone through three hands. That I found very offensive. I lived in Chicago, Illinois.

The third thing that I found offensive was the demeaning nature of the Black African Methodist Episcopal Bishopric Assistant, which was definitely a plantation, sort of, pecking order. I found that in the Black Methodist Bishop, a lot of the same tyranny that one would find in a White racist. Only, he played it out on Black people. I think it was displaced anger and hostility that came down on folks in tiers; so that the bishop put pressure on the presiding elder, who put pressure on the preacher, who put some pressure on the people, who then looped back to the bishop to try to get the preacher. I just didn't like the lack of freedom that one had in all of that, and really thought that I would probably have very little to do with the ministry. I was talking about law and dentistry and the rest. But I found that after I was really honest, there was a love for the people shown (through all of these entrapments that I have already talked about) and a love for God, as seen in Jesus Christ and as seen in heroes and heroines of the Old Testament, that made me feel that I wanted to do my ministerial role. I was not sure just where. So I think the call was not a traumatic thing that came to me. It was something that I yearned to do, but that I fought, because I thought that the political trappings and the infrastructure of my denomination mitigated against fulfilling the kind of ministry I wanted to fulfill.

The next thing that I really knew was that I wanted to have a ministry that was broad enough to let me address some political, social, and economic problems and would not be so narrow in its confines that I would have to be wedded to a particular parochial situation. I was looking for some sort of a quasi-political, theological bridge that would allow me to be comfortable in both camps, as I took the theology and tried to apply it to all these other areas. I went on to college, and while in college had opportunity to meet some Presbyterian folk. In the process of meeting them, they encouraged me to consider going into the Presbyterian church. It was for political reasons that I went into the Presbyterian church, because I saw that it gave me more freedom to be unencumbered by a number of folk, to be independent and to be able to do the kind of ministry that I wanted to do. When that opportunity for education really came on to me, then I think that the call was really sort of authenticated; because I felt that I would be able to exercise ministry in a way that would allow me to honor who I was. At heart, I was an AME. I enjoyed everything that the church was about. I reveled in the ideas of Richard Allen and other strong Black people in the 18th and 19th centuries in our denomination who had founded schools and pulled away from White denominations and established churches and hospitals and established beachheads in Africa. I admired all of that, but the present manifestations got in my way. The Presbyterian Church made me feel like I could take that tradition and blend it into whatever I wanted it to be; so that my call was not a catastrophic, vertical thing that suddenly came upon me. It was rather the accumulation of a number of experiences that nudged me on toward a ministry that was unencumbered by some political problems of infrastructure.

It is not, therefore, something that I can date in terms of a Tuesday at one o'clock when anything happened but, rather, something that I think was rather gradual. And not to sound defensive, but I believe when people stop lying, most of them will admit that it was a gradual thing that they were nudged to and not a catastrophic, one-day piece that suddenly came and hit them like a bolt of lightning out of the air. Notwithstanding what Martin Luther said about what happened to him, I think all of those stories, if we looked them up, are but the pinnacle of a long series of God's prodding and nudging us toward decision. Then we talk about one that was critical, and that was it. I can remember the day when Frank Gordon, who was pastor of Shiloh Presbyterian Church, talked to me. I could say it was on that day, after we had that talk and that prayer, that my call was confirmed, I came out of the darkness. But that would be a lie, so I'm not going do that. So, that is my answer.

My pilgrimage since then has been a long one. But if you ask specifically about how that call came into being and how I went in from Knoxville College to Union Seminary to Princeton to perfect that ministry and what happened in the ministry, that's another story. But that is how I actually was drawn to it. I was able finally to reconcile myself with a system of governance in a denomination that would not impede my view of a broad ministry and my view of a free ministry, where I would not be controlled by a people who might take personal vendettas against me, because they either didn't like my political stance or they didn't like the fact that I was not going to acquiesce to their supreme authority they thought they had because they were a part of the Episcopal ranks.

    I think there is a certain extent as to which a connectional church that has bishops who are not sensitive can be demeaning to the sacredness of human personality. It can almost be another form of slavery. I don't think that anyone should have to wonder about where they are going after a year of faithful service. But the bishop decides, and you have to run around and carry his bags and bow before him. He is but another man, and I think it is idolatry. Now there are some good bishops, and I am not putting the AME Church down, because I love it. I may, now being older, I may have been able to work in that, but it would have had to be with a particular understanding that I did not think would meet with the approval of those who were in power. It would always mean that, for me, it would be a rugged and unhappy relationship between myself and the bishop. So, that's how I got there.

Frederick C. Sampson II
Detroit, Michigan

The Reverend Frederick C. Sampson II was born in Port Arthur, Texas on August 9, 1928, called when he was in college and ordained a Baptist minister in 1948. He received a BD from Howard University and a MA from Columbia University. He pastors Tabernacle Missionary Baptist Church in Detroit. Interview recorded April 26, 1989.

68

Under a Magnolia Tree Looking Up, When God Spoke

I find it rather interesting that you would put it that way, that is, to speak of a "call," because in my attempt to get some enlightenment and equipment before the assignment, [I found] different campuses present different concepts. As you know, it got to the point where some don't even use the word "call" anymore. So, I thought it rather interesting coming from an educator, to talk about a call, because they say, "Well, you've got talents. You're interested in it as a career, and you choose it. If you don't like it, you can always get out of it."

It's of interest to me, because that's primarily what it was. We were born on the Gulf of Mexico, right on the bay right outside of Dallas, in Port Arthur, Texas, a peninsular thumb in the Gulf. Watching the ways of life was of great interest to us. Two of the largest refineries in America, the waterfronts, the Gulf of Mexico right at the back, the drawbridges with rivers and things coming through . . . We saw all those activities—people coming from Europe, Africa, landing where we were born to a mother who was married at fourteen and almost had a child every twelve months, and ended up with nine children, seven boys and two girls. And to father who, in his attempt to escape the poverty, the demands of life, the pressures, became a stevedore and from that became a merchant marine and became a world traveler, to the extent that when he came home, he found himself rather discouraged and so he didn't leave a forwarding address. So, this little Black woman without welfare, without any outside assistance, decided that she was going to be the mother that she had always been—and she had such strong convictions.

I was christened Catholic, my father was a tough Catholic. My mother signed the papers that her children would be reared Catholic, so she took us to five o'clock Mass and Catechism, etcetera, but she was truly Baptist. She had us living a double-headed religious life. She would live up to the contract, but she would also take us to the Baptist Sunday school and the church and the BYPU, prayer meeting on Wednesdays, novenas during the Lenten season, all of the activities, the parochial school, Mother Superior and all the rest.

We watched her, and we couldn't understand how the people who lived in our neighborhood were always complaining —many of them had men at their address. We couldn't understand that the kids with whom we played had shoes on (we didn't), suits on (we had patches). And when I was a boy and you wore a suit to anything, your people were really up there, we thought. But we kept watching, and we couldn't understand people complaining about what they didn't have to eat. We never heard that at our house. The word "poor," the word "poverty," the words "God does not care," the words "Lord, what am I going to do?" we never heard at our address.

We saw our mother coming from a job, going to work, but she always had time for her children. In the evening, when we sat around the table, she was there. It was a good while before I discovered folks had the privilege of choosing what they were going to eat, because when we sat at the table, that was it! And we ate as a family. I heard my mother's voice every day in prayer—every day we heard my mother's voice in prayer. Every Sunday she didn't call us, she didn't say anything, but we ended up around her bed on our knees in prayer; and we had to pray before we "became Christians." She taught us that, " You don't have a daddy to give you what you want, but you have a Father who will never let you need." And she taught us that, he was our Father. When she prayed, she called us by name and presented the case to God.

I remember the words now: "Now, you take that Robert. Now you've got to take him over, because I've done all I know how, and I don't want to hurt him." Now, he was right there! And then when she would start telling on us, we'd say, "Oh, God, don't tell him!" But we didn't know the Man already knew. She would just lay it out there. She taught us almost as much theology, as much about the nature and personality of God as we learned in seminary. And when she said "God," certain things came to our minds: words like relationship, fellowship and kinship, before we could spell them. We learned when we stubbed our toe, if we learned words from somebody else, we had learned almost immediately to say something to God, first of all from fear, of course ("He's gonna get you!"), but then all of a sudden we started getting into something else.

I kept watching her. She always talked about our going to school, but she called it "making something of yourself." "You must make something of yourself." We found out that—I grew tall for my age, I'm in the middle of all those kids, and I shall never forget being in school, tall and no shoes on. I walked about two or three miles to school one way and had to come back for lunch, because we didn't have any money to buy nothing. So we walked back, as many of us did. And I found myself sometimes dropping my pencil so I could look around and look back to see if I could see some more bare feet, so I could feel better. Because I was tall for my age, no shoes on and all that old, good stuff—patches. But she would always say to us, "Cleanliness is next to godliness." And we would talk about what others had, but she heard "God doesn't love us" and "Why doesn't God answer our prayers?" and she wouldn't talk about the people. A lot of the people had clothes because of what their families did.

When I was small, Port Arthur was wide open. Prostitution was legal, gambling was legal—all that old, good stuff. If it brought pleasure, the fathers put a tax on it and things of this sort. I mean, the prostitutes traveled in pairs just like the nuns did, because this was a Catholic town. But my mother would always talk, and so, if somebody wanted to know how much clothes a particular person had, she said, "I thought you all liked that guy." "We do, we just talked about his clothes." "Well," she said, "how many suits does he have?" I said, "He's got five." "No, he's got ten." She said, "Give him twenty. How many can he wear at one time?" She would say, "Now, the kids will laugh at you, they'll sniggle at you because of your clothes. Get some wisdom in your head, some love in your heart; and when your teacher calls on you, you stand up—they'll sniggle, but if you let something come out your mouth, they'll stop laughing before you sit down," and all of that.

We wanted to know, "What are we going to do with our lives?" And I'd say that God had always put, in absence of a father, wingless angels in my path to keep me from making crazy turns—elderly people. Miss Polter called me one time (my brother and I were in this school, the two of us went altogether all the time). She said, "Why don't you guys come to school?" She said, "You wouldn't be among the smartest; you'd leave this class."

There was a guy that had come into our home; my mother had put him out. I learned later it was common-law. And he'd walk in [saying,] "Stop wasting my money." It was my mama's house. We were in an area where they wouldn't bring the light, the electric, to ours, because most were Blacks living there. So, in the city, we experienced part of a country lifestyle, because we had outside toilets. They didn't bring the sewer in the edge of town of Port Arthur. We were right across the street from the refinery, where I was born. We had lamps in a house in the city. They'd pick up the refuse once a month. At night we had to walk through the grass to go to the bathroom. Bathing tubs in the city! But we never heard the negatives out of my mama's voice. She didn't go around cussing God or blaming him.

So we found that Miss Polter called us in—"Come to school." She was our English teacher. Miss Williams called us in, Miss Fleeks called us in. We found out later it was a positive conspiracy. "Get those boys, get 'em. Get them Sampsons!" I would come in with part of the bed in my hair. I shall never forget Miss Williams took me in the coat room, took out her comb. Have you ever tried to comb nappy hair with a comb? And she put it at the top. Well, I was scared to holler, because the kids would know what was going on. And I discovered that we said, "Okay, they helped us discover our talents."

Before I got to high school, (Lincoln) , when we got to high school we already had arithmetic, first and second year algebra, plane and solid geometry and trigonometry and introduction to calculus—that's before college! We had had social studies, etcetera, etcetera, *Arthur and the Round Table*, Shakespeare's works and all that good stuff—that's before. We had two years of Latin, Spanish. They had eleven grades, but before I graduated, they put on twelve, so they added French, and I had to take that. Now all that's before college. The humanities were almost a review for us because we had had—okay, we were reared with the Blacks, the Spaniards, the Mexicans, the Dutchmen immigrants, all lived in the same general area. We could go into what is known as the Spanish section of town, so we were exposed to all that culture.

They wanted to know, "What are you going to be?" I had an aptitude for science, so they pushed me in the sciences. I actually took a test and taught trigonometry, solid geometry while I was a senior in high school at Lincoln. I taught the guys in eleven and twelve. My brother was above me, I taught him all the trigonometry he knew. I took that test; they pushed me where my aptitude was, so I looked at that.

I got to Bishop College, where I was going to pursue the sciences, but I felt something had happened. "What can we do with all of this? What does God want?" My mother had put that in us. "You were not an accident. You were born for a reason. Your daddy didn't stay with you, but your Father sent you. So since you don't have a daddy to go to, stay with your Father. Find out what he had in mind before you became mine." The word "purpose" she didn't use; "locked into his providential plan" she didn't use; "adventuring with Jesus" she didn't use. But she convinced us. So we said, "Hey, what does he want? Why are we here? Why did he permit all of this? Why didn't he help my mama?" We kept coming with the negative, but it would always move into assignment.

I had taken up typing and worked at Port Arthur College. (I spoke there week-before-last.) And while there, I had to clean up the commercial department, and I saw these little things where they were teaching typing, so I started doing [some typing.] Somebody heard me one time, and I looked around and didn't see anybody. And each day I'd feel that presence. One day this lady walks in and she said, "So, you're the one! (This was a White college). What do you think you're doing?" I started to tell her I was just—"Well, who teaches you typing?" I said, "I don't take any typing." She said, "How do you hold that steadiness, that rhythm?" I said, "I just do this every day." And each day now there was an assignment sheet on the table, and I typed those assignment sheets every day. I learned to type cleaning the white college commercial department. Because for that year and a half, every evening she had the assignments there, and she started putting tests there; and I started taking them, and she'd mark them.

I went to Port Arthur three years ago in a revival. Dr. Briscoe was at the college. She's ninety-two years old. When we started talking, she remembered. She said, "So, you're the boy?" And then her chest went out. All right, so when I got to Bishop, we started working. They told me I was going to get a job in the commercial department, but Dr. Downing's (a graduate of Bishop) daughter wanted a job, and they gave her my job. So I told them, "Look, I still have to work," so they gave me the dormitory to clean, some of the other things. Before the year was out, Jesse J. MacNeil came to the campus to take over the school of religion. He wanted some work done, and they couldn't get him a typist; they were all busy. Somebody said, "Well, we know a boy who types." He said, "Send him to me." So I came to him. He gave it to me and he told me, "Bring it back by Friday." I brought it to him Wednesday evening. He said, "No, you keep it until you've completed it." I said, "I completed it." So he looked at me and said, "Thank you," and he didn't give me nothing. So I left.

The next couple of days he called me again, wanted me to do some typing. He was writing for the publishing board, as well as setting up this thing at Bishop. So in two months when they got time for a secretary when he moved, they gave him a list of students to choose from. He said, "If you don't mind, I'll choose my own secretary," and that's how I became secretary to the dean of the school of religion at Bishop College.

I was under a magnolia tree, looking up; and almost as if someone were there and said, "When are you going to answer me?" I said, "Pardon me?" He said, "When are you going to answer me?" I said, "About what?" He said, "What are you going to do with your life?" I said, "I'm in college, I'm doing this." He said, "No, when are you going to answer me?" And, Doc, as if a panoramic scene, scenes of light began to fall altogether. My mother had taken us to this place, taken to this theology, the understanding of God . . . enlightenment about life itself started to almost fall into place. "What are we going to do with our lives?"

So my brother and I were talking. We said, "We've got to do something to make mama proud. But we've also got to find out why God did certain things or didn't permit other things." My sister called me and said, "Are you all right?"—I haven't shared this with a lot of people. She said, "When are you coming home?" I said, "I don't know." That evening I was trying to get some things together about death, all the negative things; but much of what came in my mind that day went under the category negativity, but they had no negating power. Instead of driving me away from things, they kept me there; and I kept looking. Having been in the sciences, I knew how diamonds got made; I knew how pearls got made; I understood what nature did, and that which we call violence is sometimes just a process. When the storms come, other things happen by clearing the atmosphere, what God does with these things. All of that stuff started falling into place. So I went home in two weeks.

My sister said, "Fred, I want to share something with you. I had a dream. There was a big cloud, and I heard a voice that said, 'Where's Fred?' I looked around, and all these people are groping in darkness. That's the part where they said, 'Where's Fred?' I said, 'I don't know.' The voice said, 'Give him this,' and he gave me a lantern. I said, 'What shall I tell him?' The voice disappeared and it said, 'He'll know. Give him this.'"

That evening I was on my bed, I don't know whether I was awake or asleep. I was in church, the choir was singing (I love music, I love beauty, I love poetry, I love life), and I looked around. All the choir members appeared nude, still singing; and each one, certain clothes got on them seeming to identify each one. I looked at the congregation, and everybody was nude; then clothes started coming on them, certain faces. And they said, "You gonna answer now?" And my sister got that thing together.

I pursued science, thought I had the equipment for medicine and clinical work. A lot of guys call it a waste, but it was all preparatory. I felt an irresistible claim on my total life and an assignment without a job—almost an open arena, an "I want you." It became almost a surrender. From then on, whatever I did, I didn't have to show anything to prove I was doing it right. I didn't emphasize, "Is this working for me?" I always saw it as pursuing whatever it was. And that's why I say that in my life, it seemed as if God always put wingless angels in my life to keep me from making mistakes.

Dr. Hugo Schiff taught us scripture, exegesis of the Psalms. He was a professor at Howard University, and he brought more than academics to our classroom. He had spent some time in concentration camps in Germany and had watched his wife beaten. He would teach that scripture and live when he taught it. And all of that became part of the in-pouring of this almost total saturation of my whole spirit. I got the idea that my call was not to be a pastor. I never even discussed it with the Lord. I knew he had claimed me, I knew that he had asked me to be committed to him, I knew that he had called me with a capital "C," but I didn't know what he wanted.

I was at Howard University working in the office. I was secretary to Dr. William Stewart Nelson at Howard University. MacNeil was minister of this church. Dr. Harrison, who was minister of Shiloh, came here to Second Baptist every year. They were talking, and Harrison said they needed somebody to help set up his department of Christian education, etcetera. MacNeil says, "There's a fellow at Howard University. He doesn't tell the folk he's a preacher. Get him to come over, he'll help you." Harrison made an announcement from the pulpit, "If you see Sampson from Howard, say I'd like to see him. If not, if you go to Howard, tell him I'm looking for him." I had been working with Dr. Hill, who was dean of chapel at Howard University. Armstrong was chaplain at Howard, he left to go to the army. Dr. Hill asked me to take over that position for the rest of the year, as chaplain; and I began working on that.

Right at that end of year, Proctor invited me to come to Union to do some teaching, and then I thought that was my life. And it kept going, still, this "What are you going to do with it?" Proctor came to me one day and said, "Fred, I was in Roanoke, Virginia, and I did something I don't normally do." "So, what's that?" He said, "If anybody asked me about a teaching job or a pastorate, I give them three names, two Unionites and another. But this church, High Street Baptist Church, largely middle-class in the Shenandoah Valley, asked me about a good man. I gave them your name almost without thinking. They said, 'What about if he doesn't fit?' I said, 'You asked me for a good man. It would be contradictory if I gave you two more.'" He says, "Now, I'm not the Holy Ghost, I'm not God, but I feel there's something there. If they call, at least respond."

That week they asked me to come to Roanoke to preach. I preached. They asked me if I'd accept the church. I told them I didn't know. Somebody asked, "How much would you want?" I said, "I can't speak to that. It's hypothetical," and I went back to Howard. In a month and a half, they extended me a unanimous call to become pastor of High Street Baptist Church, and that's when I went into the ministry. Stayed there eight years, went on. But I keep reaching in the "deposit box" and the other disciplines that I won't have the opportunity to experience.

And what happens now authenticates the call that I feel he laid on my life, because I have no regrets of having not gone into medicine totally or stayed in clinical work or into the big dollar areas. To me, that long exposition says something about the call of Frederick C. Sampson II into the ministry of the Lord and Savior, Jesus Christ, which I say was an irresistible craving of the totality of my being. For me, there is no life apart from giving my life in an adventure with Jesus, living up to the claim that he placed on my life and being commited to letting the Holy Ghost make assignments for me.

Manuel Scott, Sr.
Dallas, Texas

The Reverend Manuel Scott, Sr., was born in Waco, Texas on November 11, 1926, called in 1944 and ordained a Baptist minister in 1948. He has a BA from Bishop College. He pastors the St. John Missionary Baptist Church in Dallas. Interview recorded October 25, 1989.

69

An Irresistible Compulsion

My call to the ministry was a consciousness that I felt at the earliest stages of my life. I've never dreamed or proceeded to desire any other type of life pursuit other than preaching. At the very elementary school level, I felt deeply persuaded that it was my business. The call didn't come at any ecstatic moment. It came with a growing and gradual awareness that the lesson, as far as a church's mission and to be a messenger of the master, broke on me. It was irresistible. The fulfillment of expression of my inner awareness, with respect to preaching, became an irresistible focus. The consciousness of the call and the confirmation came with gradual and increasing impact. I could no longer be satisfied with participation outside of the pulpit ranks. There wasn't no lightning flashes from heaven or no emotional tears or exceptional joy. As the intensity of awareness grew, it became a compulsion at the age of seventeen, when I acknowledged my call. The call to preach for me never came as a burden. I wasn't no reluctant prophet. It was no burden for me. Yes, there are the Jeremiah type—a reluctant prophet—and the Isaiah type, who see the world situation and see themselves in relationship to that, to the nature of things. And they just say, "Here am I, send me." I was the Isaiah type.

"*I* was eight years old and had chosen and committed to memory the fifth chapter of Matthew for the next Children's Day. When I finished speaking, the people went wild. Old women waved their handkerchiefs; old men stamped their feet, and the audience stood up, including the young, and applauded me lustily, loud and long. How could I let this crowd down? They said that I would do something worthwhile in the world, that I would be a Booker Washington or a Fred Douglass. The pastor, Rev. James F. Marshall, predicted that I would preach, and I was a 'marked' boy from that day forward."

Benjamin E. Mays,
Lord, The People Have Driven Me On
(New York: *Vantage Press, 1981*): 2.

William Shaw
Philadelphia, Pennsylvania

The Reverend Dr. William Shaw was born in Marshall, Texas, on December 13, 1933, called in 1944 and ordained a Baptist minister in 1950. He received a BA from Bishop College, a B D from Union Theological Seminary (NY) and a DMin from Colgate Rochester. He pastors the White Rock Baptist Church in Philadelphia. Interview recorded October 8, 1991.

70

"A Constant Inclination toward Ministry"

My call to the ministry goes back as far as I have consciousness of being related to a church. I have early memories of going to church as a child. I remember a commitment experience at the age of seven, when a preacher came and conducted a revival at our church and I felt the urge to respond to the invitation to discipleship. It was done, actually, in a Sunday school session, following the baptism. There was nothing that was spectacular in my life, except a constant inclination toward the ministry.

I think, specifically, the thing that caused me to acknowledge the call—by the way, it happened when I was very young; I was eleven when I acknowledged the call to ministry and did my trial sermon—was that I was at a trial sermon of a student from Bishop College who had become related to my home church. I felt the urge then to make the confession that had been always expressed as a vocational commitment by me for all of my days. At that time, I went to my pastor of eleven years and indicated that I felt called to preach. It was not surprising to him or to the church, because they had known always that I said that

A Constant Inclination toward Ministry

I wanted to be a preacher.

    I don't remember a period in my life when I did not have a sense of call. I remember two periods when the sense of commitment was definitively acted upon: one at seven when I made confession and was baptized, and one at eleven when I made confession and was given the privilege to preach.

Fred Shuttlesworth
Cincinnati, Ohio

The Reverend Fred Shuttlesworth was born in Montgomery, Alabama, on March 18, 1922, called in 1940 and ordained a Baptist minister in 1948. He has a BS from Alabama State-Birmingham and an AB from Selma University. He pastors the Greater New Light Baptist Church in Cincinnati. He was one of the key people in the Civil Rights movement of the 1950s and 60s, and was one of those in Dr. Martin Luther King, Jr.'s inner circle. Interview recorded July 6, 1989.

71

"I Was Anti-religious and Anti-God"

I think most all of my life I have always had, even from a child up, the highest respect for the ministry, and I decided to be a preacher. If I had not been a minister, I would have been a doctor, because those were two choices from childhood up. I guess from about since I was about sixteen and a half or seventeen years old, I began to feel a yearning for the ministry. I married when I was nineteen, and when I was eighteen—let me start by saying I was raised in the Methodist Church in Oxford, Alabama (Saint Matthew's AME) and I've always been studious, apt and religious. There was a time in my life when I did not try to be religious. I was anti-religious and anti-God. I was rebellious against religion. I've always had the fondest of admiration for the Lord's house, the Lord's people and the Lord's work, even if I didn't understand it. Consequently, he has been with me as you see and look beyond me.

I accepted the call to the ministry, deeply, when I was around eighteen. I had mentioned it to my minister, and had I

I Was Anti-religious and Anti-God

stayed in Birmingham, I would have gone up the the annual conference and become a licentiate, because the presiding elder was going to take my request to the bishop. I never did preach a trial sermon or a message or nothing like that in the Methodist Church. Now, I married in October of 1941, and I went to work. I was working for the Alpha Portland Cement Plant in Birmingham. It's in Birmingham's city limits now. When I married, I lived first on 8th Avenue and 24th Street South so that it made me have to catch the streetcar and go to Pilot, practically to Pilot, and walk across the mountain about six miles. I did that every Sunday. I was in Sunday school and student genesis school. I was very studious. Even the rain and snow didn't stop me from going to church.

In July, let's see—June or July, maybe June of 1943—I went to Mobile, Alabama, with two other friends. We were working, taking automobile mechanics training there for Birmingham, Vector McCones Carson Company. We wanted to go to Mobile to make money in the shipyards. So that's where we went. We went to Mobile. The one was named DeWitt Murphy, who is dead now, and the other was named Dave. I can't think of Dave's last name now. We went to Mobile, and the next day we went to Brooklyn Field Air Force Base—and all three of us were hired like that. We didn't even get to the shipyards. We would have probably made more money at the shipyards, but this was the Lord's way.

Now up to that time, I had had no theological training and didn't know a whole lot about the Bible. I don't know too much right now. But for this job we were hired as truck drivers. We had to just take the men to their jobs, whether it was working on the runway or doing this and that, we never had to put our hands on anything. Many times, we took men to a job, we'd have three-hour days; so I would use my time and read my Bible. I always kept the New Testament in my pocket. That was the biggest time that I learned about the Bible, at that time. This gave me the opportunity to talk to a lot of people, to meet people. I was quite apt, quite gifted—older people, men and women took to me. My ministry has blossomed from my years as a pastor, my involvement with the civil rights movement, for which I'am grateful.

325

J. Alfred Smith, Sr.
Oakland, California

The Reverend Dr. J. Alfred Smith, Sr., was born in Kansas City, Missouri, on May 19, 1931, called in 1948 and ordained a Baptist minister in 1948. He received a BS from Western Baptist College (Kansas City), a BD and a ThM from Missouri School of Religion (Columbia, Missouri), a Master of Church History from the Graduate Theological Union and a DMin from Golden Gate Baptist Seminary in California. He pastors Allen Temple Baptist Church in Oakland. He is a past president of the Progressive Baptist Convention. He has published numerous books, including *Making Sense of Suffering: A Message to Job's Children* (Progressive Baptist Convention, 1988) and *The Overflowing Heart* (Broadman, 1987). Interview recorded October 2, 1991.

72

The Saxophone Player Who Heard the Call of God

I was born into humble family, a single-parent family, with a mother who was very, very religious. My grandmother helped my mother rear me, and she was very very religious. My mother and my grandmother were my first teachers of the word of God. We had prayer in our home, and I learned all of the Bible stories, especially the Bible stories coming from the Old Testament. The figure of Moses loomed large in my life. I'm taking the time to say this because it was this early religious formation that provided an unconscious motivation toward God through this process. I felt the calling of God, maybe on an unconscious level; it came to full fruition as I endeavored to move away from the church in which I was reared and some of those good old Sunday school teachers and good old deacons who touched my life along with my mother and grandmother.

But the call experience was an explosion in a cataclysmic way. It took place when I was seventeen years old, working as a jazz musician in the summer months trying to earn money. There was no man to help care for me, my mother and grandmother. There was no man to help me get money to go to school. I was a saxophone player, and I was playing gigs in Missouri, Oklahoma, Kansas and Arkansas—one night stands. I enjoyed being a musician and wanted to become a Johnny Hodges or a phototype of him. But one night while doing a gig in Venita, Oklahoma, this scripture came to me: "What would it profit a person to gain the world and lose his soul?" I knew that I was made and called and created for more than that, and I realized that my people needed more than that. I realized that I had a soul hunger and a heart hunger. I couldn't be satisfied just by being a muscian entertaining people. I felt that life had more than that to offer. Life was about more than entertainment. So I told the Lord that I would go.

I left the band the next day and got on a Greyhound bus, and came back to Kansas City and went to work in the fields in order to earn my livelihood. Then I started to bargain with God and said, "God I'll go, but not now". But the fall came and I went on back to my senior year in high school and start earning money with a deacon of the church as a painter. After class I would go with him, and I would paint houses. One day I was up on a ladder painting, and the Lord reminded me that I made a covenant with him that I hadn't kept. Tears came down my face. I couldn't help myself. I came down off the ladder that day, went home and took a hot bath and cleaned myself up. I sought my pastor out. I went to prayer meeting and he wasn't there; I went up to his parsonage and somebody told him that I was looking for him. Between the parsonage and the church we met, and I announced my call to him. He said, "Son, I knew you had been called, I just been waiting for you to tell me." On Sundays, I would get up and attend a six o'clock Bible class, and I was the only young person, the only teenager in the class with men. That's my call story, in a capsule. I believe in the call. I could have done other things, made money other ways with greater materialistic success, but I'm doing what the Lord has touched my heart to do. If I had to do it all over, I would go this way; and I can't talk about my call in a non-emotional way. I get happy, and I cry as I think about it.

Gardner C. Taylor
Brooklyn, New York

The Reverend Dr. Gardner Calvin Taylor was born in Baton Rouge, Louisiana, in 1916, called in 1937 and ordained a Baptist minister in 1939. He earned a BA from Leland College in Louisiana and a BD from Oberlin College. His honorary doctorates are too numerous to list. He is pastor emeritus of Concord Baptist Church of Christ in Brooklyn and a former President of the Progressive Baptist Convention. He is considered by many to be the dean of Black preachers. His sermonic artistry and picturesque language are widely studied. He is the author of *How Shall They Preach* (Lyman Beecher lectures), *The Scarlet Thread and Chariots Aflame* (Broadman, 1988). Interview recorded April 22, 1987.

73

The Dean of Black Preachers: He Didn't Want to Be a Preacher

I was a pastor's son. I had, growing out of some of my family members' attitudes, some antipathy toward the ministry. I came by it in that atmosphere. My father was a pastor, a rather well-known pastor, and I greatly admired him. He died when I was thirteen. But together with that family influence, my own, I guess, inclinations and schooling, I became very scornful of the ministry and wanted absolutely no part of it.

As a matter of fact, I had been admitted in my senior year of college to the University of Michigan Law School on condition, because our school was not accredited. And I wanted to be a criminal lawyer. But in the Spring of my senior year in college, I had a traumatic experience with an automobile accident. I was chauffeur for the college president, and there was an accident on the highway driving his car. Three men, White, cut across me in an old Model T Ford. One was killed on the spot, one other died later. That experience—and this was a rural Lousiana highway in 1937—the only people who gathered were Whites. Now, I did not associate this directly with my call, with any call. But I would guess that this was the culmination of some disquiet that had been going on in me for some time. Within the next week or two, I went into the president's office and, I suppose to his surprise, told him that I felt called to the ministry. I would guess that this was something that had been going on inside of me for some time. But this accident brought it to the fore.

I might say about that accident that the only witnesses to it were two poor Whites, one a farmer, the other a oil refinery worker. His name lives on although it's been fifty years. Jesse Shockly was his name, a local Southern Baptist preacher, a poor, White local refinery worker. Both of those men, the next day at an inquest, testified that I had not been exceeding the speed limit. Though I was very close to exceeding it, I was not exceeding it, because I was late getting back to the campus. Another student was in the car with me, neither of us were hurt. The call grew out of this. I would not want to say that that was the cause of it. I would not want to say that I would have surrendered to this without it. I can't disentangle these things. I cannot untangle these things. I just don't know.

More than what I've said, I just don't know. I know I wasn't comfortable, I was going to the University of Michigan Law School, but I wasn't comfortable. I guess something was going on inside of me. I know I took delight in debating the young fellows who were going to be preachers. My father had some books, one of them was *The Mistakes of Moses* by Robert Ingersoll. And I read that stuff when I was thirteen, fourteen years old. I enjoyed reading that stuff, and I'd come up with some of Ingersoll's questions about the Bible and give these young preachers the devil. I do not take pride in that now. It was not kind. I was embarrassed for having done it. But I did do it. I guess something was happening inside of me then; I wanted to be a radical, hung out with fellows who were from that mold. It didn't quite work. But I can't analyze it.

I had an aunt who was a great influence on my life. She was my mother's aunt, but they were like sisters. She had very little time for churches and preachers. When I told her about it, after this experience in my senior year in college, she said, "Well, what you gonna do, Gardner?" I said, "Well, I been called into the ministry." She said, "You need to go to school for that." She never became a Christian, certainly not a confessed one. But when I would come home from school and preachers would invite me to preach here and yonder, she would always go with me. "Around there, going to church," she said, "there's something—I don't know what it is—it's a certain feeling about the preachers in the church. And it's kept me in a compromised position. I think that's what it is."

I had never felt any particular pride in being a preacher. I felt almost embarrassed. And it's only been within the last eight or ten years that I have been delivered fairly well from that. I still have some tension. I guess it was the caricature that I saw of preaching. I'm sure my aunt had some influence on that, and the low standards I think we've had for preachers, exacting of them, training and so on. On the other hand, you can't judge a preacher by his training. I realize that. So it's a grey area. But I did have that ambivalence about being a preacher. I apologize to the Lord for that now almost daily, because it was a great honor that he let me be a preacher. He let my years have the kind of strength that they have had, and let my preaching be received the way it has. But, honestly, no reflection on him, I just didn't think much of it.

I think I was determined not to preach, until finally I said, I will. I was determined not to. I don't know anything on earth that I wanted to be less, than I did a preacher. I don't know anything on earth now more I want to be, than a preacher.

I think all people have vocations. I think the vocation of the preacher is a specific vocation among other vocations. Somebody else may see it differently. But to me, now—not always, but now—it is the first among equals. I would validate anybody's call to medicine, to carpentry, to whatever. I think my calling is the first among equals. Chief among chiefs. I respect it that much. And I have grown to this: that for anybody to be allowed to be more or less the official (though that is a sort of strange word) spokesman for God to people is a tremendous privilege. On the people side, one who is in my calling is admitted into secret places of people's lives where nobody else is allowed, and almost always without embarrassment. There is no other calling in which one may speak so openly of such intimate matters as one may in the pulpit.

Charles Tunstall
Mobile, Alabama

The Reverend Charles Tunstall was born in Sawyerville, Alabama, on November 17, 1912, called in 1932 and ordained a Baptist minister in 1934. He received a BS and MA from Alabama State University and a BD from Selma University. He pastors the Stone Street Baptist Church in Mobile. In addition, he is a city councilman in Mobile. Interview recorded June 30, 1989.

74

"I Tried to Avoid It; I'm Going to Die"

My name is Charles Tunstall. I was born in Sawyersville, Alabama, which is in Hale County, just nine miles out from Greensboro. My mother passed when I was six months old, and I was reared by my cousin, who was Martha Ann. I was a young farmer during that period. I had always attended Sunday school and church as a young man. I was active in church and active in choir and all of the auxiliaries of the little church by the side of the road in the country.

I joined church quite young, about nine years old. I didn't realize that I was destined to be a minister, [but] there was always something that urged me on somehow to speak in Sunday school and church. During that period, I picked up a lot of information as a Bible student, but I had not suggested or confessed that I was called to the ministry.

When I was about eighteen years old, I got seriously ill and stayed ill for maybe a month. I felt that I wouldn't live and I had lost all the weight that I had, and I had not felt really [well]. I was called to the ministry. So, one morning after being so ill for so long, I decided—thought that I was going to die, really—and I called my cousin into the room and told her that I was going to die, but I had something to tell her before I died. She said, "What is it?" I said, "I want to tell you that I was called to the ministry and I tried to avoid it. Since I'm going to die, I'll tell you, so I won't have to preach."

That very day, it's a strange thing that when I confessed to her that I had been called to the ministry, there was a change in my condition. I had not gotten up to walk, I was weak. But after I stated to her that I was called to the ministry, that day I got up out of bed and walked. At that time, I started preaching at that house, small house—a one-room house with a kitchen. Finally, I gained all of my strength back, and the minister of that church taught me as best he could, for over a period of six months, all I knew about the Bible that I had not learned in Sunday school. During that time I had just finished ninth grade, but I was nineteen years old in the ninth grade, because that was high education back there. And there were few people who had finished high school, especially Black people, at that time.

I left there and had to finish high school. Out of that experience I got a chance to go to high school and complete high school work. I was still preaching. I had not been able to pastor in a church nor had I been ordained. I was just preaching whenever I could when, finally, I was licensed to preach by a minister. I left Sawyersville. I had an uncle who had only one sister, and that was my mother. He wanted me to come to Charleston, West Virginia, to stay with him. I went there and stayed with him for a year, and met Dr. Mordecai Johnson, who gave me a scholarship to come back to Stillman College and go to school.

On my way back from Charleston, West Virginia, I was on the train—the train traveled from Tuscaloosa to Greensboro, through Sawyersville, that's where I was going really—and I was on that train with the president of Selma University. He asked me a couple of questions. He asked me where I was going. I said I was going to my church and then I was going from there to Stillman College. And he said to me, "What are you going to that Presbyterian school for, when you're a Baptist?" I said to him I had a scholarship and I had no money to go to a Baptist school. He said to me, "Come on to Selma University, you don't need no money." That's how I got Selma University to know my name.

I lived at 1616 Loughton Street. Mrs. Matilda Meggans was the widow of a minister, Dr. Meggans who passed on, and she'd always help young preachers to try to stay in the university. She allowed me to stay with her during that period. I ate what I could get and worked the best I could. I stayed there for two years, finished junior college and then went into the theological department along with my other work, completed my theological school, got a BTS degree.

Before that time, though, I had started pastoring a small church by the name of St. Michael—that was the first church I pastored. From that church to Bethlehem, and that next church to Morning Star in Demopolis and others. During that period, I got married, and I was married when I was in Demopolis. Next year, the war broke out, World War II, and I was commissioned a first lieutenant at Craig Field in Selma, Alabama, and was sent to Harvard University at Cambridge, Massachusetts, where I studied the chaplaincy and pastored as first lieutenant. From there, I went to Camp Stuart, Georgia, and was shipped from there to France and Germany; and I was at the Bulge during World War II.

After the war was over in Germany, I went from there through the Strait of Gibraltar, back to the Far East and then to the Philippines (that's during the time the Japanese were committing hara-kiri), and we stayed there until the war was over. And you know about the atomic bomb during ... you read about it, you're too young to remember, but you've read about it, I'm sure. That atomic bomb stopped the war in the Far East.

I came back to California, came out of the army and then back to Demopolis. Then I was principal of a school up in Thomasville, and then they called me here, the oldest Baptist church you might see there, White or Black, in the State of Alabama—Stone Street Baptist, which I'm pastoring now.

Wyatt Tee Walker
New York, New York

The Reverend Dr. Wyatt Tee Walker was born in Brockton, Massachusetts, on August 16, 1929, called in 1950 and ordained a Baptist minister in 1951. He has a BS and MDiv from Virginia Union University and the DMin from Colgate Rochester. He pastors the Canaan Baptist Church of Christ in Harlem. He was a key figure in the Civil Rights movement in the 1950s and 60s and was one of those in the inner circle with Dr. Martin Luther King, Jr. He is the author of numerous books, among them *Somebody's Calling My Name: Black Sacred Music and Social Change* (Judson, 1979).

75

"No, No, No, Young Man. Not Money; Service, Service"

I believe that as a young lad, I always felt the impulse to ministry, although I was not able to decipher what it was that was in my life. My earliest recollection is when some of the old sisters of the church, at a baptizing in the river at Riverside, New Jersey—that's the Delaware river, which was not far from my home—pointed to me and said, "You're next." I was terrified that I was gonna have to make a public confession of my faith in Jesus Christ. I don't know why that frightened me but it did.

I remember very clearly the night I did make my public profession in Jesus Christ. It was at a Sunday night service. I remember sitting in a pew in my daddy's church. I'm a preacher's son. I just kept my eyes fixed on him all night and when he began the invitation, I just shot right up to the front, making my decision to join the church and become a candidate for baptism.

I went through high school and never had any ambition or idea about going to college. Under a strange set of circumstances, I ended up at Virginia Union University. I had an older brother who was a WW II veteran; he, of course, had the GI Bill available to him. He applied to my father and mother's school, Virginia Union; and they wrote back and said that his grades were below what they usually require, but since they knew my father and my mother as alumni, they would let him come on trial. He was a little bit offended by that and he decided not to go. My mother in her naivete wrote back to Dr. Ellison, the president of Virginia Union, and said that she had another son who had good grades and to know if he could come on the other son's GI Bill. Of course, that wasn't possible.

Anyway, that fall I found myself on the Havana Special going south to Virginia Union with a $100 clinched in my fist that my mother and father had given me to register. The fees were $40 per semester at Virginia Union in 1946. Needless to say, once I had a year on campus at Virginia Union, it opened my eyes to all kind of possibilities with my young life.

I had somehow determined that the last thing I wanted to be was a minister, because I had seen the impoverishment, as I determined it, of my father's family—he was so giving in his service—and the low pay and the thanklessness of people, as I looked at it through a child's eyes. So I knew I didn't want to be a preacher. I thought I would be a doctor, because doctors made a lot of money. I was rocked back on my heels by a sainted teacher named Ruby Moon Brinkley in my freshman essay about why I wanted to be a doctor. She told me, "No, no, no, young man, not money; service, service." It was a jarring reprimand to me.

As I neared the end of my college career, I was a good student, I stumbled on good study habits. My second year I began to work in the food service so that I had to manage my time. I finished my college year as a honor student "magna cum laude." I just missed "summa" by thirteen grade points. I was at the top of my division and near the top of the class.

In my junior year I took Christian ethics under Dr. Samuel DeWitt Proctor. I had never seen or heard of a minister like Sam Proctor, who wore a jacket that was different than the pants he had on. And as you probably know, Sam Proctor is very convivial and down to earth. I took his ethics class, because by this time having had three years in college, I thought I was an agnostic. Sam's ethics class awakened the roots of my personal religious faith, which was buttressed again in that same year with a visit by Gardner C. Taylor, as the week-of-prayer preacher. I found myself making a new commitment of faith under the power of Gardner Taylor's preaching in the Coburn Chapel on Virginia Union's campus.

It was then that this troubling about ministry really began to get to me. The three weeks before my graduation as a chemistry-physics major at Virginia Union, my father was re-invited to come to give the message. I remember him preaching from the subject, "The Measure of our Responsibility," from a text in Isaiah. It was that week that I decided to respond to the call to ministry. I went to see Sam Proctor in the alcove of the dining room where the faculty sat, and I asked him if he thought I could make the adjustment from the natural sciences to seminary life. He said, "It won't be no problem; whatever you didn't get, you could probably get it on your own. You are bright enough to do that." I had taken his ethics class and made a couple of A's, so he knew that I was a decent student.

I enrolled that next September in the graduate school of religion at Virginia Union. I was licensed that summer at my father's church, August 9, 1950, married that Christmas Eve, December 24, 1950. And I have never really looked back. I never had any spectacular experience except that I always had this troubling. When I would try to envision what I was going to do with my life, I could always get a picture of myself being in a pulpit somewhere speaking. I spent the summer following graduation speaking to youth groups, and I noticed that most of my speaking had to do with religious themes and Bible references. That, for me, certified that God was calling me to ministry. I don't have a single regret in the whole wide world.

Alfred Waller
Cleveland, Ohio

The Reverend Alfred Waller was born in Virginia, on December 8, 1920, called in 1943 and ordained a Baptist minister in 1944. He received a BA and a BD from Virginia Union University. He is the former pastor of Shiloh Baptist Church in Cleveland, the oldest Black Baptist church there. Interview recorded July 17, 1989.

76
When the Preacher Came, Everything Seemed Better

My call to the ministry I would classify as an indwelling desire to promote the cause of Christianity as I had observed it. It so happened that in my family I have four uncles, five cousins and two brothers ahead of me in the ministry. As a very small lad, I took an interest in the preacher of the church. It seemed as though after he paid my family a visit, that everything around the home seemed to be more happy and more pleasant. These were in the horse and buggy days of the deep south. I grew up desiring, when I became grown, that the Lord would use me and that I could take my horse and buggy and drive around and make people happy.

The Lord laid it on my heart while I was in college. I felt the desire and the ambition, not only to make it known, but to apply myself in that area of study. I was at the time at Virginia Union University in Richmond Virginia. I remained there for college and seminary days. I began my pastorate in April of 1945, and here it is July of 1989, which is approximately forty-five years that I've spent in the actual pastorate and preaching. It has been most blessed. My ministry has taken me around the world, and has taken me to Africa on a thirty-day preaching mission back in 1967 and an around-the-world trip in 1970. My wife and I went out over the Pacific and came back over the Atlantic.

Renita J. Weems
Nashville, Tennessee

The Reverend Dr. Renita J. Weems was born in Atlanta, Georgia, on June 26, 1954, called in 1979 and ordained an African Methodist Episcopal elder in 1984. She earned a BA from Wellesley College, Massachusetts, an MDiv and a PhD from Princeton Theological Seminary. She is a professor of Hebrew Bible (Old Testament) at Vanderbilt Divinity School. She is author of *Just a Sister Away: A Womanist Vision of Women's Relationships in the Bible* (LuraMedia, 1988) and *Marriage, Sex, and Violence: Hebrew Rhetoric and Audience* (Fortress, forthcoming). Interview recorded November 21, 1988.

77
"...All Right God, I Tell You What, I'm Gonna Fleece You"

I did not have a Damascus road experience like most of your Baptist friends—like the lights went on, and you were knocked down on the road and the Lord said preach, and you said no. I mean, I didn't go through all of that. I was terribly unemployed when the Lord called me. I know it's not a very majestic call. I can say that I was terribly unemployed, so that it was not a moment too soon. There has never been a time in my life when I have not known that God's hand was on me. Even when I was not terribly active in the church for a while when I moved away to college. It's just never been a time I have not known that.

I don't think I struggled with it as much, because, indeed, it was the best use of my gifts. I'm not trying to say it was a very rational decision for me, but it wasn't irrational for me. I might not have had very many role models of women in the ministry, but I had become a part of a whole circle of people where women were very active leaders in church. So female leadership was not

"...All Right God, I Tell You What, I'm Gonna Fleece You"

foreign to me. Maybe the peaching ministry may not have been absolutely known to me, but aggressive female leadership in the church was not foreign to me. So, again, I did not struggle with it too much on that level. It was the very best use of my gifts. I loved the church. I loved and I love working in the church. It makes sense. And I think that there is nothing wrong with that. I pray that we get to the place where people can feel comfortable with saying, "I love working in the church, why can't I do this full-time?" It may not be a called, ordained ministry as in preaching, but people who love the church and who do church work well, there ought to be some opportunity or some way that we can build in that those kind of people can be employed full-time by the church.

I will say that I did kind of equivocate for a few weeks once I realized, perhaps, that I had been called. Why did I equivocate even when I did? Because I remember, all I can remember, was the Sunday finally when I accepted; and I said to the Lord, "All right, God, I tell you what, I'm gonna fleece you. This preacher getting ready to preach. We both know, God, he cannot preach. Now, if this preacher says anything about being called to the ministry or if you are called to the ministry, if he talks anything about the calling, I'll know it's you. Because this ain't what he talks about. And we know he can't preach. But I'm gonna fleece you. If he says a word just about the calling, period, without ever fleeting then I'll know it was you." And lo and behold, that Sunday—it was an afternoon service—he indeed did mention the calling. I don't know what he said, but he did say it. Now I said, "Now you just done fleeced God." I couldn't up the ante and say, "Now, look here, let me tell you." I mean I had to keep my side of the bargain. I mean it sounds very carnal, but it was at the level of my personality.

God deals with you at the level of your personality. I'm not so sure I would have been the kind who could have been knocked out and slain in the spirit, etcetera. I mean, I grew up in a Pentecostal church: I knew about how much to trust that kind of stuff. So, I know mine is going to be a more carnal kind of call. I mean, that has never been the way God has spoken to me. I have never had one of those great epiphanies; I never had a great epiphany or a theophany moment. It has always been a very rigorous dialogue between God and I. Anything that has ever come to me is through God and I wrestling and arguing it out. It's not been a rational kind of argument, but it's always been a rigorous kind of argument. So, my call was in the line of tradition in which God and I used to talk to one another. I have strongly desired to have one of those other kind of things, you know, like epiphanies. But I also do know that the Lord's hand had always been on me, ever since I was a little girl. I always knew that there was something different about me. I always knew that God had already made it very clear to me that my life was being spared for something very serious. What that something serious was, I had no idea.

Like I said, I don't want to underestimate how important it is that I belong to a community of people, not only in terms of my local church, but in terms of a network of churches that I was in conversation with people of other churches. I belonged to a community of people where female leadership was not foreign. The pastors may have been male, but my closest friends were wives of pastors who exerted incredible influence in their churches, I mean, who were very active women, very articulate women and very creative women. In fact, during that same period, a number of them went into the ministry. A number of us came into the ministry at the same time, within the same six month period. So the groundwork had already been laid for me. I am not one of those who can say, "I was out in the wilderness of Oklahoma and the Lord called me." And I mean this in all sincerity, I have to stand in awe of people who were in absolute isolation and could hear God call. I cannot say that. I mean I was not somewhere where I had never seen another woman in the ministry and the brothers would not ordain me. I don't have that experience. I was in a very supportive environment.

So, at one level, I guess, I have been blessed, even pampered. But then, of course, I also was called in the Northeast. It was different in not just being called from the South, but like Mississippi south. You know, there is the Georgia Atlanta south, and there is like Twidilly, Mississippi kind of calling. So I can't say that I had that. I was in a very supportive kind of community which made my accepting the call easier than it might be for someone else. Now, that doesn't mean that when I did accept it everything just went smoothly. It didn't. And that's as much my pastor's chauvinism, as my own personality. I can be difficult to get along with, I'll admit that—in a moment of weakness, it's twelve o'clock at night, I'll admit a whole lot of things. I might not be the easiest person to get along with. Although my pastor and I now are extremely good friends. His wife and I are really tight. I suspect that if you pushed him, he would have to admit back then, when I accepted my calling, he couldn't stand me.

Eventually, I think within a month, I did preach my trial sermon. And I'll never forget it. I preached, I don't remember the title, but I remember preaching from the first chapter of Revelation. And, actually I haven't been back to the book of Revelation since. Oh, "I John was on the isle of Patmos." It's amazing, I've never had an epiphany, but I took a text about an epiphany. I never thought about that until I'm telling this story. I only came back to the book of Revelation when I was preaching this past May—when I was preaching in the same church again. And, in fact, it was probably one of my most successful sermons this past May at this same church. But I hadn't been back. I hadn't been nowhere near the book of Revelation. I hadn't even thought about Apocalyptic literature. All rather strange, you know. But that's what I preached. I came from that text, "I John was on the island of Patmos," and talking about being on an island and talking about on account of—I think that's what I really focused on. I remember focusing on that he was not only in prison, but he was in prison on account of the word and what that means.

Now, I'm realizing how the theme of suffering on account of the word, on account of the gift, on account of revelation, on account of the anointing is something I probably preach often. It's probably a resounding theme of my sermons. I preached a few weeks ago at Howard Divinity School, and one of the things I said was, "If the truth be told, all preachers only have one theme." We preach a lot of texts, but we come back to one little theme God has given us. Because that's all you have. I mean Amos had it, Hosea had it, Jeremiah had it. We all have one theme. We may take many texts, but we are all given one message. There is only one good book in all of us, one good poem, one good song, and most great preachers come back to that one theme, truly the one God gave them. As I'm thinking about it, I suspect that the notion that "your anointing of this calling will cost you something" is something that I have always preached—something I return to, certainly the notion of suffering and preferably redemptive suffering. So, that is a very important kind of theme for me.

One of the interesting things about being asked to talk about your call ten years afterwards, you know, you can interpret it the way you want to. It's one thing to ask someone about their call a week afterwards, but after ten years, you get prosaic and philosophical about it and so profound. But, see, one of the things about asking about your calling, you still haven't asked is "Called to what?" You know, you are assuming that it's preaching. And I think that one of the things that especially women bring to this new movement of the ministry is that we are reinterpreting what it means to be in the ministry. We are reinterpreting ministry—all of us that you have talked to and many of us are very, very fine preachers. However, at the same time we bring so many other gifts that you really find yourself having to re-define what ministry is itself. Because, at the same time, we are also women who are fine preachers, but we are not necessarily pastors. Yet, if you meet us, you know that we could out-pastor anybody else you got on that table and do better.

I think that our presence in the ministry forces the church, forces us, forces our colleagues to have to rethink ministry, rethink gifts, rethink the notion that in the Black church only the preaching ministry is the ordained ministry in our churches. That needs to be seriously rethought, because many of us come with all kinds of other gifts, whether it's gifts in administration, and some of the men do too. I would hope that our presence even opens doors for them to be able to exercise other kinds of gifts and really give thought to developing other kinds of gifts. There are a lot of women coming in with administrative kind of gifts, with medical gifts, former nurses. I'm amazed at how many former nurses are going into the ministry . . . chaplaincy, teachers who are teaching doing all kinds of different things.

I know that I was called to the ministry ten years ago but I think now, ten years later, I would say that it wasn't just the preaching ministry. I think that I am a fairly fine preacher and I have a fairly nice reputation as a preacher; but I would definitely resist anyone saying to me that ten years ago it was just the preaching ministry. Ten years ago I might have articulated it as the preaching ministry, because I didn't know anything else. Most of us, if we think back on it, we were probably called to the ministry or we were "set aside." I guess that is the more accurate way of saying it, not so much "called to the ministry"—that language doesn't get it as to what goes on in this whole career. It's not so much that you are called to the ministry as you finally recognize and acknowledge that you have been set aside to be used by God in a leadership capacity and leading God's people.

Because of our sociological situation and our historical situation, the preaching moment has become the central moment or platform by which you lead people, but in these last and evil days, I think that we are having to rethink all the ways that you get Black folks' attention. And it's not just through the preaching anymore. It should be through writing; it should be through radio ministries or television ministries. I mean, there are other kind of ways that we have to reach Black people, and I think men and women have to develop that.

So, then, called to what? I guess I'm saying that knowing that you have been set aside, and I guess that's what the sanctified people mean when they talk about sanctified. Sanctified means to be set aside. You know that your life is not your own. You know that God has his hands on you. You know that life is like a brother once said, "The life you choose is the life you did not choose." I live the life that I did not choose. And you really don't have any choice in the matter. Not only do you not have any choice in the matter, you are not even happy doing anything else. You are exhausted, you're tired, you're frustrated, you're mad, but it's a happy exhaustion, tiredness, frustration, and madness. It's not like the frustration and madness and exhaustion you feel when you are doing something that you absolutely do not want to do. When I come home now, after several sermons, after several workshops, after several counselings or whatever I do, after several lectures, I mean I'm mad, I'm cussing and complaining like any other Black person. However, I do know that I'm doing what I'm supposed to be doing. There is a satisfaction that is unlike any other satisfaction. (And I have been in that situation that I don't need to be doing. I mean, I have been on a job that I hate. And one of the things that I do well is when I'm miserable, I can make everybody around me miserable. I do not suffer alone. So it was in my best interest for me to be fired, because I was definitely demoting the morale of other people.)

I love what I'm doing. Complaining, I do complain. But I can't imagine living any other life. I can't imagine, like working those other kinds of jobs that would just drive me crazy. Now, I would even improve what I'm doing. I would love not to have to go to anybody's job. I would love to sit home and write. And there are days when I wonder, do I enjoy preaching more than I enjoy writing? It's a toss-up. It's a toss-up for me. I know that that may be rather scandalous language in the Black church, in the Black tradition; and that's probably because for us preaching is only an oral event. I don't just think it is just an oral event, not if you are a good writer, it doesn't have to be. If you are a poor writer, all you've got is your mouth then. But, if you can write it and say it, and again I'm not tooting my own horn ... I'm not trying to toot my own horn by any stretch of the imagination, but I am commited to reaching people with whatever the Lord will use to reach them. While my ego may enjoy, the carnal woman may personally enjoy, the preaching moment because of the power of that moment of commanding the attention of that number of people, the carnal satisfaction of the call and the response of being able to get immediate kind of response and feedback; although the carnal woman in me enjoys the preaching moment as much as anyone else, the other woman in me—and I pray its the spirit woman in me—prefers the written sermon or written word or written essay, article, whatever. Because I like to leave people with something in their hands they can work with, argue with.

With the sermon, you're only as good as your last sermon. Bette Midler says, "You're only as good as your last song, your last one minute and thirty-six second song." And the sermon—you are only as good as your last thirty-five minute sermon, and you've always got to top that last one because, you know, we are some unforgiving people. You are only as good as your last thirty-five minute sermon and then they aren't going to remember that. That is the frustrating thing about a sermon: they aren't going to remember the title; they remember that one illustration about that chicken that was on the fence. You know, you worked all night long and they remember that one illustration. That's a pain. That moment is so emotional, it's so impactful, but so transient. It is such an ephemeral experience. In that moment it's so incredibly intense, but the moment that it's over, you cannot quite remember it. I mean, you knew that it was something about it, but it's gone and that thing is so gone that it's gone. And it's out of your hand. You have to depend upon your memory to to remember it. Yes, you've got this little tape, but its not like being able to turn page by page and kind of re-think it and highlight it, putting your little yellow mark on it, writing your little comments on the side.

But again, writing is my thing, so I will think in these kind of terms. I am certainly by no means trying to push writing over speaking. I am just saying that writing gives me a satisfaction that speaking does not. There is nothing I love more than when I write a good line. A good line, to me, is just tremendous gratification, in terms of awe for myself. A good line, to me, that I have written is at the end of my book about Lot's wife, "Remember, I did not look back, I looked around." Now, even when I heard that, something inside of me bowed. It's just so unusual. I mean I'm not trying to take credit for it. It is so divine. A good line is so divine itself that you couldn't even take credit for it, because you couldn't have thought of it yourself. It's not even you. When those lines come for me, it is so divine that there is no reason that I should have even gotten that line. So I really do encourage writing.

But then there is another side. When you write something, it gets out of your hand and it takes on a life all by itself. There is nothing more interesting to me than to go around and hear people say, "You know, I read your article" or "I read your book," and it did this and thus and so. And you have no idea that, here I am sitting here at twelve o'clock at night and somebody is reading the book and being moved and changed and whatever, but I'm here. That's one of the awesome things about writing. People will tell you about what it did to their lives. It is out of your hands and it takes on its own life. A sermon, you are kind of in control in that moment. But people certainly come to you and tell you about how a sermon you preached years ago really blessed them. So there is some similarity there, but not the same kind goes for writing.

For me, the call was no so much to preaching as it was to being self-conscious about the fact that I belonged to God and not to myself.

Edward L. Wheeler
Cincinnati, Ohio

The Reverend Dr. Edward L. Wheeler was born in Long Island, New York, on June 4, 1946, called in 1961 and ordained a Baptist minister in 1969. He received a BA from Morehouse, an MDiv from Colgate Rochester and a PhD from Emory University. Until recently he was pastor of the Zion Baptist Church in Cincinnati. He is presently Dean of Chapel at Tuskegee University. He is the author of *Uplifting the Race: The Black Minister in the New South, 1865-1902.* (University Press of America, 1986). Interview recorded July 6, 1989.

78

No Girl Friends If You Are a Teenage Preacher

I was called to preach when I was fifteen years old. My family had moved to Atlanta, Georgia, when I was fourteen, and I was living with my uncle, my mother's oldest brother and his family, from August until December of 1960. That spring of 1961 or that summer, I went to Tacowa, Georgia, with my cousin, my uncle's only child, who's in the CME ministry. I went up to—he had a church in Canelia, Georgia at that time—the north Georgia mountains. I worked with him in vacation Bible School. I didn't preach, but I worked with the kids in arts and craft work during the day. Then in the evening, I would speak to them. Once again, it wasn't preaching. I just talked to them for five to ten minutes about a Bible story or something.

After that week in Canelia, I came back home and I told my mother that I felt very strange about the ministry. I had grown up in the church but I never wanted to be a minister. I wanted to be a dentist from as early as I can remember. I was going to be a dentist. I did the school work and I was doing well in school. But I had no idea about being a preacher. I grew up in the church. I sang in the choir. When I was in New York it was not unusual for us to be in church all day Sunday for Sunday school, morning worship, three-thirty afternoon program, six o'clock BTU Program and then evening worship at seven. I grew up in the church but I had no desire to be a minister.

When I came home and talked to my mother about it, she indicated to me that she would not ... I mean there was nothing I could do to make her any happier, but that the seriousness of that calling was of such that I had to be sure about it. I didn't tell my daddy, because my daddy was the kind of person who, when he became a Christian, he became whole-hog in it; and I knew that if I had mentioned to him at all, first thing he was going to do was to my pastor and tell him. Then I would have no control over anything.

My mother was more introspective, and I knew that I could talk to her without her jumping to conclusions. So she told me I needed to pray about it. I did. I prayed as fervently as I think I have ever prayed in my life, at fifteen, asking that God would show me clearly whether or not I was called to preach. I was happy when I wasn't getting an answer. I mean that was a great sense of relief when I didn't get an answer.

But on the eighth night ... I grew up in the church in Union Baptist Church in Hempstead, New York. The pastor during my young years was Lonny J. Thompson. Now Reverend Thompson was a big, strong Black man. I cannot say that I can remember him vividly now, because that was there in my younger years. He died before I was baptized. I was baptized—I joined the church when I was eight and was baptized. It was close to my ninth birthday and I was actually baptized when I was nine. Reverend Thompson was already dead at that time. When we moved to Atlanta, this is six years later, I felt the calling to the ministry.

On that eighth night in my dream, I saw him as clearly as I see you. He was dressed in a black suit, white shirt, dark tie (which was his way of dressing). He had a Bible in one hand, and he was reaching for me with the other. I knew that was confirmation that I had been called. Well, I told my mother about it, and sure enough she told my daddy. He did exactly what I thought he was going to do. He went straight to my pastor, and he told my pastor about it, and my pastor talked with me. This was later

June of 1961. After my pastor had talked to me a couple of times, he arranged for me to have a trial sermon in August. In August of '61, the second Sunday of August 1961, I had my trial sermon. I was licensed to preach by vote of the church. I have been preaching ever since.

I can honestly say that there have been times when I have wondered why I was called, but I have never regretted the call. I guess now, preaching is so much a part of who I am that, I guess, my identity is incomplete without preacher as part of that. It was a struggle at fifteen, because I wasn't sure what was expected of me. I didn't know what it was to be a preacher and wasn't sure about what all that meant. I used to love to dance and, you know, all of a sudden, I was being told I couldn't do that anymore. I always . . . my mother says there was never a time when I didn't like girls, but girls at fifteen, fourteen-fifteen year old girls, they don't understand going with a preacher. So at first I wouldn't even tell them. Eventually they would find out and the phone conversation usually went something like, "May I speak to Eddy?" And I would say, "This is Eddy." They'd say, "I just want to ask you just one question. Are you a preacher?" I'd say, "Yeah." They'd say, "Why didn't you tell me? I ain't going with no preacher. We're through." After that [I'd say], "That's why I didn't tell you."

I loved preaching from the beginning, but at about seventeen I had a conversation that really changed my life for the better, with a man that I can't even remember who it was now. I wish I could remember who it was, because I owe him a debt of gratitude. He asked me one day, he said, "Eddy, how do you enjoy being a preacher?" I said, "I love preaching." He said, "That's not what I asked you. I asked you, 'How to do you enjoy being a preacher.'" I had to admit, for the first time since my calling, that I didn't enjoy it very much. He said, "The reason why is that you're too busy trying to be somebody you're not." He said, "When the Lord called you to preach, he knew who you were. Only thing he wants you to do is to be the best you that you can be," he said, "and once you find out who you are, you'll find more enjoyment in preaching than anything else in the world." He was right.

Since then, I guess, I've been trying to find out who I am and trying to be the best me I can be. I stopped trying to imitate certain folks that I want to be like, and I started going to dances every now and then and enjoying it. It's part of growing up. I stopped being fifty at the age of eighteen. When I was at Morehouse, I even played football while I was assistant pastor of a church up in Tacowa, Georgia. Sometimes it made it tough getting to the church when I was supposed to preach when we had away games; but even that, you know, the people understood that.

They accepted me for who I was, and I owe a lot of folk a lot for what I am now the good things I am now. The bad things —maybe I owe that to myself. My parents always supported me. My family always supported me in the ministry. My "father in the ministry," Reverend J. A. Wilborn at Union Baptist Church in Atlanta, gave me an opportunity to preach and encouraged me as I was growing up. A lot of the ministers in Atlanta at that time gave me a chance to preach their youth day sermons and everything, so I had a lot of opportunities to preach as I was growing up. By the time I went to seminary, I was ordained. I went overseas for a year on a scholarship in '67-'68, which would have been my senior year at Morehouse. When I came back from that, during the time I was there, it was confirmed for me that this was really my call in life. So, I asked my pastor if I could be ordained as I got ready to go to seminary. In 1969 I was ordained. Then I graduated and went to seminary and into the ministry.

Alfreda Wiggins
Baltimore, Maryland

The Reverend Alfreda Wiggins was born in Baltimore, Maryland, on January 24, 1941, called in 1959 and ordained by the United Methodist Church in 1985. She has a BA from Morgan State, an MA from Coppin State College, an MTh from St. Mary's Seminary and an MDiv from Wesley Theological Seminary. She pastors the Edmondson United Methodist Church in Baltimore. Interview recorded June 17, 1989.

79
Confirmation of a Woman Preacher by Women Preachers

Well, I'm a native Baltimorean, and I grew up in the Disciples of Christ Church. My parents were Baptists, and they moved up from Virginia—they're originally from Virginia—and they moved to Baltimore. They joined the Baptist Church, but they weren't very active. The church directly across the street from my house was a Disciples of Christ Church. So I guess it was divine providence, or whatever, that I joined the Disciples of Christ Church where I grew up. They didn't feel like going to church, so they sent me there. Of course, I became very active in their Sunday school, and I remember at about nine years old all the kids were getting baptized. Of course, all their families belonged to that church, mine didn't. But I wanted to be baptized, too, because all of my friends were getting baptized. So I asked my parents about it, and they said, "Well, if you really know what the meaning of baptism is, then you can." I explained to them what the meaning of baptism was, and they permitted me to be baptized in the Disciples of Christ.

They became, as a result of that, active, and are still members of the Disciples of Christ today. Everybody in my family belongs to the Disciples of Christ, but me—all my siblings, my father. We just buried my grandmom in May, buried her from the Disciples of Christ. I did the eulogy, but it was at the Disciples of Christ; so it's a very rich heritage now here in my family.

I've always felt the . . . I guess, because I grew up in the church and worked in every capacity, singing and saying my little piece in Sunday school and all that kind of thing, I guess I sort of felt a call early on in my life. I remember in my last year of high school, when I was making a decision about a career and college and all of that, I spoke to my minister about ministry. I was interested in ministry even in my last year in high school. I never will forget—one of the tasks we had to do in twelfth grade was to write a letter to a college of our choice requesting an application and that kind of thing. I wrote my letter to Jarvis Christian College in Texas (which was a Disciples of Christ school). Of course, my friends laughed at the very thought of my wanting to be in the ministry and wanting to be a minister. First of all, it was unheard of in 1959 that a woman would even think about preaching, and then, secondly, me, because I was a typical teenager. I didn't wear a halo or anything. So it was made sport of by my class.

I remember approaching my minister about it and, of course, received from the church at that point no encouragement whatsoever. As a matter of fact, discouragement, that in 1959 that was just not the thing that women would do, and maybe I should think about the mission field and becoming a missionary in the Disciples of Christ. That meant, of course, going to Jarvis Christian College. Well, in '59 my parents really weren't too keyed up about my being that far away from home, and they said no. They didn't want me to go that far away from home and go to college. I could go to college at Morgan and stay here a couple years, and maybe after a couple years they might consider it.

My first year at Morgan, I met Reverend Agnes Austin. Did you get to interview her? My first year at Morgan, I met Reverend Austin. My grandmother was very active in the Elks. I don't know if you heard anything about the Elks or not, but she was really active in the Elks. They would have various affairs and things where they would have a woman come in to speak. Many of the times it was Agnes Austin who came in to speak at these. My grandmother would always take me to these little things and then, of course, I played piano and I could sing, and I would always have to sing little solos and play and that kind of thing at these little church things they would be having. Whenever Agnes was preaching, my mother or my grandmother, either one, would take me to hear her preach. So when I met her at college, I couldn't adjust to the fact that here I am eighteen, in college, and this was somebody that I had been going to hear preach since I was a little kid. I said, "Well, maybe this is another Agnes Austin." But all the kids knew she was a preacher. I mean, she was considerably older than we were as youngsters right out of high school. But the kids would all say, "Shhh, the preacher's coming." There was a great respect for the preacher there.

Finally, one day, I worked up enough nerve to say to her, "You know, my mother used to take me to hear a lady named Agnes Austin preach, is she any relation to you? Is she your mother?" She said, "No. What is your mother's name?" I told her and my grandmother's name. She said, "I'm the lady." And we struck off a real good friendship right at that point. She knew my family. I then shared with her my call and the fact that my parents had told me that if I went to Morgan a year or so, then I could go to Jarvis Christian College and become a missionary. I was eighteen at the time. Agnes said to me, "God has a call for your life closer to home. You don't have to go that far to be in service to God. Have you considered preaching?" Then I explained to her all about the talk that I had with my minister; and she said, "Well, you're going to preach."

Well, by this time I had given it up, because everybody had said, "No way." So when she told me I was going to preach, I said, "Oh, no, there's just no way I'll ever preach." I was eighteen years old then. At age twenty-four, I accepted the call to ministry. Well, what happened in between, that searching—there was a searching (and I call this all a part of my spiritual sojourn) while in college. Because I was a singer, I joined up with other kids that were singing gospel music, got involved in singing with a gospel choir that did a lot of traveling from church to church. Therefore, my horizons were broadened with different denominations and different styles of worship and that kind of thing. And one of the people, while I was going through this sojourn and this kind of searching of myself and this kind of longing and looking and knowing there was something there, but not really being able to identify it as such, but the feeling was there where there was a woman minister . . . Of course, I ended up with one of the girls I sang with taking me to her Pentecostal Church, and here began role modeling for me as a woman minister. First, Agnes Austin who told me I was going to preach at eighteen, and when

I went to this church this woman considered herself gifted in prophecy and that kind of thing; and she said to me, "God has the call on your life. Why don't you surrender to God? God wants to use you. Why don't you surrender to God?" And I said, "Oh, no, here we go again, it's the second time around—Agnes and now this woman." I never told her anything. I just went there to worship with my friend. After church she introduced me to her minister, and she said, "Are you in a hurry?" I said, "No." She said, "Stick around for a while."

After she talked to all the people, the first thing she said to me was, "God has the call on your life. Why don't you give up? You're holding out. Give up." Well, I was twenty-four, and by this time I was singing rock-n-roll music, and I wanted to be a big, famous rock-n-roller. So, I mean, the whole notion of preaching was completely alien—not alien, but sort of sidelined, and I was thinking about making big bucks and the whole bit. But there was still that gentle little nudging going on, and it's something that makes you know that indeed there is a call on your life. So finally, at age twenty-four, I accepted that call.

Strange—I went to a Pentecostal service at another church one night where another woman—all these women ministers seem to have come into my life all of a sudden, when the only one I really knew was Agnes Austin, but then these other people seem to have come into my life. Maybe it was because I was in a denomination that wasn't really heard of at that time. I went to a meeting one night. I was engaged to a young man who was Pentecostal, and he had started going to another church. He said, "You ought to come to this revival that's going on. There's a woman coming from New York to preach, and you ought to come to this revival." I said, "Well, maybe." Well, at that time, there was a struggle going on within me about the call and whether I'm going to say yes or no, and I was just kind of like staying away from church, forget being there or not being there and that kind of thing and definitely not wanting to go to another service. But somehow or another, I found myself that night at this church where I knew he was. I thought for a long period of time about going, finally got up, got out of the car and said, "Well, it's too late to do anything else. Might as well go on up there and listen to her."

I went up there, sat in the service and listened to her preach. She was okay. At the end of the preaching, of course, she gave them all the call and people came. Then she said, "I'm going to pray for some people that are in the audience today, in the congregation." And one of the first persons she called to pray for was me. She said, "Can I pray for you?" I kind of looked around, I thought maybe she was talking to somebody else. She said, "No, you." I had on a gray suit, as a matter of fact. She said, "No, you. Can I pray for you?" I said, "Yeah." I went up. I had never had this kind of experience before, this prophecy thing, people telling you stuff and all that, and I had my doubts about it. She said, "God has a call on your life." I said, "Oh, no, not again! I don't believe this!" I said to myself, "Yeah, I know, my friends that are here have already told you." Well, there was no way they could have told her, because when I came in, she was getting up to preach and I sat down. I mean, unless they had really described me to her and told her I was coming that night or whatever.

Then she said some other things about how I had been running away and some other things that were real pertinent, and I said, "Well, maybe this woman does have a direct line or some kind of contact, something going on here." Then she said to me, "I want to pray for you, and God's going to break that yoke, the yoke that's holding you and keeping you from really giving in." And I said, "Yeah, yeah, I really don't believe in this kind of stuff," because I was raised in a traditional Disciples of Christ, breaking yokes and all. Anyhow, she prayed for me that night. I didn't feel nothing, I went on back to my seat and went home, still kind of troubled, though, but yet searching and constantly searching. There was steadily a constant search going on.

I don't know if you ever heard of what's called a shut-in service. Well, in this movement they had what was called a shut-in service where they would come in and stay in the church for three days and three nights to pray—every three hours was a prayer hour, so it was around the clock. You couldn't eat anything. Some people slept in sleeping bags and stuff like that. I just kind of felt this need to have—it was kind of like a retreat, only it's right in the church. During the other times of the day, you talk about the spiritual journey and discipleship and spiritual growth and all that kind of thing. I asked whether or not persons that were not members of that congregation could participate, and they told me yes. I said, "Well, I think I want to come." I was working at the time. I took time off from work and I went.

It started on Wednesday. It was Wednesday night—no, Tuesday night after service, and it was Wednesday, Thursday and then they would come out noon on Friday, I think, or something like that. Wednesday morning in the three o'clock prayer, we were praying at three o'clock, and in that three o'clock prayer I asked if they would pray for me. So all the ministers and this lady, they laid hands on me and they prayed for me. I really began to pray, and I began to say, "Yes. Yes, Lord, I accept this call." I mean, it wasn't really emotional or anything; I didn't see flashing lights or hear bells or any of that kind of thing, but felt a sort of inner peace that the journey, the struggle, is over now. You said yes, so you don't have to keep running here, there and everywhere trying to get away from this thing.

That was on Wednesday. That Sunday, this church's choir had to go to another church to sing, and their musician couldn't go. They asked me if I could go. They knew I played, so they asked me if I could go and play for them. I said okay and I did a quick rehearsal with them and went over to this other church to play for them. Well, at this church was a Baptist lady whose church I used to go to to sing all the time; and she said, "Oh, Alfreda, I haven't seen you for years." And she was going on. She said, "Are you preaching yet?" And I said, "No, no." Now, Wednesday I had just said yes. Sunday this lady says, "Are you preaching yet?" "No." So she said, "Well, I'll tell you what, the second Sunday in November (this was 1967) is our women's day." (As a matter of fact, this is strange, I saw her this last week for the first time in about eight or ten years, I ran into her and she said, "You haven't been to preach to me for a long time.") She said, "I want you to come and preach for us on that Sunday." I said, "Fanny, tell you what. I'll come and I'll bring the choir, because this is a good choir. I'm sure the minister will come and let me bring this choir, and maybe one of their young ministers will preach for you, but not me." She said, "Oh, yeah, you're coming and you're going to preach."

So, I went to this minister whose church I did not belong to, whose choir I played for that one time, and I said, "I would like to take your choir with me to this church on the second Sunday of November for them to sing. And the lady has asked me to preach, but I'm not preaching." He said, "But you said yes to God just a couple Wednesday nights ago, and you are going to preach and that will be your trial sermon." I said, "But I belong to another church, and I've got to get this all cleared up and straightened out," and all that stuff.

As it would happen, I can't even remember the details of how it worked out, but we went to that church that Sunday and, sure enough, I preached my first sermon, "A Good Name is Rather to Be Chosen than Gold and Riches," or something like in Proverbs—something in Proverbs. It was overwhelmingly affirmed by all those that were there. I never told anybody, but they told everybody, and there were many, many, people there, and this was in a Baptist church. Then I went back to the church that I started playing for this choir, and what I did was I discontinued my membership with the Pentecostal church that I had belonged to—this was also a Pentecostal church—and joined this church since I was playing for their choir.

Then I really got involved in ministry there, stayed in that Pentecostal movement for twelve years. It was the Deliverance Evangelistic Association, Skinner—I don't know if you ever heard of him or not. He's out of New York. Anyhow, that was the movement, and I stayed there for twelve years and felt a call to a different style of ministry. During that time period, I went to St. Mary's Seminary, and I guess probably the whole exposure to the academics of theology kind of changed my mind. I had gone to a lot of these little Bible colleges around town, very evangelical, fundamentalist kind of places, and I was just not really satisfied with that. There was more of a grasping for more knowledge than what I was receiving. So I decided to go to St. Mary's Seminary, which you probably heard some others talk about. This brought on a whole different insight.

In the meantime, because I used to sing, a lot of people knew me from singing; and the same people that knew me from singing, once they heard I was preaching, would call me to come and preach for all these different occasions—mostly Women's day, of course, and youth day, because I was much younger and that kind of thing. So I got going from church to church and everybody knew me—"Oh, Alfreda's preaching now." "Oh, really?" "Yeah." "It's about time. We always knew she would go into that kind of thing." And then Agnes, who had encouraged me at eighteen, just fell right in as my mentor and was pushing me every way she could. If she was called to preach at a church and she couldn't go, she sent me. Therefore, I came to know a lot of people and a lot of people knew me.

In so doing this, I preached in a lot of Methodist churches, and they would always say to me, "Have you ever considered becoming United Methodist?" I said, "No, I'm okay where I am." But I was recruited by several different people that were United Methodists, and I wasn't really impressed. I was in law school, went to law school and, in fact, worked in criminal justice for most of my life, met a buddy of mine—do you know St. George Cross. You may know the name even if you don't know George. George is a well-known person in our town. He is now in charge of HUD in this area, and he is also an ordained United Methodist minister. He is currently on a leave of absence, because of his second job. But George and I went to law school together, and so while we were in law school, George said (George was Church of God and Christ at that time), "I'm going to join the Methodist church. Man, they got money and all kinds of..." (George was always talking about money) "and they got a good retirement, benefits and all that." I said, "Oh yeah, George, whatcha gotta do?" I called several people who had always been talking to me about joining the Methodist church. So he said, "Well, you know you're going to have to go back to seminary if you do that, because St. Mary's is not going to be enough. You're going to have an MDiv." So I said, "Well, I'll think about it. I'm going to let you do it first, and after you do it, if it works for you then I might try it."

Sure enough, George joined the United Methodist church and came to Baltimore (he first pastored in Washington), came to Baltimore and was appointed to Lewin United Methodist Church in Baltimore. I guess George had been here about a year, and I went to see him one Sunday. In the meantime, I had been talking to the pastor of my church where I belonged, that I helped to organize and everything. We had an excellent relationship, and I told her that I just didn't feel that I was going anywhere and I felt the need to do something else and to take another step in the ministry. Of course, she didn't want to hear that, but she said, "Well, if you feel if that's the way the Lord is leading you ... " And it took me four years to make that move, because I earnestly prayed about it, I really prayed about it and I asked God for a sign that it was the right thing to do.

Finally, after four years, I got God's permissive will, not necessarily the perfect will, but, you know, when a father—you have a child, and the child will say, "Daddy, I want a bicycle." And you say, "But you are not really ready for a bicycle yet, not a two-wheeled one. You need training wheels and everything." And the kid keeps saying, "But I want a bicycle! I want a bicycle!" Finally you say, "All right, go on and get the bicycle." I feel that this is God's permissive will. I don't know where I'll go from here. I don't know if the United Methodist Church will be the end of ministry, whether I'll stay till retirement or maybe I'll do some other things.

But George, of course, was at Lewin Church, and he had been there about a year. I went to Lewin Church and joined Lewin Church, stayed there under him for the year that I had to stay in the process (you have to be a member of the United Methodist church for one year). At the end of that year, I went to the district committee on ministry; and they said to me, "Well, you're coming from an organization that we do not recognize, and since you're coming from an organization that we do not recognize, you will be a layperson, and then you will start in the ministry. You cannot do anything sacerdotal." I said, "Okay. Can I preach?" They said, "You can preach." I said, "Fine. That's all I need to do is be able to preach," because by this time I had already been preaching for twelve years, and I was not going to stop preaching even for that.

The ironic thing is that I had gone to John Bryant and talked about the possibility of becoming AME, and John didn't really give me a whole lot of encouragement. After I joined the United Methodist church, both he and Cecelia jumped on my case and said, "You know you have given up the cause and turned your back on Black folk." I mean, they gave it to me. Then another friend of mine, Marshall Strickland, who is pastor of the largest AME Zion church, said, "Why'd you go and do that? Gave up on Black folk." You know. But I had already made that decision then and stayed, of course, the year that I had to stay. Then I went to Wesley Seminary, the process of going through deacon's orders, elder's ordination, serving in my first student charge, and then, being appointed. Right now, of course, I'm serving Christ Edmonson United Methodist Church in Baltimore City, and this will be year number seven for me at that church.

I guess that's it. The only thing I may have left out is preaching mentors. Early on, my preaching mentors were Pentecostals, and one person in particular, a man from New York whose name is William O'Neill, and he was really more in the spiritual church mainly, if you know anything about that. I had friends that belonged to his church, and he almost mesmerized me with preaching.

"I was on my way to Harvard Medical School. In the last half of my senior year Colgate began to install the Humanities system. I worked as an assistant to Doc Alton, who continued to influence me.... One particular night in February of 1930 I'd worked late at my desk in my room in Andrews Hall on some papers for Doc Alton. It was two in the morning. I turned out the light, looked out over the snow-clad golf course through the leaded-glass English casement window, with the moon shining in my face. Suddenly there came a voice. Something like my father's, but softer, and yet more insistent. A still, small voice: "Whom shall I send? Who will go for me?" And there in that room in that quiet, for the first time in my life God talked to me....

Early the next morning I telephoned my parents, who had never advised me or encouraged me in the slightest to go into the ministry and had no idea I was even thinking about it—because up to that time I hadn't been—and I told them I had decided to change my life's program and intended to enter the ministry. The tears of happiness flowed over the phone. My father was so incoherent that I don't even remember what he said....

On Good Friday night, 1930, I preached my trial sermon. It was a strange crowd that listened—all the girls from the Cotton Club, others from the downtown night clubs, girls of every color, bootleggers, gamblers, all the fantastic array of acquaintances I had accumulated through the years. I can still remember the sight. They all came to laugh. 'Adam's going to preach!" Adam, who played one of the best games of stud poker, who had bet every cent he had in his pocket on one roll of dice, who had slept with more women than anyone could count, and who could hold more liquor than anybody in his circle, was going to be a preacher!... Thirty-seven people joined the church that night."

Adam Clayton Powell, Jr. *Adam by Adam: The Autobiography of Adam Clayton Powell, Jr.* (New York: The Dial Press, 1971): 34-35

Ronald Williams
Cleveland, Ohio

The Reverend Ronald Williams was born in Anderson, South Carolina, on August 30, 1952, called in 1969 and ordained an African Methodist Episcopal Zion Deacon in 1975 and a Brethren Elder in 1987. He received a BA from Livingston College (South Carolina) and an MDiv from Ashland Theological Seminary. He pastors the Brethren Fellowship of the Saviour in suburban Cleveland. Interview recorded July 17, 1989.

80

"The Next Time You Hear That Voice, Answer Yes, Lord"

I was called to the ministry, I believe, at the age of fourteen or fifteen. I was sure about it then; however, I fought it because my father was a minister. He was a Zion minister, and I saw the hell that he went through. I saw how we, the family, were suffering a lot of the times because of daddy's ministry. I didn't understand it, and I knew I couldn't—if you will, "whoop"—like my dad. I thought that was all a part of it, the "whoop" and the dramatics. So I just thought I wouldn't have anything to do with it. I was involved with the music ministry, but that was good enough for me for then.

I went to Livingstone College in North Carolina, and there were a lot of young ministers there, a lot of young pastors; but I thought they were all—I didn't think they were pastoring material. Yet, at the same time, I didn't want to step out and do anything. I thought they were a bunch of weak guys who couldn't excel in anything else so, they decided to become preachers. I had this call all of my life, and the whole while it was making me miserable because everything I tried to do was failing.

The Next Time You Hear That Voice, Answer Yes, Lord

Upon graduation from Livingstone, I came home, back to Cleveland. It was June 19, 1974 that my mom said to me and my aunts said to me (my father was very quiet, he knew what I was going through but he wouldn't say anything), my mom said, "Son, you're not going to be successful in anything in life until you do what God wants you to do." It just struck hold of me. That week, that same week, I started hearing voices. I know this sounds like spooky and mysterious, but I started hearing voices. I heard somebody call my name. He said, "Ronald." And I went downstairs and I said, "Mom, what do you want?" She said, "I didn't call you." So it happened about three more times that same day—"Ronald, Ronald, Ronald." Each time, "Mom, what do you want?" She says, "I didn't call you." So my mother got on the phone, and she called my aunt. Then they called my father. Because I think my mom thought I was losing my mind. But my father said, "The next time he hears that voice, tell him to answer, 'Yes, Lord.'" The last time was late that evening; about eleven o'clock at night I heard the voice: "Ronald." I said, "Yes, Lord." I haven't heard the voice since, but I still didn't know what was going on.

It was that Sunday at—my father at this time is pastoring in East Chicago, Indiana, and it was that Sunday, no the Saturday evening—Greater Abyssinia Baptist Church, right here in Cleveland, Ohio, there was a young man there from Los Angeles, California, running a revival. After he finished with his message, and his message was "Who will go?", I went downstairs and shook his hand and told him that through his message I was going to accept God's call. I was twenty-one then. I came home and I told my aunt, no, my father (my mother, everybody's in Chicago, I called my father and I said, "Dad, don't tell anybody, but I've decided to enter the ministry. I'm tired of fighting." He did not honor my word, what I asked him, my request. He got up in front of 800 people the next Sunday and told all of them that I had entered the ministry. Then I was caught. I couldn't get out. Not only did he do that, but he set a date for me to accomplish my trial. So that is basically the story of how I became a minister.

Jeremiah A. Wright, Jr.
Chicago, Illinois

The Reverend Dr. Jeremiah A. Wright, Jr., was born in Philadelphia, Pennsylvania, September 22, 1941, called in 1959 and ordained by an American Baptist minister in 1967. He has a BA from Howard University, an MA from the University of Chicago Divinity School and a DMin from United Theological Seminary. He pastors the Trinity United Church of Christ in Chicago. Interview recorded June 6, 1989.

81
Unnatural Light in a Dark Room

When I was a teenager, a young teenager, I thought I was going to work in the church in terms of the church with a capital "C". I mean, I didn't think I was going to be preaching. I thought I was going to be ... I had a career objective of being a seminary professor. My father made us, my sister Laverne and I, always be in the house at dark when the street lights came on, and we had a rule that we could watch one hour of television only. You could pick two half hour shows or you could pick an hour show. What that meant was, you had to read. You had to do other reading, you had to study. We saw, years ago, that the boob tube was just that, a boob tube. It would rob you blind of your creative energies and juices.

So what my sister would do, she'd read ahead in her lessons. I'd read, if they said read to page 56, I'd read to 56; but I'd find me something else to read. What I found to read was my father's books in his library. He had—it was a blessing and a curse for me—gone to Virginia Union and gotten a Bachelor's in Theology, a Bachelor of Arts, a Bachelor of Divinity, later converted to the Master of Divinity; an STM, and Lutheran School of Theology for the remainder in Afro-American history.

Unnatural Light in a Dark Room

So I had a whole rich mine of books in his library to read for myself and in which to lose myself in. I saw myself heading for teaching seminary. I did not want to pastor at all, based on what I saw, in terms of his life in the pastoring of Grace Church in Philadelphia.

I went away to college, and while a freshman at college, my roommate, Smitty, would play games sometimes, playful games. We lived on the first floor. Sometimes he'd come around to the outside room, clowning, like college freshmen kids. And one night, I had gone to bed, I don't know where Smitty was, he wasn't in the room. All of a sudden, my eyes were closed, I could feel this bright light in the room, so I knew he was clowning. I said "Smitty." I called, "Smitty, come on stop playing." He didn't say anything, which was normal; he didn't say a word; and I opened my eyes to see what kind of light he was shining. There was no light coming from outside of the window. The light was just in the room.

Then I got terrified. I closed my eyes and rolled over and it just got very quiet. My heart was pounding, I was scared to find out what that was. I heard a voice saying, "Why you running?" "I ain't running." I said. "Smitty?" Then I heard Smitty coming down the hall, toward the room. And I was glad I heard him coming down the hall. When he opened the door, there was no light. I was scared, I didn't know what had happened. I was scared 'cause I said, "Were you just outside?" and he answered "No." He was at Harris's room.

Interesting thing about it, I was telling my seminary students, was that I was scared to talk about that for a long time. I wouldn't talk to people about it. I talked to my father about it. My father asked, "What *are* you running from?" I said, "I'm not running from anything, I'm not running from anything." So he asked me to pray with him. I didn't want to pray about it because I didn't want to think about it. I did not have any out-of-body experience, supernatural experience, theophanies, nothing. I didn't want to even want to deal with anything like that. And I kept trying to figure out who was playing with me. I kept reliving it over in my mind. But how could they get the light to shine like that in the room and not come from outside? I couldn't understand. I looked right at the window, and it wasn't coming from the window. There was no light in the window, no light outside the window. I did what my father said: I prayed, I prayed about it.

Then, I guess about three months, maybe four months later, it hit me that what I was running from was the parish ministry. I did not want to be a parish minister at all. I didn't want to preach at all. So I shared that with my father. He asked me, "You get an answer to what you're running from?" I told him, "Yeah." He asked me if I was trying to run from God. The long and short of it was I ended up preaching my trial sermon the first Sunday in May, my first year in college.

I still fought the thing, I still fought. I preached my trial sermon, and then I fooled around in Richmond, with Fifth Baptist Church, where Rev. Anderson pastored, as just a student at undergraduate school, in Richmond, Virginia. I still had a little problem with the organized church, and the rules, which were very . . . I didn't understand the rules. They seemed more humanly-oriented than divinely-inspired. I wished they didn't have the rules. I was in a church school back in the '50s. (1959), I was a freshman. We had *rules*. I mean, girls had to be in around nine o'clock. What biblical base? I mean, what's nine o'clock? Why do freshmen girls have to be in at nine, I just didn't understand that, as a freshman in college. Where is this in the Bible? Is three a holy number? And then three times three is nine? Is that why they had to be in? What makes that religious?

No alcohol! So that means that most preachers sneaked. No alcohol means you don't drink in front of each other. And the only graduated school at Virginia Union was the "B.D." school (the Divinity School). I knew a lot of preachers; and I saw disparity between what the rules said and what was being practiced.

When I got to my senior year, I was having some serious problems. I knew next came seminary after the senior year, right? Here I was president of choir, president of senior class, etcetera; and I quit school, because I couldn't deal with going on to the seminary. I wasn't ready for that. In terms of next steps, I just couldn't deal with it.

I saw a friend of mine, in fact, I was thinking about him tonight, driving back from the service. He lives down here, I think he's in Newport News. His life was ruined by one of these "holier-than-thou" persons. He had a reversal, that he never recovered from. He was a guy who had no parents sending him to school. He was sending himself to school. He worked, going to school and that meant he would work a semester and go to school a semester—until he finished. When he finally finished undergraduate school, he was in seminary. He did not hide his habits, because he thought that was hypocritical. So he would drink a little wine; and he had wine sitting up on his dresser. Matter of fact, it was unopened—some Mogen David. Once, when he had a girl in his room, he left the door open, because she was going to type a paper for him. He was showing her how he wanted it typed. And one of those "saved" preachers reported it to the dean: he had a woman in the dorm, some wine, and the preacher made it sound like a tryst, which it was not! They put him out of school, made him stay out a year. And I just thought that was the epitome of embarrassment, especially since the same Negro who told on him was one of those Negroes who was "getting all he could" behind closed doors. (And) Here he was the one telling on somebody who left the door wide open so everybody could see. That kind of "churchianity was a trunoff!"

I left school and went into the service. I stayed in the service six years. The rest of the call story is not as dramatic, in terms of the supernatural, but just as dramatic in terms of how God works through people. Two other things, supernatural, that I want to come back to: first thing, the non-supernatural or God working through human instruments. I was in service for six years. The last year in service I was stationed in Rockville, Maryland. No, I was stationed in Bethesda, and my partners were from Rockville.

While we were up in Rockville, Maryland, one Saturday, just a bunch of service guys, we were sitting out in front of the church drinking some wine. Nothing was going on in church, it was empty, vacated. We were sitting there, drinking a fifth of wine and talking, solving the problems of the world. And here are four or five guys on a fifth, so nobody's getting ripped. Hardly enough to have two glasses or one glass with four or five guys on a fifth. This brother walked up, he was sixty-three years old at the time, he talked like a thirty-five year old kid. He starts talking to us. We talked back. I was a chief proponent of the talking, talking to the brother because other guys were sort of mumbling half answers. I offered him a taste. We had the bottle in the bag and offered him a taste. He said, "No thanks," kept on talking. About forty-five minutes into the conversation I found out he was the pastor of this church, whose steps we're sitting on. These guys knew this. They were from Rockville. And they were easing away one by one, leaving me there talking to the guy. I'm the only one there now with this fifth in my hand, and I said, "Oh, you're the pastor here." He said, "That's okay." So, I tried to apologize. He said, "No apology necessary." We kept on talking.

The man was Dr. Houston G. Brooks. He was Henry Brooks' father. Henry Brooks' daddy. We talked for four hours. At the end of that four-hour period, he said to me, "I want to ask you a question. I don't want you to answer today, I want you to think about it. Let me know later. I don't think you have a problem with the church." We talked about it, we talked theology, we talked church history, and we talked Afro-American history. We talked racism, the whole thing. That was back in '67, '66. It was '66, height of the civil rights movement, sit-ins, the whole peace movement. And I'd been in the sit-ins of Virginia Union. I had seen White men drag Black women across the street by their heels. I resonated more with what Malcolm said than what Martin said. I was *not* non-violent. I was in the military. He said, "I don't think you have a problem with the church. I don't think you have a problem with the Lord. I don't think you have a problem with that, I think you have a problem with what people have done to the church, White people and Black people." He said, "Now the question I want to ask is this. Where do you think, (because I have the feeling you love the church deeply) where do you think you could do the most good for something you loved as much as you love the church? On the outside, by throwing stones at it, or shooting howitzers at it, which is what you're doing, trying to level it; or, on the inside, working to make it become the kind of institution you think it should become? Where do you think you can do the most good? And, don't answer that today, think about it." It was really a terrible question because I knew the answer. Even through the fog of my Taylor Port (wine), I knew the common-sense answer.

I went home, and that next morning I got up, getting ready for church. My wife said, "Where you going?" I said, "To church." She said, "You're going where?" I said, "To church." "Wait, wait, wait. You're going where?" I said, "To church." She knew I was anti-church. In the Black church, I used to sit up in church and pick sermons apart, based on all the stuff I had read, with no teacher and not knowing the whole history of intellectual history. Why German criticism, why this whole thing which attacks the scriptures from a certain kind of stance? I'm not a teacher, I'm just reading this stuff as a teenager. I would sit there and be miserable 'cause the preacher would say, "The Red Sea." I would say, "The Sea of Reeds. Seventeenth century stuff is

Unnatural Light in a Dark Room

wrong. Ya'll done messed it up, the Red Sea is no where near Mt. Sinai." I went to church to check the old brother out. I told her, "I met this old cat yesterday, he talks a pretty good game. I want to hear how he preaches." Went there and the choir was excellent, sermon was beautiful and I found myself crying, walking down the aisle. He asked me to hang around after service, and we started talking some more, that Sunday.

In a couple of months he asked me (that was the summer of '66), he said, "Why don't you study for ordination?" I said, "I can't." He said, "Why?" I said, "Several reasons. One is, I was raised American Baptist.And I know that I've got have a seminary degreeand I don't have one." So then I got to go back to finish college. I get out of the service next year. I plan to go back to school and finish my undergraduate work. I quit in my senior year. But at present, I don't have a seminary degree or a college degree, so I can't be ordained.He says, "Suppose I get the college and seminary requirement waived, would you consider it then?" I said, "Yes," thinking that would never happen, based on my knowledge of American Baptists. In another two weeks he showed me this letter from Valley Forge, saying if I scored above ninety on the test(and with the stipulation that I would go back to school,)I wouldn't have any problems. I got nervous.

That January, (third Saturday, in January,) the ordination took place.My father brought three buses down from Philadelphia, I don't know if you've seen a Baptist ordination—the ecclesiastical council, it was public. The church was packed. I had to go through the whole New Hampshire Confession of Faith with everybody there. Everybody sat there staring at me, scared to death. I passed, I was ordained. I became his assistant.

I got out of the service that summer. I got out in June and went right back into Howard University. When I say right back (I'm being transferred to Howard.) I got out the sixteenth of June, from the military and started summer school the nineteenth of June. Of course, transferring to Howard, they took away some hours from me from Virginia Union, so I could fulfill the residency requirements. I went straight through summer school, and the next academic year, I finished that following June. Went right into graduate school that following year, the same June, right after graduation. I did my first master's degreethere at Howard, and my second at University of Chicago Divinity School.

The two other supernatural things that happened: One

was my Aunt Hattie who was my great-aunt. She really wasn't my aunt, Aunt Hattie had a "second sight." I used to be afraid of my Aunt Hattie, cause she was one of those African women, born the daughter of slaves. She was born, "with a veil over here eyes," as they say. She could "see things" and she scared me. She would see things, and she'd come up to you and start talking to you about something she had seen in your life. I would stay away from her. Do you know, Myers, I sat at her funeral crying, because I kicked myself for not taking the tape recorder and just sitting down and talking with her for days. She was quite a phenomenon.

Two of the most bizarre things that stand out in my memory are not related to the call. But to show you what kind of person she was: Aunt Hattie, when we got pregnant with our first child, wanted to make sure (we were stationed in the Great Lakes), wanted to make sure the rabbit died and all. Finally we got the test results and everything was positive, went to the phone to call home. We called home and my mother said, "Oh, I know what it is you're calling about." "Oh, you do?" She said "Yeah, you're pregnant. A girl's going to be born in June, about June 23rd." My daughter was born on June 23rd, the oldest daughter.

The second thing that scared me, in fact, it scarred me, and we just have a validation for it now. I wondered if my daughter had a gift like Aunt Hattie, because of the way she was when she was sixteen months old. During that pregnancy, my grandfather was living with my parents, Infact, my grandparents lived with us for the second half of my childhood. Grandma died the night of my senior prom. Grandpa got very ill back in the '60s, and we were driving up to Philadelphia almost every other weekend to visit. Grandpa used to say to me "I ain't going nowhere till I see my great-grandson. Don't worry about me dying, I'm not going anywhere."

October, (October the 19th,) Janet my oldest girl, woke up in the middle of the night screaming. We went running into her room, "What's wrong?" "Man, man." I said, "Man, what man? There's no man there." I just took her to the window. "See how high up we are? No, man can crawl up here." She knew what "chain" was, 'cause we showed her, if we ever got locked out, how to get up on a chair and pull the chain off. "Chains on. No man," I said. She insisted. She would not go back to bed. My wife asked, "What does the man look like, Janet?" She said, "Grandpa." I said, "My daddy or your mommy's daddy?" "No, no, no. Grandpa daddy, grandpa daddy." "You mean Grandpa Henderson? Grandpa Henderson?" I said, "Baby, do you know how far away he is? We get in the car, we drive and you go to sleep. That's a long way. That's where Grandpa Henderson is." She said, "Grandpa Henderson, Grandpa Henderson." I said, "Well, what did he do, why are you crying, if it's Grandpa Henderson?" She says, "He's waving bye-bye, bye-bye." I said, "Okay, I'm sure you're right." She wouldn't get back into the crib so we took her and put her in bed between us, and all went to sleep.

Five o'clock in the morning, my mother called. She said, "Aunt Hattie told me to call you all, because" Hamp" died last night, that's why I'm calling." He saw the soul of his next great-grandchild coming. He saw that it was a girl, saw he had nothing to wait for, so he stopped to say goodbye to his only great grandchild. She didn't want the baby to be scared, and I'm laying there like on television, you know, Twilight Zone or something. What's going on with this child? She really *did* see him. She said, "Could the baby sleep? Did he scare the baby?" Well, she just wanted to know everything was okay. He was just saying good-bye." I didn't say a word!

Aunt Hattie, (she'd read you, Jack!) she would just look at you. I was doing some stuff in my life I did not want her to be reading. That's why I would stay away from her. She had told my father that I was running. "He's running, but he don't want to preach." My father told mehe prayed. I had already told him, but he didn't want to put more ideas in my head. But I had already told him. When I went to tell my father, he said, "I know, Aunt Hattie already told me."

Then one night, I never will forget that night, man, I was in the Marine Corps, out of the church. I was driving back, I was just young, dumb, married, andmy wife was living in Richmond, Virginia .That weekend, I stayed there till the last minute, jumped in the car and was trying to make it back to roll call. And I was driving back sleepy! Young people do stupid things in cars. You knew the highway, and you 'd say things like, "Hey, this is a ten mile straight stretch hereI'll take a little nap."' You'd' prop your hand up so you don't veer and try to take a little nap. Young, you running fifty five-sixty miles per hour. And I was drifting. This car started blowing behind me, flickering his lights, and blowing, pestering me. So I slowed down to let him pass me, and he wouldn't pass me. I slowed down to a crawl, I'd speed up; they'd speed up behind me. They kept that fool system going

The Irresistible Urge To Preach

until we got into to Rocky Mount North Carolina. I pulled into a service station. They pulled in behind me. It was a White lady and a White man! I said, "Oh, this is a White dude, six feet one. White folk." She said, "Are you all right?" I said, "I'm fine." So I went and got some coffee, got two cups of coffee. Drank one. We used to do this in the service, drink one and the other one you hold in your hand. Keep the top off, it's hot. So when you hit a bump, that stuff would fall right down your leg, and you're wide awake for ten or fifteen miles.

So she said, "Do you want me to drive? (Now these are white folks in the South in 1963!) Do you want me to ride with you? Do you want my husband to drive?"' No", I replied. I looked at the base sticker, they had a base sticker. My mother's a math teacher, so I have always been doing math. I took a pen and wrote down the number of the base sticker in case some stuff happened. If anything happened, I would know who these people were or would find out who they were tomorrow. They didn't have any license in the front. It was North Carolina license in the back. So I wrote down the base sticker. They stayed behind me, I got sleepy again, they started blowing and flickering their lights, staying right behind me till we got down to five miles outside the base, and they pulled next to me. They said, "Are you okay now?" I was coming around slowly. I said, "I'm fine. Thank you." They said, "No problem." They pulled on around me, and I wrote down the license number. I said,"At Liberty call today, I am going to thank these people. They sure enough kept me alive."

I went on to work. Got off at three o'clock. Went up to the Provost Marshall. Took my numbers with me. I gave them the base sticker and license number. They told me "No such number.""You must have made a mistake when you wrote them down." He said, "No, I didn't make no mistakes,." I said. He said, "You made a mistake." I said, "Check the license ." He checked the license and there was no such car. I went back to my barracks, and my mother called and said, "Aunt Hattie said, 'The Lord had to send two angels to keep Jeremiah alive last night. He don't believe this, but there are White angels! He don't like white people, so you be sure to let him know that he'll be all right. He isn't losing it, that those are just some angels the Lord had sent to protect him.' Man, I couldn't sleep. I couldn't sleep.

The key thing that struck me was you haven't done what the Lord wants. When I got out of the service and out of Howard,

I went and got accepted at the University of Chicago, at the divinity school which trains *teachers*, not preachers. The stepchild program in the whole divinity school is the program for preachers. The Divinity school had seven disciplines back then. It was founded for the professional training of scholars in religion. Not for ministers. I went there and majored in the History of Religions. It was my seminary, in terms of training to become a seminary professor. While there, working side jobs in the church I saw that the church is where the real rubber met the road in terms of where are you really needed . . . While working as an assistant pastor I worked with some kids, and these kids were struggling with their identity in the late 1960s. They had a whole lot of questions about the nature of things: being Black and living in this country, and they weren't getting any answers from these preachers who were preaching the rapture to these kids. These kids were catching hell. The preachers were preaching sermons against " the Natural" (the Afro), against their African American heritage, and all the kids were asking me questions, "Well, you're in school, talk to us!"

That, coupled with my encounter and working with Rev. Brooks working with the young and old people there at the other church, did it for me. I decided to stop running in terms of being a pastor. At the end of '71, I took my vitae downtown to several different denominations, United Methodist, Disciples of Christ, United Church of Christ, and put my applications in. (There were no American Baptist Churches in the inner city of Chicago for Blacks.) When I went to Grace Baptist Church in Germantown, the church I grew up in, a few years ago, seminarians asked me, "How did you end up in the United Church of Christ?" I said, "A deep theological issue called 'hunger.' It's how you put food on the table. It all depended on what church was open back then in 1971." I said, "God called me to pastor and I don't believe he put a denominational tag on the back of things. I went wherever I could get work. Which is why I am where I am."

Only in the course of the last thirteen years working in seminary, have I begun to talk about my call in terms of the supernatural part of things or the spooky level. I don't want to talk about things that make you sound crazy, because they don't fit into normal categories of sane, rational, educated, college-trained people. People start looking at you and saying, "Oh, yeah?" Only recently have I learned to say back to them, "Yeah!"

Prathia H. Wynn
Princeton, New Jersey

The Reverend Prathia Hall Wynn was born in Philadelphia, Pennsylvania, on July 29, 1940, called before she was born and ordained a Baptist minister in 1977. She received a BA from Temple University, and an MDiv and a ThM from Princeton Theological Seminary. Although she pastored the Mt. Sharon Baptist Church in Philadelphia at the time of this interview, she has since become Associate Dean at United Theological Seminary in Dayton, Ohio. Interview recorded June 8, 1989.

82

Awakened at Four o' Clock; "I Had Been Preaching"

Okay, I just recalled what it was that I thought I was leaving out, so let me start there because it puts the whole thing in a kind of framework. I very, very much resonate with the call of Jeremiah. A whole sense of who I am or my identity is kind of wrapped up in that experience of call and the kind of identity of preacher. So that what I said to you about not ever remembering a time when I didn't know the Lord is a part of that sense of resonating with Jeremiah's call. *Before I formed you in the womb— I knew you and appointed you a prophet to the nations*—that is just, it kind of speaks for me because of my experience in knowing the Lord, my awareness of knowing the Lord and of knowing the power of the Lord, the presence of the Lord in my life as a very young child. As long as I've known myself, I would have to say that I have known the Lord, and that my public confession, faith, was a formality which was required for me to be baptized. But it was definitely not an experience of finding the Lord or even being found by the Lord. It was just a logical progression of my experience—publicly.

My public expression or confession of faith was one in

which I was at my mother's home church in Virginia at a revival service. They had the mourner's bench. I went forward and sat there for four days from, I guess, it was Sunday to Thursday. I kept waiting for the conversion experience that I had heard in the church's testimony. That didn't happen. After a while, after being there all of those days, finally on Thursday afternoon I had a conversation with the Lord about my sitting there. I said, "Lord, why am I sitting here? You know that I love you. I know that I love You. I know that I trust you, that I believe you." That's what I heard the preacher say, that all you have to do is believe. Well, that was all or had long since been the case. It seemed to me that the Lord said, "Well, get up then." And that is what I did. I got up and I came forward, and was received as a candidate for baptism and was baptized by my father.

But all along the way, there was the experience of conversion and the sense of claim on my life, of God having a very definite claim that my life was not my own to pick and choose my career, to pick and choose what I wanted to do with it. So, from my earliest childhood while I was active in church and speaking in church and taught to recite, and taught to make speeches and that kind of thing, from my earliest teens—I guess I was about thirteen when I first spoke as a woman's day speaker or youth day speaker, that continued. But all along this time of birth, there was also this other restlessness that I either couldn't put my finger on or didn't want to. I was just very much terrified by the prospect.

I didn't know any women. I knew no women ministers. I didn't know any Baptist women. I didn't know any women well. I did have what was for me a very significant experience of going to hear an African Methodist woman evangelist who came frequently to our city to give revivals. She's a nationally known evangelist preacher, Dr. Mary Watkins Stewart of Detroit. She was the first woman that I heard preach, and there was absolutely no doubt about what she was doing. It was very clear that this was a preacher in the pulpit. She had the power and she had the authority which comes from speaking that word which God has given you. I was very impressed by her, and I got to know her. I would often go to hear her speak. We had conversations, and that was just a very ... and I recall that later in my life when I surrendered to this call, I recalled my memories of Mary Watkins Stewart and what affirmation and relief that was for me to see her. It didn't make me ... it didn't settle the issue of my own call. It didn't make me come forward, but it certainly was a marvelous affirmation for me to see her and to see how effective she was and to see the response to her ministry.

I try to remember that now, when I am preaching and I go places and those little girls. There is one every now and then that I see with that look in her eyes that I recognize. I want very much to be an affirming experience for her. I preached at Princeton University Chapel. I go there almost once a year for the last four or five years, and there's a woman and her two daughters that come to every service. One day when I left there, they just kind of chased me down. I was going to my car, and then the little girl got very shy and started hiding behind the tree while her mother kept saying to her, "Tell her, tell her what you said." So, finally, after coaxing her out, she came out and she said, "I told my mother I want to preach like you when I grow up." She was about eight years old. That was just very, very special. It's happened more than once.

I continued as a teenager to do my church work, to do my speaking at churches, to be affirmed as a speaker; and, of course, there were times when people would tell me that I was preaching. You know, they were almost accusing me of preaching. I would become very defensive and just not relate to that. It is still scary. It is still awesome. I've learned now that there is a certain amount of that awesomeness, I mean, that I want to keep. You know, I don't want to ever get... I don't ever want it to be something that I can take for granted. But in college, I had decided, after rejecting the idea of being a medical missionary... and I've read that Mary McCloud Bethune wanted to be a missionary to Africa. There are other Christian women for whom this became the kind of obvious ministry. This was an acceptable ministry for women in the church. When I really realized that that wasn't for me, then my solution was to be a lawyer, because for me, the faith, understanding, serving God and fighting injustice were very integrated. I felt that I could use the gifts that God had given me to speak, and I could, at the same time, fight injustice by becoming a lawyer.

In college I was a pre-law student with a major in political science and a minor in religion. It is interesting that now my PhD area is religion and society. It just didn't... as I became more involved in the civil rights movement of the early '60s I was also expected because I had begun taking classes at the Theology School at Temple University, I was expected to begin in the seminary upon graduation. I just chickened out. I just panicked. I wasn't ready to do that, so what I did was to go south and work in the civil rights movement and try to negotiate with the Lord. It was, "And Lord, if I do this, this is your good work and will you leave me alone? Is this all right?" I think that for several years—in fact, after going through the experience working with SNIC, coming back and getting married and having children working in a national women's organization and running for the school board in my community and becoming president of the school board, I thought that the bargain had worked. What I discovered, however, was that all this time that I was running, as we say, from the call to ministry, God was so gracious and was really holding me while I ran that I may have been running from the call, but I certainly never was running from God. Because God was right there holding me, shaping me, using every one of those experiences to prepare me for the church and to prepare me for the ministry.

So, where did I run? I ran smack into the hand of God. There came a time when I could no longer shut it out. I couldn't silence the voice. My specific call experiences were usually the experience of having the preaching. I mean, there's this uneasiness, this wrestling had been going on all my life. But then it moved to a new level. My conscious mind, it seemed, was taken over by preaching, by the preaching, even by the meaning of preaching, the ministry of preaching. I kept thinking about it all the time. I would wake up at four o'clock in the morning and would find I had been preaching. I would see myself before the people of God. I would try to read a book, any quiet moment was a time when this preaching, this—I don't want to use the word compulsion, that is not what I want to say. It is a command, but it is also something that was not outside of me. It was very much inside me. It was just everything that I did. I had no time—there was no time when it was away from me and I was away from it, no matter what my activities were. No matter what I was doing, somewhere, always with me, was this unsettled question.

Finally, after pleading and asking the Lord why was it that I had no peace and that this issue kept coming up and I wanted to know—"I'm doing your work. All these things that I am doing. I'm counseling drug addicts. That's your work. I'm working in the community, working with poor people. That's your work. This is ministry." I just experienced the spirit of the Lord saying to me, "But you're not doing it my way. You are not doing it the way that I called you to do it. You are not doing it as my ambassador." I struggled with that again for quite a while and then had what was for me, I guess, the ultimate experience of call, of just being kind of grabbed. Grabbed by the Holy Spirit and shaken and confronted: "Every thing and every gift you have, I gave you. If you can speak a word, I gave it to you. If you sing a note, I gave it to you. Even this passion for justice which burns within you, was mine before you ever tasted it. I gave you those gifts. I did not give them to you to pick and choose how you wanted to use them." That was enough. At that point I couldn't stand it any longer.

It was at that point I kind of cried out in surrender to the Lord. I made the moves. I began to talk to people about it, a few of whom were surprised. Then I took the steps. I had friends to pray with me, and took the step of going to Philadelphia and speaking to a pastor who had been a friend of my father's, Dr. Harrison Trap. I had no idea what his position was on women in the ministry. There was something that I said earlier, too, that it's interesting to me that I never heard a negative word about the ministry of women from my father. I identify my mother as one of those women from an earlier generation, similarly called, but who came along at a time when she was not able to really hear that call as a call to preaching. My own experience of, at least, probably twenty years of wrestling with it, is what I am hearing, I'm hearing. I can understand how much more difficult it was for women of my mother's generation. I see them in the church all the time. They are speakers. They are dedicated. They've done a number of different things. They've accepted and married ministers and made the ministries of their husbands their own. Some of them have taken women's work in the church. I am very interested in the women who are in the women's auxiliaries of the conventions and the Sunday school work and all that they do. They do women's work. They do youth work. But they do this all the time. I've seen and I've met them now, as I've preached.

I preached in Denver a few weeks ago. There was a mother, a deacon, in that congregation. I recognized the minute I saw her and the way that she responded to the gospel, to my preaching—and her rejoicing was not just for me, but it was also for herself. Somehow my being there was like an answer to her own call. She said, "I've been praying for this for thirty years." So many of those women do embrace us. These women who are now blessed to be able to come through and to be public about their calls and to be recognized as ministers. I've seen those women. Some others have not worked that through, but there are those women in the church who also have the call and the anointing, but have never been able to live it out themselves, personally. They rejoice when they see daughters. For me, they are real mothers in Zion. I think that covers basically what we've talked about before.

You can see what I mean about the Jeremiah experience, because it is very much a kind of sense of identity and self-definition, which is early formation. It had kind of just been there ever since I've been.

James S. Young
Pensacola, Florida

The Reverend James S. Young was born in Milton, Florida, on February 9, 1920, called in 1952 and ordained a Baptist minister in 1953. He has a BA from Florida Memorial College and a BTh from Union Baptist Seminary. He pastors the Mt. Canaan Baptist Church in Pensacola. Interview recorded July 1, 1989.

83

Lost on the Pacific When God Spoke

First of all, my call to the ministry took place my junior year in college, at Florida Memorial College at St. Augustine, Florida. It was one of the greatest experiences in my life. It is rather difficult to put in words the divine revelation that took place in '52 at the Florida Memorial College. It's like, you don't have to say to yourself that you're hungry. The mechanism of the human body will remind you of this. But when one is truly called of almighty God, he'll know it. Even though it is rather difficult to put it in chronological order, you'll know that that divine revelation has taken place. One of the assured ways of one knowing that he has been called is that he wants to preach. It's that longing desire. It's an urge. It is something that you can't ignore. So a divine call is a mystery. It's a symbol to the new birth.

I've been a born-again Christian for a long time and trying to tell it, what happened and haven't told it yet. So it is with divine call. I think it was Job who said, "One thing I know, I know that my Redeemer liveth." And it is amazing, a calling to pulpit, that you would know that there is a call to evangelism, a call to teach, a call to pastor and things of this nature. But when you've been called to proclaim the word of God, somehow or another,

God in His own omnipotent power differentiates between that call. Because the call to preach, irrespective to the other calls ... I feel that in every committed service in the vineyard of a Christian experience, whether it is in music, one is called to that, or a teacher, or one is called as witnessing, a good missionary, even a good musician, I believe that it's a call.

That is true, but when one is called to a plain ministry, the gospel of Jesus Christ, somehow or another in God's own sovereign power, he differentiates that call he wants me to do over and beyond some other service of a Christian commitment. So then a call, one cannot truly put it together in a theological concept. Number one, this happened; number two, this happened. But we do know that to be truly called by God—somehow or another through divine revelation, you know it. In ordaining preachers and things of this nature in my lifetime, I've had various comments from young preachers who I have ordained, "How did your call take place?" And it's interesting to note that none of them were the same. Some said for months and months they had a dream or a vision and they found themselves in some huge cathedral and standing behind the pulpit with thousands of folk, and they've just expounded, and things of this nature.

To me, I was sitting at my desk in my dormitory—I think I was writing a resume on the letters of the Apostle Paul—when something miraculous happened. When I knew anything, I was jumping up and shouting and such things. I never shall forget a classmate of mine, Reverend Ross, pastor in Lake City, Florida now, he jumped up. "What's the matter, Young?" I said, "I'm just fine. I feel better than I ever felt in my life." I said to him that it seemed as if I were having the experience of a new birth again and things of this nature, and something hearing just as plain as I'm speaking now: "I have a mission for you to do, and that is to proclaim the word of God to a dying world."

And it's interesting to note that this was the second revelation that I had. I remember in '45, I was on the island of Okinawa, out in that sea, on a vehicle we called a duck—it runs on land and water. And I was out there waiting my turn to get a load of bombs to bring back in to shore; and while waiting, I remember just humming "Jesus, Keep Me near the Cross." I was just sort of—not loud, just gradually was singing that while I was waiting my turn to go up against the ship to get that load. And during that period, I got spiritually ... then I started praying when I noticed the thing had drifted away from that ship. I saw as I looked back toward the shore, it looked like New York City—all the other ships and lights and things, and I never had been as afraid as I was that night in all the history of my life. I had gotten off the channel that brought me in and would take me back out and things of this nature, and was out there wondering which way to go. All around that huge Pacific Ocean, all the way around were the lights and the ships and things on the shore. I had lost all direction, and that's what happens when you are lost. Even in seeing, you lose all sense of direction. I became so afraid, and someone said, "Don't worry, God ain't through with you yet. I got something for you to do." And I looked around and the bottom of that—we call them ducks—well, I thought somebody was on there with me. I looked around that empty duck. I think that happened around about eleven o'clock at night, and this is approaching around two o'clock in the morning—and I was afraid. In that area, it is noted for typhoons, hurricanes—you name it—and things of this nature. And this thing was so frightening that I was afraid the weather might change, and that was it. That water was coming in and wouldn't pump it out or nothing.

Around three o'clock that morning, another American ship saw me and recognized it was an American vehicle, and they recognized it didn't have any business being that far out. They came to where I was and let down the bowels of the ship, and I drove up on that LSTV and they cabbed me on to another country, Okinawa, where they were headed. At that time, I understand they had airplanes out searching for me and they then called the headquarters and told them they had picked up Corporal Young. I stayed on the island about two weeks, and they drove me back to that same spot and let me down. I came on in. From that time until I was in my junior year—it was about two years from that time that happened—I had been discharged and was in my junior year in college, when I received this call. I just found myself saying, "Yes, Lord. Yes, Lord." When I said that, it was just like somebody had this house on me, and somebody came there and took it off.

I told my classmate about it. That same night, I was the chaplain for the Baptist student unit after school; and we went to the chapel for prayer service and things of this nature, and I would give the closing prayer. They said it wasn't a prayer, it was a sermon. I'm telling you, as God is my secret judge, students were falling out and just hollering and things. And the security guard, instead of coming to find out what happened, he went to the president's home and woke him up, Dr. R. W. Puryer. Went and woke him up, and they come rushing in there wanting to know what had happened, nothing but that young boy just praying and things of this nature. I found myself often just going to it, just going up and praying. It was a very unique experience and trying to come to the call in terms of what happened: number one, number two and three. Personally, that's difficult. But I do know, without a doubt, that it was a divine revelation of God that touched me and said, "I want to use you to reclaim (that is, to make known) the word of God." There has been no doubt since.

In closing, I said that to young preachers. That's the question they ask every year in the seminary in which I happen to be dean over. They seek to try to find out for sure—really was their call like mine or their call like such-and-such a person? I try to bring out the fact that God is not the God of limited abilities and how he works with one person, he doesn't necessarily have to use that same formula to work with another. Variety is his name. I said that's why out of all the fruits you got—you got an orange, you got an apple, you got grapes, you got the other; and all the trees you got—you got the oak, you got the pine. So God builds in variety. The same thing holds true with inner vision, and that's why some folk sometime are not assured, not only of the calling, but not assured of their salvation. Sometimes they get tied up, "It didn't happen to me like that," and "I don't feel the spirit like so-and-so," and things of this nature. They forget to recognize that you can't monopolize the spirit of God. The same thing holds true with the spirit: the way it effects me may not effect the next person. Some folk might just cry a lot, some folk walk, some folk just clap their hands. And we have to understand that we cannot pinpoint the power of God. Only man is limited, and God is unlimited. I think as we recognize that —and even as a theologian yourself, you have to keep in mind as you seek to differentiate these stories of men of God who said they've been called—we've got to understand that The Man that has done the calling, he has all power and he doesn't have to hound me like he hounds John Doe.

And you can rest assured, you may not be able to put it together—I wasn't sleeping, I was well aware of what happened. I hadn't had a bowl of black-eyed peas. Folks say, "Because you were dreaming" and things of this nature. But even at that, when the Lord's got something for you to do, he makes it crystal clear, and you can rest assured of that. I know that and I wouldn't change for nothing. I stopped teaching in the school system, because I was dedicated and committed; and I was thankful to God for bringing me four years and nine months and thirty-one days from the service, United States service. That was just one example.

I won't take up your time explaining the other such things that happened over there in Okinawa, and nothing but our God that brought me out. And every time it happened, I said, "You gonna come through more than conquerors, because 'I'm not through with you yet.'" The last time I had given up on that duck out there in the South Pacific, I thought about my mother, my dad. They were all living and all my brothers and sisters. I just knew that was it. Something just out of the sky—I was looking up. It was a very bright night and the stars were just twinkling and blinking, and something said, "You know, God still lives." Just like that. I looked around again. After then, I became just as cool as a cucumber, and about ten or fifteen minutes later—maybe less or more—I saw this light from the ship flashing on and kind of directed me through that night cold that I could read what to do.

When it happened in the dormitory on that campus, this miraculous type of divine revelation that came from the Lord Jesus Christ, I said to myself that night, I told this again . . . with God, [it] was only two years ago I was on the island of Okinawa. He's keeping me for some purpose. In these thirty-four years as pastor and as a servant of his, I wouldn't change with Rockefeller. That's about it.

"*K*ing's father wanted him to be a minister, but King decided quite early that he was not going to be a minister. It seemed to him then that religion could not be intellectually respectable and socially relevant. He decided, therefore, to become a doctor.... Although King said he wanted to study medicine, he continued to sharpen the non-medical skills, particularly oratory, that would later bring him fame."

Lerone Bennett, Jr.,
What Manner of Man: A Biography of Martin Luther King, Jr.
(Chicago: Johnson Publishing Co., Inc., 1976): 25..

McKinley Young
Atlanta, Georgia

The Reverend McKinley Young was born in Atlanta, Georgia on November 10, 1944, called in 1963 and ordained an African Methodist Episcopal elder in 1965. He received a BA from Morris Brown, a MDiv from Andover-Newton and a MA from the University of Chicago. He is pastor of Big Bethel AME in Atlanta. Interview recorded June 23, 1989.

84
"The Lord Is Calling . . . You Can't Ignore That"

I think it would be very difficult to pinpoint a specific time and date and place when I had any one experience that led me to believe that God wanted me to be a preacher. I wanted to be a spokesman or a prophet. I think that what my ministry represents is an accumulation of events and circumstances which led to no other conclusion than that I actually answer the call to preaching. From early childhood, five, six, seven, perhaps even earlier—I would be tagged or labeled by peers or by neighbors or by parents, adults, and others who would see me and say, "He's going to be a preacher. He will be a preacher. He sounds like a preacher." I think there is nothing that created in me more of an anxiety than that, because I think that any young person who is pegged to be something . . . it is almost like you are "wanted to be" yet unable to be, to determine what you want yourself. Someone already knows what you are going to be. That naturally threatens you. It threatens your freedom, your own personal sense of autonomy.

So, naturally, I rebelled on my own: I'm not going to be a preacher; that's not what I'm going to be. I grew up in a house where my father was a pastor. He had circled thirty-five years in the Atlanta Northern Conference, built some churches and renovated some churches, so I had that as a kind of a backdrop of the discussions. But I was just not in my early childhood, I had a sense that that was my destiny, a kind of unspoken understanding. That was what was expected of me. That would be my role in history and my responsibility, although I think I worked very diligently to demonstrate both to myself and to others that I had many other talents and many other vocational options that could be explored. I told them I was going to be a lawyer or a doctor. I had good grades in school. I was a good student and so, naturally, I was standing in good state for a number of other alternatives. But I think when I finished my first year of undergraduate school at Morris Brown, I think I came to the conclusion that the people and the witnesses that had come to me and telling me that I was supposed to be a preacher had been right. I would not be able to evade the call or to abandon it, so to say.

One very graphic experience occurred when I was in high school and I was vice-president of student body, along with Ron English. Ron English, pastor from Charleston, West Virginia—the First Baptist Church—he was president of the student body at high school, and I was vice president. Martin Luther King, Sr. gave us our campaign money. Ron was working at Ebenezer, and I grew up here in this congregation. So, naturally, we had close ties with the people and the pastors who were on the street. Martin Luther King, Sr. gave us our money for our campaign posters. We got, like, the president and the vice-president of the student body. Bishop William Wilkes, who was a bishop in our church, elected in 1948, did the inauguration of Ron and myself as the president and vice president. And in my inaugural address, when it was over, after he had installed us into office and everything, he sat there talking with us. He had not made the connection between me and my father. He would call me Lonny. Afterwards we were all standing there talking. He said, "You—you going to have to be a preacher. The Lord is calling for you. You can't ignore that. You can't go around that. You've gotta do that." But I thought that was always . . . I've always remembered his words, because he ended up being the person who ordained me as an itinerant deacon in the church in 1963. That was what—1962 then? So, it was very interesting.

At the end of my freshman year of college, I think, I came to the conclusion that I was going to prepare myself to be a minister. I did the basic training and education and everything essential in order to be able to be well prepared emotionally, academically and intellectually so that I would do a good, incredible job. Along the way there were other instances. Words from my grandmother and my grandfather... I spoke to a man one Good Friday, coming down Edgewood Avenue just walking and talking. I said hello to him. He turned around and said to me, "You know, I didn't know it was Good Friday until you spoke to me." This was out of the clear. He wasn't drunk or anything. I was just a teenager at the time. So there were many instances.

I didn't have any earthquakes or any lightning bolts to arrest me, but I think the instilled small voice of people, opportunities to pray in church, share in the leadership, and to do things which I found an enormous fulfillment in, and then to have other people say, "this is what you were cut out for..." One of the ladies out there is Joanne Vickers. She is Bishop Bearden's daughter. She came to my high school graduation. I gave a prayer at my high school graduation. She said to me, "All you need to do is go to ITC and let them give you your seminary degree." But the point was that I more than demonstrated that that was what I was to do. I think I resolved it in myself, settled it within myself during my course in college.

By the time I graduated from college, I was a fully ordained minister in my denomination. I had pastored a church down in Clarkstown, Georgia. I had preached in many places, given some youth day addresses. I think the more I did it, the more exposure and experience I had, the more comfortable I became with it and the more aware I was of "that was what I was supposed to do." I think what separated it for me was there were a lot of things I could do. Perhaps there were a lot of things that would be exciting and meaningful for me in my life, but there would be nothing more fulfilling.

The Bishop said to us when he ordained us, "If you can keep from preaching, then you should not be ordained. Because anyway that you can find in your life that is fulfilling by not answering the call, then don't answer it." I think it's the realization that there would be nothing that I would do, but to give my life to the highest level of fulfillment and would help me be totally in touch with my destiny and my reason for by being. So I settled for it. Graduated from Morris Brown and went to Boston to go to the seminary. I had a church in Providence, Rhode Island, in my senior year at Andover-Newton (Theological Seminary), and I was an assistant pastor in Boston and Chicago and then went on to another year at the University of Chicago. So, I've been at it now since, in earnest, since 1963. That's twenty-six years.

I was ordained an elder in 1965 and have been a pastor of six congregations. My first church was twelve members, down in Clarkstown, Georgia. Then I had about thirty-five to fifty members at the AME Church in Providence, Rhode Island, then a small church in Chicago on Cermak Road on the west side. I'd been at the larger church on the west side of Chicago. Then I went from there to Ebenezer Church in Evanston, Illinois, where I served and I came home to Bethel (Atlanta) where I grew up. I started in 1962. So in 1980, of course, there were about seventeen years, I came back as a senior pastor of the church where I got my license to preach—the second youngest pastor to serve since Joseph Flippet in 1888.

Johnny Youngblood
Brooklyn, New York

The Reverend Dr. Johnny Youngblood was born in New Orleans, Louisiana, on June 23, 1948, called in 1970 and ordained a Baptist minister in 1972. He has a BA from Dillard University, an MDiv from Colgate Rochester and a DMin from United Theological Seminary. Interview recorded August 15, 1989.

85

"You Know What I Want You to Do."

I am forty-one years of age and a native of New Orleans, Louisiana. I am, I guess, what you could call a child of the church. I grew up in church all my life. I was not always a part of the Baptist denomination; I grew up in an eclectic group in New Orleans called the United Metropolitan Spiritual Churches of Christ. My mother was primarily responsible for my being a part of that; when I reached the age of reason, that's where we were.

I was always involved in the church experience by way of music and, of course, always a kind of student in the missionary societies, etc. What I remember most that may have kind of upturned me toward the parish and preaching ministry was the bishop who took a liking to me, who was also a graduate of Texas Southern University. That was really my first affiliation with a college graduate in my nitty-gritty experience, other than school. Of course, there were teachers and all who had their degree, but they were my teachers, they were not a part of what I would call my everyday life outside of school. I then took on the desire to go to Texas Southern, just because the bishop went there. I used to watch the bishop, how he reasoned and dealt with folk, and he was a very impressive man.

Music was always exciting to me, because... I don't know

if it was the different rhythms of the songs, because of the dynamics or the groups, etcetera. I really did not want to preach. My first real acquaintance with preaching, first of all, made it dull and boring for me as a kid. I didn't want to sit there and listen to it. The next thing is that I started getting these Black folk in the South, particularly, who may see something a little bit extraordinary in you—or at least they would claim they see it. And the first thing they would do is they would suggest to you, powerfully, that you may be a preacher—you may be a preacher!

Well, it got to the point that folk would say that, and when they would say it, it was kind of a two-headed coin, in that heads was "That's great" but tails was "What all you can't do if you preach." In one breath, they opened this doorway to a possibility of achievement; and in another way they shut the door of normal growth. Because it's like if you become a preacher, I can remember, you can't dance—my mama got into "You can't laugh too loud, you can't hang out with the girls, you can't play ball." So, I mean, man, I am going into my teenage years. Who wants those kinds of restrictions? So I figured God and everybody else could wait until I was through that kind of stuff.

Well, from there, what I did is I automatically learned about the Christian faith. Not only was I in church most of the time, but also my schooling was in Roman Catholic schools, where I learned about the Christian faith even if I learned it from the Roman Catholic bent. I spent twelve years in Roman Catholic schools, and from there I went to Dillard University, which was a Congregational Methodist- affiliated school down in New Orleans. So I got a little religious training there, but mainly by choice, because they were elective courses—religion was not my major. And philosophy was, in a way, my methadone from the church Sunday school addiction that I had. Trying to break away from that in college life and to make more sense out of religious experience, I kind of got into philosophy, where you can at least talk it more. Because in terms of the local church, there wasn't much in terms of explanation. You know, God said it, that settled it—this kind of thing. With going to college, you started to think more and you had more questions, but you couldn't take them home.

From there, what happened is my final semester in school, which was my best semester gradewise, I had a religious experience (that's what we call it) there on the campus, where I literally heard a voice that I say was the voice of the Lord, saying to me: "Now, you know you don't want to spend the rest of your life in a classroom." My undergraduate major was Spanish education. And it was true, and it was one statement, cut level, without equivocation, there was no argument on my part, true. I immediately went into a kind of, I guess you might call it, a creative depression (if there is such a thing), where I knew I had to do something. My depression was that I had wasted four years in college, and here it was, I'm coming out and don't know what I want to do.

So I went to the chapel, there at Dillard, and I went into the little prayer room. In my own way I prayed, different from what my mother and them had taught me, because I was angry, so I prayed in anger. I said, "God, if you really exist, I've got to know why you put me here. What am I supposed to be about? Mama and them struggled to get this money for me to go to school, and here this isn't what I want to do. Now what am I going to do?" And that same voice, again, spoke in a different tone, "You know what I want you to do!"

That was my first, honest acceptance of ministry. Now, I was bootlegging the gospel before then. I had been given license when I was twelve, not requested, really unwanted, but being a child in the South, when them old folks spoke, no matter what it was, you did it. So I couldn't say I wanted license to preach, I couldn't say I'm not going to preach anymore. If I had said that, I might have died at an early age, because them folk, they knew nothing about child abuse laws and that kind of thing. So that was, I guess, my first acceptance.

I accidentally heard about a fellow who was coming to campus, Bobby Joe Sawser, to interview guys who perhaps had seminary interest. Well, my mother, though she was an avid church attender and a really prayerful lady and a disciplinarian of the first magnitude, didn't want me to go to seminary. "The Lord will tell you what to say. You don't have to worry about seminary." Well, with college exposure, the philosophy, the questions that were born, there was no way I was going to seriously undertake the ministry and not be in some kind of a setting, environment, have a mentor that I could dialogue with. So I kind of went to seminary out of rebellion against my mother. I went to college because she insisted, but I went to seminary kind of out of rebellion.

When I got to seminary, my first semester I really think I

came close to a nervous breakdown, because the academic exposure to religion and what I had gotten in terms of Sunday school and church every Sunday and junior missionary society was so radically different. The word studies, the exegesis, the Sitz-im-Leben—I mean, all of a sudden the characters of the scriptures became human. The next day, God was kind of held accountable in a way that you don't even ask God questions; and then you read the Book of Job and there ain't nothing but questions. And you start to say, "Mama didn't tell me that. The Bible is this, life is this." So I went through that dilemma which has turned out to be good, I feel.

January of '71 was when I gave myself, I surrendered, to the preaching ministry. I said, "Now, if I got to do it, if it's what's going to make my life meaningful, there's no sense in me kind of being a bastard about this thing. Do it, get into it, whatever it takes. Study, travel, talk to people, deal with your doubts, therapy—do it." So I did, and by getting into it, yes, I fell in love with it! There was a way that the pain and the struggle was eased; there was another way that it was increased, because there were depths to it that I never even contemplated.

Frederick Zak
Akron, Ohio

The Reverend Dr. Frederick Zak was born in Mobile, Alabama, on August 30, 1958, called in 1978 and ordained a Christian Methodist Episcopal elder in 1984. He earned a BA from the University of South Alabama, an MDiv from International Theological Center and a DMin from Ashland Theological Seminary. He pastors St. John's Christian Methodist Episcopal church. Interview recorded June 5, 1990.

86

From Marginal Roman Catholic to Muslim to CME Preacher

I guess I would have to start with some information about when I started a relationship with God. It started in about 1978. And, at that time, the term "call to preach" or "call to ministry" was foreign to me completely. For two reasons: one, I grew up as a part of the Roman Catholic tradition, and that was not a word or phase or term that was used during my growing up. Now, my grandmother was Methodist, and I had some exposure to the Methodist church through that. At the point at where I found God or rather where God found me, I was at church. I had been at church for serveral years, and I didn't know too much about the Protestant Church or the Roman Catholic Church. But I was on a search during that time in my life. I was in college at Slippery Rock State College, which is now Slippery Rock University. I was searching for truth and found myself really studying Black history and also national and international issues.

I had a burning compassion for oppressed people and particularly Black people. And as a result of my studies, I had a passion for what we had gone through as a people and also an anger and rage toward White people. So I continued to study and seek. And I started to study different religions. I studied the Muslim religion, particularly. I started to come in contact with people from several different faiths at school and several different nationalities. I was still on a search, and I had a kind of spirit of altruism wrestling within, where I wanted things to be ideal. But I was still searching for the truth. At one point I was in Pittsburgh with a friend of mine whose mother is an AME preacher and was talking with him—he and I used to have heated discussions, debating the Muslim religion over against the Christian religion. We talked and talked, and as I left his house one evening, his house was right near downtown Pittsburgh, a very strange feeling came over me, where I experienced a great joy. I was crying and laughing at the same time. It was a great emotional feeling. For the first time I felt like that I had come in contact with God and I knew God was real, without a doubt. I guess, through my training by parents and relatives, people had talked about God. But I was searching to find out if this was really real. And, at that point, I felt like I was just lifted off the ground. Something peculiar about that experience was that I was in downtown Pittsburgh, and there was all kinds of races of people there as I looked out—I have a great love for my people—however, it seemed like what God was telling me is that this battle is not between Black and White, but it is between good and evil. He was showing me Chinese people, Hispanic people, Black people and White people. And in a sense, he was showing me how in a sense, we are all a part of the family of God.

At that point—as I stated before, I was not familiar with the term "call to preach"—all I felt was that I knew God had something for me to do. That terminology was foreign to me at that time. But I started to search. One of the first things I did was to throughly read through the Bible and try to grasp as much as possible about that.

At that point I was in my junior year at Slippery Rock University. I was going back to school in the fall 1978. However, I became real sick that year with pneumonia. And I went back to Mobile, Alabama to finish my last year of college at University of South Alabama. But during that time that I was at Slippery Rock, it was a very lonely experience. I didn't have a spiritual guide, a person that could kind of help me out and lead me. So I tried to go to the Roman Catholic Church, but it felt empty to me. And there is a saying comes to my mind that was my feeling concerning the Roman Catholic Church. It says, "If you have the spirit without the word, you will blow up; if you have the word without the spirit, you will dry up; but if you have the spirit and the word, you will grow." The Roman Catholic experience was that they were strong in the word, but they didn't have the spiritual fervor that I was looking for and searching for. So I didn't find any fulfillment there. There wasn't any Black churches in that area. There was a Black chaplain and I tried to talk to him, but there seemed like there was some distance there. I just found myself on my own, so to speak, for a pretty good period of time.

Until I went back to Mobile, Alabama, all during this time all I knew was that God had something for me to do. I didn't know what it was. It wasn't for me to organize a church structure. So I went back to Mobile, but I decided that I was going to find somewhere that I could grow with a group of people. I had visited a church. It was Stuart Memorial Christian Episcopal Church in Mobile, and the first Sunday I visited that church. It was the first church on my search for a church family or somewhere I could grow and seek and someone could help me to find out what God wanted me do.

The first Sunday I went there, the pastor preached on membership. It was a very inspiring message, and I just felt a kind of peace come over my life when I was there in that church. So, I made an appointment that Sunday after church to talk with him. I went to his office that Wednesday, and he just allowed me to talk. I talked about what I had gone through and what I called a conversion or born-again experience which it had really transformed my life. And, yet, I felt so unfulfilled and fulfilled at the same time. So I spilled my guts out to the minister, Rev. O. R. Jackson, and he just listened (and I think I talked for about two hours), after which he asked me, "Do you feel like you are called to preach?" I said I didn't know anything about a call, and I asked him to define that. The only way he knew to define it was that he pulled out the discipline manual of our church. Within the discipline we have a definition there for "called to preach." He went through that with me, and he started to ask me some of the questions in the discipline. And as he asked me the question and explained to me that "the call" is something you receive from God, the Holy Spirit working in your life saying that he wants to use you to witness, to preach, to teach and to serve people ... he started to ask me several questions. Most of the questions that he asked me I answered in the affirmative: I did have the desire to do God's will, I did have the desire to serve people, I have the desire to teach and tell people about God and I did feel like I had some gifts and graces that would be helpful to people. Then he said, "Let me ask you this, since I have explained the 'call to preach' and I have explained what all this is about, and you've told me your experience, let me ask you this question, 'Do you feel as if you are called to the ministry?,' It was a mysterious kind of feeling in which I felt a great peace, an assurance that my answer to this question should be yes.

This was November 1981 that I talked to Rev. Jackson, and he helped me to understand what God wanted to do in my life. I answered "Yes." I said, "Yes, yes, I do feel that." I didn't understand it fully but I knew that I just had a tremendous urge to do God's will. And at the point when I said yes, it felt like a great load and burden was lifted from my shoulder, and I felt a peace in which I've learned to kind of follow that. I call it an "open-door policy" in which other persons that I talked with, really, they weren't able to open any doors; they weren't able to shed any light on what I was going through. But Rev. Jackson was able to open the door and shed some light. I felt when that door was opened, that I was called to go through that door. And that's kind of it for the most part.

Things started to happen rapidly. I acknowledged my call in November 1981. So I came into the CME church as a member and a preacher at the same time. I joined the church and acknowledged my call the same Sunday and preached my first sermon in January 1982 and was licensed to preach that year. And, really, it's been a very accelerated experience since then. I was licensed to preach and finished college in 1982 at the University of South Alabama. And just everything seemed to flow much smoother, even with college. My pastor was a graduate of the Interdenominational Theological Center in Atlanta, and he suggested that I go study there. So I finished college in June and started seminary in August 1982 and was licensed to preach that year and was also admitted into trial, which is the first step for a traveling minister within our adjudicatory.

The beautiful thing about our field is that I was really able to go to seminary and open my mind to some things. I noticed other persons, that was a part of the seminary, that was closed to a lot of ideas and fresh perspectives because of their denominational affiliations and their long history of being a part of certain denominations. But, me, coming from the world on the street, so to speak, and having some knowledge of the Roman Catholic Church and just a little of the Methodist Church, I was really open to learn a lot. I think I will stop there.

Appendix

Appendix A

Selected Data

The following charts of *Selected Data* were developed as a graph for comparison and reference. The graph lists each contributor to this study by: ***Name, Gender, Denomination, Age, Age When Called, Birthplace, Ministry Residence, Urge to Preach, Signs as Part of Call, Religious Setting, and Resistance to Call.***

Appendix B

Notes

1. **Urge to Preach**: Indicates people who specifically mention the urge to preach in their stories.

2. **Signs as Part of Call**: Indicates stories that include various kinds of divine in-breaking, supernatural phenomena or providential occurrences as part of their call experiences. These include aural, ocular and sensory experiences such as voices, dreams, visions, lights, providential timing as in accidents, meeting people, accidents, among others.

3. **Religious Setting**: Indicates that the individual was reared in a religious setting. Usually, this is the home with parents as well as the church. However, on a few occasions it may involve other relatives, like grandparents or aunts, or merely the church.

4. **Resistance to the Call**: Indicates people who specifically call attention to the fact that they resisted the call.

Appendix A

Name	Gender	Denomination	Age	Age When Called
Abernathy, Lucille	F	UCC	46	34
Adams, Charles G.	M	Baptist	56	0
Adams, John Hurst	M	AME	61	17
Anderson, Herman L. Sr.	M	AMEZ	67	33
Alston, Agnes	F	Community Ch.	69	17
Austin, Sharon	F	Baptist	35	20
Bailey, E. K.	M	Baptist	45	19
Blake, Joseph L. Jr.	M	Baptist	63	5
Booth, Charles	M	Baptist	43	14
Booth, L. Venchael	M	Baptist	71	17
Brogdon, Julia	F	Disciples	52	8
Bryant, Cecelia Williams	F	AME	44	9
Bryant, John	M	AME	47	10
Bryant, Vivian C.	F	AME	52	46
Carpenter, Delores	F	Disciples	46	14
Carter, Mack King	M	Baptist	43	9
Caviness, E. Theophilus	M	Baptist	62	17
Chappelle, T. Oscar	M	Baptist	74	16
Churn, Arlene	F	Baptist	60	5
Clark, Caesar A. W.	M	Baptist	76	9
Cotton, Earl C.	M	Baptist	68	0
Delk, Yvonne	F	UCC	51	5
English, Ronald	M	Baptist	47	23
Essek, Barbara	F	UCC	39	30
Felder, Cain Hope	M	UM	47	13
Forbes, James A.	M	UCC	55	9
Ford, Johnny	M	Baptist	48	33
Fowler, Ronald	M	Church of God	55	27
Gilkes, Cheryl Townsend	F	Baptist	43	34

Selected Data

Birth Place	Ministry Residence	Urge to Preach	Signs as Part of Call	Religious Setting	Resistance to call
MS	OH		X	X	X
MI	MI	X		X	
SC	GA			X	
NC	NC	X		X	X
VA	MD		X	X	X
NY	GA	X		X	X
TX	TX	X		X	X
AL	OH	X	X	X	
MD	OH	X		X	
MS	OH	X		X	
OH	OH		X	X	
NY	MD		X	X	
MD	MD	X	X	X	
MI	MI		X	X	X
MD	DC		X	X	X
FL	FL		X	X	
TX	OH	X		X	X
OK	OK	X		X	
PA	NJ		X	X	X
LA	TX	X		X	
TX	CA	X		X	
VA	NY			X	X
GA	WV			X	
AL	NY		X	X	X
SC	DC			X	
NC	NY	X	X	X	X
AL	AL	X		X	
OH	OH	X	X	X	X
MA	ME		X	X	X

Appendix A

Name	Gender	Denomination	Age	Age When Called
Glover, Sterling	M	Baptist	65	0
Hale, Cynthia	F	DC	38	23
Henderson, Cornelius	M	UM	56	19
Hill, Edward V.	M	Baptist	57	11
Hines, Samuel	M	Church of God	61	17
Holly, Jim	M	Baptist	47	7
Hopkins, Susan Newman	F	UCC	33	19
Hoyt, Thomas L. Jr.	M	CME	49	17
Jackson, Alvin O'Neil	M	DC	40	21
Jackson, Joseph Harrison	M	Baptist	90+	8
Johnson, Suzan D.	F	Baptist	33	13
Johnson, William	M	Baptist	48	37
Jones, Henry Wise	M	Baptist	49	24
Jones, Odell	M	Baptist	58	9
Jones, William Augustus Jr.	M	Baptist	56	22
Kemp, Arthur E.	M	Baptist	61	23
Kimbrough, Walter	M	UM	50	22
King, Bernice	F	Baptist	27	17
Knight, Carolyn	F	Baptist	34	0
Lightner, Ann Farrar	F	AME	45	36
McKenzie, Vashti M.	F	AME	43	34
Massey, James Earl	M	Church of God	60	16
McCreary, Carey	M	Baptist	73	5
McCreary, Leroy	M	Baptist	44	23
McKinney, Samuel B.	M	Baptist	64	23
McMickle, Marvin A.	M	Baptist	42	16
Mitchell, Ella P.	F	Baptist	73	21
Mitchell, Henry H. III	M	Baptist	71	20
Morgan, Eugene	M	AMEZ	72	27

Selected Data

Birth Place	Ministry Residence	Urge to Preach	Signs as Part of Call	Religious Setting	Resistance to call
NJ	OH		X	X	X
VA	GA	X		X	X
GA	GA	X		X	
TX	CA	X	X	X	
W. Ind	DC	X		X	X
PA	MI	X		X	
DC	NY		X	X	X
AL	CT	X		X	
MS	TN	X		X	
MS	IL	X		X	
NY	NY		X	X	
OH	OH		X	X	
KY	OH		X	X	X
AR	MI	X	X	X	X
KY	NY	X		X	X
NC	OH		X	X	
GA	GA		X	X	X
GA	GA	X		X	X
CO	NY	X		X	
NC	MD		X	X	X
MD	MD	X		X	X
MI	AL		X	X	X
AL	OH		X	X	X
AL	OH	X	X	X	
MI	WA	X		X	X
IL	OH		X	X	X
SC	GA			X	
OH	GA	X		X	X
AL	OH		X	X	X

Appendix A

Name	Gender	Denomination	Age	Age When Called
Moss, Otis Jr.	M	Baptist	55	17
Newberry, Andrew K.	M	AME	34	11
Newman, Ernest W.	M	UM	62	16
Payden, Henry J.	M	Baptist	67	23
Pounds, Roderick	M	Baptist	32	21
Proctor, Samuel D.	M	Baptist	69	18
Reid, Frank M. III	M	AME	39	20
Richardson, W. Franklyn	M	Baptist	41	18
Roberts, Joseph L.	M	Baptist	55	17
Sampson, Frederick C. II	M	Baptist	62	18
Scott, Manuel Sr.	M	Baptist	64	18
Shaw, William	M	Baptist	58	11
Shuttlesworth, Fred	M	Baptist	68	18
Smith, J. Alfred Sr.	M	Baptist	60	17
Taylor, Gardner C.	M	Baptist	72	19
Tunstall, Charles	M	Baptist	78	20
Walker, Wyatt Tee	M	Baptist	62	21
Waller, Alfred	M	Baptist	70	23
Weems, Renita J.	F	AME	36	25
Wheeler, Edward L.	M	Baptist	44	15
Wiggins, Alfreda	F	UM	49	23
Williams, Ron	M	Brethren	38	17
Wright, Jeremiah A. Jr.	M	UCC	49	18
Wynn, Prathia H.	F	Baptist	50	0
Young, James S.	M	Baptist	70	32
Young, McKinley	M	AME	46	19
Youngblood, Johnny	M	Baptist	42	22
Zak, Frederick	M	CME	32	20

Selected Data

Birth Place	Ministry Residence	Urge to Preach	Signs as Part of Call	Religious Setting	Resistance to call
GA	OH	X		X	
OH	OH	X		X	X
SC	TN			X	
OH	OH		X	X	X
OH	OH	X		X	
VA	NY	X	X	X	
IL	MD	X		X	X
PA	NY		X	X	X
IL	GA	X		X	X
TX	MI		X	X	
TX	TX	X		X	
TX	PA	X		X	
AL	OH			X	
MO	CA			X	
LA	NY		X	X	X
AL	AL		X	X	
MA	NY			X	
VA	OH	X		X	
GA	TN	X		X	
NY	OH		X	X	X
MD	MD	X		X	X
SC	OH		X	X	X
PA	IL		X	X	X
PA	NJ	X	X	X	X
FL	FL	X	X	X	
GA	GA	X		X	X
LA	NY		X	X	X
AL	OH	X		X	

Appendix B
Index of Call Stories by Author

Author	Title	Page
Abernathy, Lucille	"We Would Rather Have an Unqualified Man Than a Qualified Woman"	2
Adams, Charles G.	Starting a Church in the Garage at Age Eight	11
Adams, John Hurst	The Law Student Who Became Bishop	16
Anderson, Herman L. Sr.	The Bishop Who Swore Never to Be a Preacher	18
Alston, Agnes	The Woman No One Would Allow in Seminary	20
Austin, Sharon	The Lutheran Who Became a Baptist	25
Bailey, E. K.	Cracked in God's University of Hard Knocks	34
Blake, Joseph L. Jr.	"Confess the Call or Die"	38
Booth, Charles	Preaching at Camp at Age Fifteen	42
Booth, L. Venchael	The Mississippi Preacher Who Founded a Convention	44
Brogdon, Julia	Damascus Road in an Emergency Room	49
Bryant, Cecelia Williams	When God Appeared as a Light	54
Bryant, John	"Choose Me and Live, or Take Your Chances with Satan"	58

Index of Call Stories by Author

Bryant, Vivian C.	When God Called at 3:45 Every Morning	60
Carpenter, Delores	Acceptance of the Call at a Funeral	64
Carter, Mack King	"Now That Your Grandmother is Gone, You Must Move Up"	71
Caviness, E. Theophilus	Movies and Dancing or Preaching: Which Will It Be?	74
Chappelle, T. Oscar	Young Preacher Influences Future Baptist Congress President	76
Churn, Arlene	Boy Preachers Yes, Girl Preachers No	78
Clark, Caesar A. W.	From a Seventh Grader to the Leading Revivalist	81
Cotton, Earl C.	A Divine Seizure	84
Delk, Yvonne	"God's Yes Was Louder than My No"	88
English, Ronald	A Scary Question at Ordination	95
Essek, Barbara	"Fear Not, I Have Chosen You. . ."	99
Felder, Cain Hope	The Troubler of Biblical Waters	104
Forbes, James A.	When God Spoke through Tchaikovsky's Symphony # 4 in F Minor	111
Ford, Johnny	The Preacher Who Is Also Mayor	114

Appendix B

Fowler, Ronald	God Called through a Little Boy without Shoes	116
Gilkes, Cheryl Townsend	"I Think I'm Going Crazy"	124
Glover, Sterling	"You are No Longer to Work with the Dead, but with the Living Dead"	137
Hale, Cynthia	When Her Father Said, "I Won't Support You if You Go to Seminary"	143
Henderson, Cornelius	From a Physical Education or Music Major to District Superintendent	147
Hill, Edward V.	"Are You Ready to Preach?"	151
Hines, Samuel	"Nobody with Your Color Eyes Can Be a Preacher"	157
Holly, Jim	"The Calling Came as a Fact That I was Raised by God"	169
Hopkins, Susan Newman	"Who in the World Would Marry a Woman Preacher?"	172
Hoyt, Thomas L. Jr.	Considered Most Likely to Be Bishop in High School	179
Jackson, Alvin O'Neil	Influenced by an Old Testament Professor	183
Jackson, Joseph Harrison	The Most Dominant President of a Baptist Convention	186
Johnson, Suzan D.	When God Spoke in a New York Traffic Jam	188

Index of Call Stories by Author

Johnson, William	"It Was like My Body Was on Fire"	195
Jones, Henry Wise	Two Similar Accidents—Is God Speaking to Me?	197
Jones, Odell	"I Would Not Be a Boy Preacher"	199
Jones, William Augustus Jr.	"I Was Down in the Motor Pool Preaching to Trucks"	201
Kemp, Arthur E.	Rebellious Soldier in Two Armies: Man's and God's	204
Kimbrough, Walter	"God, If You Want Me to Preach, Wake Me Up at 3:00 or 4:00 o'Clock in the Morning"	211
King, Bernice	One Regret: Daddy King Wasn't There	213
Knight, Carolyn	"I Don't Come from a Lineage of Preachers"	216
Lightner, Ann Farrar	"I Never Wanted to Be a Preacher"	220
McKenzie, Vashti M.	From a Broadcasting Career to Preaching	226
Massey, James Earl	Called While Reading a Score of Chopin	230
McCreary, Carey	Betwixt and Between: Blinded at High Noon	233
McCreary, Leroy	The Presence of God in the Wind	242
McKinney, Samuel B.	"I Didn't Call You to Be Your Father's Clone"	245
McMickle, Marvin A.	When a White Candle Turned Red	254

Appendix B

Mitchell, Ella P.	"In the Same Year That Mama Died, I Also Saw the Lord"	259
Mitchell, Henry H. III	Has Anyone Written More on Black Preaching?	264
Morgan, Eugene	"I Made a Bargain with God"	270
Moss, Otis Jr.	The Urge to Preach	275
Newberry, Andrew K.	The Influence of Being a Preacher's Kid	277
Newman, Ernest W.	"I Had No Choice"	280
Payden, Henry J.	Awakened by the Hand of God	283
Pounds, Roderick	An Overwhelming Burden	286
Proctor, Samuel D.	Isolation, Separation, and Confrontation with the Brutality of Fraternities	289
Reid, Frank M. III	"Called from My Mother's Womb"	300
Richardson, W. Franklyn	Called in the Midst of a Medical Mishap	304
Roberts, Joseph L.	Rebellion of an AME Preacher's Kid	307
Sampson, Frederick C. II	On a Magnolia Tree Looking Up, When God Spoke	311
Scott, Manuel Sr.	An Irresistible Compulsion	320
Shaw, William	"A Constant Inclination toward Ministry"	322
Shuttlesworth, Fred	"I Was Anti-religious and Anti-God"	324
Smith, J. Alfred Sr.	The Saxophone Player Who Heard the Call of God	326

Index of Call Stories by Author

Taylor, Gardner C.	The Dean of Black Preachers: He Didn't Want to Be a Preacher	328
Tunstall, Charles	"I Tried to Avoid it; I'm Going to Die"	331
Walker, Wyatt Tee	"No, No, No, Young Man. Not Money; Service, Service"	334
Waller, Alfred	When the Preacher Came, Everything Seemed Better	337
Weems, Renita J.	"…All Right God, I Tell You What, I'm Gonna Fleece You"	338
Wheeler, Edward L.	No Girl Friends If You Are a Teenage Preacher	346
Wiggins, Alfreda	Confirmation of a Woman Preacher by Women Preachers	350
Williams, Ron	"The Next Time You Hear That Voice, Answer Yes, Lord"	360
Wright, Jeremiah A. Jr.	Unnatural Light in a Dark Room	362
Wynn, Prathia H.	Awakened at Four o' Clock; "I Had Been Preaching"	372
Young, James S.	Lost on the Pacific When God Spoke	378
Young, McKinley	"The Lord Is Calling…You Can't Ignore That"	384
Youngblood, Johnny	"You Know What I Want You to Do"	388
Zak, Frederick	From Marginal Roman Catholic to Muslim to CME Preacher	392

www.ingramcontent.com/pod-product-compliance
Lightning Source LLC
Chambersburg PA
CBHW071226290426
44108CB00013B/1306